POSTER POWER

AUCTION: SUNDAY, NOVEMBER 12, 2000 AT 11:00 AM

**THE AUDITORIUM, Armenian Diocese,
2nd Avenue at 34th Street, N.Y.C.**

**EXHIBITION: Friday and Saturday,
November 10 & 11, from 9AM to 9PM**

This sale is organized by
Mr. JACK RENNERT and Ms. TERRY SHARGEL.
This catalogue is edited by Mr. TIM GADZINSKI.

For more information on this sale, as well
as to place bids if unable to attend,
please contact Ms. Terry Shargel.

POSTER AUCTIONS INTERNATIONAL, INC.
601 West 26th Street, New York, N.Y. 10001
Telephone (212) 787-4000.
Fax (212) 604-9175
Email JRENNERT@ANGEL.NET

CONTENTS

Mistinguett, Dranem and the French Music-Hall	1-74	Olympic Posters	173-196
		International Posters	197-705
Motorcycle Posters	75-84	N.Y. World's Fair	563-566
Automobile Posters	85-124	Salon des Cent	622-634
Ship Posters	125-160	Spanish Festivals	649-656
Aviation Posters	161-172	Books & Periodicals	706-713

ACKNOWLEDGMENTS

I am most grateful to the many individuals who have given their full support and assistance to us in the preparation of this POSTER POWER sale. First and foremost, our thanks to the 95 consignors in 21 States and 11 foreign countries who entrusted their finest works to us for this very special occassion.

Our staff has been materially helpful in all aspects of this auction, and I wish to especially single out the work of my associate, Ms. Terry Shargel. Our editorial department was headed once again by Mr. Tim Gadzinski who is responsible for the lively and incisive text in this book. Helping with many of the administrative aspects were Mr. Giovanni Cohen, Mr. Xavier Serbones and Ms. Julie Press. Mr. John Greenleaf handled all the computer matters. And no sale could be smoothly organized without the help of Ms. Valerie Beale and Ms. Barbara Rennert.

We take great pride in making all our annotations as complete and accurate as possible, and we are helped enormously in this task by being able to call upon very knowledgeable colleagues throughout the world. Helpful in answering our many questions for this book were Ms. Laura Brass, Ms. Peggy Bronstein, Mr. Chester Collins, Ms. Laura Corwin, Mr. James Dierks, Mr. Andre Farkas, Mr. Bill Jackson, Mr. Ronald Keats, Mr. Eric Kellenberger, Mr. Jean-Louis Lamot, Dr. Maura Mansfield,

Ms. Barbara Rennert, Ms. Terry Shargel, Mr. Kurt Thaler, Mr. Alain Weill, Mr. William Worthington and Mr. Christophe Zagrodzki.

In the production of this catalogue, I was again fortunate to be able to call on the talents and devotion of fine craftsmen: Mr. Guenter Knopf is our very able photographer; the staff of Harry Chester, Inc. was in charge of design and production, and I especially want to thank Ms. Susannah Ing; the excellent color in this volume is the result of the careful and caring work of Mr. Benny Perez at Jalor Color; Mr. Sandy Rosenblum and Mr. Joseph Nazianzeno at Sanford Graphics printed it all with style and under great time pressure. Mr. Gene Litz of Short Run Bindery wrapped it all up in timely fashion.

Advertising for this sale was again handled by Global Marketing Group. Public relations is most ably directed by Mr. David Reich.

The staff of the Diocese of the Armenian Church continues to make us very welcome; our thanks especially to Mr. Frank Stoneson.

To all of them and to all the others who offered help, suggestions and encouragement, many thanks.

—Jack Rennert

SNEAK PREVIEW

Most of the posters in the French Music-Hall section are on view at our headquarters (The International Poster Center, 601 West 26th Street, New York City, between 11th and 12th Aves. on the 13th floor) Monday to Friday, 9am to 5pm and Saturday 10am to 6pm, until November 6.

CONDITIONS OF SALE

We call your attention to the Conditions of Sale printed on the last pages of this book. Those bidding at this sale should first familiarize themselves with the terms contained therein.

OUR NEXT SALE

We are pleased to announce that the PAI-XXXII sale of rare posters will be held on Sunday, May 6, 2001, in the Auditorium of the Armenian Diocese in New York.

Consignments are accepted until January 15, 2001.

BID WITH CONFIDENCE—EVEN IF YOU CANNOT ATTEND

If you cannot attend the auction of November 12, please use the Order Bid Form on the next-to-last page. It should be mailed or faxed to arrive at our office no later than Friday, November 10.
Note that all illustrations in this book are of the item being sold—we never use stock photos.

Jack Rennert—License 0797440

MISTINGUETT, DRANEM & THE FRENCH MUSIC-HALL

There never was a performer like Mistinguett (1873-1956). From the time she made her debut as a nightclub singer in 1890 at the age of 17, until she stopped touring in 1948 at a well-preserved 75, she was the French music hall incarnate–delicious and dazzling. How Mistinguett got her nickname is retold by critic Alain Weill: "Her friends from Enghien nicknamed the youthful Jeanne Bourgeois, Heylette, the heroine of an opera by Audran, whom they claimed she resembled. Inventing a play on words based on the popular refrain 'La Vertinguette,' the Miss hummed, 'It's la Vertin, Miss Heylette, it's la Vertin . . . It's Mistinguette.' The songwriter Saint-Marcel, who was at her side told her, 'If you ever appear on stage, my little girl, call yourself Mistinguette,' and that's what she did!" (Weill, p. 13).

1

2

3

G. K. BENDA (Georges Kugelmann)

1. Mistinguett. ca. 1913.
44³/₄ x 60 in./113.7 x 152.5 cm
Philippe G. Dreyfus, Paris
Cond B+/20" tear at bottom paper edge. Framed.
Ref: PAI-XXX, 572
Benda is the pseudonym of a painter and graphic artist who resided in Paris a good many years, as there are records of his having exhibited paintings in various salons between 1907 and 1921. He produced only a handful of posters, with this Mistinguett design being especially memorable. Catching her in this whirling moment breezily communicates that she was a breath of fresh air, a fact to which all of those who were fortunate enough to see her perform uniformly agree.
Est: $2,500-$3,000.

CHARLES GESMAR (1900–1928)

2. Mistinguett/Moulin Rouge. 1926.
30¹/₂ x 46³/₄ in./77.4 x 118.7 cm
Imp. H. Chachoin, Paris
Cond B+/Usual tears and stains at folds.
Ref: Folies-Bergère, 63; Hillier, p. 249;
    Theaterplakate, 155; PAI-XXIX, 509

Mistinguett achieved her greatest success at the Moulin Rouge, where this 1926 revue was simply called "Mistinguett." Weill indicates: "It is one of Gesmar's most beautiful posters: without jewels or fancy dress, it's the Miss, child of Paris, which he shows us here. . . alluring, tender, and roguish with the rose between her lips which we would like to pluck." (Folies-Bergère, p. 11). In his tragically short life, Gesmar created more than 50 posters, all filled with zest and colors; he designed posters and costumes for Mistinguett from about 1918 until his death.
Est: $2,500-$3,000.

3. Mistinguett. 1925.
45¹/₂ x 61³/₄ in./115.5 x 156.8 cm
Imp. H. Chachoin, Paris
Cond B/Slight tears and stains at folds.
Ref: PAI-XXX, 576
The fluff of the white ostrich feathers is a perfect foil for the famous music-hall star's irresistibly flirty quality. Even the sparkling jewels that give the poster its informal name can't outdazzle her green eyes and winning smile.
Est: $2,500-$3,000

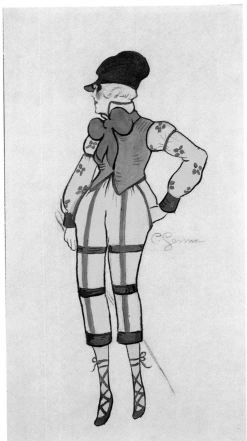

4

5

6

7

MISTINGUETT/Gesmar (cont'd)

4. Top Hat and Polka Dots.
8 x 15 in./20.2 x 38 cm
Hand-signed drawing. Framed.
Perhaps Mistinguett's greatest talent was her ability to fling herself into any situation, equally at ease draped in pearls or in a ragamuffin's patches. Regardless of the exaggeration or overstatement, she filled the stage with a verve that was all her own. Take for example this hand-signed, gouache and ink Gesmar costume drawing—a foppish assemblage of polka dots, bows and somewhat muted tones, an ensemble that neither plays up nor down Mistiguett's femininity. And yet knowing what we do of the artist, it is not far-fetched to imagine her making this design as much a part of her personna as her dazzling smile.
Est: $2,000-$2,500.

5. Stripes and Laces.
7³/₄ x 15¹/₄ in./19.7 x 38.7 cm
Hand-signed drawing. Framed.
This version of Gesmar's clothes horse in gouache and ink utilizes a virtually identical physical form as the previous lot—barely altering the clothes as a matter of fact. Hats have been switched, colors brightened, stripes swapped for polka dots and laces replacing high-buttons. But with these few changes, a totally different look emerges, with charm being the only remaining unifying element.
Est: $2,000-$2,500.

6. Mistinguett Unleashed.
6 x 13⁵/₈ in./15.2 x 34.5 cm
Hand-signed drawing. Framed.
Caught in a gouache and pencil musical maquette

8

moment of wild-eyed abandon, Mistinguett is a Gesmar study in contrasts: an eclectic jumble of wardrobe elements inexplicably working in accord with an electrostatic coif that acts as a sun-bursting halo about the singer's face while redefining tressful disarray.
Est: $2,000-$2,500.

7. Mistinguett Costume Design.
18⁷/₈ x 11³/₄ in./48 x 30 cm
Original drawing; signed verso.
Somewhere between a flapper's wardrobe and a humongous painted daisy, Gesmar found the inspiration for a Mistinguett costume rendered in watercolors and pencil. Outside the flash-and-trash confines of Las Vegas, the art of the Ultra-Costume has all but been forgotten. Which is a shame, as this rosy reminder points up the notion that a little exaggeration can create an unforgettable impact.
Est: $1,700-$2,000.

DANIEL DE LOSQUES (1880-1915)

8. Mistinguett. 1911.
41³/₈ x 75³/₄ in/105 x 192.2 cm
Imp. H. Chachoin, Paris
Cond A.
Ref: PAI-XXIII, 44
An early, rather demure full-length portrait of Mistinguett as a sweet, simple country girl. But even under that bonnet and covered-up dress, you can see the slender torso and long legs that became part of her stage persona. The poster was popular enough to have been done in at least two different color versions (*see* PAI-XXIII, 45). De Losques was the pseudonym of David Thoroude, who studied law and started out as a law firm employee before switching to art. This is one of the many theatrical posters he created, along with magazine illustrations and caricatures during the period 1904-1914. His career was cut short by his death in aerial combat during World War I.
Est: $2,500-$3,000.

JEAN-DOMINIQUE VAN CAULAERT (1897-1979)

9. Mistinguett/Vedette Columbia. 1938.
451/8 x 621/2 in./114.7 x 159 cm
Cond A–/Slight stains at folds and edges.
Ref: PAI-V, 305
One of the best of all the Mistinguett posters—the line, the color, the composition—it all adds up to a most compelling and appealing design. And it's also quite rare today. The insouciant, inviting come-hither look and provocative pose are caught with an elegant flair that does full justice to the renowned performer.
Est: $6,000-$7,000.

10. Mistinguett/Théâtre Mogador. 1937.
46 x 60¹/₂ in./117 x 154 cm
Atelier Girbal, Paris
Cond A.
Ref: PAI-XXIX, 513
With the trademark sophistication and refinement for which his celebrity portraits were known, Van Caulaert paints Mistinguett in her rags-before-riches street urchin personae for an appearance in *ça c'est Parisien* at the Théâtre Mogador.
Est: $2,700-$3,000.

EMMERICH WENINGER (1909-1971)

11. Mistinguett. 1933.
48³/₄ x 106³/₈ in./124 x 270 cm
Waldheim-Eberle, Vienne
Cond A—/Slight tears at paper edges.
Ref: Phillips I, 604
This huge 3-sheet poster, printed in Vienna, shows Mistinguett at her absolute toothy-best. Vienna-native Weninger designed many film posters up until World War I; he then moved to Holland and worked for Phillips, the electronic conglomerate, designing album covers and other graphics.
Est: $2,000-$2,500.

MISTINGUETT

CASINO DE PARIS
MISTINGUETT

PARIS QUI BRILLE
LA PLUS BELLE REVUE DU MONDE
MATINÉES _ JEUDIS. DIMANCHES & FÊTES

13

12

MISTINGUETT (continued)

ZIG (Louis Gaudin, ?-1936)

12. Mistinguett. 1932.
$62^3/4$ x $46^7/8$ in/159.3 x 119 cm
Imp. H. Chachoin, Paris
Cond A–/Slight tears and stains, largely at edges.
Ref: PAI-XXIX, 511
After Gesmar's death in 1928, Mistinguett entrusted
all her design work—costumes, sets, programs and
posters—to Zig. Here, Zig poses Mistinguett coquettishly
in a bare-back swimsuit, sporting an enormous black
cartwheel hat that serves to halo her face. Mistinguett
gives us proof that at 59 she is still as attractive as ever.
Est: $6,000-$7,000.

13. Casino de Paris/Mistinguett/Paris Qui Brille.
   1931.
31 x 86 in./78.8 x 218.5 cm
Cantral Publicité, Paris
Cond B/Slight tear at horizontal fold; slightly light
      stained. Framed.
Ref: PAI-XVII, 541
The poster is for Mistinguett's revue at the Casino de
Paris called "Paris Adazzle," and the poster more than
lives up to its designation: a bejeweled Mistinguett,
pink-tinged feather in one hand, reins of her playful
team of blue horses in the other, spotlit against a
black background. *This is the larger format.*
Est: $3,000-$4,000.

14. Casino de Paris/Mistnguett/Paris Qui Brille.
   1931.
$15^3/4$ x $35^1/4$ in./40 x 89.4 cm
Central Publicité, Paris
Cond A–/Unobtrusive horizontal fold.
Ref: Folies-Bergère, 67; Delhaye, p. 35; PAI-XXIII, 540
In yet another promotion for "Paris Adazzle," Zig depicts
Mistinguett perched on a stool, with the city at her
feet, displaying most of her visible assets. Setting off
all that skin: long red gloves, oodles of dripping jewelry
and an insouciant little hat. *This is the smaller format.*
Est: $2,500-$3,000.

CASINO DE PARIS
MISTINGUETT

PARIS QUI BRILLE
LA PLUS BELLE REVUE DU MONDE
MATINÉES   JEUDIS . DIMANCHES & FÊTES

CENTRAL PUBLICITÉ _ PARIS

14

15. Casino de Paris/Mistinguett/Paris Miss. 1930.
$16^1/4$ x $23^3/4$ in./41.4 x 60.3 cm
Central Publicité, Paris
Cond A–/Slight stains at paper edges.
Ref: Femme s'Affiche, 64; Folies-Bergère, 65;
   Delhaye, p. 36 (var); PAI-XXIV, 577

In this poster for the singer's *Paris Miss* revue, it's a
wonder how she can be wearing so much—a cascading ostrich-plume headdress, a sumptuous full-length
ermine cape, above-the-elbow gloves, yards of jewels
—yet be covering so little. She's partnered by twin
greyhounds whose contours match her sleek elegance.
Est: $2,000-$2,500.

16. Mistinguett. 1928.
$46^3/4$ x $62^5/8$ in./118.8 x 159 cm
Imp. H. Chachoin, Paris
Cond A–/Unobtrusive folds.
Ref: PAI-XXX, 577
In 1936, Zig also died prematurely, although his exact
age was never established. The artist had been a
habitué of Montmartre cabarets where he sang and
recited at the drop of a beret. Both of them affected a
flamboyantly showy style, which exactly suited the
Miss persona. Here, Zig gives us Mistinguett as a country girl complete with a basket of flowers. Beyond its
graphic flair, it's Zig juxtaposing the star's saucy sexi-
ness with *naïf* trappings—like Brigitte Bardot in her
gingham bikini—that makes the image so effective.
Est: $5,000-$6,000.

15

16

DRANEM

"The son of a workman jeweler, himself an apprentice jeweler for a time, (Dranem) became a store clerk who launched himself into amateur theater in 1890. After diverse contracts that scarcely resulted in making him a known name, Dranem was engaged by the Electric Concert in 1894, followed in 1895 by the Concert Parisien. During these years, he presented himself in the manner of Polin (see Nos. 60, 65 & 69), dressed in military uniform. The role was merely moderately suited to him and when in 1899 he was hired by the Eldorado, . . . he created the personage of Dranem. . . . (He) established a privileged relationship with the public that never got in the way of him being a man of the people. He was one of the premier comic singers who would actually converse with his public" (Collectioneur, p. 104).

17

18

ANONYMOUS

17. Dranem/Truffard. 1912.
15^1/$_8$ x 23 in./38.4 x 58.4 cm
Imp. G. Delattre, Paris
Cond B+/Slight stains at edges.
"Dranem, truly named Armand, Ménard (1869-1935), was a unique sort of figure of the café-concert . . . Playing the perfect idiot, . . . he created a liberated personality, an outlet from the repression of all that was moral and sophisticated" (Collectioneur, p. 104). Never an artist to deny his public the simpleton pleasures they craved, Dranem's workhorse ethic is manifested in this announcement for a one-night only appearance at the Theatre de Poitiers. In addition to playing the title role of Truffard in the military comedy of the same name, Dranem also presented an intermezzo of favorites from his repertoire between the opening piece, "Well Married!," and the bill's featured presentation. "Stupidly-willed, (Dranem) presented himself on stage dressed in checked pants, both too big and too short, a coat that fit too tightly, an oversized bow tie and a little hat, without forgetting enormous, unlaced shoes . . . From the moment the curtain rose, Dranem . . . unleashed general hilarity" (Collectioneur, p. 104). The uncredited designer of this poster was thoughtful enough to give Henri Mannel photo credit for the image upon which he based his creation.
Est: $1,200-$1,500.

19

20

22

21

world of comic artists and we recall that the money collected goes to them, divided between those most in need" (Collectioneur pp. 192-193).
Est: $1,400-$1,700.

21. Les On Dit. ca. 1918.
$61^3/4$ x $44^7/8$ in./157 x 114 cm
Devambez, Paris
Cond B+/Slight tears and stains at folds.
Ref: Paillard, 210
The mood is rather serious in this post-World War I poster for an Alsace-Lorraine weekly publication whose name translates as "The Way It Is." It's an understandable stance taking the time period and the paper's creed—Strength-Victory—into account. And considering that the journal's primary beat was Politics, Parisians and Literature, having notables from those fields whispering the latest news into the gigantic central auditory organ, including French statesman and writer Georges Clemenceau, was to be expected. But proving that jocularity should never be left out of the mix, the unknown artist allows Dranem to sneak his way into the illustrious gathering, unobtrusively to the right of Clemenceau.
Est: $1,400-$1,700.

22. Jeu de Cubes Comiques.
$8^1/2$ x $14^1/2$ in./21.5 x 36.8 cm
Cond A. Framed.
Ostensibly a children's block stacking game makes a fitting memorial to a blockhead comic the likes of Dranem. Actually a nod to his popularity with audiences of all ages, Dranem is but one of four comic characters that can be created with the proper cube assemblage. Advertised as the centerpiece of a child's fantasy wonderland, it bears noting how closely the on-looking lumber bears an uncanny resemblance to the unruly apple trees in "The Wizard of Oz."
Est: $500-$600.

ADRIEN BARRÈRE (1877-1931)

23. Dranem. ca. 1905.
$30^1/4$ x $46^3/4$ in./77 x 118.7 cm
Imp. Charle Verneau, Paris
Cond B+/Unobtrusive tears and stains at folds and edges.
Ref: DFP-II, 49; Musée d'Affiche, 29 (var); Weill, 67; Caradec/Weill, 183 (var); PAI-XXIV, 155

DRANEM/Anonymous (continued)

18. Alcazar/Ca Mousse!
23 x $31^1/2$ in./58.3 x 80 cm
Imp. Ch. Wall, Paris
Cond B+/Slight stains at edges.
Far more salacious translations could be provided for the "That Sparkles!" revue playing at the Alcazar, especially taking into consideration Dranem's advantageous petticoat junction box seat view. But since the disconcerted, yet riveted expression on the performer's face seems to say it all, why restate the obvious.
Est: $1,000-$1,200.

19. Dranem.
11 x $14^3/4$ in./28 x 37.5 cm
Imp. Marcel Picard, Paris
Cond A. Framed.
"Stumbling onto the scene, lost as if he was ignorant to the locale where he now found himself, Dranem was an inspired pantomime clown who breathed real life into his creation. The costume surely called to mind the outfit of a clown, his makeup as equally painted on. . . . He played with the incongruity of his presence, . . . who would go on to sing songs composed of monumental rubbish. Lyrics overflowing with

bawdy and scatological allusions in which the rhymes made very little sense, proffered in a pose no less relaxed, body rigid and eyes closed" (Collectioneur, p. 104). Regardless of the identity of the unknown artist who captured this éssence of Dranem, the hilarious self-glee portrayed delightfully infects the viewer with its unchecked lunacy.
Est: $1,000-$1,200.

20. Loterie des Artistes. 1909.
47 x $61^3/4$ in./119.5 x 156.7 cm
Lithographie Parisienne, Paris
Cond B+/Slight stains, largely at edges.
Ref: Collectionneur, p., 193
It's only appropriate that Dranem is drafted into service in order to drum-up awareness for this artists' lottery, seeing as he was the "founder of the music hall artist's retirement home in Ris-Orange . . . The posterist, sensitive to the aspects of official announcements, places a rural constable on the scene, beating out the call to the public and unveiling the placard. But the thrown-together uniform for the venerable gentleman with his gendarme cap, his bow tie, his motley pants and untied shoes induces us into the

23

24

25

26

24. Dranem/Entrée des Artistes. 1908.
38³/₈ x 54⁵/₈ in./97.5 x 138.7 cm
Imp. Ch. Wall, Paris
Cond A–/Slight stains at paper edges.
Ref: Café-Concert, 49; PAI-XXIV, 156
The famous comedian arrives at the theater, song-
sheets, gloves, coat and umbrella in hand. Together
with the previous lot, these are among the best of all
Barrère posters.
Est: $3,000-$4,000.

25. Eldorado/Dranem dans la Revue.
38³/₄ x 54¹/₂ in./98.5 x 138.2 cm
Imp. Robert, Paris
Cond B–/Slight tears and stains at folds and edges.
In a true stroke of genius, Barrère removes Dranem
from the stage and the bright lights of the city, plop-
ping him back into what one can easily imagine to be
his original element. Draped in a mixed bag of striped
apparel, a full beard softening his features, this even
more humble Dranem goes about his country tasks
with an eye-closed passivity, totally free of his on-stage
angst. Potentially the most intriguing question that the
poster raises is this: What possibly could have lured
this simple rural fellow away from his home to take
the stage at the Eldorado? Simply fantastic.
Est: $1,700-$2,000.

26. Alcazar/Ce Que Je Peux Rire.
28³/₄ x 44³/₄ in./72.8 x 113.8 cm
Cond B+/Slight stains at folds.
With star power like Dranem and Campton acting as
the bait, Barrère needed to look no further for a hook
than the wide-eyed visages of the bill-sharing pair, set
down to caricuturistic perfection, and unerringly appropriate for the wryly-titled "What Makes Me Laugh," an
appellation as wonderfully self-deprecating as it is
promotional.
Est: $1,400-$1,700.

Barrère capitalizes on Dranem's compellingly homely
face and affected burlesque hick appearance as he
sincerely croons one of his patented, eyes closed,
nonsense songs. The color, composition, movement
and sympathetic treatment here make this one of the
best—and potentially most true-to-life—of Barrère's
works for the performer. A variant of this image
displays the Ambassadeurs theater name in the blank
area at top (see PAI-XV, 113).
Est: $1,700-$2,000.

27

29

DRANEM/Barrère (continued)

27. Dranem/Eldorado.
38³/₄ x 55 in./98.2 x 139.7 cm
Imp. G. Bataille, Paris
Cond B/Slight stains in background.
Ref: PAI-XXVI, 158 (var)
Dranem appeared on all the great music hall stages of
the day and went on to star in nine films, but it was at
the Eldorado that he had his greatest success, from
his first appearance in 1900 and continuing for 20
years thereafter. Barrère is well known for his portraits
of French stage personalities. He also produced many
film posters, especially for Pathé. His caricature-like
treatments and flat colors yielded delightful and witty
designs—yet their depth and sensitivity often tran-
scended caricature; this portrait, for example, of the
comedian at the end of a performance—deservedly
showered with roses. *Rare!*
Est: $2,000-$2,500.

28. Dranem.
13³/₈ x 19⁷/₈ in./34 x 50.5 cm
Cond B/Staining, largely in edges. Framed.
Ref: PAI-XXVI, 158 (var)
This is the smaller, before-letters version of the pre-
vious image, with a cordial, hand-signed dedication
from the artist to one Dominique Bonnaud.
Est: $1,000-$1,200.

GUS BOFA (Gustave Blanchot, ?–1968)

29. Eldorado/"la patate."
47¹/₄ x 63 in./120 x 160 cm
Imp. Charles Verneau, Paris
Cond B/Tears at folds; image and colors excellent.
Ref: PAI-XXVIII, 148
Though the finer plot points of this 2-act Dranem
extravaganza presented at the Eldorado music hall
have been lost to the ages, we can only imagine that a
play brave enough to call itself "The Sweet Potato"
must have been confident in its ability to deliver a feel-
good diversion to Parisian theatergoers. Whatever the
content of the piece, the cartoonish charm of its pro-

28

motional material is undeniable. Bofa, son of an Army
colonel, was a colorful personality with a checkered
career, from infantryman to metallurgical engineer, who
inexplicably suddenly drifted to humorous drawings
and caricature. His incisive, witty work was so good
that he became a member of the editorial staff of *Le*
Rire, Le Sourire, La Petite Semaine and *La Baion-*
nette; together with printer Devambez, he founded the
Salon de Araignée, a haven for independent artists.
Est: $1,400-$1,700.

30

30. Dranem/Alfred!
46³/₈ x 62 in./117.8 x 157.3 cm
Charles Verneau, Paris
Cond B/Slight tears and stains at folds and edges.
"Alfred! Justice of the Peace in Spite of Himself." It's
not out of the question to imagine that being the
name of Jim Carrey's next release. And yet, if that
assumption were to be made, the person making it
would have missed the boat by close to a century, as
the title in question belonged to Dranem and one of

31

32

33

34

35

ROGER CARTIER

33. Miche. 1931.
22 x 30 in./55.8 x 76.2 cm
Imp. de la Cinématographie Française, Paris
Cond B/Slight stains and tears at edges.
This palette of brightly splashed frivolity was called into promotional duty for *Miche*, a light romantic comedy produced by the French branch of Paramount Pictures. Miche is a young lady who falls for a painter, who, she soon discovers, isn't ready for a serious commitment and prefers the freedom of "safe" affairs with married women. After learning of his plans to do some work in an Alpine hotel, she shows up at the resort pretending to be married to a somewhat inept small-town lawyer she has persuaded to go along with the joke, played by none other than Dranem. Not surprisingly, her quarry falls in love with her against his better judgment and proposes. The romantic fare is presented with a great deal of verve and élan, most especially by pseudo-husband Dranem. He effortlessly steals every scene in which he appears, and has a great counterpart in Marguerite Moreno who plays Miche's busybody aunt; the scenes the two of them play together are the highlight of the film.
Est: $1,000-$1,200.

L. CHARBONNIER

34. Eldorado/Dranem.
22^1/$_2$ x 31 in./57 x 78.7 cm
La Lithographie Nouvelle, Asniers
Cond B/Restored tears at folds and edges.
Charbonnier gives credit to photographer Paul Darby for establishing the celluloid inspiration for this work, one which portrays the perennial goofball with a gentle humanity not overwhelmingly present in the lion's share of Dranem's promotional material.
Est: $800-$1,000.

35. Eldorado/Si T'Aurais Vu!!
31 x 44^3/$_4$ in./78.6 x 113.8 cm
Lithographie Nouvelle, Asniers
Cond B+/Unobtrusive folds.
Turning once more to Paul Darby for photographic inspiration, Charbonnier places a mischievously startled Dranem in the spotlight, whose mug is a perfect match for a revue titled "If You Would've Seen It!" Because quite frankly, he apparently can't believe that you haven't. Because if you had, you'd already know why you should've. So, the only sound plan would be to get to the Eldorado as quickly as possible to get in with the "In" crowd.
Est: $1,200-$1,500.

his 2-act vaudeville distractions. But from the look of things in this Bofa scenic rendition, Alfred may not have been the best judge when it came to romance. Ah, the irony.
Est: $1,500-$1,800.

31. Eldorado/La Revue de l'"Eldo".
43^1/$_8$ x 60^3/$_4$ in./109.6 x 154.2 cm
Imp. Ch. Verneau, Paris
Cond B/Slight tears and stains at folds.
Dranem the toreador? Why the heck not, since his societally-challenged persona made practically every situation ripe with possibilities, putting him in a bull ring seems like the only comically wise thing to do. Judging from the debris being flung his way in the poster for this "Eldo" revue, he made bull fighting as successful a venture as every other botched enterprise he undertook. And the Paris cabaret scene wouldn't have wanted it any other way.
Est: $1,700-$2,000.

32. Eldorado/"Badigeon".
45^3/$_8$ x 60^1/$_4$ in./115 x 153 cm
Ch. Verneau, Paris
Cond B-/Restored tears and losses, largely at paper edges.
Delving back into his repertoire to pull out his Polinesque military clown, Dranem headlines the vaudeville operetta, *Badigeon*, or "Whitewash" as is the case via translation. The title definitely applies to Bofa's background, but Dranem—sidetracked on a return trip from the market—has other plans slowly brewing in his bumpkin mind, formulating an equation involving the pastel-filled paint pots at his feet and the blank canvas wall behind him, verging on painting the town red, green, yellow and blue, and more than happy to take the audience along for the ride.
Est: $1,500-$1,800.

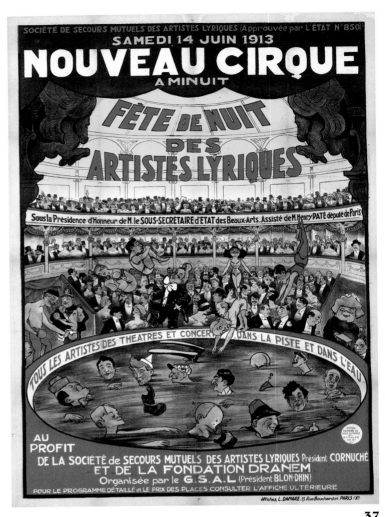

DRANEM (continued)

L. DAMARÉ (?-1927)

36. Vélodrome Buffalo/Fête Sportive des Artistes Lyriques. 1908.
$34^5/_8$ x $48^1/_2$ in./88 x 123.2 cm
Affiches L. Damaré, Paris
Cond B/Slight tears and stains at folds and edges.
For this annual one-day benefit performance for retired artists, Damare creates a panorama of tireless artists willing to cheer and peddle themselves for a good cause. The crowd is peppered with notables—Polin, Vilbert, Yvette Guilbert, Polaire, Mayol—but what sets this event apart from your everyday charity concert is the fact that the artists themselves will be competing in between-concert athletic challenges. And it's easy to see why Dranem would be working up a hefty sweat, taking into consideration that not only is Jeanne Bloch his partner in the tandem race, but the expansive comedienne has also decided that his lumbar region makes for an excellent breast stop. The Vélodrome Buffalo in the Paris suburb of Neuilly was under the direction of Tristan Bernard since 1895 and it is there that Toulouse-Lautrec became a frequent visitor and sketched several prints as well as two of his posters, the Cycle Michael and the Chaine Simpson.
Est: $1,700-$2,000.

37. Nouveau Cirque/Fête de Nuit des Artistes Lyriques. 1913.
35 x $48^3/_8$ in./89 x 122.8 cm
Affiches L. Damaré, Paris
Cond B/Slight tears and stains at folds and paper edges.
Talk about your "Night of 1,000 Stars!" This midnight festival of lyric artists held at the Nouveau Cirque promises to deliver "all the theatrical and concert artists in the ring and in the water." For about 40 years, until its demolition in 1926, the Nouveau Cirque was noted for its nautical shows in the summer, having a huge pool outfitted with the latest in hydraulic lifts and pumping stations. The convened throng of performers is a veritable "Who's Who" of the French music hall—and that holds true for even the handful of artists that

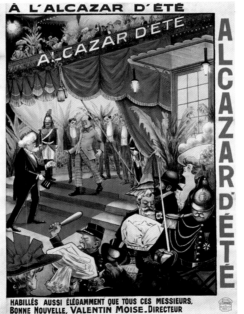

we've been able to identify. Mayol, Jeanne Bloch—her steamroller figure impressive even in miniature—and designer Sem all appear perfectly content with their water-free placement, while others—Polin, Polaire, Max Dearly, Maurice Chevalier (who made his first impression on the music hall crowds as a Dranem impersonator known as "Petit Maurice"), Dranem himself and an unidentified bare butt from an artist apparently unashamed to put his—or her—best face forward. This one-night aquatic show was a benefit for needy actors and one of its beneficiaries was none other than Dranem's own foundation.
Est: $1,500-$1,800.

38. Alcazar d'Été.
$44^3/_8$ x $60^3/_4$ in./112.6 x 154.5 cm
Affiches L. Damaré, Paris
Cond B/Recreated left margin.
No mention of his name need even be made and the throngs gather to regale themselves with the wonder of Dranem, arriving on the scene at the Alcazar d'Été with oafish aplomb, greeted by dignitaries and relieved from the burden of fan-induced mingling (which was utterly the opposite of the artist's real conduct) by a somewhat suspect police presence. A marvelously overstated testimonial to the timeless nature of celebrity profiling.
Est: $1,700-$2,000.

40

41

42

43

—the character that is, not the actual performer— would be a quality pair of boots from the Fayard line after taking a look at the arch-unsupportive, ankle-wrenching tatters currently passing for his footwear. And if a rube like him can tell quality when he sees it, there's no reason to not give Fayard the nod the next time it's shoe time. And if your tastes run a little more refined than the music hall, Fayard is quick to point out that they are also the primary shoemakers for the opera. One of many endorsements which attest to Dranem's overwhelming popularity. Larramet produced posters—the bulk of them for this printing firm—and was also known as an etcher. A student of Benjamin Constant and J.-P. Laurens, he exhibited at the major Salons between 1904 and 1923.
Est: $1,200-$1,500.

AUGUSTE ROUBILLE (1872-1955)

42. Eldorado/Cassons du Sucre.
31 x 46³/₈ in./78.7 x 117.8 cm
Charles Verneau, Paris
Cond B+/Slight tears and stains at folds.
Roubille, one of the great caricaturists of the time and a frequent contributor to such humor magazines as *Le Rire, Le Sourire* and *Cocorico*, spins a confectionary encounter to call Paris' theatrical attention to "Sugar Bread," a Dranem vehicle playing at his music hall home away from home—paired here potentially with a svelter than usually drawn Jeanne Bloch with which he partnered for many a music hall extravaganza— that was undoubtedly as comfortingly sweet as its title suggests.
Est: $1,700-$2,000.

SEM (Georges Goursat, 1863-1934)

43. Smarting House.
7¹/₂ x 13⁵/₈ in./19 x 34.5 cm
Signed gouache and ink drawing. Framed.
One wonders what smirk lies beneath the newly applied redrawn facial tip-on on this Sem maquette for a clothier to which Dranem has lent his image. Nothing more than a jovial trifle—one which may never have seen its way to poster fruition—which gives the singer a fashion makeover, showing one possible version of what Dranem, the sophisticated man about town, may have looked like had his career path veered a bit closer towards champagne wishes and caviar dreams. The career of caricaturist Sem started modestly enough in his home town of Perigueux where he published his first collection of local celebrities' portraits in 1895. Only after doing the same for Bordeaux in 1897 and Marseilles in 1898 did he venture to Paris where he charmed the city folk with his talent. Hardly anyone of note escaped being captured for posterity.
Est: $2,000-$2,500.

NOËL DORVILLE

39. Eldorado/Tête à l'Huile. 1903.
23¹/₄ x 31¹/₄ in./59 x 79.5 cm
Imp. M. Belleville, Paris
Cond A–/Unobtrusive folds.
Dranem takes a gypsy turn in this Eldorado production, whose theatrical-slangy title and setting refers to the game day-players, who much like the star, were willing and able to jump into the comic fray without inhibitions or, for that matter, shame: "The Extra." And the latter-clad love interest is none other than Mistinguett, who stars here in her first true theatrical role. This career-launching event was noted not only in the press, but also by its prolific author, Lafargue, and she quickly became his mistress. Dorville was best known for his drawings and caricatures, especially political ones, that he contributed to many satirical journals of the day, and his talent for capturing personalities is wonderfully evident in this design.
Est: $1,400-$1,700.

CANDIDO ARAGONESE DE FARIA (1849-1911)

40. R. Bertin.
85 x 53³/₈ in./215.8 x 135.6 cm
Affiches Faria, Paris

Cond A–/Unobtrusive folds.
If imitation is the sincerest form of flattery, then R. Bertin was the most complimentary man in all of turn-of-the-century Paris. If we're to believe this sweeping poster panorama, every single person attending this "A-list" salon, be they man or woman, is portrayed by none other than the versatile Monsieur Bertin, whose own portrait serves as the focal point of the star-studded hall. Some of the illustrious enclave include such diverse stars as Paulus, Mayol, Mistinguett, Dranem, the ill-fated Fragson, Yvette Guilbert, Polin and Théodore Botrel.
Est: $1,500-$1,800.

HILAIRE Z. LARRAMET

41. Fayard.
23¹/₈ x 31⁵/₈ in./58.8 x 80.3 cm
B. Chapellier-Jeune, Paris
Cond B+/Slight tears and stains at folds and edges.
It doesn't take much to believe that Dranem 's dream

44

47

DRANEM/Sem (continued)

44. Mayol and Dranem.
9³/₄ x 12¹/₄ in./24.7 x 31.2 cm
Signed gouache and ink drawing. Framed.
The unlikely dance team of bumpkin and gigolo creates
a delightful odd couple in this Sem design. This unexpected whirl around the dance floor comes complete
with the following message at bottom: "Des gouts et
des couleurs" ("The style and the colors"), no doubt
scrawled at the last minute as instructions to the printer.
Est: $2,000-$2,500.

45. Le Garcon.
8¹/₂ x 14³/₄ in./21.6 x 37.5 cm
Signed ink and crayon drawing. Framed.
The drinks in this ink and crayon drawing appear to be
destined to take a tumble in this Dranem as waiter
concoction, with Sem's printer's instructions included
in the lower right. Once again we see a newly sketched
face for Dranem pasted over an apparently unsatisfac-
tory original version, pointing to the fact that not only
was Sem adept at capturing his subject's personalities,
but also a stickler for personal accuracy.
Est: $1,700-$2,000.

RAOUL VION

46. Dranem.
46¹/₄ x 122¹/₂ in./117.5 x 311 cm
Imp. G. Delattre, Paris
Cond A–/Unobtrusive slight tears and creases.
Ref: Collectioneur, p. 105
Although little is known about the artist who created
this 2-sheet advertising portrait, the exuberant humor
that fills his few known designs is very much on display, presenting the singer with such yokel candor and
vitality that one nearly expects him to shamble free of
his graphic confines and favor us with a traditional
"Idiot Song."
Est: $1,400-$1,700.

45

46

WAGNER

47. Rasoir "Le Touriste".
28¹/₄ x 40³/₄ in./72 x 103.3 cm
Imp. Clément, Le Roy, Paris
Cond B/Restored tears at folds.

As the perennially out of place Dranem seemed to almost always appear to be a stranger in a strange land, who better to extol the virtues of "The Tourist" razor, the ideal shaving blade for artists, officers, sailors, voyagers, explorers et al. And just in case you'd just

returned from an extended stay in a foreign land, bottom accompanying text identifies the large-headed fellow as none other than the Eldorado's favored son, who gleefully proclaims, "Oh! The Tourist razor is first-rate."
Est: $1,200-$1,500.

FRENCH MUSIC-HALL

49

50

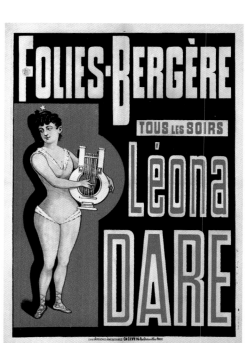

48

ANONYMOUS

48. Folies-Bergère/Léona Dare.
35¹/₄ x 48¹/₂ in./89.4 x 123.2 cm
Ch. Levy, Paris
Cond B/Slight tears at folds.
This healthy-hipped harpist is none other than Léona Dare, an accomplished American acrobat (real name: Adeline Stuart) who became a popular music hall fixture during the late-1880s. Obviously, for this announcement, the Folies-Bergère felt that the public was sufficiently aware of Dare's acrobatic accomplishments and decided to focus on the performer's lyrical side.
Est: $1,000-$1,200.

BAC (Ferdinand Bach, 1859-1952)

49. La Loïe Fuller/Aux Folies Bergère. 1892.
43¹/₈ x 59¹/₂ in./109.6 x 151 cm
Imp. Lemercier, Paris
Cond B/Slight tears and stains at folds.
Ref: Loie Fuller, 5; Takashimaya, 29; PAI-XIV, 110
German-born illustrator, posterist and writer Ferdinand Bac (his real name was Bach) had the honor of introducing American dancer Loïe Fuller to the Parisian public at the Folies-Bergère on November 5, 1892. He met the challenge nobly, catching the intriguing kaleidoscope of colors with which she dazzled the public in her dance.
Est: $3,000-$4,000.

LEONETTO CAPPIELLO (1875-1942)

50. Folies Bergère/Louise Balthy. 1902.
37¹/₈ x 52¹/₈ in./94.2 x 132.3 cm
Imp. Vercasson, Paris
Cond B–/Restored tears and losses at folds and edges. Framed.
Ref: Cappiello, 215; Cappiello/St. Vincent, 4.2 (var); Wine Spectator, 182; PAI-XXIX, 244 (var)
"Louise Balthy (1869-1926), a remarkably talented performer who was trained in ballet but broke into show business with comic songs, which secured her an engagement at the Eldorado at the age of 17. A native of Bayonne near the Spanish border, she sometimes affected some Spanish mannerisms, and Cappiello makes it clear in this design. At the time he portrayed her, she was much in demand as a star of lavish revues and spectacles" (Wine Spectator). And if Cappiello graphically captured even half of Balthy's moxie, it's easy to understand why she commanded the attention of the City of Lights.
Est: $1,700-$2,000.

la jolie Fagette

LIDIA

L'HORLOGE

Champs-Elysées

LE SEUL CONCERT D'ÉTÉ
COUVERT EN CAS
DE PLUIE

Yvette Guilbert

IMP. V. PALYART & FILS., PARIS.

FOLIES BERGÈRE

Cléo de MÉRODE

AMBASSADEURS
PARIS
TOUT NU

AMBASSADEURS
DRANEM
MISS CAMPTON

REVUE
de M.Mrs
H.DE GORSSE
& G. NANTEUIL

French Music-Hall (continued)

ANONYMOUS

51. L'Horloge/Yvette Guilbert.
$15^3/_4$ x $23^1/_2$ in./40 x 59.6 cm
Imp. V. Palyart, Paris
Cond A.
The immortal Yvette Guilbert, the greatest *chanteuse* of the period, wearing her customary chignon, famous long black gloves and a faraway look of wistful melan-choly, stands alone in this announcement for the Hor-loge, marking her singular summer appearance at the venue which has been equipped with an audience cover to ensure spectator aridity in case of rain.
Est: $1,500-$1,800.

ANONYMOUS

52. Folies-Bergère/Cleo De Mérode. ca. 1901.
$30^3/_4$ x $46^3/_8$ in./78 x 118 cm
Imp. Charles Verneau, Paris
Cond B–/Slight tears at folds; slightly light stained.
Ref: DFP-II, 960; Dance Posters, 26; Spectacle, 1156; PAI-XXVII, 203
Called "the reigning belle of Paris," Cléo de Mérode, the fabulous beauty of the Belle Epoque, danced not only at the Folies-Bergère, but performed at the Opéra and Opéra-Comique, winning praise for her appear-ance in *Danse Cambodgienne*, as well as the roles she created in other ballets. She is seen here, most

56

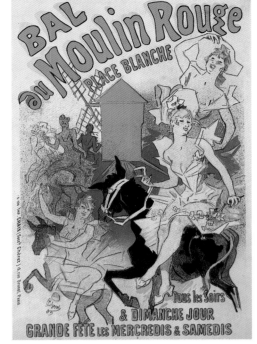

57

59

58

likely, in *Lorenza*, the ballet of Rudolphe Darzens, with Music by Franco Alfano, which opened at the Folies-Bergère on November 4, 1901. She had a romantic affair with Leopold II, King of the Belgians, whose enemies nicknamed him "Cléopold." Although this design cannot be attributed to a specific artist, it is winning in its simplicity and grace.
Est: $1,700-$2,000.

CARLO DALI

53. Ambassadeurs/Paris Tout Nu.
30¼ x 46⅝ in./77 x 118.5 cm
Publicité Wall, Paris
Cond A–/Slight tears at paper edges.
The Ambassadeurs café-concert on the Champs-Elysées was so named for its proximity to the Hotel Crillon, which used to house foreign ambassadors. In its belle epoque heyday, the café presented music hall stars from Yvette Guilbert to Aristide Bruant. In fact on this occasion, a well-sauced poster paster informs us with a semi-censoring sweep of his brush that Dranem and music hall fixture, Miss Campton, are currently appearing in a revue at the Ambassadeurs.
Est: $1,500-$1,800.

JULES CHÉRET (1836-1932)

54. Ambassadeurs/La Jolie Fagette. 1901.
34⅛ x 48⅜ in./86.6 x122.8 cm
Imp. Chaix, Paris
Cond B–/Slight tears and stains at folds and edges. Framed.
Ref: Broido, 201 & Pl. 11; DFP-II, 269; PAI-XXX, 475
The singer Fagette is portrayed in a bright yellow dress and hat and holding sprigs of narcissus against the blue-green background. Both flirtatious and coy, this songbird definitely lives up to her billing.
Est: $2,000-$2,500.

55. Lidia. 1895.
34½ x 49¼ in./87.7 x 125 cm
Imp. Chaix, Paris
Cond B+/Restored tears and losses at paper edges.
Ref: Gold, 171; Broido, 174; Maindron, 154; DFP-II-250; Maitres, 25; PAI-XXX, 112
"Using only her last name, Lily de Lidia graced some of the most popular music-hall stages of the day with her *gommeuse* (double-jointed) act. This poster . . . announces Lidia's appearance at the outdoor Alcazar d'Eté. Chéret depicts the artist almost life-size in a half-length view that's rare for him. Her expression is winsome, the creamy expanse of her décolletage

appealing, and the overall design full of movement—from the sweeping ribbons of her hat to the swaying letters of her name" (Gold, p. 120). An especially rare version of the poster without the Alcazar d'Eté lettering appearing at top.
Est: $2,500-$3,000.

56. Bal du Moulin Rouge. 1889.
37 x 51½ in./94 x 131 cm
Imp. Chaix, Paris
Cond C+/Restored tears and losses at folds and edges.
Ref: Broido, 309; Maindron, 253; DFP-II, 181; Maitres, 53; Reims, 275; Wine Spectator, 6; PAI-XXVII, 342
The Moulin Rouge, which virtually single-handedly created the cancan craze, opened its doors on October 6, 1889, and this is the historic poster for that very occasion. (The same image was used again for the 1892 season.) The donkeys are not Chéret's imagination—the two shrewd creator/promoters, Joseph Oller and Charles Zidler, actually had girls riding donkeys outside to attract attention to the place.
Est: $2,000-$2,500.

57. Bal du Moulin Rouge. 1889.
15¾ x 23⅛ in./40 x 59 cm
Imp. Chaix, Paris
Cond B+/Slight tears at top paper edge. Framed.
Ref: DFP-II, 181; Broido, 310; Maitres, 53 (var)
Smaller version of the previous image.
Est: $1,500-$1,800.

58. Casino Paris/Camille Stefani. 1896.
34 x 97½ in./86.2 x 247.5 cm
Imp. Chaix, Paris
Cond B+/Slight tears, largely at folds.
Ref: Broido, 219 & Color Pl. 5; Maitres, 93; PAI-III, 259
The auburn-tressed stage luminary graciously acknowledges her ovation from an unseen audience in this two-sheet whirlwind of color, allowing Stéfani to unabashedly shine in her element.
Est: $2,500-$3,000.

59. Musée Grévin/Fantoches de John Hewelt. 1900.
33¼ x 47⅞ in./84.5 x 121.6 cm
Imp. Chaix, Paris
Cond A. Framed.
Ref: Broido, 471; DFP-II, 267; PAI-XXIX, 301
This is the before-lettering version of Chéret's charming poster for Les Fantoches, a puppet-show extravaganza staged at the theater of the Musée Grevin, a frequent Chéret client—in fact, the design was so eye-catching that it was also used to announce a *Fête des Artistes* at the venue (*see* PAI-XV, 222). Some versions of the image, such as this, show the printer's name, while others have no text at all. Text or word-free, Chéret's fine sense of composition and great lithographic skill shine.
Est: $2,500-$3,000

FRENCH MUSIC-HALL (continued)

ALFRED CHOUBRAC (1853-1902)

60. Scala/Paris Fin de Sexe.
$22^1/4$ x $30^3/4$ in./56.5 x 78.2 cm
Ateliers Choubrac à Colombes-Seine
Cond A.

Choubrac was one of the pioneers of French poster art; in 1884, when Maindron published his first article on posters, he listed only nine active posterists known to him, and included the three poster artists whose work made up the first poster exhibition, held that same year in the Passage Vivienne in Paris: Alfred and Léon Choubrac and Jules Chéret. Clear, deliberate outlining of his subjects was one of Choubrac's trademarks; the other was gentle humor and whimsy. Both traits manifest themselves charmingly in this design for the "Paris—The End of Sex" revue playing at the Scala music hall. Whether this title refers to the French capital providing the last word in carnality or that the new century has ushered in a new Puritanism isn't made precisely clear as Choubrac includes both elements—the curvaceous charms of busty chorines and the decidedly unsexy presence of Polin. It may well be that the revue "Paris-Fin de Sex" may be a play on words with "Fin de Siècle," the magazine for which Choubrac's 1891 poster was censored for revealing a bit too much of the model's charms (see Wine Spectator introduction).
Est: $1,500-$1,800.

PAUL COLIN (1892-1986)

61. Rosario et Antonio. 1949.
$45^1/4$ x $61^1/2$ in./115 x 156.3 cm
Imp. Bedos, Paris
Cond A–/Unobtrusive slight tears at paper edges.

An especially popular dance team in the 1949-1950 season when flamenco dancing reached new heights of popularity in France, Rosario and Anonio—as portrayed by Colin—are Latin dance perfection, a sultry combination of personal flair and pheromonic union. Colin executed at least one other poster for the pair (see PAI-III, 274). Colin started his poster career in the late 1920s in the music hall and film fields, with art

deco as his guiding inspiration. He adapted it, however, to his own style, evolving as he embraced symbolism and abstraction in later years. He was a master of depicting movement in deceptively simple ways, creating dozens of posters for performers in all media, reflecting the history of Paris show business and public life during his lifetime perhaps better than any of his contemporaries.
Est: $2,500-$3,000.

CHARLES GESMAR (1900–1928)

62. Harry Baur. 1928.
$47^1/4$ x $62^5/8$ in./120 x 159 cm
Imp H. Chachoin, Paris

Cond B/Slight tears and stains, largely at folds.
Ref: PAI-XXVIII, 314

A marvelously incisive character study of one of France's premier stage and film personalities. Harry Baur (1880-1943) was one of the giants of the French performing arts. Trained in stagecraft from an early age, he was at his best portraying powerful characters, both fictional and historical; in that regard, he was the Paul Muni of the French cinema in the 1930s. He essayed Jean Valjean in "Les Misérables" (1934); Emperor Rudolph II in "Le Golem" (1936); Beethoven in "Un Grand Amour de Beethoven" (1936); Rasputin in "La Tragedie Imperiale" (1938); and he was both "Rothschild" (1934) and "Volpone" (1939). During the Nazi

64

66

65

H. GRAY (Henri Boulanger, 1858–1924)

63. Chaumière Tivoli.
36³/4 x 51¹/4 in./93.2 x 130.4 cm
Imp. Pajol & Cie., Paris
Cond B/Slight tears at folds.
Ref: PAI-XXVI, 311
A voluptuous pumpkin-pantalooned real-life Judy raises her arms in victory over a hapless wooden Punch, who is powerless versus her charms. She appears to be unaware that danger is still afoot as an evil clown prepares to pounce in this oddly engaging work for a café-concert at the Place de la République. A prolific caricaturist and illustrator who worked for a half-dozen Paris periodicals, Gray also designed posters for music halls and other clients using several different styles.
Est: $1,500-$1,800.

JULES-ALEXANDRE GRUN (1868-1934)

64. La Boite à Fursy. 1901.
33¹/2 x 48³/8 in./ 85 x 123 cm
Imp. Chaix, Paris
Cond B+/Restored tears, largely at paper edges. Framed.
Ref: DFP-II, 439; Spectacle, 926; Gold, 148; PAI-XXX, 127
The music hall Tréteau du Tabarin (Tabarin's Stage) had opened in 1895 at 58 rue Pigalle—former performance site of a famous clown, Tabarin. For four years, the singer Henri Fursy was the chief attraction; but in 1895 a disagreement with the owners induced him to leave and open his own club, the Boite à Fursy—to which the entire audience of the Tréteau du Tabarin promptly followed him. Facing bankruptcy, the Tréteau invited Fursy back, and in 1901 it reopened as the new Boite à Fursy—Henri Fursy, Director. Earlier posters for the Tréteau and the Boite appear in the background of this poster to signify the merger. The chorus girl in the foreground expresses "the very mood of the Parisian tenderloin, light-headed and insouciant, with fun occupying every thought . . . with a hint of naughtiness that is Grün's own" (Gold, p. 104).
Est: $3,000-$3,500.

65. Polin.
15³/8 x 23¹/4 in./39 x 59 cm
Imp. G. Gerin, Dijon
Cond B/Tape stains, top and bottom edge. Framed.
For over 40 years, café-concert legend Polin (the stage name of singer Pierre-Paul Marsalés, 1863-1927) reigned supreme over the musical halls of Montmartre and the Champs-Elysées. Making his debut in 1886 at *Concert de la Pépinière*, he would go on to delight audiences well into the next century with the timid sincerity and naive charm of the character he created. This poster portrait of the performer isn't precisely the fare one has come to expect from the most titillating chronicler of the Montmartre nightlife scene. Grün does an admirable job of capturing the essential Polin, setting down "Paris' Premiere Comic Singer" with impish delight, decked out in his trademark ill-fitting uniform, with his beloved security handkerchief clasped firmly in his hand.
Est: $1,200-$1,500.

CHARLES KIFFER (1902–1992)

66. Maurice Chevalier. 1954.
45¹/2 x 62¹/2 in./115.6 x 158.7 cm
Imp. Bedos, Paris
Cond A.
Ref: Folies-Bergère, 100; Kiffer, p. 18 (var);
     PAI-XXVI, 343
"Christian Dior had just launched his 'string bean' line. Kiffer uses it as a pretext for a new representation of Chevalier: the projectors beam, which catches the red background, takes on the shape of a bean; four leaves (also from the bean) and a branch constitute the individual who is only identifiable by his straw hat." (Folies-Bergère, p. 15). Of the many posters Kiffer designed for Chevalier over a period of 40 years, this has become one of the rarest. *Hand-signed by the artist.*
Est: $2,000-$2,500

occupation, the German authorities somehow got wind of the fact that Baur's wife was Jewish and they promptly arrested her; Baur refused to comply meekly and so he, too, was taken and subjected to torture as a suspected Allied agent. A few days later, he tragically died from internal injuries sustained during his interrogation.
Est: $3,000-$4,000.

67

68

FRENCH MUSIC-HALL (continued)

MAURICE MILLIÈRE (1871-?)

67. Le Divan Japonais.
34⁵/₈ x 48¹/₄ in./88 x 122.6 cm
Imp. Bourgerie, Paris
Cond B/Restored tears at folds and edges.
A painter, illustrator and etcher, Millière was well-known for his humorous sketches and magazine drawings of half-clad young women. Clearly his penchant for the demi-clad lasses is in evidence in this sprightly promotion for the Divan Japonais—the cabaret made immortal by Henri de Toulouse-Lautrec—but his caricaturistic skills show that they're up for any diversionary activity, from high-steppin' seniors to frolicking monuments. Lautrec it ain't, but it's a lively foray into the night in its own right.
Est: $1,500-$1,800.

68. Divan Japonais/La Revue Nouveau Jeu.
35⁵/₈ x 50³/₄ in./90.5 x 129 cm
Imp. Bourgerie, Paris
Cond B/Unobtrusive tears, largely at folds and edges.
All the ingredients are in place for a perfect Millière evening at the Divan Japonais: disrobed chorus girls, romance, sophistication, one (most probably) nutty old lady and more chorus girls. And with a name like "The New Toy Revue," it sounds like the perfect recipe.
Est: $1,400-$1,700.

A. MELLIÉS

69. Polin/Madelon.
19³/₄ x 56⁷/₈ in./50 x 144.6 cm
Gouache and ink signed maquette.
This maquette commemorates Polin's twilight years career, still the military clown, perhaps a bit more paunchy than in his youth, but still able to translate the human condition through the naiveté of a simpleton's verse. And though "Madelon" would appear to be a boozy recollection of a particularly favored waitress, the final line expresses with bittersweet melancholy that regardless of their drunken antics, all Madelon would do was laugh, because that "was all the bad she knew," proving once more that contemporary definitions of comedy have grown perilously narrow.
Est: $1,700-$2,000.

PAL (Jean de Paléologue,1860–1942)

70. Olympia/"Mauvais Rêve." ca. 1895.
32³/₈ x 48¹/₄ in./82.2 x 122.6 cm
Imp. Paul Dupont, Paris
Cond A–/Unobtrusive folds.
Ref: Reims, 943; Maindron, p. 102; DFP-II, 689;
    PAI-XXV, 441
It appears that in the pantomime "Bad Dream," playing

69

70

at the Olympia, Irma de Montigny played a boy's role, but there is decidedly nothing masculine about her lovely face and engaging smile. Pal, a maven of feminine allure, was a genuine Rumanian aristocrat, his family in Bucharest having descended from venerable Byzantine rulers. He, however, had no desire for the idle life of a nobleman, and having a talent for draftsmanship, opted to go to work in London as a magazine illustrator. In 1893, he was lured to Paris, where he turned to posters and introduced his finely proportioned, realistically depicted maidens whose abundant charms could sell anything. After blasting such a spectacular trail of opulently endowed beauties, Pal, in 1900, left Paris as abruptly as he had left London, and moved to the United States, where he settled down to a career of working mostly for the automobile, film and animation industries; and that's where he died in 1942, in Miami.
Est: $2,000-$2,500.

71. La Jolie Théro. 1898.
36³/₄ x 51³/₄ in./93.3 x 131.5 cm
Imp. Chardin, Paris
Cond A–/Slight tears at edges.

Ref: DFP-II, 692
Rising like untamed spin art from a carnival color wheel, La Jolie Théro launches her way into an unbridled flamenco, castanets at the ready and arched in sultry abandon. A superb tonal whirlwind from Pal, more than equal to the design he created for another Spanish dancer one must assume influenced this particular one's choice of stage names: La Belle Otero. *Rare!*
Est: $4,000-$5,000.

THÉOPHILE-ALEXANDRE STEINLEN (1859-1923)

72. Mothu et Doria. 1893.
35⁵/₈ x 48¹/₄ in./90.5 x 122.2 cm
Impressions Artistiques, Paris
Cond B/Restored tears; image excellent. Framed.
Ref (All Var): Bargiel & Zagrodzki, 12A.2; Crauzat, 490;
    DFP-II, 780; Maitres, 46; PAI-XX, 447
A gentleman rather disdainfully proffers a light to a lowly ruffian on the street in this poster for a pair of singers. We get just the right hint of the social tensions of the period. *This is the rare, previously unseen black and white proof of the design.*
Est: $4,000-$5,000.

71

72

73

74

73. Chat Noir/Prochainement. 1896.
15³/₄ x 24¹/₄ in./40 x 61.5 cm
Imp. Charles Verneau, Paris
Cond A. Framed.
Ref: Bargiel & Zagrodzki, 22.B1; PAI-XXIX, 639
This is the smaller format of the classic design for the Black Cat cabaret; the text here promotes the opening, boasting of a "highly illustrious troupe" presenting shadow plays, poetry readings and songs.
Est: $6,000-$7,000.

YONI

74. Moulin de la Galette.
43³/₈ x 29⁵/₈ in./110 x 75.4 cm
Imp. Draeger, Paris
Cond A.
Ref: PAI-XXV, 546
The Moulin de la Galette, from all accounts, was a dance hall that tried to pattern itself after the Moulin Rouge, right down to parading girls on donkeys outside the place to get noticed. But even though it was bigger and had a somewhat better location on the crest of Montmartre, it never reached the same level of reputation. Here, it proclaims its reopening after a renovation with a poster in which it's personified by a bawdy broad with wildly buoyant hair—presumably representing the wild abandon that will reign in the redecorated hall. Since "yoni" is an ancient symbol of female pudenda, we speculate that the designer may have, in fact, been a woman hiding behind an allusive pseudonym.
Est: $1,700-$2,000.

MOTORCYCLE POSTERS

75

76

77

ANONYMOUS

75. Harley-Davidson. 1928.
41 x 57^1/$_2$ in./104 x 146.2 cm
Printed in U.S.A.
Cond B+/Restored tears at folds and edges.
As the opening page of the Harley-Davidson website states: "It's one thing to have people buy your products. It's another for them to tattoo your name on their bodies." Now, although there is no visible ink on this spiffy traveling tandem, their apparent unfettered satisfaction is unmistakable and puts a face to the devotion which those who give themselves over to the motorcyclic lifestyle feel towards the Harley—a dedication which borders on the sacramental. Another point made apparent in the talented hands of "CHS" is that this poster was intended for European distribution in spite of the English text—were it for American advertising, the sidecar would have appeared on the other side of the cycle. An amusing side note: Most people, regardless of their affinity for the twin-wheeled muscle machines, have heard them referred to as "hogs," a somewhat curious pet name for a ride of such intensity. One possible explanation to the Harley-Davidson-exclusive reference dates back to the 1920s. During this decade of dominance, the factory racing team would bring their mascot pig along with them to every challenge. Since this team ruled the tracks and was known by all, their entrance, legend has it, had everyone exclaiming, "Here comes the Harley team and their Hog." *Both these Harley-Davidson images are extremely rare!*
Est: $5,000-$6,000.

76. Harley-Davidson. 1928.
40^5/$_8$ x 57^3/$_4$ in./103.2 x 146.7 cm
Printed in U. S. A.
Cond B–/Restored tears and losses.
In 1901, in the Midwestern blue-collar Mecca of Milwaukee, Wisconsin, two men in their early 20s, William Harley and Arthur Davidson, began experimenting with "taking the work out of bicycling." After making innumerable changes and adjustments to their engine design, along with the addition of a new looped frame, production of three separate models of motorcycle began in 1903. By 1920, Harley-Davidson had become the largest motorcycle manufacturer in the world, boasting dealers in 67 countries. The Twenties were indeed an innovative decade for the motorcycle magnates, including the introduction of the teardrop gas tank in 1925 and, in 1928, the front brake. This poster—masterfully created by in all probability a local artist who identifies himself with the initials "CHS"—can be numbered as one of the company's late-'20s innovations as well, having the savvy to green-light exhilarating, near-epic artwork that equals the machines they promoted. It also points out that, regardless of the quality and in spite of the master craftsmanship that goes into creating the 350cc sidevalve ride, Harleys, without a doubt, are babe magnets, effortlessly hypnotizing the lasses as it surges through a Dutch port town. You've got to tip your hat to the rider, a man of the world who obviously knows what he likes and perfection when he sees it.
Est: $4,000-$5,000.

77. Moto "Ultima".
31^3/$_4$ x 47^1/$_4$ in./80.7 x 120 cm
Affiches Corbe-Rouzet, Dole
Cond A–/Slight stains at paper edges.
This chap out for a spin through the mountains obviously isn't going to pin the needle on the testosterone

78

79

80

81

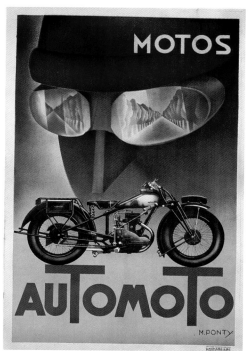

82

meter—when was the last time you saw someone riding a motorcycle while smoking a pipe, I ask you—but that may be precisely the point: Ultima motorcycles are the make for everyone, well-constructed for high performance but definitely not too intimidating. The unidentified artist conveys this sense of refinement and escape with colorful reserve.
Est: $1,700-$2,000.

ROGER CARTIER

78. Motoconfort/Hutchinson.
30^1/2 x 45^3/4 in./77.5 x 116 cm
Imp. Max Courteau, Paris
Cond B–/Restored tears at folds and edges.
Unleash your inner centaur with Hutchinson tires. Though at first glance this scene of mythological release appears to be for a brand of bike whose name would seem to hint at the comfort their ride provides, the lack of detail given to the motorcycle itself indicates otherwise, therefor placing attention firmly on the tires that make you feel as if they aren't even touching the road. A design of legendary proportions by Cartier, an artist primarily known for his work for the film industry (*see* No. 33).
Est: $1,200-$1,500.

LAJOS MARTON (1891-1952)

79. Motos Peugeot. 1928.
31 x 46^1/2 in./78.9 x 118.2 cm
DAM Studio; Et. & L. Damour, Paris
Cond B+/Unobtrusive tears and stains at folds.
Ref: Affiche Réclame, 28; PAI-XXIX, 79
The zooming motorcycle is only a dark blur, but being a French make, it leaves a blue, white and red streak in its wake—a very simple, yet imaginative way to inject a nationalistic tone into the design. Although previously offered as the work of an anonymous hand, the poster's inclusion in the above reference material has led us to identify the designer as Marton, an artist employed by the DAM Agency between 1928 and 1931.
Est: $1,200-$1,500.

MILO MARTINET (1904-?)

80. FN.
27^1/2 x 37^7/8 in./70 x 96.2 cm
Imp. Bénard, Liège
Cond A.
An intense design for Belgium's Fabrique Nationale d'Armes de Guerre, or FN, a firm which produced everything from bicycles to armaments, and symbolized it appropriately in its logo—albeit modifying it to indicate the armament branch with the subtle sighting of a scope rather than the inclusion of a rifle (*see* PAI-XXVIII, 41). The sheer mechanical prowess of the cycle is pleasingly overpowering, getting right up in the face of the passerby with object poster singularity while refraining from overblown swagger.
Est: $1,700-$2,000.

POZZI

81. Motor Club Imola. 1954.
39^3/8 x 53^3/8 in./100 x 135.6 cm
Lithografica Marzocchi, Bologna
Cond A.
Dust and thunder combine with futuristic uniformity in this head-on 2-sheet promotion for the 1954 European Motocross Championship sponsored by the Imola Motorcycle Club. The Northern Italian town situated in the Bologna province has a long-standing association with tests of speed and endurance, stretching back to two-wheeled charioteers in 80 BC and remaining a Formula One hotbed to this day.
Est: $1,400-$1,700.

MAX PONTY (1904-1972)

82. Automoto.
31^5/8 x 47^1/8 in./80.4 x 119.7 cm
Hachard, Paris
Cond B+/Slight tears at folds.
Ponty's known designs are few, but more than suffice to establish him as a foremost Art Deco posterist. Here he turns his angular attention to Automoto motorcycles, creating a futuristic photomontage dreamscape for the French firm that produced their machines from 1901 through 1962. Contrasting the curvy sensuality of the photographed bike against the angular overlord face, the open road reflected in his goggles and the entire scene drenched in graded shades of moody violet, Ponty creates a cyclic fantasia, capturing both the thrill, speed and inherent danger of the ride without ever placing a bike in simulated motion.
Est: $2,000-$2,500.

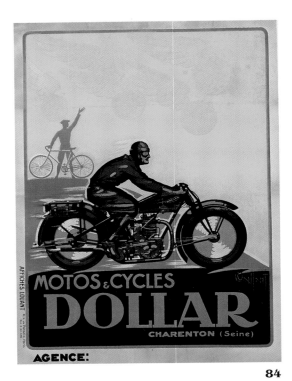

83

84

MOTORCYCLES (continued)

FRANÇOIS-LOUIS SCHMIED

83. La Motosacoche. ca. 1908.
55 x 42³/₄ in./139.7 x 108.7 cm
Klausfelder, Vevey
Cond B/Restored tears at folds and edges; image and
 colors excellent.
Ref: Genève, 27
One of the first posters created for the celebrated
Genevese make of motorcycles. Quite simply, a beautiful poster, romantic to a fault, breathtaking to the
extreme and noble beyond compare, the sort of epic
cinematic scope one might associate with "Gone With
The Wind," but not with a motorbike firm regardless of
the quality of the product. "Switzerland had some

twenty motorcycle manufacturing companies, starting
in 1899, the year in which Motosacoche was founded.
Henri and Armand Dufaux started out producing small
engines for bicycles, but devoted themselves almost
immediately to the production of motorcycles and
engines of 250 cc to 1000 cc, under the MAG trademark" (*One Hundred Years of Motorcycles*, Massimo
Clarke, editor, p. 190). In the early part of the century,
horsepower was related to engine size, usually for tax
reasons. So the 350 cc V twin engine on this motorcycle was credited with 3 hp. Such was the racing success of this motorcycle, however, that the power
output can safely be put at between 10 and 12 horsepower, an astonishing figure for that time.
Est: $7,000-$9,000.

VAILLANT

84. Motos & Cycles Dollar.
45³/₈ x 61⁵/₈ in./116.3 x 156.5 cm
Imp. Affiches Louant, Paris
Cond B/Staining and tears in yellow background and
 along folds.
The golden heavens of solitary transportation all but
envelope these two riders—pedal-powered and motorized alike—focusing our attention on the graded violet
and milky-indigo vehicles, the cyclist saluting the
winged Indian dollars whizzing through the aureate
sky, the gold coins a clever nod to the speed, economy and brand name of the French cycle manufacturer.
Est: $1,500-$1,700.

AUTOMOBILE POSTERS

ANONYMOUS

85. Le Camion 6 Cyl. Chevrolet.
46 x 62 in./116.8 x 157.5 cm
Office d'Editions d'Art, Paris
Cond A.
During the mid-1930s, Chevrolet began converting
their trucks to meet European standards and one of
those models is on display here: the 6-cylinder
flatbed. The dockside formalistic treatment given to
the General Motors workhorse is a paragon of utilitar-
ian simplicity, but at the same time, the unknown
artist imbues the design with a hazy romanticism that
leaves the viewer with a blue collar yearning not at all
dissimilar to the current "Like A Rock" Chevrolet television commercials.
Est: $1,700-$2,000.

86. Cycles Terrot/Automobiles. ca. 1900.
44⁷/₈ x 61⁵/₈ in./114 x 156.5 cm
Imp. P. Vercasson, Paris
Cond A-/Unobtrusive folds.
Ref: Meisterplakate, 251; PAI-II, 3
The Terrot firm originated in Dijon during the 1890s
as a bicycle manufacturer; at the turn of the century,
they also began to produce automobiles. The chain,
which this poster features, was used as late as 1910
on high-powered racing cars and evolved from the
earlier belt drive. As automobile engines improved
and vehicles began to operate much faster, the more
secure chain was used to replace the belt, a device
which would slip easily at fast speeds. And it's speed
that is emphasized here, with the festively frocked

85

89

automobilist tooting her own horn and flippantly ges-
turing to the train that she has just raced—and
beaten!—through the tunnel. The dismissive gesture
was something of a trademark for the early Terrot

advertising, first established by Tamagno (*see* PAI-XXX,
296), who would exploit the outdistancing motif in a
series of various race-like conditions. But no matter
what the competition, the young woman never neg-

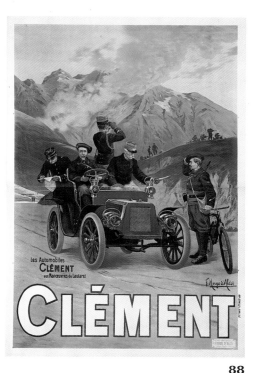

88

with a regimental flair. As a battle rages, the field marshals and generals, dispatch an envoy via a stalwart bicycle messenger (possibly riding a Clément cycle?). Notice, however, that they do not even step out of their swift, reliable mobile strategic headquarters just in case the line collapses and they need to beat a hasty retreat. *This is the larger 2-sheet format.*
Est: $1,400-$1,700.

ARCO

89. "Crosière."
23 x 31 in.58.6 x 79 cm
Cond A. Framed.
I pose this question to anyone who has ever driven a car for more than a three-block stretch: What would you do without your radio? No matter what type of music, regardless of which talk you prefer, the car stereo has become an absolute essential, to the point where compact disc players and 8-speaker systems are becoming a part of your basic package. But my friends, things weren't always so cush. Sometimes just having a quality radio could make an everyday drive in the family sedan seem like a luxury junket. To that end we present the "Cruise," the international class wireless car radio, from the Electromobile corporation, a system so refined that only classical visual allusions will suffice for its advertising. *Rare!*
Est: $1,500-$1,800.

GUS BOFA (Gustave Blanchot, ?-1968)

90. Rudge-Whitworth. 1912.
46¹/₂ x 62¹/₂ in./118.2 x 158.8 cm
Imp. Ch. Verneau, Paris
Cond B/Slight tears and stains at folds and edges.
If a group of elves can be responsible for creating quality footwear, then why can't a well-equipped gnome take credit for the mechanical aspects of the easily removable Rudge-Whitworth detachable tire? Not to mention that Bofa's jolly elemental utterly distracts the viewer from the actual messy process of tire changing and almost makes the enterprise seem like a fairly pleasant diversion. Almost.
Est: $1,500-$1,800

lected to let her adversary know in no uncertain—if not precisely ladylike—terms who the champ was.
Est: $2,000-$2,500.

87. Donnet Zedel. 1925.
47¹/₂ x 60 in./120.5 x 152.2 cm
Imp. H. Chachoin, Paris
Cond A–/Unobtrusive folds.
Ref: PAI-XXVI, 20
The handsome yellow Donnet is silhouetted against a blue Mediterranean sky as it climbs a road above the Cote d'Azur. It is, as the slogan punningly tells us, "The car that climbs, the brand that's climbing."

90

One of two very effective designs for this car that are known to us from the "Atelier A.B." (*see* PAI-XVII, 66).
Est: $3,000-$4,000.

F. HUGO D'ALESI (1849-1906)

88. Clément.
63¹/₄ x 160.5 in./93¹/₈ x 236.5 cm
Imp. Cornille & Domicile, Paris
Cond A.
Ref: PAI-XXVI, 23 (var)
D'Alesi, who is often credited as the "inventor of the 'landscape poster' typical of the first period in poster design" (Affiches d'Azur, p. 19), gives us a panoramic mountainscape without sacrificing the focus of the object of desire: the Clément automobile, presented

91

94

93

95

AUTOMOBILE POSTERS (continued)

MAURICE BARBEY

91. Amilcar. 1932.
62^1/$_8$ x 46^5/$_8$ in./158 x 118.4 cm
Imp. H. Chachoin, Paris
Cond B+/Unobtrusive slight tears and stains.
Ref: PAI-XV, 55
By giving us a close-up view of the car, with mountains and valleys behind, and especially by projecting an exaggerated shadow of the Amilcar hood ornament so that it becomes a veritable cliffside billboard, Barbey has given us a poster as much appreciated for its powerful design as for its nostalgia. Amilcar was a company launched by two Paris businessmen, Emil Akar and Joseph Lamy, in 1921. It started with a small car which became progressively larger, as this 1932 model shows. The company could not escape the worldwide Depression, however, and went out of business in 1939. Barbey was primarily a landscape painter whose work was exhibited at the Salon des Indépendants from 1912 to 1938.
Est: $2,500-$3,000.

MARIO BAZZI (1891-1954)

92. Fiat. 1950.
35^3/$_4$ x 50^1/$_4$ in./91 x 127.7 cm
Roggero & Tortia, Torino
Cond B/Slight tears at folds.
Fiat's traditional concern is "producing ordinary, everyday cars for ordinary, everyday people" (Fordyce, p. 138). Nevertheless, the company has always leaned towards the spectacular in its advertising. This poster, for example, has the company's name thrusting mono-

lithically alongside a country lane, the poster-within-the-poster of the firm's original model blown gently by the wake of its latest model, the Fiat 1400. This was the first all-new, post-WW II Fiat model, designed with an American-style bearing body instead of the traditional chassis. Its engineering and stylistic innovations required a total plant overhaul to produce. An act, in and of itself, worthy of monumental advertising. This is something of a departure for Bazzi, a painter and illustrator who leaned more towards caricature than iconoclastic platitudes. Stylistically, his poster work tends to run in a Cappiello-esque vein (black background, colorful central figure), opting to dismiss detail in favor of persuasive imagination.
Est: $2,000-$2,500.

HENRI BELLERY-DESFONTAINES (1867–1909)

93. Automobiles Georges Richard. ca. 1904.
59^1/$_8$ x 34^3/$_4$ in./150.2 x 88.2 cm
Imp. Eugène Verneau, Paris (not shown)
Cond A–/Slight tears at paper edges.
Ref: Auto Show III, 26 (var); PAI-XXVIII, 10
A racing spirit forms a figurehead for the speeding automobile as it kicks dust into the starry midnight sky. Simultaneously poetic and dramatic, it is one of the most spectacular automotive posters ever created. Several versions of the image are known; this particular variant comes to us before the addition of lettering in the top text panel. Possibly the firm did not yet know that their car won the prestigious Gordon Bennett race in 1904—something heralded in the version with top text (see PAI-XXII, 41). Bellery-Desfontaines had a short but successful career as a painter, decorator and

designer of furniture, books and typefaces. Two of his color lithographs were included in the prestigious *L'Estampe moderne* (1897 & 1898).
Est: $5,000-$6,000.

A. BOSWALL

94. Grand Prix/Peugeot. 1913.
20^5/$_8$ x 14^7/$_8$ in./57.5 x 37.8 cm
Imp. Camis, Paris
Cond A–/Slight tears at edges. Framed.
Regardless of the fact that a singular Peugeot is shown muscularly banking its way through a turn, the thunder of engine—spewing forth a patriotic tricolor blast—and bite of petrol surges off this design while modestly boasting of the automobile's "world record of the hour," having bested the field in the American Grand Prix and The French Grand Prix for both 1912 and 1913. Although Peugeot was a pioneer firm at the birth of the sport, participating in automotive races from 1894 on, the year 1912 heralded in Peugeot designs as the true progenitors of the modern racing car. And at the French Automobile Club event of the following year, covering nearly 580 miles with twenty-nine laps at Amiens, the Peugeot dominance bore itself out in spectacular fashion. The race itself was settled by a single incident: the leader of the race, Guyot, ran over his own mechanic with his Delage. He wasn't seriously injured, but the mishap allowed Boillot in his Peugeot to take the lead and never relinquish it, in spite of a hose bursting and a snapped ignition lever. Though not the most spectacular of all races,

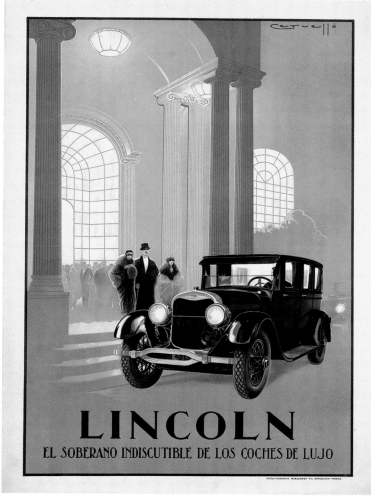

92

96

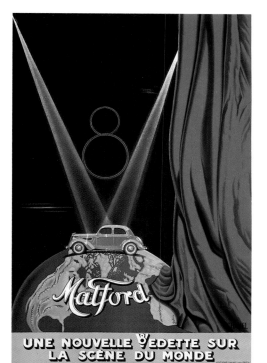

UNE NOUVELLE VEDETTE SUR
LA SCÈNE DU MONDE

97

Boillot summed up his victory thusly: "'I finished, glad to have the honour of winning the Grand Prix for the second year in succession'. Georges Boillot was the hero of France" (*The French Grand Prix 1906-1966*, by David Hodges). Later that same year, the second place finisher in the A. C. F. race, Jules Goux—also behind the wheel of a Peugeot—would go on to win

the second running of the Indianapolis 500, marking the first time that a European car and team would claim victory at Indy.
Est: $1,400-$1,700.

LEONETTO CAPPIELLO (1875-1942)

95. Pneu Velo Baudou.
$46^{1}/_{4}$ x $62^{7}/_{8}$ in./117.5 x 159.8 cm
Imp. Vercasson, Paris
Cond A.
Ref: PAI-XXVII, 38
Since the tire is named "La Sirène," it is appropriately a radiant siren that rises out of the startlingly blue sea to sell it to us, her red hair flying in the wind, a few strands semi-decorously obscuring her bosom, while tendrils of seaweed do their best to conceal the remainder of her ample charms.
Est: $2,500-$3,000.

CERVELLÓ

96. Lincoln.
$20^{3}/_{8}$ x $28^{3}/_{5}$ in./51.8 x 72.2 cm
Fotolito Grafia Rieusset, Barcelona
Cond B+/Unobtrusive tears at folds.
Emerging complacently through the mist of some gala or another, this well-heeled trio heads for the confines of their awaiting Lincoln limousine, whose flowing lines and classic design rival the vaunted archway and columnar thrust of the backing architecture. It's hard to imagine aping the threesome's blasé attitude towards their sophisticated surroundings, but perhaps that's just the message the designer was putting

across: With Lincoln there's no need to prove a thing. Lincoln equals class and if you need any more explanation, then maybe you're not ready for a such automotive pampering. And just in case the splendid graphics don't get the point across, the bottom text line puts a fine point on the lush decadence with unblinking brevity: "Lincoln: The Indisputable Supreme Luxury Car." *Rare!*
Est: $6,000-$7,000.

CHANEL

97. Matford. 1936.
$30^{1}/_{8}$ x $45^{1}/_{2}$ in./76.3 x 115.5 cm
Imp. Editions Chanel, Paris
Cond B/Restored tears in top background.
The curtain is paged back to reveal the new star on the automotive world scene—the Matford V8. Literally sitting on top of the world, spotlit and glinting like a chrome and steel sapphire, this poster gives the newest everyday sedan the automobile "Queen for the Day" treatment. " Before 1934 the only Ford peculiar to France was a forward conversion of the European 8hp Model-Y, the Tracford, but in 1934 an agreement was signed with the ailing Mathis concern whereby their factories were at first partially, and then entirely turned over to the manufacture of Ford vehicles. The cars were closely related to their American prototypes, the small 2.2-litre V8-60 being added to the range for 1936. . . . In 1947, the company was reorganized as Ford S.A.F. and cars were marketed under the Ford name" (*Encyclopedia of Motorcars*, p. 405).
Est: $1,200-$1,500

100

101

98

99

AUTOMOBILE POSTERS (continued)

GAMY

98. Charron. 1910.
29⁷/₈ x 15 in./75.8 x 38.2 cm
Maribeau, Paris
Cond B/Stains at edges.
Dropping in the subtle "Everyone's going in a Charron" catchphrase in the lower left is a nice bit of advertising moxie, but simply putting the name of the convertible in question might have been message enough. Because if this group's speedy little jaunt down the coast isn't enough to convince the passerby that Charron is the only way to take a spin, then no amount of textual manipulation will do the trick. Fernand Charron, who won the first Gordon Bennet Cup in a car of his own design in 1900, eventually took over the Charron firm and manufactured large, comfortable—and expensive—sedans.
Est: $800-$1,000.

99. Fabrique Automobile Belge. 1913.
17 x 34¹/₄ in./43 x 87 cm
Mabileau & Cie., Paris
Cond A.
Ref: PAI-XXI, 186
Given the usual muscular quality of most automobile posters, this unusual specimen for the Belgian Automobile Manufacturing Association has the formality of a Japanese woodcut rendered with delicacy and charm. It is probable that Gamy was, in fact, Marguerite Montaut, wife of automobile artist Ernest Montaut; her nickname was Magy, an anagram of Gamy. All Gamy-signed works are in the same spirit and use a similar technique as Montaut's, but date after his death in 1909.
Est: $1,200-$1,500.

GEORGES GAUDY (1872-?)

100. Voitures Mors. ca. 1910.
37¹/₄ x 24⁷/₈ in./94.7 x 63 cm
La Lithographie Artistique, Tournai
Cond A.
Ref: Auto Show II, 1; PAI-VII, 402
Milady's frock is coral, but nearly everything else—car, pageboy and background foliage—is green in this 2-sheet poster, providing a distinct impression of the manufacturer's ideal clientele image. Emile Mors was a racing enthusiast who built his first car in 1895; he later opened a factory which was at one time run by André Citroën. In 1927, Citroën, by then a far more successful manufacturer, bought Mors out. Gaudy was a Belgian painter, magazine illustrator and posterist whose masterful handling of bicycle and automotive subjects reflects his own interests.
Est: $2,500-$3,000.

H. GRAY (Henri Boulanger, 1858-1924)

101. Gladiator.
61¹/₂ x 45 in./156.3 x 114.4 cm
Imp. E. Bougard, Paris
Cond B+/Slight stains and creases.
Finally. A poster that dares to ask the question, "What would Rome have been like if Ben-Hur had been a stock car driver?" An intriguing query, to be sure. Actually, Gray's concept is a completely logical one, what with the company named Gladiator, but an audacious one no less. Framed within columns that reflect the grandeur and pomp of the inner Coliseum proceedings, these high-octane charioteers show no fear as they jockey for position in their tweaked-out Gladiators, but one really has to admire the icy daring of the riders who chose to take on the competition atop the Gladiator cycles. Let's see Chuck Heston top that!
Est: $2,500-$3,000.

GEO HAM (Georges Hamel, 1900-1972)

102. Grand Prix Automobiles/Meeting Aviation/ Nimes. 1947.
31¹/₈ x 47¹/₈ in./79 x 119.7 cm
Sadiac, Nimes
Cond A–/Unobtrusive tears.
Ref: PAI-XXII, 59
A pair of race cars streak up and over a dusty hill, but they're no match for the plane zooming overhead in this Ham poster for the 1947 Nimes Grand Prix and Air Show, the proceeds of which benefited war veterans.
Est: $3,500-$4,000.

102

103

103. Monaco/22 Avril 1935.
$31^1/_2$ x 47 in./80 x 119.4 cm
Imp. Monégasque, Monte-Carlo
Cond A.
Ref: PAI-XXIX, 19
With the Nazi regime now in full sway in Germany, the Mercedes-Benz team arrived with the most powerful cars yet used in the Grand Prix, and earned first prize easily. With Italian driver Luigi Fazioli at the wheel, the 3.99-liter Mercedes W25 model led from start to finish, never seriously challenged by the three Alfa Romeos and the Maserati that took the next four spots. On the poster, Ham puts us right in the action, against the glittering background of sun-drenched Monte Carlo.
Est: $6,000-$7,000.

HRAST

104. Michelin Pilota. ca. 1938.
$39^1/_2$ x $55^1/_2$ in./100.5 x 141 cm
F. Milani, Milano
Cond B/Slight tears and stains at folds.
Regardless of the country in which the tire conglomerate advertised their Pilot tires, the sales pitch remained the same in every language: Steer the road like you're riding the rails. To that end, the designer has cleverly laid down the route for his lithographic motorist amidst his sketchy surroundings, backed by the monolithic magnificence of the tire that practically does the driving for you. And since no Michelin advertisement would be complete without Bibendum, the segmented man holds up a tread sample for all to see.
Est: $2,000-$2,500

104

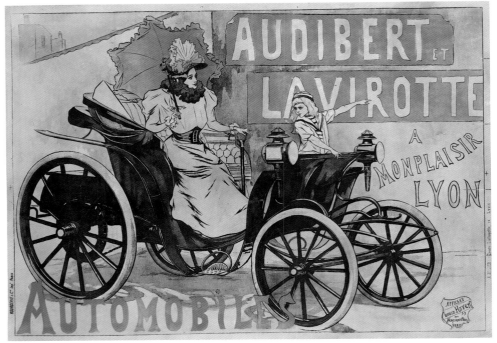

105

106

107

108

110

LOUIS HUVEY

105. Audibert et Lavirotte. 1896.
$51^5/_8$ x $42^7/_8$ in./151.3 x 109 cm
Imp. Bougerie, Paris
Cond B/Slight tears; restored stains.
Ref: Khachadourian, p. 42
Welcome to the birth of the automotive industry. This true horseless carriage, without a door or seat belt in sight, represents one of the earliest visions of the public taking to the roads in a motorized four-wheeled vehicle. It's almost unfathomable how much advertising—and vehicular safety—has changed in little more than a century. The obvious consideration being addressed here for the Audibert and Lavirotte manufacturers is freedom and ease, the sheer facility of getting behind the wheel—or more accurately, steering pole—with such lack of effort that a woman need not abandon the gentility of a parasol nor take a watchful eye from her free-roaming child/passenger. Such a proposal would be laughed off the market today, but at the turn of the 20th century, it was just the message needed. Especially, one must imagine, to housewives wanting a broader horizon than their parlors could afford. Of all automotive posters, this is "arguably the earliest surviving one. The make survived until 1901, turning out some 50 cars" (Khachadourian, p. 49). The firm, which sprung from the mechanical imaginations of Lyonaise automotive pioneers Emile Lavirotte and Maurice Audibert, began production of motorized tricycle voiturettes some two years before they were granted a license to produce their cars. Lavirotte and Audibert would eventually be bought out by Marius Berliet and go onto be successful commercial directors for, respectively, Rochet-Schneider and Berliet.
Est: $3,500-$4,000.

H. J. LECOQ

106. Automobiles P.-Génestin & Cie.
45 x $60^5/_8$ in./114.2 x 154 cm
René Walch, Paris
Cond C/Several restored tears.
With the road unwinding behind her like a river of gold directly streaming from the blazing sun of progress, this unflappable motorist can prettily sit behind the wheel of her Génestin with utter security, at ease with the swift hill-climbing prowess of her vehicle. "The Génestin was a light car which used a variety of engines. The touring models came in four sizes, from an 1,100cc 4-cylinder to a 1,681cc 6-cylinder, the engines being made by Chapuis-Dornier" (*Encyclopedia of Motorcars*, p. 271).
Est: $2,000-$2,500.

HANS LISKA (1907-)

107. Tripolis 1939/Mercedes-Benz.
$19^1/_8$ x $27^1/_4$ in./48.5 x 69.2 cm
Cond A–/Slight tears near paper edges.
Ref: Khachadourian, p. 46; PAI-XIX, 71
In a high-powered blue and yellow design, Mercedes-Benz announces (in German naturally) the debut of its new 1.5-liter race car in the 1939 Grand Prix of Tripoli, Libya (then an Italian colony). Driving for the Mercedes team are Hermann Lang and the Italian Rudolf Caracciola, who drove to victory for Mercedes-Benz in the 1936 Monaco Grand Prix. The car is described as "a unique achievement of the Daimler-Benz company" and the two drivers "victorious through devoted work and great effort." If this sounds heavy-handedly propagandistic, well, in 1939, a German-Italian collaboration did have a certain larger significance. Besides his steady work for Daimler-Benz, the Austrian-born Liska did work for various publications and for the 4711 cologne manufacturer in Cologne.
Est: $1,200-$1,500.

109

111

112

PIERRE LOUYS

108. Citroën. 1924.
46 x 62³/₄ in./117 x 159.3 cm
Imp. Chaix, Paris
Cond A–/Unobtrusive folds.
Ref (Both Var): Auto Show III, 78 & color plate;
   PAI-XIX, 73
The 1924 Citroën roadster is being admired by two elegant young ladies who seem to have just stepped out of the pages of a fashion magazine. The bottom text panel—seen here before the addition of letters—was imprinted with the names and locations of various dealers.
Est: $1,700-$2,000.

MEZQUITA

109. Good Year.
27⁷/₈ x 39³/₈ in./70.7 x 100.1 cm
Los Tiroleses S. A.
Cond B+/Unobtrusive tears, largely at edges.
Although technically the name of the tire itself (Air-

wheel), Mezquita takes a brand name to literal new heights, elevating the wheels from the road—along with the Pinewood Derby trademark body and leggy, flag-waving passenger—and places them in their deserving spot in the cloud-free blue sky. In other words, the tire that makes you feel like you're riding on air. Which, in fact, you are. Wonderfully packaged redundancy that unfailingly plants the name of the product that promises beauty, comfort and durability in the mind of the consumer.
Est: $1,700-$2,000.

MONACO GRAND PRIX

110. Monaco Grand Prix: 13 Posters. 1973-1996.
Each approx.: 16¹/₄ x 23¹/₂ in./41.2 x 59.8 cm
A. I. P., Monaco
Cond A/P.
A genuine treasure trove for the Formula-1 fanatic. Not only are there thirteen spectacular graphic visions of mechanical excellence wending its way through the fashionable Riviera speed hub, but every poster—

beginning with the 1973 race on to the 1996 challenge—is hand-signed by the legendary winning drivers of the modern era: Clay Regazzoni, Jean Pierre Jarrier, Piercalo Ghinzani, Ricardo Patrese and Johny Herbert, to name but a few of the signatory racers.
Est: $2,500-$3,000. (13)

OTTO LUDWIG NAEGELE (1880-1952)

111. Forstenriederpark Prinz Heinrich Fahrt. 1909.
34³/₈ x 45⁵/₈ in./87.5 x 116 cm
Kunstanstalt J. G. Velisch, München
Cond A.
Ref: DFP-III, 2331; Plakate München, cat. no. 214;
   PAI-XXVI, 2
Naegele was primarily a painter, but did produce a number of powerful posters. Here he gives us a roadster confidently thundering through the speed trials of the 1909 Prinz Heinrich Race held at Munich's Forstenriederpark.
Est: $3,000-$3,500

114

"Au delà des Pyrénées." Renault

113

118

AUTOMOBILE POSTERS (continued)

ANDRE NÉVIL

112. Two Roadside Races. 1905.
Each: 29¹/₂ x 18 in./75 x 45.7 cm
Minot, Paris
Cond A–/Slight tears and stains at edges. Framed.
It's stupefying when you stop to think of just how many modern day toys we take for granted on a daily basis. Communication devices. Airplanes. Cars. As a society, we've become so jaded that the technological has become blasé. But not so long ago—less than a century in fact—things were startlingly different. The emerging automotive age was the focus of unparalleled fascination, excitement and danger. And these two Névil prints capture the many facets of the dawning obsession with an artistry born of sensationalism. Both spectacularly capture the commotion caused on a rural stretch by racing automobiles—most especially in the ranks of the animal kingdom. *Both posters are hand-signed by the artist.*
Est: $2,500-$3,000. (2)

113. Renault/Au delà des Pyrénées. 1912.
33³/₈ x 16¹/₈ in./85.6 x 41 cm
Mabileau, Paris
Cond B+/Slight tears and stains in borders.
Renault was founded in 1899. By 1911, it was the best selling car in France, its popularity won, to a great extent, on the track. Both Louis and Marcel Renault began racing their cars at the turn of the century. But sometimes, speed doesn't amount to a hill of beans. Sometimes what matters is where a car can take you. And in the case of this pochoir print, it's the Pyrenees mountains. Or more to the point, beyond the Pyrenees, to a landscape awash with sunset splendor and rustic Basque charm. Because any car can take you for a ride, but only the Renault can take you to the "most satisfactory of France's frontiers" in such style.
Est: $1,500-$1,800.

PUNCH

114. Automobile Club dell'Aquilla. 1930.
39³/₈ x 55¹/₈ in./100 x 140 cm
N. Moneta, Milano
Cond B/Slight stains at edges; restored tears at folds; image and colors excellent.
The Abruzzi Massif, the highest of the Apennine range, is a harsh region that, due to its isolation and climate, has preserved its beautiful landscapes. The Gran Sasso massif is the highest peak of the region, marked for its variety of landscapes composed of gorges, sheer gullies, forests, desolate high plateau and verdant pastures. And it is to this harsh, breathtaking area that the Italian Automobile Association extends an invitation to witness the driving prowess taking place in the 4th Gran Sasso Cup. Punch creates a

spectacular call to spectate, flattening the perspective with nearly construction paper-like precision, a technique which still gives the mountainous course its due while calling into prominence the vehicle surging forward with such surety that it appears ready to break free from its two-dimensional trappings. *Rare!*
Est: $4,000-$5,000.

GIUSEPPE RICCOBALDI (1887-1976)

115. Fiat/La Nuovo Balilla. 1937.
39³/₄ x 55¹/₈ in./101 x 140 cm
IGAP, Milano
Cond B/Slight tears and stains at folds.
Ref: Fiat, p. 205
Posters for the bold little Balilla, the first Italian "people's" car, typically ranged from the command-

115

116

117

119

FEDERICO SENECA (1891-1976)

118. Coppa Della Perugina.
38 1/2 x 55 5/8 in./ 97.8 x 141.2 cm
Gino Borrani, Firenze
Cond A. Framed.
A spectacular promotion for the Perugina Cup, its overhead perspective focusing on the the truest elements of automobile racing: the driver, his car and the short expanse of open road that it occupies as it roars through its course. Making the design all the more sweet is the fact that the automotive competition was sponsored by the Perugina company, purveyors of fine chocolate. Seneca, who settled in Milan at the end of World War I, was one of Italy's most original and innovative designers, with an illustrative style that was both supple and explosive. And with Cappiello as his primary influence, his works have a timeless quality that rise above topicality. *Rare!*
Est: $5,000-$6,000.

FRANCISCO TAMAGNO (1851-?)

119. Pneumatique Condor A. Soly.
43 5/8 x 61 in./110.8 x 155 cm
La Lithographie Parisienne, Paris
Cond B+/Slight tears at folds and edges.
Placed within the unbroken circle of a Condor A. Soly vulcanized rubber tire, serving both as frame and portal into a prosperous world of radiant industry, the sun rises in the name of superior pneumatics, its potent rays unable to refrain themselves from crowning the Condor the best tire in the world. Perhaps more pomp than one is accustomed to in a tire promotion, but an energized, unexpectedly potent image all the same.
Est: $1,200-$1,500.

ingly elegant (*see* PAI-X, 42) to somewhat iconoclastic (*see* PAI-XXX, 261). Riccobaldi, who executed a total of three posters for the automotive producers, takes a more direct route for the 508 C Balilla 1100, toning down all nonessential elements so that our sole focus is the car in question. Riccobaldi began his career as a set designer before committing himself totally to poster production, creating some fifty posters noted for their originality and concision.
Est: $2,000-$2,500.

ANDRÉ ROBERT

116. Voiturettes Automobiles Léon Bollée. 1896.
54 3/4 x 38 1/2 in./139.2 x 97.7 cm
Imp. Charles Verneau, Paris
Cond A.
Ref: Auto Show III, 5; PAI-IX, 461
Bollée was one of the mechanics and machine shop owners who, in the days before mass production was introduced into the auto industry, offered to build custom bodies for the early enthusiasts. In this three-wheeler, the fastidiously-dressed passenger is perched semi-comfortably *in front* of her chauffeur. And

though the dangling blanket and lack of a safety belt might make the modern motorist a bit uneasy, it's an excellent portrayal of the devil-may-care naivety of the early automotive age. As foreign as they appear to the contemporary eye, these tricycle demi-cars gained nearly instant popularity upon their introduction and their presence on the European roadways were fairly commonplace, disappearing completely only after World War I.
Est: $3,000-$3,500.

ROY

117. Grand Prix/Bordeaux. 1953.
31 3/4 x 47 1/4 in./80.7 x 120 cm
Imp. Rousseau Frères, Bordeaux
Cond A.
Ref: PAI-XVIII, 91
Roy omits outlines, creating his image out of only essential, cut-out-like areas of color: here, a few blue, red and gray shapes magically become the Bordeaux Grand Prix. *Not* left to the viewer's imagination, of course, is the name of the sponsor.
Est: $2,000-$2,500.

AUTOMOBILES/Tamagno (cont'd)

120. Cottereau Cycles & Automobiles.
46 x 62¹/₈ in./117 x 157.8 cm
La Lithographie Parisienne Romanet, Paris
Cond B+/Slight tears at folds and edges.
Ref: Collectionneur, p. 228; PAI-XXIII, 39
To emphasize the fact that the Cottereau automobile
and bicycle factory is located in Dijon and is of industrial importance to the area, Tamagno uses not just a
map—but a *road* map of France—as the background
in his design. That done, he ruptures it with a scene
that takes place in front of the smoke-stacked factory:
a driver and passenger in a splendid open Cottereau
leading a parade of similar models off the production
line. The cavalcade contains only a single cyclist, but
Tamagno covers that base with a windblown beauty
looking on from her handlebars at the lower-left corner. The poster indicates that the lithographic stones
are by A. Gallice from Tamagno's design. Worked out
to the last detail and showing the artist's customary
impeccable craftsmanship, the image itself is unusual,
and the poster is *rare!*
Est: $2,000-$2,500.

E. V. STANEK

121. Barthélemy. ca. 1898.
62¹/₂ x 46 in./458.9 x 116.8 cm
Imp. Bourgerie, Paris
Cond A.
Put yourself in this position: It's almost 1900, you've
noticed these newfangled "automobiles" chugging
around the streets of Paris and, quite frankly, you'd
like to see what they're all about firsthand. But where
could you go to transform yourself from pedestrian to
motorist? Though dealerships didn't pepper the landscape the way they do today, Prague-born Stanek's
design makes it clear that the stylish choice was
Barthélemy, located on the Passage Dubail, the ideal
locale for buying, selling or merely repairing your automotive obsession.
Est: $3,500-$4,000.

WALTER THOR (1870-1929)

122. Naphta-Cycle.
31¹/₄ x 43¹/₈ in./79.2 x 109.6 cm
Affiche Cohen, Marseille
Cond B-/Restored tears.
There's no getting around the fact that this advertisement is for a motor oil, which at its core is not that
romantic a subject. You wouldn't know that, however,
judging from Thor's interpretation of his subject; that
the vehicular recipients of said product are primarily
rendered in deep brown hues are about the only hint

we're given. The rest of the artwork is bathed in sumptuous sunset tones, casting a spell of instant nostalgia
that resonates far more than any Pennzoil commercial
ever could. Thor, a member of the Salon des Artistes
Français, is best known for his humorous turn-of-the-
century transportation posters.
Est: $2,000-$2,500.

RENÉ VINCENT (1879-1936)

123. Michelin.
46¹/₈ x 62³/₄ in./117.2 x 159.2 cm
Imp. Draeger
Cond B+/Unobtrusive folds.
Ref: PAI-XV, 353
O'Galop's wonderful creation continued to live a long
fruitful life even after he no longer drew him. Here,
Vincent—himself an avid motorist—renders him the
kindly savior of a stranded family in an endearing
roadside scene.
Est: $8,000-$10,000.

WEILUC (Lucien-Henri Weil, 1873-1947)

124. "Bayard." 1908.
61¹/₄ x 45³/₄ in./155.5 x 116 cm
Société Nouvelle d'Art et Décoration, Paris
Cond C+/Restored tears and stains.
Ref: Auto Show II, 22; PAI-XXV, 59
Clément was a hugely successful bicycle in France in
the late 1800s, but in 1903, one of the family scions,
Adolphe Clément, set up an auto workshop in the
town of Mezieres. There is a statue in the town of
Bayard, a legendary knight who supposedly saved the
city from an invasion in the 16th century, and Clément
chose to name his car after him. He operated the factory until 1922. Weiluc quite frequently took a humorous approach to posters for clients who appreciated it;
here, he makes the Bayard fly through the air with the
greatest of ease and, by gum, it works.
Est: $2,000-$2,500.

122

123

SHIP POSTERS

125

126

ANONYMOUS

125. Holland-America Line/Rotterdam-New York.
35⁵/₈ x 22¹/₄ in./83 x 56.5 cm
Lith. Lankhout, Den Haag
Cond B/A few unobtrusive tears and creases; image
  and colors excellent. Framed.
Ref: PAI-XXIX, 87
An image of calm seas and prosperous voyage with a
small clipper ship sternward to reinforce the notion of
modernity, this portrait-poster of the Statendam
seems better suited to the boardroom than to the
street. The liner was completed in April 1929 (probably the occasion for the poster), the third vessel to sail
under its name. Normally carrying 153 passengers in

first class, 793 in tourist and 418 in third, she was an
economical, popular ship, well-deserving of her nickname "Queen of the Spotless Fleet." Her signature
triple lemon-and-green stacks, however, were something of a sham: the aft funnel was a dummy added to
give her a sleeker profile. The signature of the painter
in the lower-left corner is indecipherable.
Est: $1,200-$1,500.

126. La Veloce/"America".
54¹/₄ x 38¹/₄ in./137.8 x 97.2 cm
Stab. Richter, Napoli
Cond A–/Unobtrusive tears and creases in margins only.

A peculiar blend of sweeping romanticism and no-frills
utilitarianism creates an altogether pleasing promotion
for the Veloce Line's *America*. Interestingly enough,
no record exists of either the line—whose name literally translates as "rapid"—or the vessel. Though an act
of pure conjecture, judging from the poster, it would
appear as if the *America* was a turbine steamer built
either in Trieste or Genoa circa 1915. She was probably a twin screw, approximately 11,000 gross registered tons and about 535 feet long. At least that's our
best guess.
Est: $1,700-$2,000.

127

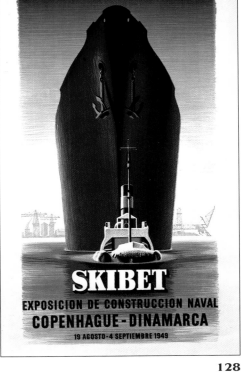

128

129

131

SHIP POSTERS/Anon. (cont'd)

127. Mala Real Inglesa. 1924.
24¹/₂ x 38³/₄ in./62 x 98.4 cm
Printed in England
Cond B+/Slight offsetting of ink.
The Royal Mail Steam Packet Line, a British steamship company serving far-flung locations not on the routes of the major carriers of the time, utilizes a powerful, no-frills approach to promote a special South American cruise—departing from Avon and arriving in Almanzora in precisely two-weeks' time—their uncredited vessel plowing through the surging Atlantic froth with such determination that it forces a flock of seagulls right out of the frame and into the text. The Spanish-language advertisement also encourages rapid reservations as accommodations are limited in the specified third-class berths. It is interesting to note that two fares are clearly pointed out—those for passengers between the ages of two and ten, and one for passengers further into their double digits—indicating that, although no overt evidence is presented on the poster, the cruise would make for an excellent family getaway.
Est: $800-$1,000.

128. Skibet. 1949.
24³/₈ x 39¹/₄ in./62 x 100 cm
Cond A/P.
This towering advertisement for an exposition of naval shipbuilding being held in Copenhagen clearly borrows a page from the *Normandie* handbook (*see* No. 132), going so far as to include a stylized tug leading the russet cruiser out of the harbor and throwing in the dwarfed portscape of Copenhagen in for good measure. However, as the poster, for all intents and purposes, serves as an extolment of military prowess, an element of looming domination pervades the design, creating a piece that practically dares you to question its authority.
Est: $1,200-$1,500.

129. White Star Line/West Indies. ca. 1931.
15¹/₂ x 22 in./39.2 x 55.8 cm
Cond A–/Unobtrusive tears near top paper edge. Framed.
A tropical invitation from Great Britain's White Star Line to leave the drip and drizzle of jolly old England behind for the sunnier, lush environs of the West Indies—complete with gracefully wading flamingos of course—aboard the *Megantic*. Actually, this design comes from the last legs of the life of a ship launched on December 10, 1909. Though the bulk of her time at sea was spent serving Liverpool to North America routes, during the winter months and the Depression

130

of the 1920s, the *Megantic* made cruises to the West Indies. However, the staggering decline of business by 1931 forced the White Star Line to lay up the ship and in February of 1933, she was sold to shipbreakers in Osaka, Japan.
Est: $1,200-$1,500.

ALO (Charles Hallo, 1884-1969)

130. Red Star Line/"Belgenland".
24¹/₂ x 37³/₈ in./62.2 x 95 cm
E. Stockmans, Antwerp
Cond A–/Slight tears at paper edges. Framed.
Ref: PAI-XVII, 83
Hallo, a Beaux-Arts-trained painter, is perhaps best known for his 100-odd posters for the SNCF, the French national railway. But clearly, he was an equally gifted artist with regard to the romance of ocean travel. His painterliness is much in evidence here, and the star-speckled, emerald sky and light-splashed waters

are wonderfully moody. The Red Star Line was founded with Anglo-American capital in 1871 and stayed afloat until 1935. Its ships flew under the Belgian flag.
Est: $1,700-$2,000.

OTTOMAR ANTON (1895-1976)

131. Hamburg-Amerika Linie. 1935.
23³/₄ x 33 in./60.5 x 83.7 cm
Kunst im Druck, München
Cond B+/Slight tears and crease, largely near edges.
The Hamburg-Amerika Line extends a golden invitation to the German-speaking globetrotter for escaping the traditional fuss and tumble of the holiday season aboard the newly refit and refurbished, all 1st-class motorship *Milwaukee* as she steams to the Atlantic Islands on a sixteen day Christmas and New Year's Eve cruise on a celebratory "second" maiden voyage. And without a Saint Nick or noisemaker in sight—the *Milwaukee* itself unobtrusively tucked into the horizon — the exotic flora and arid landscape provide more than enough incentive to set sail to anyone who's had their fill of "Ho-ho-ho!" Originally painted black, the ship's hull was painted white after its conversion to carry its 559 passengers. Anton was a native of Hamburg who

132

133

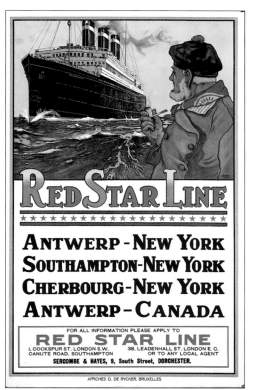

134

started working for a local agency there, but from 1921 on, had his own studio where he produced a large body of work for Hapag, the big transatlantic conglomerate. Later, he became an art instructor at the Bremen High School of Art.
Est: $1,000-$1,200.

A. M. CASSANDRE
(Adolphe Mouron, 1901-1968)

132. Normandie/Service Regulier. 1935.
24$^1/_2$ x 39$^1/_8$ in./62 x 99.4 cm
Alliance Graphique/L. Danel, Paris
Cond A.
Ref: Mouron, 56; Brown & Reinhold, 53;
Cassandre/Suntory, p. 91; Weill, 345;
Deco Affiches, p. 33; PAI-XXIX, 92
An advertisement for the *Normandie* and her "First Arrival in New York City on June 3 [1935]" touted that "The arrival in New York Harbor of the gigantic superliner *Normandie* will inaugurate a new era of transatlantic travel. She will set new standards of luxury and speed, steadiness comfort and safety . . . not merely the largest liner afloat (79,280 tons) . . . but in almost every respect a *new kind of liner!*" And in almost every respect, this Cassandre masterpiece was a new way of selling the glamor and excitement of ocean liner travel. A deceptively simple, but impressive design with the ship towering above us, a flight of small birds at bottom giving the image as much scale and strength as the imposing hull itself. The classic design appeared with several variants of text at the bottom; this is the version with the ship's name emblazoned over its ports of call.
Est: $10,000-$12,000.

HENRI CASSIERS (1858-1944)

133. Red Star Line/Antwerpen-New York. 1901.
44 x 62 in./111.8 x 157.4 cm
O. DeRycker & Mendel, Bruxelles
Cond B/Slight tears and stains at folds and edges.
Ref: DFP-II, 1003; PAI-XXVI, 226
Cassiers depicts the "Zeeland" vessel on a delft blue tile wall, with navy blue text on unfurled banners and a decorative sepia border. This is an inspired device that only augments the marvelously detailed rendering of the ship, with its figures visible on deck.
Est: $3,000-$4,000.

134. Red Star Line/Antwerp-New York.
24$^3/_8$ x 39$^3/_4$ in./62 x 101 cm
O. de Rycker, Bruxelles
Cond A–/Unobtrusive folds.
Ref (Both Var): DFP-II, 1005; PAI-II, 142
The hallmark of all Cassiers posters is a sympathetic and colorful rendering of native people, usually farmers, fisherman or sailors, and it is from their vantage point that we see the promotional item. This very human touch adds a great deal to the appeal of his posters, as is evidenced by this puffing tar taking in the "Belgenland" as she cruises into port for the Red Star Line. A distinguished Belgian painter and magazine reporter/illustrator turned posterist, Cassiers became an aquarellist of note at an early age, placing his work at many exhibitions and earning various kudos. In the 1890s, he traveled as a roving magazine contributor. In poster work, he stays with his painterly style, most of the time depicting a folksy scene to which text is added.
Est: $1,200-$1,500

135

137

136

138

SHIP POSTERS/Cassiers (cont'd)

135. Red Star Line/Antwerpen-New York. 1899.
49³/₈ x 36¹/₂ in./125.5 x 92.7 cm
O. de Rycker, Bruxelles
Cond B+/Slight tears at folds. Framed.
Ref: DFP-II, 996; Cassiers, 67; Belle Epoque 1970, 11;
    Belgische Affiche, 13; Timeless Images, 53;
    Wagner, 56; PAI-XXX, 156
The rich colors and fine design of this poster for the Red Star
Line make it a picture of enduring grace and beauty.
The Red Star Line, operating from Antwerp under the
Belgian flag, was a serious competitor to the Holland-
Amerika Line, but the Depression hit the company
quite hard and by 1935 the last of its ships were sold.
The 16,000-ton "Westernland" shown in this poster was
subsequently repurchased by the Holland-America Line
in June 1939, with the right to operate on the Antwerp-
New York run under the name of Red Star Line.
Est: $7,000-$9,000.

136. Red Star Line.
28⁷/₈ x 24¹/₄ in./73.2 x 61.7 cm
O. De Rycker, Bruxelles
Cond A.
Ref: PAI-VII, 91
One of the rarest and best for the Red Star Line by its
leading graphic exponent: as is his wont, Cassiers gives
us some sturdy rustic types observing a departing ship
from an oceanside knoll, but the treatment here is somewhat more sensitive—more melancholy, if you will—
than one would expect for a steamship corporation.
Est: $1,500-$1,800.

PAUL COLIN (1892-1986)

137. Transatlantique/1855-1955.
24³/₈ x 39¹/₈ in./62 x 99.4 cm
Imp. S. A. Courbet, Paris
Cond B+/Slight ink splatter at top.
Ref: Colin Affichiste, 185; PAI-XVII, 212

Colin helped celebrate the centennial of the Transat-
lantique shipping company by flying the golden years
like flags from the mast. Classic design precision executed with dignified flare.
Est: $1,200-$1,500.

TOM CURR

138. Summer Holidays by Cunard.
12¹/₄ x 19⁵/₈ in./31 x 50 cm
Cond B+/Slight tears and stains at edges. Framed.
Ref: Mer s'Affiche, p. 135; Golden Age of Travel, p. 195;
    PAI-X, 14
A shipboard flirtation between a pert passenger and a
weathered seaman suggests the promise of fun and
high seas intrigue to be had on the Cunard summer
cruises. On a purely technical note, the soft yellow of
her dress makes for a fine contrast with the salty dog's
deep blue uniform.
Est: $1,500-$1,800.

139

140

141

CHEMINS DE FER DE L'ETAT & DE BRIGHTON

PARIS-LONDRES
(St LAZARE)   (VICTORIA)
VIA DIEPPE - 2ʰ-45 ET NEWHAVEN
DE TRAVERSÉE MARITIME

142

BECK & ANONYMOUS

139. Empress of Britain: 2 Posters. ca. 1930.
a: 24 1/4 x 39 3/8 in./61.7 x 99.8 cm
b: 23 7/8 x 35 7/8 in./60.7 x 91 cm
Sir Joseph Causton & Sons, London (a only)
Cond B+/Slight tears and creases, largely at edges.
Ref: Canadian Pacific, 40; PAI-XXI, 29 & 64
The period between the two World Wars was the hey-day of luxury cruising. During these years, Canadian Pacific operated more than 350 cruises to the West Indies, the Mediterranean, the Canary Islands, Scandinavia and around the world. And the crown jewel of their fleet was undoubtedly the *Empress of Britain.* "To compete with such majestic ships as the Cunard Line's *Aquitania,* the French Line's *Ile de France* and the United States' Line's *Leviathan,* Canadian Pacific Steamships launched the 45,000-ton *Empress of Britain* in 1930, the second ship to bear the name. A somewhat bulky looking three-funneled vessel,

claimed by some of its admirers to be the most luxuriously-appointed ship to have ever sailed, it was the largest ship operated by the Canadian Pacific and proudly took its place as the flagship of the fleet (Canadian Pacific, p. 44). Beck sets the *Empress* assail beneath a globetrotter's fantasy frieze of exotically colored travel vignettes. In the accompanying anonymous piece, the oversize image dwarfs Neptune's golden chariot flying under its bow, with only the sunset sky capable of approaching her grandeur.
Est: $1,700-$2,000. (2)

GEORGES GAUDY (1872-?)

140. Cercles Coloniaux.
34 5/8 x 47 3/4 in./88 x 121.5 cm
Lith. J.E.-Goossens, Bruxelles
Cond B/Slight tears at folds.
An illustrator, posterist and painter, as well as an accomplished cyclist, Gaudy created images that almost always centered on a bicycle or automobile. It is, however, the exceptions to this rule that impress upon the poster aficionado how facilely he could

translate his talents to areas of non-specialization. Take for example this wistful invitation to roam the world aboard the Belgian federation of Colonial Circle ships. This vaunted allegory places the pith-helmeted explorer in the embrace of mother Belgium under the stony-gaze of Leopold II, king of the Belgians from 1865 to 1909—an ideal patron saint to the Belgian traveler as he led the first European efforts to develop the Congo River basin, making possible the formation of the Congo Free State in 1885, which was annexed in 1908 as the Belgian Congo.
Est: $1,200-$1,500.

LUDWIG HOHLWEIN (1874-1949)

141. Norddeutscher Lloyd Bremen.
10 3/4 x 17 3/8 in./27.3 x 44.2 cm
Wilhelm Jömzen, Bremen
Cond B+/Slight tears and stains at edges; grommet holes at top for hanging. Framed.
Ref: Hohlwein Posters, p. 24; PAI-XXIV, 325
The steamship line invites Italians to travel with this image of a smiling crew member delivering rose bouquets bound for departing passengers. With the decorative border suggesting confetti and streamers, you can almost hear the accompanying sendoff cheers. The placard served as a hanging calendar, with the calendar pad slipping into the slits on the right side and obscuring the artist's signature. In another version of the calendar, the pad was inserted into three slits on the bottom panel which is empty of type.
Est: $1,200-$1,500.

SANDY HOOK
(Georges Taboureau, 1879-1960)

142. Paris-Londres/"Versailles".
28 3/4 x 40 3/4 in./73 x 103.5 cm
Imp. L. Dufay, Paris
Cond A–/Slight tears at paper edges. Framed.
Ref: PAI-XVII, 306a
Sandy Hook was almost exclusively a marine artist. Serving in France's submarine command in World War I, he received the title of Navy Painter. He went on to design posters for 28 shipping and shipbuilding companies. "His style (is) at once precise and lively . . . a critic called him a 'portraitist of ships' because he could discern and render the differences even between two ships of the same series, and express the personality of each" (Mer s'Affiche, p. 272). And that is precisely what he does in this poster for the good ship "Versailles." Since Channel service relies on reliability and dependability, Hook doesn't gussy up the vessel, simply presents it as the solid workhorse that it is, steaming determinedly on its appointed solitary rounds.
Est: $1,500-$1,800.

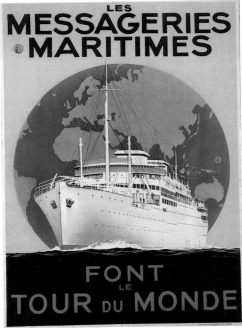

143

144

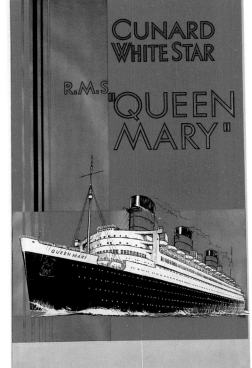

145

SHIP POSTERS/Sandy Hook (cont'd)

143. Messageries Maritimes/Tour du Monde.
28¹/₈ x 39⁵/₈ in./71.4 x 100.6 cm
Imp. Réunies, Paris
Cond A–/Unobtrusive tears at paper edges.
Ref: PAI-XVII, 306c
Though the vessel is not singled-out by name, Hook's message for the maritime stalwarts resounds with singular force: The Messageries Maritime service the world. End of story. The only elements necessary—a ship slicing through the open sea and a globe to cast her against. Powerful simplicity expressed with uncluttered elegance.
Est: $1,200-$1,500.

144. Messageries Maritimes/Japon-Extrême-Orient.
28⁵/₈ x 40⁵/₈ in./72.7 x 103 cm
Imp. F. Champenois, Paris
Cond B+/Slight tears and stains at folds and edges. Framed.
Ref: PAI-XVII, 306b
Hook frames the harbored ship within the striking confines of a Japanese *torii* temple gate with two decorative Japanese women thrown in for good measure to up the exotic ante in this design for service to The Orient. The imaginative framing device used in this poster transforms it into something quite spectacular and places it among the best of this genre.
Est: $1,400-$1,700.

JARVIS

145. Cunard/White Star/"Queen Mary". ca. 1936
24¹/₂ x 39³/₄ in/62.3 x 101 cm
British Colour Printing, London
Cond B/Slight tears at paper edges; image and colors excellent. Framed.
Ref: Fantastic Voyage, p. 29; PAI-XXIII, 307
Work on Cunard #534—the future *Queen Mary*—had begun on December 27, 1930. But the Depression affected every North Atlantic steamship line, and construction was halted a year later, not to resume until April 1934. The funds for the restart came from the British government, who agreed to supply them on the condition that Cunard merge with the White Star line. The merger occurred, and it took two years more to complete the ship; she sailed on her maiden voyage (Southampton-Cherbourg-New York) on May 27, 1936. The joint name continued until 1960 when the *Britannic*, the last ship to carry the White Star name, was retired. The poster reflects much of the elegance that White Star was known for (Cunard often promoted itself on speed). The Art-Deco design is a handsome, restrained geometric arrangement of red, gold and black. The distinctive Jarvis signature appears on several posters for the Royal Mail Lines dated 1958, but

147

we have been unable to locate any information on the artist.
Est: $1,400-$1,700.

ANDREW JOHNSON

146. Orient Cruises.
25 x 40 in./63.5 x 101.6 cm
Cond A–/Slight wear at folds.
Ref: PAI-I, 119
Johnson was best known as "an agreeable landscape painter (who) expertly rendered the scenic views he was entrusted with" (Weill, p. 226). The designer himself, however, had some simple ground rules for poster making that he adhered to no matter what the designated subject matter: "If the poster forces attention by its dramatic presentation or its 'newness' its first object is achieved. It has been seen" (Richmond, p. 149). Certainly one would have difficulty disputing the voracity of his goals after catching a glimpse of his work for the Orient cruise line, with the ship's funnels

148

towering monolithically over the unfazed elegant passengers indulging in a round of shuffleboard.
Est: $3,000-$3,500.

JOHNSTON

147. Union-Castle.
25 x 39⁵/₈ in./63.5 x 100.7 cm
Cond B+/Restored tears at edges.
An expansive sky and a calm briny expanse lend added heft to the painterly treatment given to the voyage of the *Windsor Castle*, a vessel in the Union-Castle fleet, an English line which specialized in seagoing excursions to the Dark Continent. The 36,123-ton liner, built just across the Mersey from Liverpool in Birkenhead, was named by Her Majesty Elizabeth, the Queen Mother, who used a special bottle of South African wine for the ceremony held on June 23, 1959. The ship sailed on her maiden voyage to the Cape a year later, on August 18, 1960. The *Windsor Castle* was

146

150

149

the fastest liner ever to sail on the South African run. It was known as the "Big" ship because of her large 623,000 cubic foot cargo capacity, 352,000 of which

were used for refrigeration. Her accommodations were considered the most luxurious on the Cape Mail run and incredibly spacious.
Est: $1,000-$1,200.

LOUIS C. KALFF (1897-1976)

148. Holland Amerika. ca. 1927.
23 x 34⁵/₈ in./58.5 x 88 cm
Cond A-/Slight tears and creases at edges. Framed.
An effortlessly spectacular Kalff output for the Holland-America line, featuring the Rotterdam on the distant horizon, her tendrils of blue-grey smoke binding her to a watery framing device—spraying forth from the deep with geometric surety—while focusing our attention on the central gull, whose pixilated reflection transforms another of the whitecaps that gently tug the eyes to the ship in the distance. In June of 1926, the Rotterdam was converted into a four-class ship, and rerouted around the time of this poster's production on the New York-Cherbourg-Southampton-Rotterdam run in either direction. She was one of the first large Atlantic liners to be built with two major oceanic innovations: a glassed-in promenade deck and elevators, of which she had three. One of the finest luxury liners of the day in terms of both revenues and appearance, the *Rotterdam IV* was an exquisite example of the Edwardian class cruise ship, made to sail with a moderate amount of speed and a maximum of plush interiors.
Est: $1,700-$2,000.

JAMES SCRIMGEOUR MANN (1883-1946)

149. Allan Line/Canada.
25 x 39³/₈ in./63.6 x 100 cm
Turner & Dunnett, Liverpool & London

Cond A-/Slight tears at folds.
The Allan Line was a Scottish-based steamship company offering service from Great Britain and France to Canada, with ships sailing from ports in London, Plymouth, Glasgow, Liverpool and Le Havre. The dual bright-red and black stacks draws one's attention to the outward grandeur of the unidentified quadruple-screw, 18,000-ton steamer—both in profile and lording over tugs and other insignificant ships with which she deigns to share the harbor—as she steams on her way to the Atlantic Ocean and St. Lawrence Seaway. The oft exhibited Mann utilized his talents both as a posterist and marine painter.
Est: $1,200-$1,500.

MICHAEL

150. India Australia & Intermediate Ports/P & O.
24¹/₂ x 39³/₄ in./62.2 x 101 cm
R. H. Perry, London
Cond B+/Restored tears at top edge.
The sheer romantic indulgence of ocean travel practically gushes off the surface of the paper in this promotion for the British P & O Line and their service to India, Australia and points in between, including ports in the Straits of China and Japan. As opposed to other advertisements for the company that emphasized the mysteries of the exotic East (*see* PAI-XXVIII, 544), Michael chooses the shipboard life itself as the seductive thrust of his design, bathing the scene in golden wash, upping the ante of the swoon of the ladies for the dashing officer in starched dress whites. And what daily drab could resist this allure, especially seeing as all this wish fulfillment is available for the affordable indulgence of a tourist class fare.
Est: $2,500-$3,000.

151

155

152

158

SHIP POSTERS (continued)

FRED PANSING (1854-1912)

151. S. S. Potsdam.
$44^7/_8$ x $31^1/_8$ in./114 x 79.2 cm
O. de Rycker & Mendel, Bruxelles
Cond B+/Slight creases, largely near paper edges.
Pansing presents us with the stately port entry of the Holland-America Line's *S. S. Potsdam* in the escort of a number of rather lesser vessels. The Potsdam's single stack was heightened considerably in 1908 due to her poor exhaust performance as her boilers didn't steam very well. The augmentation would earn the vessel the nickname "Funneldam." Sold in 1915 to the Swedish-American Line for a high price and renamed *Stockholm*, the ship would be sold off once again in 1928, renamed *Solgimt* and converted into a whale factory ship by the Norwegian Odd Company A/S. Fred Pansing was born in Bremen, Germany, and came to the U.S. at age 11. He started out as a sailor, and after becoming a painter, he returned to the sea, specializing in maritime scenes. He eventually settled in Jersey City.
Est: $1,500-$1,800.

R. S. PIKE

152. United States Lines/"Leviathan". ca. 1923.
$24^1/_2$ x $39^1/_8$ in./62 x 99.4 cm
Cond A–/Unobtrusive fold. Framed.
Ref: PAI-III, 382
It's not exactly a secret that Americans on the whole enjoy living out the axiom that "Bigger is Better." As proof of this sweeping generalization, we would like to present Exhibit A: The *Leviathan*, the gargantuan oceanic "American Way to America," as she crushes her way out of port, in the process making her accompanying tug appear to have no more right to share the surrounding waters than would a child's bath toy. One of a parcel of vessels ceded by the Germans after World War I—originally christened the *Vaterland*—which became the nucleus of a new company organized under the name United States Lines. Chief among these was the *Leviathan*, whose operators used her great size and basic patriotic appeal to try and keep her filled. Sadly, their strategy failed. As majestic a liner as she was, the ship earned the reputation for being the "Great White Elephant" as she never turned a profit. The *Leviathan* was broken up in Rosyth, Scotland, by June, 1938.
Est: $2,500-$3,000.

153

154

156

157

GIUSEPPE RICCOBALDI (1887-1976)

153. Lloyd Sabaudo/The Famous Counts. 1927.
25³/4 x 38⁷/8 in./65.7 x 98.7 cm
Barabino & Graeve, Genova
Cond B–/Slight tears and stains; trimmed at left and
right edges. Framed.
Ref: Golden Age of Travel, p. 206
The razor-sharp, iconographic Italian futurist style so
popular during Mussolini's tenure trumpets in The
Famous Counts—the nickname for the four great liners of the Lloyd Sabaudo Line. Ushered along by the
nationalistically-toned Four Horsemen of Recreational
Travel, the *Conte Verde, Conte Rosso, Conte Bianco*
and *Conte Grande* surge en masse through the placid
waters beneath their imposing escort. Not that you
could tell from the understated rendering of their
hulls, the interiors of these ships were over-ornate,
over-decorated, over-gold leafed, ostentatious gilded
stucco that closely resembled operatic sets. And for
all the fanfare of the poster, the facts and figures of

these four vessels is fairly commonplace: two—the
Conte Verde & Conte Rosso—were destroyed during
WW II, while the remaining two both sailed until 1960.
And so ends the tale of the Famous Counts.
Est: $2,000-$2,500.

HARRY HUDSON RODMELL (1896-1984)

154. French Line/Plymouth to New York/"Paris".
24³/4 x 40¹/8 in./62.8 x 102 cm
Pierre Lafitte, Paris
Cond B+/Slight tears at paper edges; image and colors
excellent.
The *Paris* was not the luckiest of ships. Begun in 1914,
she was obliged to vacate her slip for warship construction before she was completed. She didn't make
her first voyage until 1920. Six years later she sank a
tugboat in Le Havre, the incident bringing about the
loss of ten lives. In 1929, her interior was ravaged by
fire. In 1939, on the eve of sailing for New York, another
fire broke out in her bakery. Fire crews brought it under
control, but like the *Normandie* three years later, she
was sunk by the tons of water from the pumps. None
of this unhappy destiny can be gleaned from this
design, however, with its celestial union of tricolored
French/American patriotism, set off by the exclamatory
presence of the conjoining presence of the Statue of
Liberty. After attending the College of Arts in his native
Hull, Rodmell worked extensively for the Swedish-
Amerian Line and for the Norddeutscher Lloyd.
Est: $1,700-$2,000.

RICHARD RUMMELL (1848-1924)

155. French Line/The "France". ca. 1920.
42⁵/8 x 26⁷/8 in./108.2 x 68.2 cm
Cond B/Slight tears and creases near paper edges.
Ref: PAI-XXVI, 525
The majesty of the big luxury liner as it glides past
the New York skyline is impressively depicted, with
small tugs and other vessels paying homage. An
excellent maritime poster in all respects. Rummel
grew up in Brooklyn and remained active in New York
City all his life.
Est: $1,500-$1,800.

FRITZ C. RUMPF (Carl Georg, 1888-1949)

**156. Laurenburger Dampfern/Burmester & Base-
dow.**
16⁷/8 x 23¹/8 in./42.8 x 58.7 cm
Curt Behrends, Berlin

Cond B–/Stains from verso tape at edges; creases in
bottom text area; image and colors excellent.
Ref: DFP-III, 2768 (var)
The simple joy of getting away from the ordinary trumps
ports of call or amenities in this breezy Rumpf design
for the Burmester and Basedow line and its steamship
excursions from Hamburg to various day trip destinations, the firm's flag unfurling behind the couple,
blissfully free, if only for a while, from the rigors of the
daily grind. Rumpf studied in Berlin and Tokyo, became
something of an expert on Oriental art, and even
wrote some books which he illustrated himself. He
executed numerous posters for various Berlin clients,
but men's fashion posters were his specialty.
Est: $1,500-$1,800.

ALDA SASSI (1929-)

157. Italia. 1954.
24¹/4 x 36¹/4 in./61.5 x 92 cm
A. Mondadori, Verona
Cond B+/Slight tears and creases.
Ref: Bolaffi, p. 199
Rather than advertising a single ship, the Italian Line
opts to promote their Central American tours with a
cruiser gently slicing through mango-tinged waters,
accompanied by the stylized gyrations of an exotic
couple in a carnival mood chaperoned by a pair of
abstract gulls. Nothing in the way of specifics, but the
contagious esoteric exotica refuses to be ignored.
Sassi created the bulk of her designs for navigational
firms, executing eye-snagging works marked by an
effective use of extreme modernism.
Est: $1,200-$1,500.

ALBERT SEBILLE (1874-1953)

158. Transatlantique/"France".
39¹/2 x 28⁷/8 in./100.5 x 72 cm
Imp. F. Champenois, Paris
Cond B–/Tears at folds and edges; framed to text at
bottom.
Sebille was a successful and prolific maritime artist,
many of whose paintings adorned the staterooms of
French Line ships. His maritime posters for the company are some of the best ever done—not least, this
superb view of the *France* steaming her way into the
open seas that lay beyond the harboring embrace of
Miss Liberty. Completed in January of 1912, the *France*
was one of the fastest ships in the CGT fleet at the
time, making her maiden crossing in five days and sev-
enteen hours. She was also the most luxurious French
liner of her day, as well as the only four stacker.
Est: $1,700-$2,000

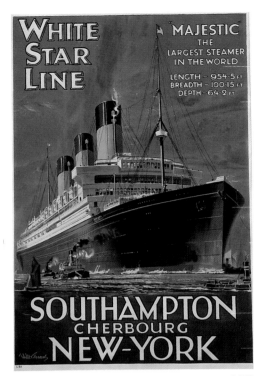

SHIP POSTERS (continued)

WALTER THOMAS (1894-1971)

**159. White Star Line/Southampton/Cherbourg/
New York.** ca. 1923.
24¹/₂ x 37³/₈ in./62.3 x 95 cm
Cond B+/Unobtrusive tears, largely in bottom text
area. Framed.
Ref: PAI-VI, 278
An impressive depiction of the *Majestic*, at the time
the star of the White Star Line. The company acquired
the German liner *Bismarck* which had been seized by
the British government as part of the German war
reparations, and renamed it the *Majestic*. Originally

built in 1914 in Hamburg, the 56,000-ton liner was
955 feet long, its eight steam turbines and quadruple
screws capable of propelling it at a speed of 24 knots.
The ship was turned over to the British Admiralty in
1936 and used as a training vessel, until a fire gutted
it at Rosyth off the Scottish coast, and it sank with the
loss of 12 lives. Thomas was a marine painter and
poster artist who did most of his studies and work in
Liverpool.
Est: $2,000-$2,500.

NORMAN WILKINSON (1882-1971)

160. White Star Line. 1904.
43 x 32¹/₄ in./109.2 x 82 cm

The Liverpool Printing
Cond B/Recreated margins.
Wilkinson's skill as a maritime specialist is evident in
the moody, churning blue waters of the Atlantic in this
poster for England's White Star Line. The understated
majesty of the line itself is the thrust of the design, as
the ship shown surging through the choppy seas could
be any one of the line's "Big Four"—the *Celtic, Cedric,
Baltic* and *Adriatic*—holding court on the high seas,
its beige and black funnels belching smoke skyward
en route to varied ports of call. Wilkinson designed
posters for the British railways, and organized the
series by Royal Academy artists for the LMS railway
in 1924.
Est: $1,400-$1,700.

AVIATION POSTERS

ANONYMOUS

161. Airplane Rides/Boeing Clipper. ca. 1929.
25¹/₈ x 37³/₈ in./63.8 x 96.2 cm
Cond A–/Slight tears at top paper edge.
Ref: Airline Artistry, p. 3 (var); PAI-II, 70
"Was there ever an aviation poster with more in it than
this? Art and Rolley Inman had the biggest aircraft ever
used in a Flying Circus—the 20-passenger Boeing 80-
A, which was, in 1931, used by United Airlines in its
fastest coast-to-coast service. In addition, they had the
famous Ford tri-motor, used by several U.S. airlines in
mail and passenger service before the advent of the
DC-2. They were responsible for introducing hundreds
of thousands of people to the safety and comfort of
airline travel. Special rides at 50 cents were a bargain.
Parachute jumps were featured, with a collection
taken up for the jumper. Margie Lee Inman, Rolley's
wife, had been doing wing walking for years on their
biplane, with which they had previously barnstormed.
This Flying Circus was formed in the 1920s, and flew
until the late 1930s. . . . In 1942 both Art and Rolley .
. . were flying across the South Atlantic and Africa, fer-
rying lend-lease twin-engined bombers for PAA Ferries.
Rolley, who survived a crash in Africa, was killed in a
crash in Maine in 1944. Margie died in 1987 at age
76." (Airline Artistry, p. 3).
Est: $1,500-$1,800.

162. Groot Vliegfeest.
28³/₄ x 43 in./73 x 109.2 cm
Leon Beyaert, Sioen Courtai
Cond A.
The Flemish city of Turnhout near the Dutch border
announces an air show extravaganza with a jumble of
planes and the tumble of aerialists without the slight-

Affiches Photographiques ROBAUDY, CANNES

est hint of danger, as if hanging from a biplane by your ankle was as natural a thing to do as opening a can of soup. Sponsored by the "Aeronautical Propaganda and Popularization Squadron" of Brussels and the city council, some of the performers at this in-flight hoot-enanny include: Miss Denise Mercier, parachutist; Vadime, a flying trapeze artist and wing walker who specialized in snagging flags off the earth below; and Serge, a Russian pilot and parachutist.
Est: $1,500-$1,800.

ANDREY

163. Castrol/Mrs. Amy Mollison. 1932.
22⁷/₈ x 30 in./58 x 76.2 cm
Cond B–/Restored tears at folds.

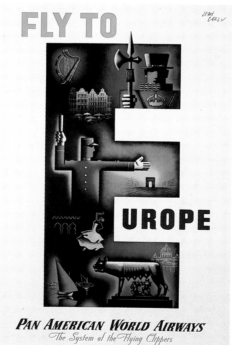

Though the rendered craft is a tad more muscular than the Puss Moth used by the aviatrix to make her one-hundred and two hour flight from London to Cape Town, the dramatic airborne isolation of Mrs. Molli-son's flight is panoramically captured by Andrey for Castrol motor oil, a lubricating firm with a solid associ-ation with avionic records (see PAI-XXVII, 96 & 97). "As a long distance pilot, fame came almost overnight to 26-year old Hull-born typist Amy Johnson . . . . In her de Haviland Moth Jason, . . . she left Croydon on 5 May 1930 and reached Australia on the 24th of the same

month. . . . In August 1932 Miss Johnson married James Mollison . . . Later in the year Amy Mollison deci-sively bettered her husband's time to the Cape, using a more powerful Puss Moth" (*History of Aviation*, by John W. R. Taylor and Kenneth Munson, p. 208). The Mollison's became one of the most active and accom-plished husband/wife flying teams of the 1930s. Dur-ing the 1940s, they both served as members of the British Air Transport Auxiliary, in whose service Mrs. Mollison tragically lost her life.
Est: $1,000-$1,200.

CHARLES LÉONCE BROSSÉ

164. Meeting d'Aviation/Nice. 1910.
30⁷/₈ x 42¹/₂ in./78.2 x 108 cm
Affiches Photographiques Robaudy, Cannes
Cond B+/Slight tears at folds.
Ref: Looping the Loop, Cover & Pl. 34;
Affiches Azur, 315; PAI-XXIX, 111
From a bird's eye view above the cockpit of a fantasti-cal flying machine, we share in the pilot's vertiginous, breath-taking vista of Nice and the Gold Coast as he scatters a bouquet of roses to the town quite literally at his feet. Brossé, a graphic chronicler of the city of Nice, not only provided us with a magnificent poster for the 1910 air show, he was also one of the event's key organizers.
Est: $4,000-$5,000.

JEAN CARLU (1900-1997)

165. Pan American/Europe. 1949.
27⁵/₈ x 42¹/₄ in./70.2 x 107.2 cm
Cond A.
Ref: Carlu (checklist)
All of Europe's most tantalizing sights and citizenry are corralled into the confines of the continent's prominent capital first letter, save for the beefeater's halberd getting straight to the point with regard to Pan Am's World service to Europe courtesy of their fleet of Flying Clippers in this Carlu bauble. The service was introduced to the public in 1947.
Est: $1,200-$1,700

167

170

171

172

AVIATION POSTERS (continued)

A. M. CASSANDRE
(Adolphe Mouron, 1901-1968)

166. Air-Orient. 1932.
$23^1/_2$ x $31^3/_8$ in./59.7 x 79.7 cm
Alliance Graphique, Paris
Cond A–/Slight stain at top.
Ref: Mouron, ill. 144; Cassandre/Tokyo, 51;
    Cassandre Suntory, 57; PAI-XXIII, 167
Superimposed images are a Cassandre specialty, and
here the technique works exceptionally well. Unusual
for him, however, is the use of photography—seen
here as a background—yet he handles it with equal
mastery. Air Orient was formed in 1930 by a merger of
two smaller airlines; three years later it became one of
the components of Air France.
Est: $10,000-$12,000.

LUCIEN CAVÉ

167. French Aviation: 7 Commemorative Posters.
Each: $11^1/_8$ x $14^5/_8$ in./28.5 x 37 cm
La Publicité Synchronissée, Lyon
Cond A–/Slight tears at paper edges.
Ref: Looping the Loop, 19
A series of posters that celebrates Gallic aeronautic
achievements that range from Montgolfier's 1783 balloon ride to the first East/West North Atlantic crossing
in 1930, with each poster emblazoned with the head-
line, "The World Owes its Wings to France." Other
events covered in the septet include Bleriot's flight
across the Atlantic (1909), the first hydrofoil flight
(1910), the first commercial crossing of the South
Atlantic (1930) and the first sustained one-kilometer
flight of 1908. "Henry Farman . . . won a prize of fifty
thousand francs by flying a Voisin biplane around a
closed course of one kilometer on 13 January 1908.
In doing so he proved to Europeans, who had refused
to believe that the Wright brothers had accomplished
the same feat and more three years earlier, that con-
trolled and powered flight was possible" (Looping the
Loop, p. 30). The series was published by the Secre-
tary General of Air Defense.
Est: $2,000-$2,500. (7)

HANS RUDI ERDT (1883-1918)

168. Flieger Zur See. 1915.
$37^1/_4$ x $55^1/_4$ in./94.7 x 140.2 cm
Hollerbaum & Schmidt, Berlin
Cond A–/Unobtrusive slight tears at seam.
Ref: PAI-XXX, 309
For what would appear to be a wartime film in praise
of military might, Erdt gives us this sweeping 2-sheet
design focusing on the swashbuckling nature rather
than the destructive aspects of the life of a *Sea Flyer*.
At the time, naval biplanes were catapulted from the
ship's deck in order to scout the skies surrounding the
fleet. As no landing gear was available to the planes,
they would set down in the water to be recovered by
specially built cranes. No record of the film exists however in German film chronicles, which leads us to
believe that it must have been an import whose name
was altered to suit Germanic consumers. Although he
only lived to age 35, Erdt amassed an impressive
record as a graphic artist and lithographer in the single
decade form 1908 to 1918. He depicted upper-class
people in their sports and luxuries, and had a keen
eye for reducing a scene to a few essential forms and
flat colors.
Est: $4,500-$5,500.

DOMINIQUE CHARLES FOUQUERAY
(1872-1956)

**169. Exposition Internationale Locomotion Aéri-
enne.** 1919.
$31^3/_4$ x $47^1/_4$ in./80.6 x 120 cm
Imp. Lapina, Paris
Cond A–/Unobtrusive folds.
This Fouqueray design for an International Parisian Air
Show in the winter of 1919 conveys a rousing, decidedly nationalistic bent that seems altogether apropos
in the pride-restoring days following the end World
War I. The slashing pencil work and sepia color scheme
conjure a sense of eddying motion and liberation, the
only color present being the tritone swatch draped
from the unfettered Marianne, heralding the event as
she soars amidst flanking Fokker-style aircraft above
the Grand Palais.
Est: $3,000-$4,000.

UMBERTO DI LAZZARO

170. Il Volo in Massa Italia-Brasile. 1931.
$27^1/_4$ x $39^7/_8$ in./69 x 101.3 cm
IGAP, Roma
Cond B–/Restored tears at folds and edges.
It's an arduous task to decide which feature is more
impressive in this poster commemorating the 1931
massive Italian formation flight to Rio De Janeiro—the
surreal shrunk-world perspective of the landscape
which places Rome on the shimmering lemon horizon,
a relative stone's throw across the South Atlantic,
Savoia-Marchetti flying-boats suspended gracefully in
the air above, or the assembled headshots of the
pilots and flight crew, centered by General Italo Balbo,
commander of the mission and Minister of Aviation.
This was the first of two massive Italian formation
flights over the Atlantic Ocean—the second transpiring
some two years later (*see* PAI-XXIX, 114)—that would
effectively demonstrate how flight was rapidly shrink-
ing the planet, with both missions headed by the dash-

168

169

ing Italian Air Minister. After serving in World War I, Balbo joined the Fascist movement and in 1922 was one of the four top leaders of the March on Rome, which brought Mussolini to power. A general of the Fascist militia, he held several cabinet posts and efficiently developed aviation in Italy. Ironically, he was killed in 1940 when his plane crashed at Tobruk, Libya, apparently shot down accidentally by Italian antiaircraft artillery
Est: $2,000-$2,500.

C. PUB

171. Sabena Helicopter.
63 x 29¹/₂ in./160 x 75 cm

Cond A.
During the 1950s, Sabena, the national airline of Belgium, was the first European aeronautic transportation company to operate helicopter passenger service from town to town—from Brussels to Paris and Cologne. In Brussels, the departure point was actually operated from the center of town. And it's one such Sikorsky S-class transport choppers that we see here—an image that may possibly be a part of a larger billboard—prismatically slicing its way with commuter convenience through a fractured stained glass sky. Credit is no doubt for the agency which prepared this image.
Est: $800-$1,000.

BERNARD VILLEMOT (1911-1989)

172. Air France/Côte d'Azur. ca. 1952.
24³/₄ x 39¹/₄ in./62.9 x 99.8 cm
Cond A.
Ref: Affiches Azur, 28; Air France, checklist
In most of his posters Villemot created during his ten-year tenure with Air France from 1946 to 1956, he evoked destinations with picturesque scenes, his images rendered with splashy elliptical brushwork. Though his approach here is a bit more angular than the Villemot norm, he evokes the chic sleek of the Riviera with Colorform zest.
Est: $1,000-$1,200

LOOPING THE LOOP—Posters of Flight

THE SHOW: The third venue for this exhibition of early aviation posters is the Virginia Air and Space Center in Hampton, Virginia (telephone 757-727-0900) from October 28, 2000, to January 7, 2001. For more information, visit their website: http://www.nasm.si.edu/nasm/pa/nasmnews/pr/loop/loop/htm.

THE BOOK: This hardcover 160-page book, measuring 10 x 13 inches, contains 102 full page color reproductions. Written by Henry Serrano Villard and Willis M. Allen, Jr., with foreward by Jack Rennert. Available from Posters Please, Inc., 601 W. 26th Street, N.Y.C. 10001. Price: $40. Add $3 for shipping in U.S. and $10 for foreign orders.

173

174

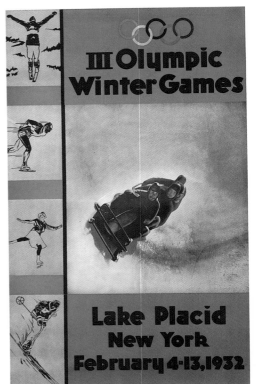

175

176

177

COX

173. Scribner's. ca. 1896.
12 x 23$^1/_8$ in./30.5 x 58.7 cm
Cond A–/Unobtrusive tears.
Although we could not find any referential evidence to unquestionably connect this Scribner's poster with the Athens' Olympics of 1896, the circumstantial connection appears obvious. First off, Scribner's April 1896 issue carried an Olympic feature as its headlining story (see PAI-XXIV, 29); this certainly could have advertised that installment of the magazine with its obvious torch-bearing sculpted classicism. And secondly, the promotional aspect of looking into "The Last Quarter Century In America" is beyond speculation, as our participation in the modern games was indisputably a major event.
Est: $2,000-$2,500.

EDOUARD ELZINGRE (1880-1966)

174. XXeme Anniversaire du Rétablissement des Jeux Olympiques/1894-1914.
28$^1/_2$ x 40$^3/_8$ in./72.3 x 102.5 cm
Affiches Atar, Genève
Cond A–/Unobtrusive tears at paper edge.
Ref: Olympics, p. 152; Sport à l'Affiche, 88; PAI-XXIX, 551
In 1914, members of the sixth Olympic Congress met in Paris to plan the forthcoming Olympic events. They used the occasion to hold a special ceremony in the large amphitheater of the Sorbonne where, in 1894, the International Olympic Committee had been created and the ancient Greek games officially revived. This heroic poster celebrates the 20th anniversary of that event. At the ceremony, Pierre de Coubertin, the Frenchman who had conceived the whole project, was honored by being presented with the flag from the first modern Games, which were held in Athens in 1896.
Est: $2,500-$3,000.

ANONYMOUS

175. III Olympic Winter Games/Lake Placid 1932.
24$^3/_4$ x 40$^1/_2$ in./63 x 103 cm
Cond A–/Slight tears at edges.
Ref: PAI-XXVI, 462
Part photo, part design in blue and yellow only, this completely uncredited design for the 1932 Winter Games is one of the rarest of all Olympic posters. The official poster, by Witold Gordon, showed the profile of a jumping skier in silhouette; this was evidently an alternative design not known to the International Olympic Committee. *This is the larger format.*
Est: $1,700-$2,000.

KRAUSS & DZUBAS

176. XIth Olympiad Berlin 1936/Germany.
25$^1/_4$ x 39$^7/_8$ in./64.2 x 101.3 cm

Reichsbahnzentrale für den Deutschen Reiseverkehr, Berlin
Cond A–/Slight creasing in bottom text area.
Ref (Both Var): Olympics, p. 47; PAI-XXIX, 55
Friedel Dzubas (1915-?) and a designer named Krauss (no data known) produced this preliminary poster for the Olympics that was to earn their place in history on several points: this was the last meet before World War II, and black American runner and jumper, Jesse Owens, earned gold medals in stunning victories that earned an angry snub from Hitler. The design shows the Roman chariot on top of the Brandenburg Gate, a triumphal arch in the center of Berlin. For the Games themselves, a different official poster by Franz Würbel

178

179

180

(see No. 178) was later adopted—coincidentally also using the Brandenburg Gate but from a different angle. *This is the English version.*
Est: $2,000-$2,500.

LENG

177. Course Relayée au Flambeau Olympie 1936.
25^1/$_8$ x 39^3/$_8$ in./64 x 101.2 cm
Reichsbahnzentrale für den Deutschen Reiseverkehr, Berlin
Cond A.
Ref (Both Var): Olympics, p. 47; PAI-XXVIII, 463
The torch route for the 1936 Olympic Games, from its smoldering naissance high atop Mount Olympus to its Berlin destination, is laid out with cartographic flair. A charming poster, pin-spotting the major European cities the torch will be passing through en route while almost creating a general travel poster for the Continent, complete with architectural highlights and sketches of indigenous folk costumes. Even though the road to Berlin doesn't pass through Italy, its historical landmarks find inclusion here. *This is the French version.*
Est: $1,700-$2,000.

FRANZ WURBEL (1896-?)

178. Juegos Olímpicos/Berlin 1936.
25^1/$_4$ x 39^7/$_8$ in./64.1 x 101.4 cm
Reichsbahnzentrale für den Deutschen Reiseverkehr, Berlin
Cond B/Unobtrusive tears in bottom text area and paper edges.
Ref (All Var): Olympics, p. 45; Sport à l'Affiche, 92; PAI-XXVIII, 464
The official design for the 1936 Olympics in Berlin shows the city's Brandenberg Gate silhouetted against the golden image of an athlete wearing a triumphant crown of laurel. The poster, sponsored by the German railways, was printed in 19 languages and allegedly distributed in 34 countries. Here we see the Spanish version.
Est: $2,000-$2,500.

LUDWIG HOHLWEIN (1874-1949)

179. Allemagne 1936/IVes Jeux Olympiques d'Hiver.
25^1/$_4$ x 39 34 in./64.2 x 101 cm
Reisbahnzentrale für den Deutchen Reisverkehr, Berlin
Cond B/Slight tears at folds and edges.
Ref (all var): Olympics, p. 49; Hohlwein/Stuttgart, 411; Hohlwein 1874-1949, p. 256 ; PAI-XXVI, 464
This poster for the 1936 Winter Games, held at Garmisch-Partkirchen, was designed by Hohlwein in 1934 and distributed throughout the world the following year in 13 languages. Deceptively simple, the image shows a skier hailing an unseen friend. The gesture makes a forceful statement, and the Olympics emblem does the rest. *This is the rare French text version.*
Est: $2,500-$3,000.

WERNER WEISKONIG (1907-1982)

180. Olympic Winter Games 1948/.St. Moritz. 1946.
25^3/$_4$ x 40^1/$_4$ in./65.3 x 102 cm
Orell Fussli, Zurich
Cond A.
Ref: Olympics, p. 57; PAI-XXVII, 139 (var)
Four official posters were printed for the 1948 Winter Olympics at St. Moritz. The sun was the theme of two. In Weiskonig's design, the solar face looks benevolent and—contrary to most mythology—not especially male. The Swiss National Board of Tourism found the image so agreeable that they used it simply as a general travel poster as well (see PAI-XXVII, 139).
Est: $1,000-$1,200.

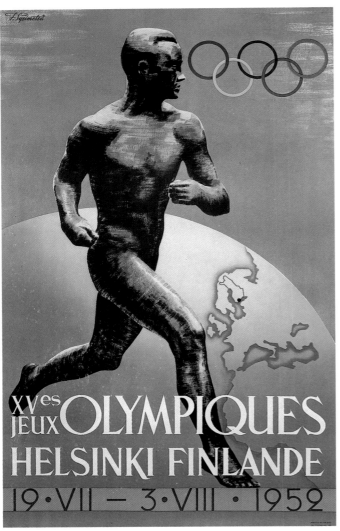

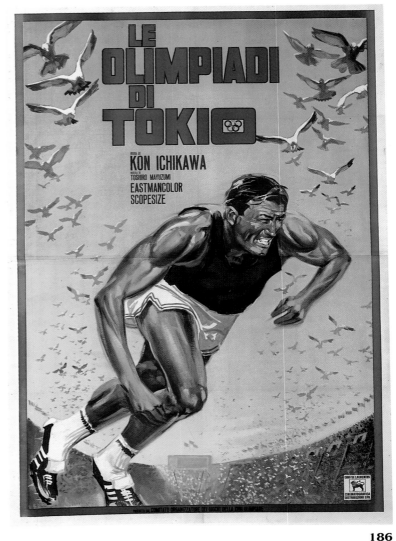

181

186

185

OLYMPIC POSTERS (continued)

ILMARI SYSIMETSÄ (1912-1955)

181. XVes Jeux Olympiques/Helsinki Finland. 1959.
24³/₈ x 39³/₈ in./62 x 100 cm
Oy. Tilgmann, Finland
Cond A.
Ref (All Var): Olympics, p. 59; Sportissimo, pp. 14, 59; PAI-XXVI, 466
By the time World War II broke out in Europe in 1939, preparations had
been completed for the scheduled 1940 Games in Helsinki—including the
official poster chosen in competition from among 72 Finnish artists. When
the war canceled the event, Helsinki had to wait until 1952 to host the
Games, and it was decided to use the old poster, substituting only the new
dates. The designer chose to depict a bronze statue (by Waïmo Aaltonen)
of the most famous Finnish athlete, Olympic runner Paavo Nurmi, together
with a globe on which the location of Finland is highlighted.
Est: $2,000-$2,500.

GREGORI

182. Giornata Olimpica. 1959.
38³/₄ x 54¹/₈ in./98.3 x 137.5 cm
Vecchioni & Guadagno, Roma
Cond A.
Ref: PAI-XXII, 132
The passing of the Olympic torch from the ancients down to our time is
conveyed brilliantly in this offset-printed poster for the "Olympic Days,"
preliminaries to the Rome Olympics of 1960.
Est: $1,200-$1,500.

ARMANDO TESTA (1917-1992)

183. Rome 1960 Olympics.
27¹/₈ x 39 in./69 x 99.6 cm
IGAP, Milano
Cond A–/Unobtrusive tears at folds.
Ref : Olympics, p. 73; PAI-XXVI, 467
The official (and only) poster for the 1960 Olympics held in Rome was
chosen from 212 designs submitted in a nationwide competition held three
years in advance. The wolf that allegedly weaned Romulus and Remus is the
symbol chosen to represent Italy; in the center, the winning athlete is putting on his crown, according to Roman custom. *This is the Chinese version.*
Est: $1,400-$1,700.

182

183

184

187

188

ANONYMOUS

184. Roma/Stadio Olympico. 1960.
26³/₄ x 39³/₈ in./68 x 100 cm
Vecchioni & Guadagno, Roma
Cond A.
A beautiful photographically rendered poster—both in terms of the view it affords and its advertising potential—that from its hilltop vantage point lays out Rome's 1960 Olympic stadium in all its classically traditional glory. It also provides us with a spectacular contrast to virtually all sports promotions, Olympic or otherwise—the empty field of competition, free from athletic grace and rabid fandom, a calm before the storm of strength and endurance.
Est: $1,200-$1,500.

**185. Squaw Valley 1960 Winter Olympics:
  2 Posters.** 1959.
Each approx.: 24 x 35³/₄ in./61 x 91 cm
Kaiser Graphic Arts, Oakland, California
a: Cond A.
b: Cond B–/Restored loss lower right area.
Ref (All Var but PAI-XXVI, 468) : Olympics, pp. 77 & 75;
  PAI-XXVI, 468 & 469

The eighth winter Olympic games were held in Squaw Valley, California in February 1960. 648 athletes—about a quarter of them women—from 30 countries participated. Two official posters were selected and distributed at the end of 1959. The first image shows the star-like official emblem of the event against the photographic background of a field of snow. The second of the two official designs uses the motif of pennants on a slalom run and serves with a twin purpose: It shows the site of the games on an outline map of the United States, and it provides the exact dates of the games, which were unknown at the time of the first official announcement. Both posters were issued in five languages, and we see the Italian version of both designs.
Est: $1,000-$1,200. (2)

186. Le Olimpiado di Tokio. ca. 1965.
54⁷/₈ x 77³/₄ in./139.4 x 197.3 cm
Policrom, Roma
Cond B/Slight tears at folds and edges.
In an exception to official Olympic films, the Japanese had enough sense to assign this job to an established director of profound imagination—Kon Ichikawa—and then give him a 566-person staff and 164 cameras

with which to do it. The result was a 170-minute spectacle, universally praised as brilliant in its own right and a masterpiece of the genre. Rather than simply reporting the events and who won them, Ichikawa stressed the human element—the efforts of the athletes and the reactions of spectators to them—producing a work that moved one critic to call it a "hymn." Americans had a right to feel cheated: We got a shorn, 93-minute version and the critics damned the U.S. distributor. This poster for the Italian release of the movie shows a runner exploding from a starters' position, which upon closer inspection, would appear to be the unknown artist's interpretation of an action still from the film. So interpreted, in fact, that this sprinter appears to have changed races: In a previously seen photo-collage version of the image (*see* PAI-XXV, 55), we see the identical runner, down to the muscular striations and stripe of his socks. However, the decidedly black athlete became markedly Caucasian, in all likelihood for marketing purposes.
Est: $2,000-$2,500.

YUSAKU KAMEKURA (1915-1997)

187. Tokyo 1964 Olympics.
28¹/₂ x 41³/₈ in./72.3 x 105 cm
Dai Nippon Printing Co., Japan
Cond B/Slight stains and tears near paper edges.
Ref: Olympics, p. 81; PAI-XV, 437 (var)
Up until the Tokyo Olympics of 1964, there was customarily a single official poster for each of the Games. Kamekura, however, prepared a total of four, breaking the precedent and setting a new trend of multiple Olympic posters. By clearing the landscape of all extraneous elements, Kamekura presents the trek of the torch and the solitary focus of its bearer with isolated dignity.
Est: $800-$1,000.

188. Tokyo 1964 Olympics.
28¹/₂ x 41³/₈ in./72.5 x 105.6 cm
Dai Nippon Printing Co., Japan
Cond B/Slight tears and creases, largely near paper
  edges.
Ref: Olympics, p. 81; Kamekura, 59;
  Plakatkunst, p. 160; PAI-XXVIII, 456 (var)
Bursting forth from the blocks in a churning jumble of limbs and focused determination, these sprinters photographically captured by Kamekura snare the essence of the race for The Grail of amateur athletics. Founder of the Nippon Design Center, Kamekura is one of a small group who helped chart the course of Japanese graphic art after World War II.
Est: $1,000-$1,200

189

191

190

196

OLYMPICS/Kamekura (continued)

189. Tokyo 1964 Olympics.
28^1/$_2$ x 41^3/$_8$ in./72.4 x 105 cm
Dai Nippon Printing Co., Japan
Cond B/Slight tears and creases, largely near paper
    edges.
Ref: Olympics, p. 81; Kamekura, 60;
    Plakatkunst, p. 161; PAI-XXVIII, 468 (var)
Grace, strength and determination. These unifying
factors set to the page by Kamekura define Olympic
resolve with moments of motion frozen by the
camera for eternity. And in this piece, the contrast
between the frothing butterfly stroke and glassine
waters dazzles the eye with hypnotic simplicity.
Est: $1,000-$1,200.

PEDRO RAMIREZ VASQUEZ, EDUARDO TERRAZAS & LANCE WYMAN

190. Mexico 1968 Olympics.
24^1/$_2$ x 47^5/$_8$ in./62 x 121 cm
Miguel Galas, Mexico
Cond B+/Slight tears at fold.
Ref: Olympics, p. 87 (var); Ateny-Atlanta, 15;
    PAI-XXIV, 57 (var)
All the official posters for the XIXth Olympiad were the
combined teamwork of three artists: Mexicans Vasquez
and Terrazas collaborating with Wyman from the U.S.
Guided by the motto "Information, esthetics, function-
alism," the trio incorporated native Mexican motifs
into their designs, particularly the concentric pattern-
ing found in the art of the Cuichol Indians, which
made its way into the logo. Central to the design here
is a medallion with Mayan motifs. As opposed to the
most commonly seen version of the poster (*see*
PAI-XXIV, 57), this variant strips the medallion to its
most essential details, streamlining it into a compass
for athleticism backed by the bright simplicity of a teal
and pink pattern.
Est: $800-$1,000.

ANONYMOUS

191. Mexico 1968 Olympics.
34^3/$_4$ x 34^3/$_4$ in./88.3 x 88.3 cm
Miguel Galas, Mexico
Cond A.
Square in shape, but not in construct, this uncredited
design—labeled "Periodico Mural No. 15"—strays
somewhat from the native motif incorporation of the
Olympiad's official trio of artists, laying out Mexico
City as a bustling cartoon cityscape that calls to mind
the style popularized by the "Pink Panther" animated
series. As the bottom Spanish text offers a worldwide
welcome from Mexico to the 19th Olympics—the first

games held in "Hispanoamerica"—a blimp floats
through the concrete skyscraper canyon encouraging
the citizens below to "Make Our City More Beautiful,"
in the process creating an all-inclusive positivist feeling.
Est: $800-$1,000.

GRENOBLE: 1968

192. Xes Jeux Olympiques d'Hiver/Grenoble. 1968.
Each Approx: 24^3/$_4$ x 39^1/$_8$ in./62.7 x 99.5 cm
Cond A–/Slight tears and creases at edges of "a."
Ref: Olympiques, pp. 93 & 95; Sport à l'Affiche, 94 (a);
    PAI-XXII, 136 (var)
a. Artist: **Jacques Rolet (1925-)**
Imp. Georges Lang, Paris
A graphic artist and photographer, Rolet rendered the
Olympic torch via photomontage with an overhead
shot of Grenoble's main thoroughfare for the handle
and the surrounding mountains for flames. Ingenious,
yet entirely simple.
b. Jean Brian (1915-)
Imp. Generale, Grenoble
Designer/advertising executive Brian placed the inter-
locking Olympic rings right into the midst of the action
as a kind of modified bobsled team, which, like the
rings, represents the spirit of utmost cooperation.
c. Constantin
Imp. L. Delaporte, Paris
A photomontage sets a quartet of flags flapping in the
crisp mountain air against a bluer-than-possible sky,
the French standard getting equal billing—without a
doubt a host country's prerogative—with its Olympic
lock-ringed neighbor.
Est: $1,200-$1,500. (3)

MUNICH OLYMPICS—1972

193. Collection of 22 Posters. 1970.
Each: 33 x 46^3/$_4$ in./83.8 x 118.6 cm
Mandruck, München
Cond A–/Slight tears at some posters' paper edges.
Ref: Olympics, pp. 96-99; PAI-XVII, 41(var)
For the Munich Olympiad of 1972, there was a main
poster, designed by Otl H. Aicher of Ulm, who also
served as art director for the event, plus separate
posters for each of the twenty-two sports in the com-
petition; this is the sports series (for the art series, *see*
next lot). Among the designers were Otte Hesse, Erich
Baumann, Peter Cornelius, Albrecht Gaebele and others.

In order to create a unity of style, Aicher specified that
all the individual sport posters start with a photograph,
solarized to achieve unusual effects and printed in
bright color combinations. In addition to the Olympic
rings, each design also includes a spiral rosette, the
emblem of the 1972 Games chosen from 2,333 submitted entries.
Est: $4,000-$5,000. (22)

194. Artistic Series: 23 Posters
Each: 25^1/$_4$ x 40^1/$_8$ in./64 x 102 cm
Cond A–/Slight tears at edges on a few/P.
Ref: Olympics, pp. 100-102; Sport à l'Affiche, 95;
    PAI-XXI, 137 (var)
There were two poster series for this event: one group
of 22 posters featuring individual sports (*see* previous
lot); the other of 28 posters commissioned from top
international artists. It is from this latter group that
this selection is taken. Artists of every age, background and style are represented, including Joseph
Albers, Allen d'Arcangelo, Max Bill, Piero Dorazio,
R. B. Kitaj, Allen Jones, Charles Lapicque, Jan Lenica,
Marino Marini, Serge Poliakoff and Victor Vasarely.
Although the 1972 Games were marred by an act of
terrorism against the Israeli team, the posters glorify
the international spirit of peaceful competition in eloquent graphics. *This is the most complete set from
the Artistic Series that we have ever offered.*
Est: $2,000-$2,500. (23)

GRENOBLE
VILLE OLYMPIQUE

FRANCE   1968

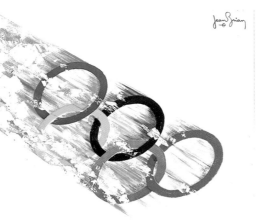

X^mes JEUX
OLYMPIQUES
D'HIVER
6/18 Février 1968
GRENOBLE FRANCE

X^mes JEUX OLYMPIQUES
D'HIVER FRANCE 1968
GRENOBLE

192

Olympische Spiele München 1972

Olympische Spiele München 1972

194

XI Olympic Winter Games

XI Olympic Winter Games

195

München 1972

München 1972

Kiel 1972

193

flake which is an ancient Japanese ideogram and the Olympic rings), plus Kamekura's skills in creating an impressive design from the assembled elements.
Est: $1,000-$1,200. (2)

PRIMO ANGELI

196. Atlanta. 1995.
29^1/2 x 45^1/4 in./75 x 114.8 cm
Cond A/P.
The Atlanta Games—commemorated by Angeli in this limited edition (No. 7 of 250) silk-screened, hand-signed officially sanctioned design that combines classic figure study with modernist, color-block flair—were far and away the largest modern era games ever held with a record 197 nations competing. These Olympics had some of the best stories ever: Muhammad Ali's return to the global stage as he ignited the Olympic cauldron, Kerri Strugg's hobbled, gutsy final vault and the horror of a terrorist bomb ripping apart a peaceful Friday evening in the Centennial Olympic Park, reminding the world of the tragedy of Munich in 1972. But as they did in '72, the games would go on, propelled by the fierce beauty of amateur athleticism.
Est: $600-$800.

YUSAKU KAMEKURA (1915-1997)

195. XI Olympic Winter Games: 2 Posters. 1970.
Each: 28^1/2 x 41^3/8 in./72.5 x 105.2 cm
Toppan Printing Co.
Cond A.

Ref: Olympics, pp. 106 7 107; Kamekura, pp. 61 & 62; PAI-XVI, 303
Two designs for the 1972 Winter Olympics in Sapporo feature brilliant photographs (skier: Kiyoshi Fujikawa; skater: Takayuki Ogawa), the official emblem of the 1972 Winter Games (the rising sun, a six-prong snow-

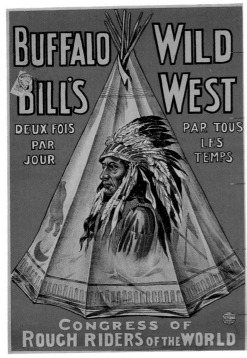

197

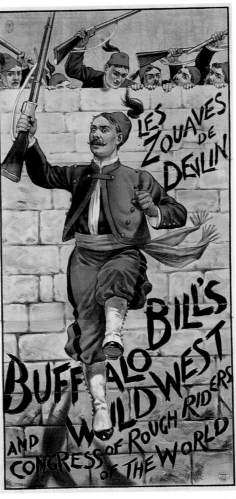

198

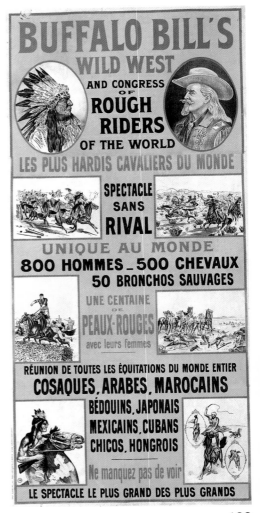

199

ANONYMOUS

197. Buffalo Bill's Wild West. 1905.
19¹/₈ x 29 in./48.6 x 73.7 cm
Imp. Weiners, Paris
Cond B/Restored tears at folds and edges.
The Indians in the Wild West posters (and in the show itself) were always treated with great respect. They were given top billing, along with the cowboys, and in these portraits are depicted as warm, stoic and dignified. Cody insisted that only authentic tribe members participate and that the material in which they appeared be historically accurate and respectful. In this image, the noble, unidentified chief is superimposed on top of a traditional—yet still foreign to a majority of the world—prairie domicile.
Est: $3,000-$3,500.

198. Buffalo Bill's Wild West/Les Zouaves de Devlin.
1905.
Artist: **D. Hand**
38³/₈ x 81⁵/₈ in./97.5 x 207.5 cm
Imp. Weiners, Paris
Cond A–/Unobtrusive folds.
Military spectacles were a big part of the Rough Riders of the World, featured in all of Buffalo Bill's shows. As Russell indicates, "The Zouave drill and uniform of baggy red trousers, gold-braided blue vest, and red fez derived from the Zouaoua tribe in French service in Algeria in the 1830s . . . The drill was executed in a double-time half-step with the men in close order, touching elbows, and consisted of intricate wheelings and patterns, usually performed in sequence without orders other than whistle signals. Its climax was wall-scaling, in which a human pyramid was formed and used as steps by the rest of the men, who were tumbled to the top, the last two or three being drawn up the wall by their rifles and rifle-slings" (*Lives of Buffalo Bill*, p. 381). This wall-climbing aspect was so popular that it was used in several military spectacles, including "The Rescue at Pekin" (*see* Buffalo Bill, 75). Although almost all Wild West posters are unsigned, this one does bear the signature of "D. Hand."
Est: $4,000-$5,000.

199. Buffalo Bill's Wild West. 1905.
39 x 84 in./99 x 213.3 cm
Imp. Chaix, Paris
Cond C/Restored tears and losses.
One of the rarest and, historically, one of the most interesting of the Wild West posters. All told, an excessively impressive design, filled with boasts ("The Greatest of All Great Spectacles"), overstatement ("800 men,

500 horses, 50 Savage Broncos, 100 redskins and their Women" may have been something of an inflated series of numbers) and statistical honesty ("A Reunion of Horsemen from Around the World: Cossacks, Arabs, Moroccans, Bedouins, Japanese, Mexicans, Cubans, Hungarians"). The vignettes running up and down the sides of the 2-sheet marvel illustrate the voracity of the claims. But perhaps the most astounding point of all was Cody's insistence on giving the Native Americans equal billing, a point born out in the cameos up top, where the Indian chief is rendered with the same attention to detail, size and dignity as Buffalo Bill himself.
Est: $3,000-$4,000.

200. The Buffalo Bill Stories: Eight Covers.
Each: 8¹/₄ x 10⁷/₈ in./21 x 27.6 cm
Street & Smith Publishers, New York
Cond B/A few tears at edges; some pencil notations.
One of the most significant tools responsible for the canonization of William Cody into the lexicon of con-

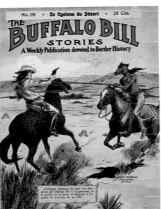

200

temporary mythology was the dime-novel. "Buffalo Bill and his national entertainment were the first to effectively capitalize on the merchandising of the Wild West, with dime novels, souvenir books, . . . programs . . . The art of slick promotion owes a great deal to Cody's master promoters and merchandisers" (Buffalo Bill/Legend, p. 3). The concept quickly caught fire, spreading the name of Buffalo Bill to the four corners of the country—and eventually the world—with frontier adventures both real and imagined. These super-sized adventures, published and printed by Street & Smith of New York, chronicle eight of the imaginatively-tweaked heroic tales from "The Buffalo Bill Stories," ranging from the tale of "Joe the Mosquito" to "The Mystery of the Adobe Castle." This "Weekly Publication devoted to Border History" doubtlessly saw a wide domestic distribution, but the boxed teaser text on most of the covers clearly indicates that the French couldn't get enough of high plains excitement either.
Est: $800-$1,000. (8)

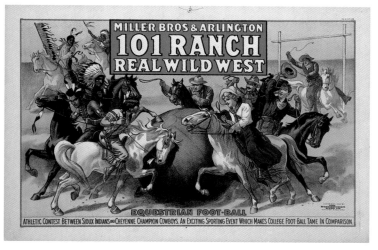

201

202

204

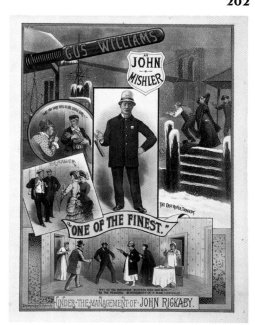

205

203

201. Miller Bros & Arlington/101 Ranch/Real Wild West. 1911.
28 x 18¹/₂ in./71.1 x 47 cm
Strobridge Litho Co, Cinncinnati
Cond A. Framed.
Ref: Phillips VIII, 268
The Miller Brothers of Ponca City, Oklahoma, owned and operated a giant ranch of allegedly 101,000 acres. In 1908, they founded their own Wild West traveling enterprise which was named after their ranch—The Miller Bros. 101 Ranch Real Wild West, sometimes merged with the name Arlington. It operated through 1916 during which season Buffalo Bill performed his last hurrah. The Millers reopened their Wild West in 1925, this time keeping their version of the West running through 1931. This poster of extraordinary vigor shows a variant of the tried and true "Cowboys vs. Indians," only this time it's an "Athletic contest between Sioux Indians and Cheyenne Champion Cowboys" butting heads in a giant ball competition that purportedly "makes college foot-ball tame in comparison." Spicing it up even further was the presence of coed teams, an unthinkable concept to the university mind of the time.
Est: $1,400-$1,700.

202. Barnum & Bailey/Tom Thumb. 1891.
37¹/₂ x 29¹/₄ in./95.2 x 74.4 cm
Strobridge, Cinncinnati
Cond A–/Slight creasing and tears, largely at edges.
Ref: Phillips VIII, 12
In 1885, at St. Thomas, Ontario, the great elephant, Jumbo, was killed by a locomotive while accompanying a baby elephant, "Tom Thumb," which survived. Circus press agents launched the legend that Jumbo had "nobly sacrificed his own life," as is spelled out on this lithograph six years after the event, along with five spectacular cameos which clearly demonstrate the "elephantine intelligence" of the "diminutive dwarf clown elephant."
Est: $2,000-$2,500.

203. The Great Kaufmann Troupe. 1905.
41¹/₄ x 80¹/₄ in./104.7 x 203.8 cm
Courier Company, Buffalo, NY
Cond B–/Restored tears at folds and seams.
"Balancing acts took every form imaginable, as bicycles (or their parts) became novel appendages of the body that seemingly transformed the performer into half-person, half-bicycle" (*The Bicycle*, p. 149). It's difficult to tell where one bike begins and another ends in this 3-sheet cluster truck for the The Great Kaufmann Group, the internationally renowned clan of trick cyclists. Whether working as a units or individually balancing along, the homogenous uniformity of the apple-cheeked gang is indisputably impressive.
Est: $1,500-$1,800.

204. Come and See Us at the Circus.
18⁵/₈ x 24 in./47.4 x 61 cm
Stafford Netherfield, Nottingham
Cond B+/Unobtrusive folds.
Though no specific circus is singled out for patronage, this facially extravagant design from an artist who identifies himself only with the initials "J. P." utilizes its distinctively-painted plethora of clowns to create a hallucinogenic grease paint kaleidoscope that, even though a bit terrifying, is an image of undeniable power and distinction.
Est: $1,000-$1,200.

205. Gus Williams/One of the Finest". ca. 1882.
29¹/₂ x 39⁵/₈ in./75 x 100.6 cm
Strobridge Litho, Cincinnati
Cond A–/Unobtrusive folds.
To cram any more melodrama into this poster might actually be a crime. And no one wants to break any laws on John Mishler's beat, the night stick swinging voice of justice in Joe Bradford's cautionary tale of the mean streets of New York, turn-of-the-century style. The role was something of a departure for Gus Williams (1848-1915), a vaudeville performer and Brooklyn native. The vignettes are classic kitsch at their best, from "The Masher" to "The East River Tragedy" to the climactic scene at bottom wherein the dedicated patrolman obviously dragged himself from death's door to resolve a domestic dispute. Mishler's the man!
Est: $1,400-$1,700.

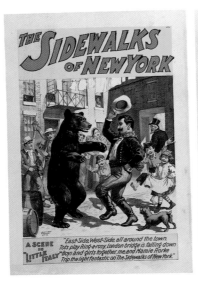

206

207

ANONYMOUS (continued)

206. The Sidewalks of New York: 2 Posters. 1895.
Each: 20 x 30³/₈ in./50.8 x 77.2 cm
Strobridge Litho., Cincinnati
Cond B+/Slight stains in border.
The melodrama splashes off one of the designs for "The Streets of New York," while the other poster couldn't be much more of a hoot if it tried. An excellent pairing for the late-19th century emotional spectacle, demonstrating that without a bit of levity the dramatic would carry significantly less impact. And though the unfortunate occurrence of the occasional out-of-control domestic dispute is still a reality in the Big Apple, there haven't been too many dancing bears roaming the streets in recent memory. Especially in Little Italy.
Est: $1,200-$1,500. (2)

207. A Modern Cinderella.
27¹/₂ x 20⁵/₈ in./69.7 x 52.3 cm
Ackermann-Quigley Litho., Kansas City
Cond A.
The beauty of the Cinderella tale is its simplicity, its ability to translate itself through the story's clear iconography into any time period. Take this "Modern Cinderella." Set in the good times before The Crash, it only makes sense to transform Prince Charming into a wholesome playboy being pursued by a bevy of beauteous chorines. And since our title character is conspicuously absent from the promotion of this "notable production of the last word in musical comedy," it's left up to us to speculate as to the lowly social niche occupied by our heroine. Cigarette girl? Cleaning woman? Gal Friday? Regardless of her station, there's little doubt that there could be any other ending than Happily Ever After.
Est: $1,000-$1,200.

208. Fiske O'Hara/Dion O'Dare. 1907.
30¹/₄ x 40 in./76.7 x 101.4 cm
Strobridge Litho., Cincinnati
Cond B+/Slight tears and stains at folds.
There's no way that the title and star of this poster for the Charles Blaney romantic comedy could be any more Irish unless the unnamed artist used a decorative border of potatoes and shamrocks to frame the action. This scene, entitled "The Sprained Ankle," attempts to attract an audience with its turn-of-the-century randiness, as Mrs. O'Dare comes between her son and the obvious interest of his romantic intent. Playwright Blaney may never have made the big time, but he created a large body of work comprised of melodramas, tear jerkers and farce comedies.
Est: $1,500-$1,800.

209. Peg O' My Heart. 1913.
19³/₄ x 30³/₈ in./50.4 x 77 cm
Strobridge Litho, Cincinnati
Cond A-/Slight tears at paper edges.
Just as the Chichester family learns that they're bankrupt, word arrives that Mrs. Chichester's brother has passed onto his reward. Though he gives them nothing by way of a will provision without strings attached, her

208

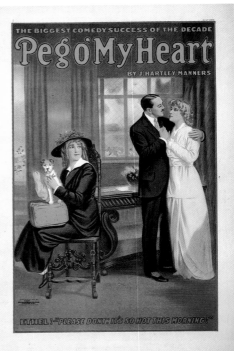

209

late brother does offer an annuity to look after his youngest, Margaret, known to all by the more familiar Peg. As the family is in dire financial straits, they accept the offer. Young Peg arrives just in time to catch her cousin Ethyl and her cad of a boyfriend, Christian Grant, in the midst of a passionate embrace, a scene which this poster trots out with posed decorum. At first, the familial strangers mix like oil and water,

the Chichesters not caring for Peg's homely mutt and dowdy dress, with Peg caring not one bit for her relative's haughty, uncaring nature. However, when Peg convinces Ethyl not to elope with Christian, things take a decided turn for the better and in the end, Peg accepts the hand of her benefactor in marriage.
Est: $1,000-$1,200.

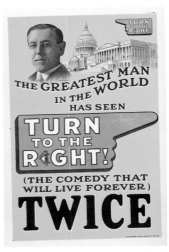

211

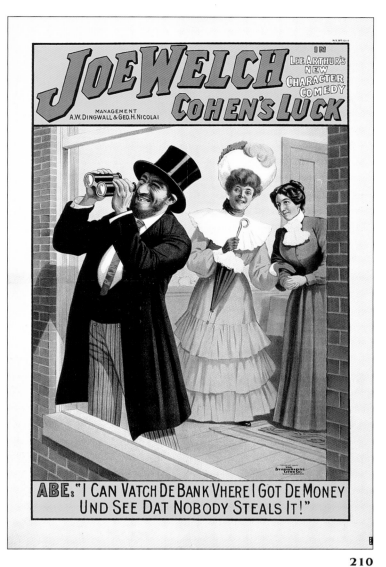

TAKING THE PLUNGE.

212

213

210

210. Joe Welch/Cohen's Luck. 1904.
20 x 30 in./50.5 in./50.5 x 76.2 cm
Strobridge Litho., Cincinnati
Cond B–/Slight tears at folds; slight paper loss at center fold.
Is it right to use racial stereotypes as a basis for generating humor? The politically correct answer, of course, is no. And in these intensely correct time, a "No!" chorus would rise up loud and strong from across the land. But, for all our polite civility, do these stereotypes, at least occasionally or even involuntarily, result in eliciting a response of laughter? If we were to be honest, the answer would be yes, whether we liked to admit it in these enlightened times or not. Not to lecture, because some things are so outrageous that it's impossible not to react. Take this poster for "Cohen's Luck," a popular early-20th century comedy starring the talented Joe Welch in the title role. The sight of this Jewish gentleman absolutely taken with his savings is so out there, so not correct, that it verges on the astounding—and take a gander at the phonetically spelled-out dialogue beneath! Potentially offensive, but in terms of the time period, no more so—and perhaps even less—than the dipping of a Black caricature in bleach to show the product's blanching power. And as today's popular entertainments are rife with racial-based humor, perhaps we've just gotten better at integrating the stereotypes instead of irradicating them.
Est: $1,400-$1,700.

211. Turn To The Right: 3 Posters. 1917.
a & c: 20 x 30$^1/_2$ in./50.6 x 77.6 cm
b: 19 x 28$^3/_8$ in./48 x 72 cm
Strobridge Litho, Cincinnati
Cond A.
If this play was good enough to have reeled in the man who conceived of the League of Nations, well then, by golly, "Turn to the Right" was the only sensible theatricality to attend. The warmhearted melodrama by Winchell Smith was by all accounts an extremely popular lighthearted feel-good affair, essentially the story of a prodigal son returning home to the family farm after all but his dear old mother had long since stopped believing that he would return. That reunion is one of the scenes shown here, as is

the roustabout camaraderie of the wandering lad and his undisciplined, but well-meaning friends. And the poster endorsement of Woodrow Wilson is nothing short of patriotic pandering at its finest.
Est: $1,500-$1,800. (3)

212. Turkish Bath.
37$^1/_2$ x 27 in./95.2 x 68.5 cm
Strobridge Litho., Cincinnati
Cond A–/Unobtrusive folds.
According to Webster's dictionary a Turkish bath is "a bath in which the bather passes through a series of steam rooms of increasing temperature and then receives a rubdown, massage and a cold shower." Judging from the shenanigans going on in this poster for the musical comedy version of "A Turkish Bath," it's a pretty safe bet that the minstrel wallowing in the fountain has arrived at the end of the spa equation. But as to what increasingly overheated comedic escapades led him to this dripping conclusion is a plot line left for our imaginations to concoct as no trace of the play seems to exist.
Est: $1,700-$2,000.

213. Exposition Universelle de Paris 1889.
36$^1/_4$ x 25$^1/_4$ in./91.7 x 64 cm
Cond B+/Slight tears and stains, largely at edges; image and colors
        excellent.
Ref: PAI-XXVII, 211
A wonderful panorama of the 1889 World's Fair of Paris, made all the more spectacular with the inclusion of richly detailed insets of its various pavilions and attractions. With the focus placed on global advancements in the fields of industry, commerce, art and science united under a banner of peace, the crowning glory of the exposition was, and is, the Eiffel Tower. Constructed in 26 months, the structure is evidence of the architect's imagination and daring: in spite of its weight, height and 2.5 million rivets, it is a masterpiece of lightness. It is difficult to believe, but the tower actually weighs more than the volume of air surrounding it and that the pressure it exerts on the ground is that of a man sitting on a chair.
Est: $1,400-$1,700.

214

215

216

ANONYMOUS (continued)

214. Rellos.
39³/₄ x 87³/₄ in./101 x 223 cm
Moody Brothers, Birmingham
Cond B+/Unobtrusive folds.
Though it was common poster practice to show magicians in league with satanic elements during the first part of the 20th century, it's not with any sort of frequency that you're going to see a practitioner of the illusionary arts hoisting a glass with Old Scratch himself. And with the flames of Hades spewing forth from the oversized magnum of Lucifer's brew, you have to believe that the Goat Lord himself is proffering the 3-sheet toast, "Here's to Rellos" as his minion handle the pouring amidst a swirl of attending goblins and fairies. A truly spectacular image. *Rare!*
Est: $4,000-$5,000.

ANONYMOUS

215. Kubelik. 1903.
38³/₄ x 85⁷/₈ in./98.5 x 218.2 cm
Dangerfield Printing Co., London
Cond B/Unobtrusive tears and stains, largely at folds
    and seams.
Ref: PAI-XXIII, 103
When Czech violinist and composer Jan Kubelik (1880-1940) set out on his career in 1898, he was acclaimed "a second Paganini." Beginning with concerts in Vienna and other European cities, he went on to tour the USA in 1902 and ultimately performed in South America, the Far East, Australia and Africa before his retirement in 1940. This three-sheet design takes advantage of Kubelik's tall, handsome figure; credit for the photograph from which it was made is given to "Alfred Ellis & Walery." This is a stock poster, meant to be used throughout an entire tour; the text at the top for a concert in Amsterdam is a tip-on.
Est: $1,700-$2,000.

ANONYMOUS

216. Eagle Pencils.
11⁵/₈ x 28 in./29.4 x 71.1 cm
Eckstein & Purr, Fulton St, NY
Cond B/Restored tears, largely at edges; image and
    colors excellent.
Give me your tired, your poor, your huddled masses yearning to write down their thoughts with a superior instrument. A slight paraphrase perhaps, but in the Eagle Pencil universe, that would seem to be the sentiment being expressed. A very clever design that transforms Lady Liberty into the patron saint of the scribes and artists of the earth, pedestaled and adorned with seemingly the entire Eagle Line. Not wanting to boast, yet finding themselves powerless not to drop in a bit of discreet braggery, the writing concern places the following inscription on the statue's tablet: Highest Award at Centennial Exhibition for Cheapness (no doubt translating to "affordability") and Good Quality.
Est: $2,000-$2,500.

217. The Yashmak.
20¹/₈ x 29³/₄ in./51 x 75.7 cm
David Allen, Belfast
Cond B/Resored tears at folds.
It appears as if this societal beauty is about to begin a trip that will lead her down the primrose path to hell, getting set to place lip to pipe and opiate her way through "A story of the East." A story best told as "The Yashmak." There's nothing sinister about the design, but it seems as if the Art Nouveau serpentine presence of the hookah and the title of the play—the name of the veil worn by Muslim women to facially hide all but their eyes—points in the direction of this perfectly lovely woman's life about to take a drastic detour from familiar territory.
Est: $1,000-$1,200.

ANONYMOUS

218. Henry Clay/Habana. ca. 1900.
19 x 25 in./48.2 x 63.5 cm
Cond B–/Restored tears. Framed.

217

The Julian Alvarez company of Havana is justifiably proud of their product, displaying the various smokables with medals they have garnered in competition around the globe, including the 1896 Philadelphia International Exposition and the Paris World's Fair, as well as a portrait of the namesake Henry Clay. Here is one of the most

218

219

220

221

celebrated old Cuban marks, who owes its name to an American senator and shareholder from the last (19th) century with interests in Havana. There exist only three varieties, today manufactured in the Dominican Republic, noted for their thickness and full-bodied taste and rolled with a *maduro* wrapper" (*Le Cigare: Guide de l'Amateur*, by Anwer Bati, p. 112). One element that has remained constant in the company's promotional presentation is the rendering of the original factory, still proudly displayed in an identical manner as it appears on this poster.
Est: $1,500-$1,800.

219. Orient-Express. 1891.
33³/₄ x 47⁷/₈ in./85.6 x 121.6 cm
Imp. F. Champenois, Paris
Cond A–/Slight tears at paper edges.
Ref (All Var): Wagons-Lits, 4 & 5; Orientalist, p. 42;
Golden Age of Travel, p. 117
As the song states, "Istanbul was Constantinople," and this Wagons-Lits advertisement for its Orient-Express service is awash with the sultry exotica of the oriental city. This unsigned design gives all pertinent travel information in the lower right, but the true crowning glory of both the poster and the city could be none other than the Hagia Sophia (Greek for "holy wisdom"), constructed under the authority of Emperor

Justinian between 532 and 537 A.D. The Orient-Express was inaugurated on June 5, 1883, shortening the journey from Paris to Constantinople by thirty hours.
Est: $1,400-$1,700.

220. Hastings & St. Leonards.
24³/₄ x 39⁷/₈ in./63 x 101.2 cm
F. J. Parsons, Hastings
Cond B/Slight tears at folds and edges.
This tony twosome, the very picture of poised healthful perfection atop the cliffs overlooking the historic resort, share the spectacular, vertiginous sweep of this vaunted pictorial window into the 4-mile stretch of seafront magnificence situated in the heart of "1066 Country," so dubbed for the historic battle of that year. The panorama includes microscopic views of the historic resort's traditional Victorian pier, town center and the ruins of Hastings Castle, visible in the central cameo. The uncredited designer does a spectacular job of transferring the sweep of the resort in this French-language invitation to "The Sunniest Health Resort" of the East Sussex area.
Est: $1,400-$1,700.

221. Miracolosa Injezione. ca. 1900.
32³/₄ x 46¹/₂ in./83.2 x 118 cm
Cond B–/Restored paper loss at bottom margin;
unobtrusive tears and stains.
A nice bit of graphic misdirection gives this poster a bit of additional zip—most especially if the viewer doesn't speak Italian. At first glance, the promotion would appear to be a fairly standard allegorical nod to the illuminating power of some light bulb or another. However, the real illumination comes post-translation when one discovers that the product being touted is, in fact, Professor Costanzi's Miracle Cure, discreetly held aloft in the right hand of the bare-cheasted envoy of public health. And what a cure it is: the good professor's elixir not only obliterates genital and urinary syphilis, it ousts anemia as well and is available at finer drugstores throughout Napoli. An unusually nude advertising approach taking into consideration the nature of the medicinal curative, but an undeniably effective one at that.
Est: $1,000-$1,200

223

222

224

ANONYMOUS (continued)

222. Clément/Bicycles, Tricycles. ca. 1887.
$35^3/_8$ x $48^1/_2$ in./90 x 123.4 cm
Imp. Edw. Ancourt, Paris
Cond B+/Slight tears, largely near paper edges.
Ref: PAI-XXVII, 1
The many varieties of two and three-wheeled Clément cycles converge to charming effect in this breezy street scene, clearly demonstrating that there is a perfect pedal-powered vehicle for every walk of life. Clément was one of the giants of early bicycle manufacturing and advertising, here proudly touting the fact that they took the *Diplôme d'Honneur* in 1886, as well as the fact that they supply the Ministry of War with their models.
Est: $2,000-$2,500.

223. Di Cola's Macaroni. ca. 1890.
17 x 10 in./43 x 25.3 cm
Favaloro, Palermo
Cond A. Framed.
The Di Cola company gives their finest Sicilian macaroni a regal send-off—without exhibiting a single strand of pasta. Obviously meant for export, this uncredited designer takes us on a journey from the tracks to the docks to a far away land in the hazy distance, the implication being that the final destination for the crated noodles are the dinner tables around the world —specifically in the U.S., with the two countries' flags prominently draped together in the foreground. In addition to the numerous medals awarded this macaroni, it is also duly noted that the pasta "Furnished to Their Royal Highnesses the Duke of Aosta and Genoa."
Est: $800-$1,000.

224. M. Hommel. ca. 1894.
$26^1/_2$ x $20^1/_4$ in./67.2 x 51.5 cm
Wittemann Litho. Co., N.Y.
Cond A–/Unobtrusive tears at edges.
Ref: PAI-II, 68
When one thinks of Sandusky, Ohio, one is more likely to have the Cedar Point Amusement Center pop to mind than fine wine and top-shelf liquor. But apparently, that wasn't always the case. This poster for the

M. Hommel distillery boasts the highest award for American champagne at the 1893 World's Colombian Exposition held in Chicago. Bottles of champagne, vermouth and brandy frame a view of their Sandusky factory. Fine lithography in subtle earth tones, with details in gold and silver.
Est: $1,000-$1,200.

225. Esposizione Internazionale d'Arte/Feste Veneziane. 1895.
$27^7/_8$ x $39^1/_4$ in./70.8 x 99.7 cm
Tipo Litografico C. Ferrari, Venezia
Cond A.
The placard hanging from the bow of the blossom festooned gondola announces the 1895 Venice International Art Exposition. And what a festival it was, celebrating artistic expressions both athletic and esoteric—regattas, fireworks exhibitions, theatrical spectacles, an international fencing tournament, open air concerts, light shows, serenaders, various athletic competitions and the Savior's Bacchanal, no doubt a grand marshal's reception, but the literal translation sounds like so much more fun. An enchanting design with one peculiar element: Not to come off like a conspiracy nut, but why does the sail in the background sport a Masonic eye? Artistic intrigue in a secretive city.
Est: $1,200-$1,500.

226. Grand Skating Lyonnais.
$15^3/_4$ x $23^1/_2$ in./40 x 59.8 cm
Affiches Courbe-Rouzet
Cond B+/Slight tears at folds.
This expansive outdoor roller skating rink serves as an ideal rendezvous spot for the sophisticated Lyonaise skater of every age. Although the stoic foreground officer sets a rather serious skating tone, the folks he shares his whirl with appear to be having a bit more fun than he, dance skating or taking a conversation break, although one background woman does appear to be scant seconds away from an impending fall. The throngs ringing the rink make it clear that if physical activity isn't your idea of fun, the roller park is an excellent people watching post as well.
Est: $1,200-$1,500.

225

227. Anton Tichler.
37 x $48^3/_4$ in./94 x 123.7 cm
Grimme & Hempel, Leipzig
Cond B/Slight tears aand stains, largely at paper edges.
Ref: PAI-XXIII, 104
"Now how do you like this hat?" asks the satisfied customer. "They only flatter you when they're made by Anton Tichler." He's nicely dressed in the longish coat of his day, but everything about him is handled flatly in comparison with the portrait treatment of his face— all the better to show off his headgear.
Est: $1,700-$2,000.

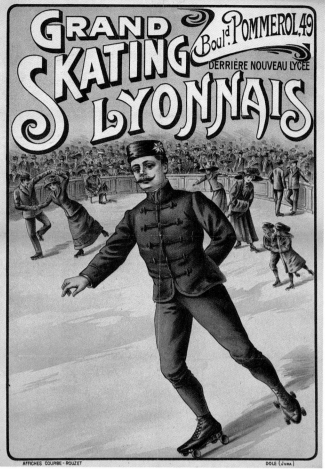

226

227

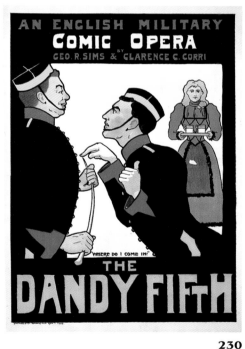

228

229

230

228. C. Terron/Au Coin de Rue.
38¹/₄ x 54¹/₈ in./97 x 137 cm
Imp. H. Laas, Paris
Cond A.
Proving that you didn't have to travel all the way to
Paris for the latest fashions, the C. Terron clothiers of
Avignon strut out this natty quartet of gents that you
might find on the fashionable street corner decked out
in the season's newest looks. Apart from varied cra-
vats, hats and high collars, it looks like the waxed han-
dlebar mustache was also all the rage—leaving the
sailor-suited lad left to dream of facial hair to come.
Est: $1,700-$2,000.

229. C. Terron/Au Coin de Rue.
38³/₈ x 54³/₈ in./97.4 x 138 cm
Imp. H. Laas, Paris
Cond A.
And what, we ask, is a fashionable man without a fashionable lady to accompany him? Since there's more
than enough room on the C. Terron corner to accom-
modate everyone, the Avignon fashion house displays
the latest additions to their ladies line, which, in tandem with the previous poster, shows them to be the
complete clothing source for the Mediterranean berg.
Est: $1,700-$2,000.

230. The Dandy Fifth.
19⁵/₈ x 28³/₈ in./50 x 72 cm
Stafford Netherfield, Nottingham
Cond B+/Restored tears at folds.
"The Dandy Fifth" doesn't sound like the most rough
and tumble regiment to have ever graced the stage,
but it no doubt delivered all the militaristic comic
opera goods a British audience could endure during
its time on the boards. Here, a moment of tension
seems to have popped up between a pair of musical
theater comrade-in-arms, most likely caused by the
root off all friction between regimental dandies—a
woman. Some things never change!
Est: $1,000-$1,200.

231

232

233

ANONYMOUS (continued)

231. Mode Feminine. ca. 1899.
$38^3/_4$ x $50^1/_4$ in./98.6 x 127.7 cm
Affiches Camis, Paris
Cond B+/Slight tears and stains at folds.
Ages before the glut of far-ranging mail order couture catalogues could flood the postal boxes of a fashion-hungry female populace, designers and merchants needed to get the word out about their latest style offerings. Once again, the publicizing world turned to the poster. In this case, a virtual template of what the style-minded woman or girl needed to be seen in this particular season, from fur-trimmed capes to brocaded waistcoats, from the plume-topped hats to discreetly feminine frill, this poster has everything any fashion plate could ever want, all awaiting the addition of letters from a merchant wise enough to recognize its promotional portent.
Est: $1,200-$1,500.

232. Mode Masculine. ca. 1899.
39 x $51^5/_8$ in./99 x 131.2 cm
Affiches Camis, Paris
Cond B+/Slight tears and stains at folds.
Conversely, the men folk of the late-19th century didn't want to walk around like a band of roving schlemiels. Once again, the poster rises to the occasion, saunter-ing out the latest outfits for men and boys, in a variety of stripes, plaids and checks, as well as the sailor suit, a fashion statement for the lads that never seems to go out of style. A natty testament of stylish promotion.
Est: $1,200-$1,500.

233. Rêve de Parfum.
$14^5/_8$ x 20 in./37.2 x 50.8 cm
Cond A. Framed.
The relaxed sensuality of this perfume design before the addition of letters is so palpable that one can practically catch a whiff of the fleshy blossoms filter-ing through the fantasies of the reposeful Art Nouveau beauty being carried off by the effortless potency of scent memory. Too bad that no trace of the producers of this fragrance could be found as the image creates a keen desire to be transported along with this entrancing miss, a yen that only could be satisfied with a hint of a brand name.
Est: $1,500-$1,800.

234. The Gentlewoman.
$19^1/_2$ x 30 in./49.5 x 76.2 cm
Marlborough Pewtress Lith., London
Cond B/Slight tears at folds.
Published between 1890 and 1926, when it was merged with "Eve," this magazine reached a huge circulation of 250,000 by the mid-1890s. One of their announcements makes their formula for success quite clear: "Astute advertisers will observe *The Gentle-woman* is bought by women and read by women, and as women spend nine-tenths of what men earn, the

234

moral is obvious." In this promotion announcing an amateur photographic competition, cash prizes are offered to both men and women—presumably, if one judges from the previous advertising line, to give men a chance to recoup some of their wifely-squandered assets and women to get some money they wouldn't have to meticulously account for. The flattened per-spective and stained glass-like design choice create a perfect backdrop for the announcement, rendering a perfect balance of marketing and art.
Est: $1,200-$1,500.

235. H. B. Claflin Co. ca. 1910.
$19^7/_8$ x $29^3/_4$ in./50.5 x 75.7 cm
Sacket & Williams, New York
Cond A–/Unobtrusive tears at edges.
Tranquility. Just a pinch of time to oneself in the company of an effortless read and and languorous cat, whiling the hours away on a hammock as far from re-sponsibility as possible. As attractive a desire a century ago as it is today. But what to wear for such a retreat from concern? Well, in more decorous times, the obvi-ous choice was the high collar/full length "Specialty E" corded silk chiffon frock from the H. B. Claflin Com-pany, the ideal outfit for both comfort and propriety.
Est: $1,000-$1,200.

235

236. Etrennes Jouets.
$38^1/_8$ x $102^3/_4$ in./96.7 x 261 cm
Affiches-Camis, Paris
Cond B/Slight tears and stains at folds and edges.
An advertisement for an unnamed store's gift and toy sale that verges on religious iconography—framed within an archway, head at a benign tilt, light bulb acting both as halo and descending spirit of charity, this matron is transformed into the Madonna of Con-sumerism. And though this woman and her children's hearts are in the right place during the graphic season of giving, might it not have been a better idea to provide the less fortunate with food for a holiday repast instead of a clown doll? But then, that wouldn't have made much of a commercial endorse-ment, now would it?
Est: $1,400-$1,700.

ANONYMOUS

237. Au Pauvre Jacques. 1896.
$36^5/_8$ x $60^3/_4$ in./93 x 154.2 cm
Lith. Th. Dupuy, Paris
Cond B+/Slight tears at folds.
This golden girl lilts her way back into the eddying snows, her visage graced with a genteel smile of the successful shopper and ornamented with her select

236

240

237

239

gifts from Poor Jack's. And with a name like that, any Parisian feeling the holiday pinch will most assuredly find the toys and presents they're after at a price they can appreciate during their announced one-day sale.
Est: $1,700-$2,000.

ANONYMOUS

238. Yost Typewriter Co. 1898.
10¹/₈ x 19 in./25.7 x 48.2 cm
Alf Cooke, Leeds
Cond A–/Unobtrusive slight tears and stains in border.
"George Washington Yost produced his first machine in 1887. The models that followed knew great success not only in the United States but also in Europe, where part of his production was exported" (Crayons, p. 156). This promotional poster for the Yost typewriter, whose superior manufacture had already garnered sixteen gold

238

medals, has an 1899 calendar as part of the design—a calendar, that coincidentally, is identical to the one used for the year 2000! And though this junior stenographer is already getting a hand up in the typing department, she's got her work cut out for her: the Yost upstroke machines had no shift keys, instead possessing two sets of keys, one for lower case and one for capitals. Another difference from later machines was the absence of ribbon, relying instead on an inked pad to transfer characters to the page. And as was the case with many early typewriters—and as is visible in the poster —the Yost was mounted on a hardwood base on a stand resembling those of the old treadle sewing machines.
Est: $800-$1,000.

239. McCormick Harvesting Machines/ 1906 Calendar.
13³/₈ x 20¹/₄ in./31.5 x 51.5 cm
Cond B+/Slight creasing at edges and in calendar. Framed.
This future farmer of America advises a newly-arrived immigrant tiller of the earth that the McCormick Harvesting Machines are okay. Not the flashiest of recommendations, but with the McCormick reputation firmly established by the distribution time of this 1906 promotional calendar, perhaps this pint-sized folksy approach was just the ticket.
Est: $800-$1,000.

240. Palavas Les Flots.
36⁵/₈ x 51¹/₈ in./93 x 130 cm
Firmin Montone, Montpellier
Cond A.
"The Queen of the Mediterranean Beaches" plays host to a duo of impeccably sporty fashion plates, no doubt whisked to the southern French resort of Palavas-les-Flots by the efficiency of the P. L. M. rail line, the winsome twosome currently engrossed with a regatta of sorts or some particularly scintillating people watching. During the 1890s, this popular seaside development had all the picturesqueness which red balconies and green shutters could afford, possessing every kind of cafe, from the best to the humblest,and two little stone piers jutting out into the blue of the Mediterranean at the mouth of the Lez river.
Est: $2,700-$3,000

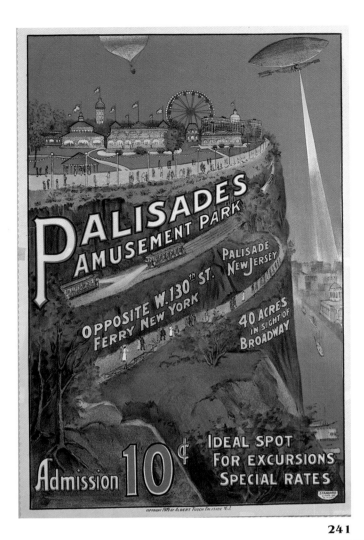

241

242

243

ANONYMOUS (continued)

241. Palisades Amusement Park. 1909.
$19^3/8$ x $29^1/2$ in./ 49.2 x 75 cm
Standard Litho. Co., N. Y City
Cond B+/Tape stain and slight tears at left paper edge. Framed.
Ref: PAI-XXVII, 226

What started out in 1898 as a New Jersey picnic grove designed by a local trolley car company to increase weekend ridership, Palisades Park grew to become one of the world's most famous fun centers, a carnival wonderland unlike any other which instilled a life's worth of magical memories to anyone fortunate enough to have passed through her gates. A trip to the park was not a mere excursion—it was a wildly anticipated event. High atop the Palisade cliffs, the attractions, which at its naissance were comprised of humble benches, tables and concession stands, exploded to include the Cyclone roller coaster, the Tunnel of Love, the world's largest saltwater wave pool, a carousel, various rides and a Wild West show. The famed open-air entertainment venue at the Amusement Park played host to

244

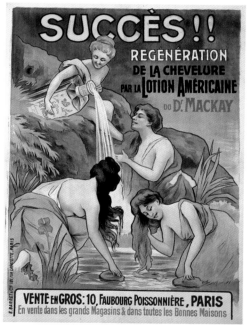

245

246

248

247

Cond B/Restored paper losses near edges.
Nothing fancy. Just simple canine graphics at their finest used in the promotional service of Lausanne International Dog Show. This poochy trio—a Belgian Shepherd prototype (today's Chien de Berger Belge no longer looks this way due to breeding enhancements), St. Bernard and Irish Setter—puts a rather dignified face (or trio of faces) on a featured event within the city's 8th Agricultural Expo, peering through the opening of a slat board enclosure. And as an added attraction: a police dog demonstration. All told, a veritable dog lover's feast.
Est: $1,000-$1,200.

246. Reid's Flower Seeds.
21$^1/_8$ x 14$^5/_8$ in./43.8 x 37.2 cm
Stecher Lith. Co., Rochester, N.Y.
Cond B+/Unobtrusive folds.
If you trust the humorous—if not precisely kind—theory put forth by this uncredited designer, not only is buying Reid's Flower Seeds a good idea when it comes to getting your garden to grow, it may well be a biological imperative as well. For what male would not choose the bounteous maiden at left over the piteous, withered crone at right, thus enabling natural selection to weed out the barren, non-Reid seed buying consumer. Who knew that purchasing the right seeds held such grave consequences?
Est: $1,500-$1,800.

247. Léon Chandon.
12$^1/_8$ x 25$^5/_8$ in./31 x 65 cm
Cond A. Framed.
The merest touch of wry humor and spectacular beauty combine to create one of the loveliest designs we have ever come across for Reims' champagne producer Léon Chandon. Framed within a climbing bower of vines and clusters, the sky behind her itself effervescing from the splendor of the sweet intoxicant, the Art Nouveau flirt peers deeply into her crystal chalice, searching for the champagne's secret as she gazes deep into its amber fizz. As she breaks free ever so slightly from her arboreal enclosure, the crook of her arm leads us to the helmeted griffin crest and its accompanying motto: Why not. Why not, indeed. The name of the Italian distributor for the French bubbly is listed at bottom.
Est: $2,000-$2,500.

248. Lotion Americaine du Dr. Mackay/Succès!!
36$^1/_4$ x 49$^7/_8$ in./92.1 x 126.7 cm
E. Barret, Paris
Cond B+/Unobtrusive tears at edges.
A Grecian statue comes to life, pouring forth the rejuvenating balm of Doctor Mackay's "Americain Lotion" Hair Regenerator from the confines of its enormous flagon into the spring where a trio of appreciative demi-clad amazons dip their tresses into the healing waters for the restorative treatment they so desperately deserve. Precisely what makes this potion "American" or regenerate follicles matters not a jot in this classical overstatement for the product on sale in all the finer stores and already on the shelves of all good homes. Success hardly begins to sum up the effect of this fantastic design.
Est: $1,500-$1,800

everyone from Benny Goodman to The Jackson Five to The Junior Miss America Pageant. One constant remained from the venue's inception: The breathtaking view of Manhattan. In this wonderful bit of graphic nostalgia, many of the park's attractions are visible, as well as Grant's Tomb across the Hudson. Sadly, Palisades Amusement Park closed its doors on September 12, 1971.
Est: $5,000-$6,000.

242. The South Manchuria Railway.
30$^1/_4$ x 41$^1/_4$ in./77 x 104.8 cm
Cond B/Slight foxing, largely at far bottom; slightly trimmed at bottom edge.
Peering through a portal set into a graded jade sky, the viewer is treated to an assuaging vision of Far Eastern beauty filled with pastel heavens reflecting off rippling waters in the presence of poised subservience. But, the South Manchurian Railway also wants to call attention to the fact that their service "Completes the 'All Rail' Route across Europe and Asia, and brings London within a fortnight's journey from Tokyo, Peking or Shanghai," and to that end, includes an inset of their connecting portside rail service. The Japanese-devel-

oped enterprise, with a trackage totaling 701 miles, originally belonged to the Russian-built Chinese Eastern Railway, but came into Japanese hands as a part of the indemnity in the Russo-Japanese War.
Est: $1,700-$2,000.

243. Sang und Klang.
18$^1/_8$ x 13$^1/_4$ in./46 x 33.7 cm
Hollerbaum & Schmidt, Berlin
Cond A–/Slight stains at edges.
Rendered in the rich browns befitting the most elegant luxury volume of bound sheet music available in Berlin, this trio of music lovers—one singing, one playing and a third party simply allowing the majestic sounds to cascade about her—seem more than pleased to have a copy of "Song and Sound" in their possession. The musical tome brings home all the heavy hitters from the 19th century popular music scene, their instantly recognizable names appearing in the partial list to the right of the poster.
Est: $1,000-$1,200.

244. Sunlight Soap.
60$^1/_2$ x 77$^3/_4$ in./153.7 x 197.5 cm
Cond B–/Restored tears and losses, largely at paper edges.
This pint-sized homemaker may be setting about her domestic rounds so early in the morning, but Sunlight, the cheerfully-named British-made laundry soap, turns even the most mundane of chores into a lyrical experience.
Est: $1,500-$1,800.

245. Exposition Canine Internationale. 1910.
38$^1/_2$ x 29$^1/_4$ in./97.7 x 74.3 cm
Imp. A. Denéréaz-Spengler, Lausanne

249

250

251

252

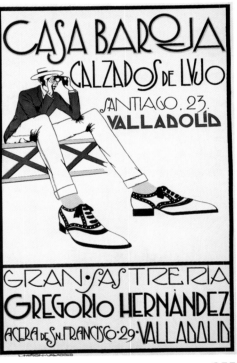

253

ANONYMOUS (continued)

249. Agfa. ca. 1923.
20 x 37¹/₈ in./51 x 94.2 cm
Rolph-Clark-Stone, Canada
Cond B/Restored tears at horizontal fold and top border.
In 1888, a factory in Berlin that had been producing color dyes since 1867 began manufacturing material for the new rage of photography. That factory, Aktiengesellschaft für Anilinfabrikation, soon adopted the acronym AGFA as its official name, a name which remains prominent in the global imaging industry. The apple-cheeked photo-enthusiast greeting us against a mountain lake panorama prettily promotes the Readyset camera—a model introduced in the early 1920s—and the Agfa All-Weather film, the perfect photographic option for the partly cloudy conditions pictured in the design.
Est: $1,200-$1,500.

250. The South Eastern & Chatham Railway. 1926.
24⁷/₈ x 39⁷/₈ in./63 x 101.2 cm
McCorquodale, London
Cond B/Restored tears at folds.
Prettily sitting on top of the world, the auburn-maned muse of day tripping doesn't appear to have a care in the world as she invites gulls to alight upon her diaphaneity. And why should she look concerned, considering the "world" over which she holds court is the more than manageable one of England's southeast coast. Not to mention the fact that she has the South Eastern and Chatham railways in her pocket for jaunts to the sea, along with connecting service to the continent aboard "The Queen." Grace and reliability combined with Art Nouveau panache.
Est: $1,200-$1,500.

251. Tee-Konzert.
27 x 39¹/₄ in./68.7 x 99.7 cm
Hubacher, Bern
Cond A-/Bottom border cut.
The unifying factor in this promotion for Rinner's Viennese Cafe's 4 o'clock Tea Concert can be distilled to one brief syllable: class. Regardless of age or beverage selection—where tea, incidentally would hardly seem to be the refreshment of choice—the masses gather round the string quintet, drawn by the elegant ambiance and teeming socialization. Unfortunately, the creator is identified only as "AMB."
Est: $1,400-$1,700.

252. Arroz Granito.
26³/₈ x 38¹/₄ in./67 x 97.2 cm
Imp. y Lit. Ortega, Valencia
Cond A.
Ref: Publicidad, 210; PAI-XXIX, 199
"It's not a party without Granito rice" claims the poster, as the jolly chef tosses a large beribboned saucepan of the glistening white grains in the air to prove it. Reined and ready for the pot are other fine ingredients for a first-rate paella: rabbit, lobster, scallions, peppers, tomatoes and artichokes.
Est: $1,500-$1,800.

253. Casa Baroja.
25³/₄ x 39³/₈ in./65.5 x 100 cm
L. Minon, Valladolid
Cond B/Slight tears and stains in background.
You know what they say about a man with big feet. And judging from appearances, those are no small shoes to fill. Spectating in his spectators, this spidery dandy puts out the word that Casa Baroja is Valladolid's spot for luxury footwear. Additionally, since one should never leave

the house simply togged in saddle shoes, the poster informs us that Baroja is more than up to the challenge of making the clothes that make the man, under the watchful eye of tailor supreme, Gregorio Hernandez.
Est: $1,400-$1,700.

254. Tipper's.
33¹/₂ x 44⁵/₈ in./85.2 x 113.3 cm
Cond A.
Ref: America for Sale, p. 108
Quack veterinary products had better watch their backs, and that ain't no bull! Well, actually, as a matter of fact, it IS a bull, raging his way through a brick wall to debunk the quackery of animal medication in order to break on through to the other side of natural quality—the B. C. Tipper and Son Works of Birmingham, England. And having gored away the competition, this rabidly frustrated beast reveals the "3 Tips" destined to keep your animal in tiptop shape: a vitamin elixir, a cod liver oil condiment and a somewhat dubious proposition named "Tipper's Mystery," a tonic apparently intended for equine exclusivity.
Est: $1,200-$1,500.

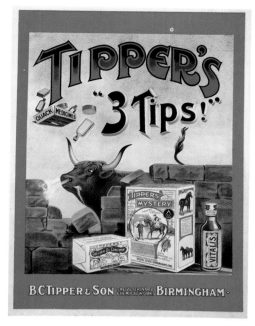

254

255

256

257

258

259

255. Sparton Radio. ca. 1926.
46¹/₂ x 70¹/₄ in./118 x 178.3 cm
Morgan Litho, Cleveland
Cond B/Restored tears at folds and edges.
A super bit of advertising reverse psychology for Sparton Radio. Rather than showing an artistically created version of their product, Sparton, via the talents of an unknown hand, takes you all the way to the other side of the transmission and into the company of this dashing violinist, thereby reinforcing the idea that the quality of their sound reproduction is just as fine as if you were in the studio yourself. Simple brilliance. The Sparton Corporation was founded with 15 employees and $15,000 capital in 1900 in Jackson, Michigan, by Philip and Winthrop Withington. Shortly, thereafter, the Withington's took on a third partner by the name of William Sparks and became known as the Sparks-Withington Company, which in 1911 adopted Sparton as its trade name. In 1926, Sparton introduced the first all electric radio, known as "Radio's Richest Voice," the item being promoted here. The company exists to this day, involved in diverse electronics manufacturing.
Est: $1,700-$2,000.

256. Pemartin.
34¹/₈ x 45³/₄ in./86.6 x 116.3 cm
Tipo-Lit. Salido Hnos. Jerez.
Cond B/Unobtrusive tears at folds and edges; slight
    staining in left margin.

Looking ferocious—or perhaps just ferociously thirsty—this lounge leopard doesn't to concern the allegorical billowing majesty of sensible consumption one jot as she uses him as a throne from which to promote Spain's Pemartin Vermouth. And as unlikely as it is for this kitty to change his spots, it's doubtful that, after one sip of the amber ambrosia, any knowledgeable tippler will be able to switch to a different aperitif.
Est: $1,200-$1,500.

257. Cigares Caraïbe.
16 x 21³/₄ in./40.8 x 55.5 cm
Imp. Gouweloos, Bruxelles
Cond B–/Slight tears and stains, largely at edges.
Uniting the world with its nicotinic might, Caraïbe cigars satisfy the most divergent of global male populations—from Native Americans to European gadflies—with its big tobacco satisfaction. A literally pleasant design for the Antwerp manufacturer of Cuban cigars, whose globe contains the only two countries necessary in the hand-rolled equation.
Est: $1,200-$1,500.

258. Le Bas Perfecta. ca. 1935.
31⁵/₈ x 47¹/₄ in./80.2 x 120 cm
Imp. Provençale, Marseille
Cond B/Restored tears at folds.
Ref: PAI-XIV, 90
A marvelous cheesecake poster for Perfecta stockings worn by this bookish, albeit leggy young lady. And only a fool would question the finding that Perfecta is the most popular brand because it's the best and the most "chic." Artist's initial's appear to be "C. A.," but they could easily be the reverse of that.
Est: $1,500-$1,800.

259. Canfranc/Hotel Candanchy.
27¹/₄ x 39 in./69.4 x 99 cm
Graficas Lavborde y Labayeu, Tolosa
Cond A–/Slight tears at paper edges.
Set behind the planted poles as if you were returning from a long exhilarating day on the slopes, the viewer gets a welcoming view of the Hotel Candanchy, a ski destination named after the well-known Aragón resort town. Situated in the international rail link and summer mountain resort of Canfranc, fifty-nine miles north of Jaca near the French border, the feel of the poster is definitely more Tyrollean than Iberian. But the gently billowing Spanish flag on the wrap-around terrace porch immediately sets the record straight.
Est: $1,200-$1,500

261

CASTAGNOLA LUGANO

262

263

260

ANONYMOUS (continued)

260. Chesterfield Cigarettes.
$14^1/_2$ x $32^1/_2$ in./36.8 x 82.4 cm
Cond B-/Restored tears and stains; image and colors excellent.
Recognizing that giving good face is the most important element of promotion once a model becomes central to a marketing strategy, an uncredited artist allows this beaming cutey's wardrobe to camouflage itself flatly into her arboreal surrounding as she sunnily swings her way to popularity in the name of Chesterfield cigarettes. A crafty design from the days when ten cigarettes cost a nickel (now costing as much as six dollars a pack in some downtown Manhattan watering holes) and tobacco could use the word "popularity" in their advertising.
Est: $1,200-$1,500.

261. Bueter Baking Company: 5 Posters.
Each: $28^1/_8$ x 11 in./71.5 x 28 cm
Cond A-/Slight staining at edges; each mounted on board.
If you can't trust an adorable transient to bring across a sense of bakery freshness to the bread buying public, then who exactly can you trust? These five Bueter Bakery trolley advertising cards—four for the aforementioned Hobo Bread and one Rockwellian design for their Butter-Krust brand—serve as kitschy calling cards from a less-delicately balanced era. In this age of correctness, the thought of having a vagrant—even one with a cute pooch—as a spokesperson for a food item would be thought of as tasteless at best, but who can resist a slogan like "Loaf with nature, Romance with health." Bueter, founded in 1910 in Quincey, Illinois, is no longer in business, but as the text which appears verso on these trolley cards attest, they were once proud producers of sandwich bread, cinnamon rolls, sandwich buns and raisin bread.
Est: $700-$900. (5)

262. Castagnola Lugano.
$25^1/_4$ x 39 in./64 x 99 cm
Brügger, Meiringen
Cond A/P.
Lake Lugano is the sight of innumerable fêtes, an Italian/Swiss tourist destination and health resort known as the "Queen of the Ceresio," lying nestled in a beautiful bay and framed by Mount Brè (pictured in the background) and Mount San Salvatore. Set among the steep, but beautiful slopes of the Alps, it is the ideal location for warm-weather fun and frolic. Though this Swiss travel poster would seem to be promoting the blanched San Lorenzo cathedral pictured on the shores of the lake, it truly refers to the entire area. The line of text, which translates as "Lugano Fireworks," finds its pyrotechnics in the flourishing flora and dazzling sunlight laid down with both care and flare.
Est: $1,000-$1,200.

263. Esports d'Hivern. 1927.
$11^3/_8$ x $20^1/_2$ in./29 x 52 cm
Imp. Oliva de Vilanova
Cond A-/Unobtrusive slight tears.
Located one-hundred miles from Barcelona, at 8,315 feet above sea level, the ski-hungry traveler will find La Molina, Spain's very first winter sports resort, founded in 1911 and still a popular destination to this day. And as this downhill maven can attest, stark against the gilded heavens as he gets some serious air, it's a chilly Catalan trip well worth making.
Est: $1,200-$1,500.

264. Fed Malay States Rlys. 1933.
$21^1/_4$ x $31^3/_8$ in./54 x 79.7 cm
Ying Wah Litho, Kuala Lampur
Cond A-/Unobtrusive slight tears and stains at edges.
The Malay Peninsula of southeast Asia for centuries has been an active player in export commerce, relying on their natural resources to establish economic ties to various world powers. It was, in fact, the 2nd Century astronomer and geographer, Ptolemy, who dubbed the area the "Golden Chersonese" ("chersonesos" is the Greek word for "peninsula"), as it was an important source of that particular precious metal for the Roman market. This rarely seen railway advertisement, however, focuses on the indigenous tourism of the land, attempting to import visitors with the sinuous vision of a state locomotive winding through the lush jungle and aureate landscape. Though the initials "HMLF" appear in the bottom center of the poster, no specific artist could be matched with these letters to make a positive identification.
Est: $1,200-$1,500.

265. Les Wagons-Lits de 2e Classe. 1929.
$25^3/_8$ x $39^1/_2$ in./64.5 x 100.2 cm
Imp. Editions d'Art, Paris
Cond A.
Ref: Wagons-Lits, 217
The gist of the message being conveyed by the P. L. M. railroad for their sleeper car service is very direct and extremely effective—whether it's lounging you're after

264

265

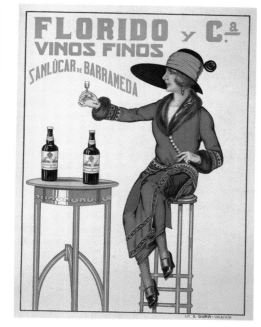

266

267

268

269

or a good night's rest, their spacious, well-appointed accommodations are without a doubt the way to go. And even though it's not pointed out specifically in the text the underlying pitch would nearly need to be spelled out as "First Class travel for Second Class Prices."
Est: $1,700-$2,000.

266. Florido y Ca./Vinos Finos.
21³/₈ x 29 in./54.4 x 73.8 cm
Lit. S. Durá, Valencia
Cond A.
Ref: PAI-XXIX, 194
As opposed to a goodly portion of their French counterparts, the Florido company of Sanlúcar de Barrameda chooses the poised sophistication of elegance in moderation instead of intoxicating abandon to promote their fine wines, namely Mari-Ana, their premium manzanilla. Located on the Cádiz Coast at the mouth of the Guadalquivir River, the fishing port of Sanlúcar is the home town of the uniquely Spanish sherry, with credit going to the sultry sea air for its special flavor.
Est: $1,200-$1,500.

267. Hannelore Ziegler.
27³/₈ x 43³/₄ in./69.5 x 111.3 cm
Wilhelm Jüntzen, Bremen
Cond A.
This poster for German dance sensation Ziegler has a particular bit of promotional text: the phrase "Eigene Tänze" can mean either that she is presenting an evening of her own choreography or a set of "peculiar dances." Both of which seem fitting for the modified, pale arabesque displayed here by the dancer, a blend of modernity and tradition, posturing and positioning. An artist's mark appears lower right, but the lattice-work signature could not be assigned to any known individual.
Est: $1,000-$1,200.

268. Kaffee Hag. 1930.
35¹/₈ x 50 in./89.2 x 127 cm
Gebr. Fretz, Zurich
Cond A.
This chortling gourmand—quite obviously a man who appreciates the finer things that life has to offer—serves as an ideal poster boy for Kaffee Hag. Comfortably

nestled into his favorite chair, a stogie smoldering in one hand and a cup of the decaffeinated brew steaming away in the other, he invigorates the textual underscoring, demonstrating that rest and Hag coffee are the ultimate keys to blissful relaxation. The Hag water process, used in Europe by Nestlé today, produces superior tasting results that no other technology has ever bettered.
Est: $1,000-$1,200.

269. Kassner/Der Grosse Zauberer. 1930.
36⁵/₈ x 54¹/₈ in./93 x 137.3 cm
Adolph Friedlander, Hamburg
Cond B+/Slight tears, largely near edges.
Ref: Magic Posters, 91; PAI-XIV, 71
"In the twenty years before World War II, Alois Kassner (1887-1970) was Germany's major illusionist. The Krassner extravaganza was a magic show in the style of Thurston's in the United States. The show carried tons of equipment and twenty people and was transported in two railway cars. Among Kassner's big features was The Vanishing Elephant" (*Magic Posters*, p. 14). Which, if you judge from the poster, was achieved with the mere wave of a wand and soon thereafter, a rapidly dissolving pachyderm.
Est: $1,200-$1,500.

270

G. KNIGHT
57, 59, 61 Castle Road, Southsea

For All "KODAK" Supplies
Developing & Printing-Rapid Service.

271

272

WOOLWORTH'S STORES

273

274

ANONYMOUS (continued)

270. Visite España.
45¼ x 63¾ in./114.8 x 162 cm
Ortega, Valencia
Cond A–/Slight staining in margins.
Ref: PAI-XXX, 369
Most posters promoting Spanish tourism typically
execute the concept in a similar fashion: a slogan
that states "Visit Spain" in a "foreign" language and
a black-haired, hoop-earringed, mantilla-wearing
señorita. But this one serves up the standard ingredients with such flamboyance that we find ourselves
unable to resist the invitation.
Est: $1,500-$1,800.

271. Kodak/G. Knight.
18¾ x 29¼ in./47.7 x 74.2 cm
Cond A.
There she goes again. The Kodak gal in the blue and
white striped dress is at it once more, this time with
her back uncustomarily to us as she snaps a seashore
shot of someone else capturing in celluloid his family's
time with a burro on the beach. A wonderfully self-
referential design.
Est: $1,200-$1,500.

272. Visitez la Yugoslavie.
24⅝ x 37 in./62.5 x 93.8 cm
S. C. I. P., Paris
Cond A.
This prismatic Yugoslavian mountainscape, with its
flattened perspective and fiery locomotive about to
pierce the ebon cliffs with molten precision, was originally printed in an indigenous shop in Ljubljana and
accompanied by a single word of text: "Traveler." This
information still appears in the poster's lower left corner. When attempting to attract the French tourist to
indulge in a Slavic getaway, a bit of Francophonic text
—and a new French printer—never hurts, if for no other
reason than to announce that it's the Yugoslavian
State Railways extending the kaleidoscopic invitation.
Est: $1,200-$1,500.

273. Woolworth's Stores.
30⅝ x 42¾ in./80.3 x 108.8 cm
Cond B/Slight tears and stains at folds.
Though he ran his multimillion dollar chain of five-and-
ten cent stores from what he dubbed a New York City
"cathedral of commerce," Frank W. Woolworth was
savvy enough to embrace a down-home advertising
simplicity that would most appeal to his nationwide
clientele. And to that end, we are presented with an uncredited floral field of dreams, overflowing with gladio-
las, peonies and lilies of all sort, an arrangement whose
flowery panache nostalgically reminds the viewer of
the subtlety of a less "In-Your-Face" era long gone by.
Est: $1,200-$1,500.

274. Gala de Ministère de la Guerre. 1950.
21¾ x 29¾ in./55.2 x 75.6 cm
Cond A.
Entrenched as they were in fighting to maintain colonial power in Vietnam, the French war department
certainly needed to maintain a strong home front to
put a positive face on what would escalate into the
most-protested conflagration of the 20th-century. To
that end, the citizens of Paris were presented with the
Minister of War's Gala, a sophisticated soiree as far
removed from the realities of their military situation as
possible. And in order to convey this sense of love not
war, an unnamed designer finds Colin-esque inspiration in his two faceless couples box-stepping their way
through the flat black night.
Est: $1,000-$1,200.

275. San Sebastian/Piscina Familias.
19¾ x 27½ in./50.2 x 69.9 cm
Thomas, Barcelona
Cond B/Unobtrusive tears and creasing.
Barcelona's San Sebastian spa advertises its "family
pool," and the thrust of their message is perfectly
clear: this is a first-rate establishment, perfectly suited
for women and children, classically appointed without

a hint of the brutish vulgarity one might find at other
watering spots. Despite our best efforts, we were
unable to reveal the particular identity to match the
exotic initials that appear down left.
Est: $1,200-$1,500.

**276. Eventyret I Sydexpressen (Adventure on the
South Express).** ca. 1934.
25¾ x 34½ in.65.4 x 87.7 cm
Bolvig Reklame
Cond B–/Restored tears at folds.
Romance on the high rails, combining Art Deco locomotion with the impending musicality of a Nelson
Eddy and Jeanette MacDonald duet to a spectacularly
stylish end. A poster for the Danish release of the German film *Adventure on the South Express*, a film that
for all its Viennese-style operetta trappings harnessed
quite a bit of legitimate musical talent: Charlotte Susa
appeared on most of the major stages of the world,
including the Met; Ralph Roberts was a popular comedic
actor with a good voice; musical director Robert Stolz
penned a few operettas of his own. The plot of this forgotten gem revolves around Lisa, a wealthy widow
aboard a train traveling to the south of Europe. She
catches the eye of a Hans, the dining car waiter, as
well as a prince named Tarnoff. When her jewels turn
up missing, Hans is suspected even though no con-

275

276

278

277

277. Hires Root Beer. ca. 1940.
57 x 33¹/₂ in./145 x 85 cm
Cond A–/Restored tears in lower left corner.
Ref: PAI-XXVI, 143
As sophisticated as root beer gets. A stunning socialite, for what else could she possibly be, taking into account her poise, fine features and enticing gardenias, enjoys a light repast of Hires and delicate, crustless finger sandwiches. Charles G. Hires discovered his formula, made with real root juices, in the 1870s and led the way in the early advertisements for "soft drinks."
Est: $1,200-$1,500.

278. Free and Easy Blues. 1959.
30⁷/₈ x 48⁵/₈ in./78.5 x 123.5 cm
Imp. F. Tytgat, Bruxelles

crete evidence can be found and he is fired. Fortunately, when the train arrives in Santa Margarita, he is lucky enough to find employment as an assistant porter at a hotel where the prince and Lisa coincidentally happen to be staying. Musical happenstance occur, and with the help of an eccentric professor who was also aboard the South Express, it is revealed that the Prince is a phony and is—gasp!—a known jewel thief. Lisa recovers her diamonds and pearls, but in exchange loses her heart to Hans.
Est: $1,000-$1,200.

Cond B/Restored paper losses at right edge and top corners; unobtrusive tears, largely at edges in top text area.
Four years before Quincy Jones took home his first Grammy Award for his arrangement of Count Basie's "I Can't Stop Loving You," he served as the band leader of The Free and Easy Orchestra—no doubt comprised of expatriate jazz musicians residing in Paris such as Clark Terry and Phil Woods with whom he was jamming in the late-1950s and early '60s. This big band provided the groove for its namesake theatrical/dance piece, heating up the cold midwinter nights at Brussels' Palais des Beaux-Arts. The poster, by an artists whose lower right electrocardiogram signature couldn't be deciphered, hints at the moody sensuality of the piece being performed as a side project by the cast of a production of "Porgy and Bess."
Est: $1,000-$1,200.

279

280

282

284

F. HUGO D'ALESI (1849-1906)

279. Connemara.
34⁵/₈ x 49 in./88 x 124.5 cm
Imp. A. Bellier, Paris
Cond A.
"Connemara is a savage beauty" is how Oscar Wilde described the unspoiled magnificence of the Gallway county town, whose name translates from the Irish as "Conneely's Village." In Connemara, the light constantly changes the mood and tone of the landscape and who better to set this to paper than d'Alesi. Long regarded the jewel of Ireland, the promotion, with text in English, yet still printed in France, is an extremely rare foray into the foreign field for the French designer, though it is possible this was also intended for domestic distribution for the chicest of Parisians. Whatever the situation, the artist is as comfortable with the gothic chill of a 6th century graveyard as he is with the brooding thrill of the dewy, undulant landscape.
Est: $1,000-$1,200.

H. AMORO

280. Anjou Vins. 1932.
15 x 23³/₄ in./38 x 60.5 cm
Affiches Gaillard, Paris
Cond A.
The angle being taken by the makers of Anjou sparkling wine is that Art Deco will provide the perfect advertising bent to get the message out with regard to their product. And Amoro succeeds in spectacular fashion, reinforcing the *vins* "v" at every opportunity, keeping the tones muted and the expressions to a purse-lipped minimum while allowing the effervescence to take center stage with nary a ticklish nose to be found.
Est: $1,200-$1,500.

LILI ARKAY (1896-1959)

281. Ifjusagi Kiallitasa. 1916.
25 x 37¹/₂ in./63.4 x 95.2 cm
Cond A–/Unobtrusive fold.
The stark simplicity of this design—utterly flattened perspective, flat tones, abundant use of paper stock as third color—creates an indelible impression of watching the watcher as she peruses the entries in the Hungarian Royal Academy of Fine Art's Youth Exhibition being held as the Castle Hill Gardens Bazaar. Powerful without excessive ornamentation. It comes as little surprise that this painter would one day become a premiere stained glass artist.
Est: $2,500-$3,000.

BERNARD J. ARTIGUE

282. Parfumerie Semiramis.
9¹/₂ x 24³/₈ in./24.2 x 61.8 cm
Imp. F. Champenois, Paris
Cond A. Framed.
A genre painter and a student of J.-P. Laurens, Artigue obviously also absorbed the Art Nouveau teachings of Alphonse Mucha. It seems that when Mucha failed to renew his contract with Champenois in 1904, the printer experimented with several artists in an attempt to find a worthy successor to his star designer. And though Mucha's influence is present, Artigue breathes his own decorative life into the design, combining the traditional natural Nouveau elements with the tantilization of an Eastern seduction, submissively entrapping the eye while suggesting a thrilling unfamiliarity to every remaining sense.
Est: $1,700-$2,000.

LOUIS AUBRUN

283. Centenial International Exhibition 1876.
  1874.
23³/₄ x 18³/₄ in./60.5 x 47.7 cm
Tho. Hunter, Philadelphia
Cond B/Slight stains. In period frame.
Utilizing an architectural bent to lure the monumentally minded to the Centennial International Exhibition taking place in Philadelphia's Fairmont Park, we are shown two buildings in an impressively detailed rendering. But, in the bigger-is-better mindset of the times, we are further compelled by the dimensions of each given building: the Art Gallery, at 365 feet long, and the Main Building, an astounding 1880 feet long—a structure more than six football fields in length! If you still maintain that length doesn't matter, also keep in mind that 20 acres of exhibition space exists here on the ground floor alone! Published for the Centennial Board of Finance, the poster was used as an advertisement by Joel J. Baily & Co., importers and jobbers of hosiery, white-goods and notions.
Est: $800-$1,000.

281

283

285

MARCELLIN AUZOLLE (1862-1942)

284. Inconnue Liqueur.
45¹/4 x 61¹/4 in./115 x 155.6 cm
Imp. P. Vercasson, Paris
Cond B/Slight tears and stains at folds and edges.
Ref: PAI-XXIV, 149
Draped in huge swaths of red and green fabric and sporting an enormous
pair of blue wings, this figure provides some strikingly colorful reasons to
try a liqueur with a perverse name—it translates as "unknown," odd for a

brand which claims to be "found in all the best homes." Auzolle remains
someone of whom we know little. The Bibliothèque Nationale has 34 of
his posters dating from 1898 to 1927, but they're missing his best-known
work: the 1895 poster announcing the opening of the world's first movie
house, the Lumière Brothers' cinématographe (see PAI-V, 7).
Est: $1,000-$1,200.

LEON BAKST (1866-1924)

285. Caryathis. ca. 1916.
51¹/8 x 88⁷/8 in./130 x 225.7 cm
Cond C/Restored tears and losses.
Ref: Hillier, p. 252; PAI-XXVII, 201
This is the rarest of all Bakst posters and possibly his most magnificent
assay into the medium. The dancer, Elise Jouhandeau, elongating herself
in an interpretive representation of the ritualistic sacrifices performed by
maidens at the Grecian Temple of Artemis Caryathis, is poised to take off
amidst swirling scarves and bright hues. Probably no painter is as closely
identified with ballet, in all its aspects, as Bakst and in his stage and costume designs, as well as the rare lithographs, he showed not only a fine
sense of draftsmanship and composition, but most especially a great love
of the exotic. His subjects are always caught in a dramatic moment and
colors are always vibrant. And if one work can embody all this, it is the
poster for Caryathis. *The Provenance for this poster announces that it
comes from the "Collection of Elise Jouhandeau, Paris," the dancer
Bakst chose to immortalize in this design.*
Est: $7,000-$9,000.

286

287

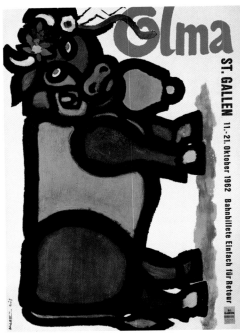

288

289

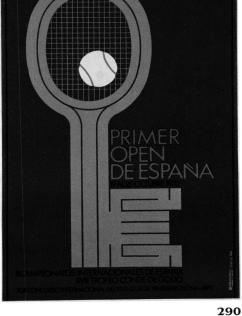

290

291

PAUL BALLURIAU (1860-1917)

286. Le Pole Nord. ca. 1893.
36¹/₂ x 51¹/₈ in./92.8 x 130 cm
G. Bataille, Paris
Cond B+/Unobtrusive folds.
Ref: DFP-II, 33; Reims, 215
A fantastic work for the fashionable Parisian "North Pole" ice skating rink, an establishment that offered "Perpetual Skating on Real Ice" to the city's gliding-minded citizenry, skating away to the accompaniment of a forty-piece orchestra. And though it's a bit unlikely that the actual decor could have matched the artist's "Fortress of Solitude" backdrop, the breakaway mother/daughter tandem appear to be but two of a multitude enjoying themselves beneath the bathing aurora borealis shimmer of the frigid gathering place. Balluriau worked on *Gil Blas*, and many of his later posters are imbued with the colors and dramatic appeal of his colleague Steinlen.
Est: $2,000-$2,500.

FRANCO BARBERIS (1905-1992)

287. PKZ. 1948.
36 x 50¹/₄ in./91.5 x 127.4 cm
Wolfsberg, Zurich
Cond A.

Ref: PAI-XX, 388
The ever-urbane PKZ man shows his *gemütlich* Alpine side in a brown tweed jacket, yellow muffler, loden hat and pigskin gloves. Even out for a casual stroll, he completes his impeccable PKZ image with a boutonniere and pocket handkerchief. Figuratively speaking, Barberis doffed one hat for another throughout his career, as he alternated between poster and fashion design and children's book illustration.
Est: $1,200-$1,500.

288. Olma. 1962.
35³/₄ x 50 in./91 x 127 cm
Cond A.
Barberis takes a bovinic approach to advertise the fall festival in the northeastern Swiss municipality whose events range from ballooning to industrial arts. The earthy color block approach is a subtly bullish approach, relying on the fair's reputation to flesh out the details. And there is something about the look this cow shoots at the viewer, something a bit more confrontational and expecting than we're used to from promotional cattle that gives the artwork a surprisingly grounded impact. Strangely enough, this horizontal image was presented in a vertical format, adding new meaning to the phrase "cow tipping." That's one way to get attention!
Est: $800-$1,000.

289. Berner Oberland. 1945.
27¹/₂ x 39⁷/₈ in./70 x 101.2 cm
J. C. Müller, Zürich
Cond A.
The illustrative wit of the designer comes more to the fore in this design for the Swiss railway, although with a bit more sly salaciousness than he allowed to eek through in his children's book work. Granted the Bern country is without a doubt beautiful, and the available skiing is beyond reproach, but there's no question what pretty thing this drooling overstuffed teddy bear has his sights set on. The only real question that remains is who does the giant carrot belong too? Intriguing, to be sure.
Est: $800-$1,000.

BAS

290. Primer Open de España. 1970.
19¹/₈ x 27¹/₂ in./48.6 x 70 cm
Pellicer & Pena, Barcelona
Cond B/Unobtrusive creasing and tears.
A deceptively simple design for the 1970 Spanish Open, its few elements conveying a promise of exceptional athleticism, a key to excitement, as well as creating a neo-hieroglyph of sport and venue, all set against a deep burgundy background absolutely suited to the host country. An ideal example of the perfection attainable when concise detail meets clarity of purpose.
Est: $1,000-$1,200.

292

293

294

OTTO BAUMBERGER (1889-1961)

291. Restaurant/St. Gotthard. 1913.
$35^7/_8$ x $50^1/_8$ in./91 x 127.4 cm
J. E. Wolfensberger, Zürich
Cond A–/Unobtrusive slight tears at edges.
Ref: Baumberger, 11; Margadant, 251;
    Schweizer Hotel, 37; PAI-XVII, 89
A native of Zurich, Baumberger regarded himself primarily as a painter, creating posters merely to generate some income. Nonetheless, he produced a magnificent body of more than 200 posters, distinguished not by a style, but by stylistic diversity—each perfectly suited to

the clients' needs. One of two posters Baumberger designed during the same year for the swank hotel/restaurant/cafe, both with the image set rather like a cameo in a ring. They must have been successful—four years later, Baumberger was commissioned for another one (*see* PAI-XXIX, 209).
Est: $1,500-$1,800.

292. Zoologischer Garten Zürich. 1929.
$35^7/_8$ x $50^1/_4$ in./91 x 127.5 cm
Gebr. Fretz, Zürich
Cond B/Restored tears at edges.
Ref: Baumberger, 151; Margadant, 138;
    Plakatkunst, p. 109; PAI-XXIX, 212
Here, the unlikely juxtaposition of pachyderm and preening fowl announce the 1929 opening of the Zurich zoo. The massive elephant and the delicate flamingo, both on view, share but a single common characteristic—long appendages.
Est: $3,000-$3,500.

293. Jecklin. 1950.
$35^1/_2$ x $50^3/_8$ in./90.2 x 128 cm
Gebr. Fretz, Zürich
Cond A–/Slight creases in bottom corners. Framed.
Ref: Baumberger, 232 ; Timeless Images, 150;
    Müller-Brockmann, 67, PAI-XXIX, 216
Baumberger's design for the Zurich piano store is a

deceptively artless one, making use of large areas of undifferentiated flat color and the paper reserve. The design was first created by Baumberger in 1919 (*see* PAI-XXIII, 139) and was printed by Mentor Verlag. The only change to this later edition is a minor one: the addition of some text with the company's name, address and stock in trade at the top of the open music sheets.
Est: $1,700-$2,000.

294. Löwenbräu. 1927.
$35^1/_4$ x $50^1/_2$ in./89.3 x 128 cm
J. C. Müller, Zürich
Cond A.
Ref: Baumberger, 130; Litfass-Bier, 215
Long before Löwenbräu ("lion's beer") was enjoyed by beer lovers around the world, it was a local Zurich beer. This foaming stein, as well as another design he created for the company a bit earlier (*see* PAI-XXII, 200), uses the product's rampant red lion with black banner logotype to affix the product to the viewer's tippling subconscious. "Apart from posters with global theses like 'beer is something good,' beer drinking is promoted through the simple illustration of the product. The full, large . . . glass with the oversized head . . . (has) the same effect on the thirsty person as the bone has on the dog. The product itself . . . is ultimately the most convincing advertising argument" (Litfass-Bier, p. 19).
Est: $1,200-$1,500.

INCREMENTS

Bidding at our auction will be strictly by the following increments:

To $2,000	by $100
$2,000–$5,000	by $200
$5,000–$10,000	by $500
$10,000–$20,000	by $1,000
$20,000–$50,000	by $2,000
$50,000–$100,000	by $5,000
$100,000–over	by $10,000

1 9 3 7

exposition internationale

GRANDS RÉSEAUX DE CHEMINS DE FER FRANÇAIS

IMP. JULES SIMON, S.A. PARIS

EN SAVOIE

BRIDES LES BAINS

OBÉSITÉ ▲▲▲ FOIE

PLM LA MER A LA MONTAGNE

296

299

LUCIEN BAYLAC (1851-1913)

295. Cycles de la "Metropole". 1893.
35$^1/_2$ x 49$^1/_8$ in./90 x 125 cm
Imp. Kossuth, Paris
Cond B+/Resored tears at folds.
Ref: Reims, 223; Maindron, p. 120; PAI-VII, 379
Baylac created only a dozen or so posters in the mid-
1890s, and no one has ever come up with any particu-
lars on him, but his small oeuvre was distinctive
enough to have made him a "name" which collectors
at that time sought. Here, a girl in a pale green dress
joyfully waves at us as she pedals effortlessly by.
Est: $2,500-$3,000.

EUGENE BEAUDOIN (1898-?)
& MARCEL LODS (1891-1978)

296. Paris 1937/Exposition Internationale. 1936.
25$^3/_4$ x 37$^3/_4$ in./60.3 x 96 cm
Imp. Jules Simon, Paris
Cond A. Framed.
Ref: Purvis, p. 84; PAI-XXII, 207
The skywriting, the night scene, the hint of futurism,
all contribute to the sense of romance and excitement
in this most effective design. The milky azure image
with its shimmering pink and white flashes of light won
first prize in a poster competition held by the French
Ministry of Commerce for the Paris 1937 World's Fair.
Its co-creators were architects who were involved in
several construction projects together around Paris,
including the overall design for the upcoming 1937
World's Fair; they entered the competition on a whim,
and regrettably, never produced another poster. After
a partnership that extended from 1925 to 1940, Beau-

CYCLES DE LA "MÉTROPOLE"

MARIÉ & Cᵒ
17 Rue Sᵗ Maur
PARIS

Représentés par M

295

MENTON
CÔTE D'AZUR
PLM

doin left to become director of architectural studies at
a school in Geneva, while Lods stayed in private practice in Paris. *This is the smaller format.*
Est: $1,700-$2,000.

297

300

301

298

CHARLES BÉGLIA

297. Menton. 1935.
24¹/₄ x 39 in./61.5 x 99 cm
Imp. Moullot, Marseille
Cond A–/Unobtrusive folds.
Ref: Affiches Azur, 251
An exhilarating window into the Riviera from the PLM, its flock of seagulls greeting us as we marvel at the tiered view of the city stretching out along the waterfront as it retreats into the mountains with sun-slathered Cézanne-esque grandeur. And though pristinely delivered and placidly executed, there is a certain unseen dulcet clamor interwoven into Béglia's design, the muted sounds of the sea and unharried bustle of the town arriving at our senses through skilled manipulation of color and perspective.
Est: $1,500-$1,800.

PETER BEHRENS (1868-1940)

298. Darmstadt/Ein Dokument Deutscher Kunst.
    1901.
9 x 26¹/₈ in./22.9 x 66.3 cm
Jos. Scholz, Mainz
Cond B+/Unobtrusive tears in top and bottom text
    areas. Framed.
Ref: DFP-III, 90; Wember, 20; Plakatkunst, p. 53; Inter-
    nationale Plakate, 206; Weill, p. 99;
    PAI-XXII, 209
For the Darmstadt show titled "A Document of German Art: The Exhibition of Art Colony," the influential industrial and graphic designer, Peter Behrens, created one of his most important works. He "began his career as a painter but after 1890 was attracted to design and the crafts under the influence of the teachings of William Morris. In this period he designed typefaces and produced Art Nouveau graphics. These pursuits led to an interest in the problems of industrial design. In 1903 he was appointed Director of the Dusseldorf School of Art. In 1907 Behrens received an epoch-making appointment when he was named coordinator of design for A.E.G., the German General Electric Company. Behrens was also important as a teacher of a generation of architects that included Walter Gropius, Le Corbusier and Mies van der Röhe" (Avant Garde, p. 195). *This is the smaller format.*
Est: $12,000-$15,000.

LEON BENIGNI (1892-?)

299. Brides-les-Bains. 1929.
24¹/₂ x 39¹/₄ in./62.3 x 99.6 cm
Office d'Editions d'Art, Paris
Cond A.

Ref: Train à l'Affiche, 250; Montagne, p. 186;
    Deco Affiches, p. 101; Voyage, p. 50;
    Chemins de Fer, 118; PAI-XXIV, 164
For the PLM (Paris-Lyon-Méditerranée) railway, geometric mountains frame and focus our attention on two women—one *sportive*, the other *à la mode*, both *très chic*, as befits guests at this "elegant woman's spa." (Another version of the poster refers discreetly to weight and liver problems.) Christophe Zagrodzki names Benigni among those Art Deco travel posterists (led by Cappiello and Domergue) whose "elegant and mannerist design derives from fashion illustration, and who like using feminine grace as an argument in favor of this or that resort" (*Train à l'Affiche*, p. 76).
Est: $2,700-$3,000.

LUCIAN BERNHARD (1883-1972)

300. Rem.
59³/₄ x 44³/₄ in./151.6 x 113.7 cm
Cond A.
Bernhard, one of the most influential graphic artists of the century, studied in Munich. In 1901, he settled to work in Berlin, where he helped to develop the modern "object poster" in cooperation with E. Growald, co-owner of the Hollerbaum and Schmidt printing firm. In 1920, he became professor of poster art at the Berlin Academy; in 1925, he moved to the United States where he taught at the Art Students' League and New York University; he died in New York City in 1972. Here, he delivers a frozen frieze for Rem cough syrup, its grey clad family making their way through the bluster and most surely in need of a little fast relief. Bernhard created a significant number of posters for the makers of the "good tasting" cough syrup for the temporary relief of coughs due to minor throat and bronchial irritations, from 1926 to 1946. Rem, an old and trusted friend in the cough suppressant department still soothing throats today, is, as its name hints at, the answer to a good night's sleep. For a variant of this image, with three men replacing the family, *see* Bernhard, p. 73.
Est: $2,000-$2,500.

301. Rem.
59¹/₂ x 45³/₄ in./151.2 x 116.2 cm
Cond A–/Slight tears at paper edges.
Another Bernhard hieroglyph for the good people of Rem, once more keeping the details of the afflicted to a minimum while starkly spelling out the name of the product against a solid orange circle, thereby turning it with uncluttered ease into the sun in the soggy lives of the scratchy-throated.
Est: $2,000-$2,500.

302

303

306

304

305

LUCIAN BERNHARD (continued)

302. 20 Jahre Deutscher Plakatkunst. 1908.
23¹/₂ x 17¹/₂ in./59.7 x 43.8 cm
Druckerei Schenkalowsky, Breslau
Cond B+/Slight tears in margins and at folds. Framed.
Ref: Bernhard, p. 29 (var); Chaumont/Exposons, p. 39
A far wordier design than one would expect to see from the graphic artist most closely associated with object poster designs featuring an outlined central image against a flat color background with as little text as possible. In fact, this work from earlier in his career is almost the polar opposite of the style he would later help to define. Though text heavy, the simplicity he strove for still shines through in this promotion for an evening sponsored by the Breslau Friends of the Poster celebrating twenty years of German poster design. And though this shadow of a woman may be perusing any of the two-hundred and forty works in the exhibition through her lorgnette, it's safe to assume that the highlight of the evening was a lecture by none other than the illustrious Dr. Hans Sachs, sharing his wealth of poster knowledge with the

assembled, lecturing on the finer lithographic points through the assistance of one-hundred and fifty color slides. It was Sachs who commissioned this Bernhard logo for his *Das Plakat* journal and his Friends of the Poster Society.
Est: $1,700-$2,000.

PAUL BERTHON (1872-1909)

303. La Joyeuse de Flute.
18¹/₂ x 24¹/₂ in./47 x 62.2
Imp. Chaix, Paris
Cond B+/Unobtrusive tears at folds. Framed.
Ref: PAI-V, 110
"Berthon was a romanticist whose style was best suited to decorative panels. He produced about 60 of them, in fact, in contrast to his handful of posters for poetry books and art shows" (Gold, p. 120). The tender pastels which he calls forth from his palette mingle to perfection in setting the stage for this haunting, doe-eyed flautist, allowing an eerily lyrical atmosphere to burnish the scene.
Est: $2,000-$2,500.

304. Almanach d'Alsace et de Lorraine. 1896.
15³/₄ x 23¹/₈ in./40 x 59 cm
Imp. Chaix, Paris
Cond B/Slight tears and stains at folds. Framed.
Ref: DFP-II, 62; Berthon & Grasset, p. 94; PAI-XI, 122
Announcing the publication this almanac, Berthon put his model in the regional peasant costume of Alsace/Lorraine. But even garbed in rustic finery, she is still a typical Berthon creation, with a soulful expression and a fragile vulnerability that are the unifying characteristics of all his females.
Est: $1,500-$1,800.

305. Le Livre de Magda. 1898.
18¹/₂ x 25¹/₄ in./47 x 64.2 cm
Imp. Chaix, Paris
Cond A.
Ref: DFP-II, 66; Berthon & Grasset, p. 97;
Timeless Images, 29; PAI-XVII, 114
An advertisement for a book of poetry by Armand Silvestre. One may doubt whether the poems themselves were as lyrically lovely as Berthon's ethereal, Art Nouveau illustration of a nude forest nymph, who seems—her hair especially—part of the landscape. "Berthon's small but characteristic body of work . . . epitomizes the Art Nouveau style on paper" (*Berthon & Grasset*, p. 8).
Est: $1,700-$2,000.

307

308

309

310

311

306. Sarah Bernhardt. 1901.
19³/4 x 25³/4 in./50 x 65.3 cm
Cond A/P.
Ref: Berthon & Grasset, p. 90 (var); Gold, 173;
PAI-XXX, 102
"This is (Berthon's) most famous lithograph, a portrait of Sarah Bernhardt in the title role of 'La Princesse Lointaine' ('The Faraway Princess') which she first played in 1894. In this design Berthon transformed her costume tiara with its flowery jeweled garland into real irises framing her idealized face" (Gold, p. 120).
Est: $1,400-$1,700.

GEORGES PIERRE BEUVILLE

307. Dijon/9e Foire Gastronomique. 1929.
30¹/2 x 46⁷/8 in./77.4 x 119 cm
Imp. Moullot, Marseille
Cond B/Slight tears at folds.
Things look grim for this chicken in the hands of this rather maniacal looking round-faced cuisiner. But even though she may be at dinner's door, the hen appears as if she may be looking to take in a last repast of her own as she eyes the creeping snail slowly closing in on the array of Dijonaise gastronomic specialties

available at that city's ninth annual food festival. A wry Beauville nod to the powerful pecking order of the food chain.
Est: $1,500-$1,800.

KARL BICKEL (1886-1982)

308. Scheidegg Hotels. 1930.
35³/4 x 50¹/2 in./90.8 x 128.3 cm
Wolfsberg, Zürich
Cond A-/Slight tears at paper edges.
Ref: Schweizer Hotel, 86; PAI-XVIII, 180
For a hotel near Jungfrau (or as the German idiom charmingly puts it, "under the spell of the Jungfrau"), a simple flower design, rather than the usual grand view of building and landscape, suggests a resort confident in its elegance—far too tasteful for vulgar boasting.
Est: $1,200-$1,500.

BOB

309. Captivante.
23¹/2 x 31¹/2 in./59.8 x 80 cm
Imp. Delcey, Dole
Cond A.

Though no date could be firmly attached to the production of this design, there is a contemporary sensibility created by the enigmatic Bob that certainly predates the arrival of the Japanimation it so closely resembles. Looking part Astro Boy, part porcelain figurine and comprised primarily of circular motifs, this lad is so captivated with the bike whose name mirrors his attitude, that he allows his equally far-out pup to do the talking, proclaiming that the "Captivator" always arrives first, regardless of the meteorological conditions.
Est: $1,000-$1,200.

GUS BOFA (Gustave Blanchot, ?-1968)
For other works of Bofa, see Nos. 29-32.

310. Marque a l'Ours.
38³/4 x 53⁷/8 in./98.5 x 136.8 cm
Imp. Ch. Verneau, Paris
Cond B+/Unobtrusive tears at folds.
There are plenty of things that you might expect to see a bear doing if you would happen upon one by chance during an alpine trek. Trying on rubbers, however, probably wouldn't be one of them. That attitude is reflected by the poster trailblazer in this wonderful Bofa creation for the Bear Mark brand of waterproofing slip-ons, with the ursine pair ecstatic that they finally can keep their paws on the dry side.
Est: $1,400-$1,700.

ROBERT BONFILS (1886-1972)

311. Paris-1925.
25³/4 x 39¹/4 in./65.3 x 99.5 cm
Imprimerie Vaugirard, Paris
Cond A.
Ref: Weill, 316; Delhaye, p. 2; Phillips I, 70
"All of the elements that the transient style of Art Deco comprised were displayed and celebrated in Paris in 1925 at the famous Exposition. The Exposition had been planned for 1915 as a stimulus to French designers, but was postponed because of World War I. In the intervening decade, particularly after 1920, Art Deco style developed rapidly, so that what was originally intended as an effort to provoke modernism became a display and celebration of the new style. It was an elaborate event of unprecedented proportions . . . Avant-garde paintings and graphics were widely displayed . . . Three posters were commissioned to promote the event, from Robert Bonfils, (Andre) Girard and Loupot (see PAI-XXVIII, 386)" (*Art Deco Graphics*, p. 31). Bonfils, a decorator and printmaker who contributed regularly to *Gazette du Bon Ton*, came through in spectacular fashion with his promotion for the exhibit, generating an angular pastoral model of clarity, the ideal combination of the mythical and the technical.
Est: $1,500-$1,800.

LOUIS BORGEX (1873-?)

312. Bounty of the Sea: Two Decorative Panels.
1900 & 1901.
Each: 15⁷/₈ x 39⁵/₈ in./40.2 x 100.6 cm
Cond A.
The polar opposite of an Old Spice ad. This decorative homage to the seafaring life is filled with a carefully balanced romanticism, paying due to the laborious nature of the fisherman and the bittersweet under-standing of the women they daily leave behind, while transposing the rugged beauty and untamed force of the ocean to the page. And their borders incorporate portions of its bounty, framing the scenes in scallop and shrimp, transforming the practical into the artistic with sure-handed ease.
Est: $2,000-$2,500. (2)

FIRMIN BOUISSET (1859-1925)

313. Chocolat Menier/Eviter les Contrefacons.
ca. 1895.
21¹/₈ x 32¹/₈ in./53.6 x 81.6 cm
Imp. Camis, Paris
Cond B/Slight tears and stains, largely at paper edges.
Ref (Both Var): Karcher, p. 75; PAI-VIII, 277
Most frequently, Bouisset's design of this young female graffiti artist shows her scribbling "Chocolat Menier" on the blank slate of a wall she has happened upon. In a lesser-seen, later version, the young girl is writing "Eviter les Contrefacons" ("Avoid Substitutes"). This particular version goes one step further, sliding the text to the bottom of the design and removing the tot's umbrella typically present in the "Substitute" version—and reduces the size as well. Regardless of version, the seductive charm of the composition remains, making it one of the most appealing posters by this artist who frequently used children as his theme.
Est: $2,200-$2,600.

MICHEL BOUCHAUD

314. La Plage de Monte Carlo. 1929.
30⁵/₈ x 45³/₄ in./77.8 x 116.2 cm
Tolmer, Paris
Cond B/Unobtrusive tears, largely at folds and edges.
Ref: Tolmer, p. 81; Karcher, 408; PAI-XXIII, 167

Beach scenes in true Art-Deco style are uncommon—and this is one of the best. The figures are stylized and the scene Cubist, with decorative details and dramatic colors.
Est: $3,000-$4,000.

ROGER BRODERS (1883-1953)

315. St. Pierre de Chartreuse. 1930.
24¹/₂ x 39¹/₂ in./62.3 x 100.4 cm
Imp. de Vaugirard, Paris
Cond B+/Unobtrusive tears at paper edges.

Ref: Broders, p. 60; PAI-XIX, 228a
A magnificent view across a French Alpine valley to the pink-purple-greenblue-hued peak of Chamechaude. The valley's color matches the region's name, Char-treuse, which derives from the Carthusian order and monastery founded there by St. Bruno in 1084. The color's name derives from the famous liqueur the monastery produces. A poster Broders designed the same year, advertising St. Pierre as a winter resort (see PAI-XXVI, 187), is more like milk—but in both, the view we drink in is intoxicating.
Est: $1,200-$1,500.

314

317

318

319

317. Grasse. 1927.
30³/₄ x 42 in./78 x 106.8 cm
Imp. Lucien Serre, Paris
Cond A.
Ref: Broders, p. 89; PAI-XXVIII, 162
This PLM poster features stylish vacationers enjoying a sunny terrace in the Alpes Maritimes resort of Grasse, overlooking the Côte d'Azur (Cannes is a scant 10 miles away). The Old City rises behind like a man-made mountain, crowned by the ancient cathedral. Delicate coloring evokes the delicious mixture of southern warmth and the chill of the mountains; one virtually shares the rarefied air.
Est: $2,500-$3,000.

318. Golf de la Soukra Tunis. 1932.
24¹/₄ x 39¹/₄ in./61.7 x 99.6 cm
Imp. de Vaugirard, Paris
Cond A–/Unobtrusive tears at edges.
Ref: Broders, p. 111; PAI-XIX, 236
In collaboration with the Tunisian tourist bureau, the PLM railroad entices golfers to cross the Mediterranean and play in the then French colony in North Africa. Broders evokes the brilliant southern sunshine with bright greens, blue, pink and white; a folk motif in the text area adds to the exotic appeal.
Est: $1,700-$2,000.

319. Hyères. ca. 1931.
24⁵/₈ x 39¹/₄ in./62.5 x 99.6 cm
Imp. Lucien Serre, Paris
Cond B+/Slight tears and creases at paper edges.
Ref: Broders, p. 83; PAI-XIX, 234
The text boasts Hyères as "the Côte d'Azur's most southerly resort" and Broders reinforces this message by framing his view with a canopy of palms. Their deep cool shadows set off the hot sun on the yellow stucco walls of the Mediterranean town and make the lush green golf course most inviting.
Est: $1,700-$2,000.

316. Gorges de la Diosaz. ca. 1930
24⁵/₈ x 39³/₈ in./62.5 x 100 cm
Imp. Lucien Serre, Paris
Cond B+/Unobtrusive folds.
Ref: Broders, p. 64; PAI-XIX, 228b

Broders takes our eyes on a spectacular walk through one of the Diosaz gorges in the French Alps near Chamonix. In contrast to his more impressionistic works, here edges are sharp, outlines distinct and black, as though to tell us not a rock of this scenic wonder is to be missed.
Est: $1,200-$1,500.

320

325

322

323

ROGER BRODERS (continued)

320. Marseille/Porte de l'Afrique. 1929.
24⁵/₈ x 39¹/₂ in./62.5 x 100.5 cm
Imp. Lucien Serre, Paris
Cond A. Framed.
Ref: Broders, p. 81; Mer s'Affiche, p. 189; PAI-XXIX, 90
Smokestacks, vents and tackle in close-up with clusters of ships in the busy harbor beyond create a striking collage of cones and triangles. One of Broders' finest and most powerful designs.
Est: $3,000-$3,500.

321. Vichy/Ses Sources. 1928.
30 x 41³/₈ in./76.4 x 105 cm
Imp. Lucien Serre, Paris
Cond A-/Slight creases at edges.
Ref: Broders, p. 54; Train a l'Affiche, 230; PAI-XXV, 205

Broders in his element: subdividing his design into several segments, he gives a capsule guide to the diverse attractions of the region, in letters as well as in pictures. Golf seems to be the favorite recreation, with tennis not far behind; then comes music, theater and those famous mineral springs.
Est: $2,500-$3,000.

322. Castle Courtyard.
11³/₄ x 6⁵/₈ in. x 30 x 16.8 cm
Signed gouache drawing. Framed.
"Roger Broders was the creator of a very graphic style, whose simplified lines mark a new period in the tourism poster and usher in the style of the 1930s. His large flat areas of color recall the Cubists, Kandinsky, Severini, La Fresnaye and Delaunay. His color harmonies are very strong, even audacious, but always

evocative of and close to the spirit of the subject" (Broders, p. 11). It's completely justified to drop the Broders name amidst the others mentioned above, to which this gouache on paper maquette clearly attests. Though the specific courtyard we've been graced with is left to conjecture, the expert artistic vision of the designer is without question, the turrets and arches merging into a playfield of light and shadow, placing us both physically and atmospherically in the heart of unadorned palatial splendor.
Est: $1,700-$2,000.

323. Village at Water's Edge.
14³/₄ x 8¹/₄ in./37.5 x 21 cm
Signed gouache drawing. Framed.
In the period between the wars, Broders was the finest designer of French travel posters. He was especially

321

327

324

326

OSCAR M. BRYN

324. Pacific Northwest. 1934.
$26^7/8$ x $41^1/8$ in./68.2 x 104.5 cm
Cond B+/Slight tears at edges.
With an almost Japanese woodblock sensibility, this previously unseen artist lays out the splendor of the rarefied air of the Pacific Northwest like a stained-glass portal into the cathedral of nature. By keeping the colors essentially flat and the panorama essentially unpopulated, Bryn allows the viewers to place themselves anywhere they deem appropriate—be it tramping through the foothills, ascending the mountain or enjoying the more civilized repose of the mountain lodge. As no specific railroad or park destination is mentioned on the poster, it's tempting place a WPA label onto the work; no specific mention of that being the case, however, could be found. Thus, it stands on its own as a creation of beatific simplicity.
Est: $1,200-$1,500.

DMITRI A. BULANOV

325. Ego prevoskhoditel'stvo (His Excellency).
1927.
$26^3/4$ x $42^1/2$ in./68 x 108 cm
Belgoskino, Tashkent
Cond B+/Slight tears at stains and edges.
Ref: PAI-XXIII, 67
Released in the U.S. as *Seeds of Freedom*, this film is one of several during the period that dealt with the dilemma of Soviet Jews. It was inspired by the real-life tragedy of Hirsh Lekert, a Jewish shoemaker executed in 1902 for attempting to kill the czar's governor-general of the city of Vilna (today's Vilnius, capital of Lithuania) for his harsh treatment of the Jewish minority. In this adaptation, the governor of an unnamed city is killed, and the Jewish leaders fear that the entire Jewish community will be blamed and persecuted for the action. The conservative rabbi, played by distinguished stage actor Leonid M. Leonidov (he was also the assassinated governor), plans to send a delegation to the new governor pleading for mercy—even as his own daughter abandons her orthodox Jewish background to join the Communist rebels. The propagandistic idea behind the film and similar others was to suggest to the Soviet regime that young Jews were always on the side of the Reds even if their elders were reluctant to accept Soviet thinking. Jews nevertheless remained second-class citizens in the Soviet Union. Bulanov was a poster designer who was active in Leningrad in the 1920s and early 1930s. His split design underscores the film's central Jewish-Soviet conflict and Leonid's performance as the two opposing characters.
Est: $2,500-$3,000.

DAVID BURNAND

326. Suffrage des Femmes.
$31^1/2$ x 47 in./80 x 119.2 cm
Imp. Vaile et L'Hotellier, Paris
Cond B/Slight tears and stains at folds and edges.
Burnand, a Swiss-born painter living in Paris, throws open the shutters of equality for Marianne as she bathes in a golden age of enlightenment, arms spread wide to embrace the idealism set forth by the French Union for Women's Suffrage, an olive branch bearing dove taking to the air and heralding this new peace. As women in France were not granted the right to vote until shortly after World War II in 1945, the peaceful power imagery speaks to the credit of a candidate named Fronts, whose signature appears at bottom, obviously running with equal voting rights as a key component to his platform. It's interesting to note that of the 150-million worldwide women mentioned as being active female voters, not one of them haled from the United States. Since the women's suffrage movement achieved its immediate objective in this country with the ratification of the 19th Amendment in 1920, we have to imagine that the focus being placed here is with the rights specifically of European women.
Est: $1,400-$1,700.

DUILO CAMBELOTTI (1876-1960)

327. Rom-1911.
$11^1/2$ x $22^3/4$ in./29.4 x 57.8 cm
Chappuis, Bologna
Cond A.
Ref: Italia che Cambia, 181 (var)
An imposingly puissant convocation of eagles perch atop chiseled column, making a lasting immediate impression for the 1911 Rome International Exposition, an event featuring extensive displays of art, archeology, music, Italian ethnography and sports. A perfect blend of living majesty and ancient tradition. The design was produced in several languages; here we are presented with the German version in its smaller format. As this was intended for indoor display, the poster came complete with metal strips for the top and bottom edges to ensure proper hanging. Cambelotti, the great Italian panoramic relief artist, is also known for his book illustrations, engravings, sculptures and, most importantly, his publicity posters. Influenced by the Roman cultural environment of the era, Cambelotti frequently used elements of ideological socialism in his compositions.
Est: $1,000-$1,200.

masterful at setting up his compositions, framing his panoramic sweep so as to focus interest just where desired. The results were always effective and engaging—one doesn't just view the scene, one comes upon it. This gouache on paper design of a village comfily nestled at water's edge is a striking example of Broders' command, calling upon blossoms and clouds to frame the unnamed hamlet, laying it out with such picturesque beauty that it seems almost like a materialized settlement from a fairy tale. Though never making its way to full poster, the work's postimpressionist sensibilities allow it to stand on its own merits.
Est: $2,000-$2,500.

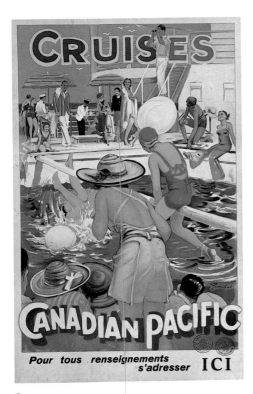

a

b

330

328

GASPAR CAMPS (1874-1931)

328. Ch. Lorilleux.
20³/₄ x 30 in./52.7 x 76.3 cm
Cond B/Unobtrusive tears and staining in margins only.
This señorita with a decidedly Theda Bara flare works
her sultry charms in the name of Lorilleux lithographic
tints. And what a lush seduction it is, her detailed fan
and mantilla displaying the depths to which the Barce-
lona-based hue merchants can indulge their clientele.
A rare Spanish commission for Camps, a Spaniard who
spent most of his career in France and was one of a
number of artists hired by the Champenois printing
house to fill the void when Mucha left for America in
1904. Creating both advertising and decorative works,
Camps eventually found his own groove—less graphic
than Mucha and more akin to oil painting, marked by
soft edges and shadings, as well as loads of sentiment.
Est: $1,500-$1,800.

329. Rhum Caiman.
15 x 29³/₄ in./38 x 75.5 cm
Cond A–/Slight tears and stains in margins.
Granted, his women may have verged on objects of
unattainable idolatry, but Camps could hold his own
among Art Nouveau giants without feeling like an out-
sider. Take for example this curvaceous temptation
plying her luscious essence in the promotional name
of Caiman rum, her ensemble an exquisite conver-
gence of flow and form, her face a passive invitation
to inebriation. But beware! This beauty has a bite the
design doesn't reveal, unless you speak French of
course. For if you did, you'd realize that "caiman"
mean "crocodile." And as everyone knows, if you're
not careful, a croc can sneak up and chomp one's
derriere when you least expect it.
Est: $2,000-$2,500.

CANADIAN PACIFIC

330. Canadian Pacific: 2 Posters. ca. 1930.
Artists: **William H. Barribal & Kenneth Denton
    Shoesmith (1890-1939)**
Each: 13¹/₄ x 21³/₄ in./32.8 x 55 cm
a: Cond A–/Slight stains at edges.
b: Cond B/Trimmed at edges; slight staining at edges.
Ref: Canadian Pacific, 74 & unnumbered;
    PAI-XXVIII, 542 (var)
Though best known for their highs seas frolics, Canadian Pacific also offered opportunities for the wandering soul to explore the beauty of the Great White North.
While the Barribal design swankily tickles us with the
opportunities of shipboard folly, Shoesmith transforms
a picture window frame into a living portrait of the

329

Canadian Rockies, the splendor of Lake Louise shimmering like a jewel amidst the dwarfing summits of
the snowy peaks. Two completely effective designs for
utterly divergent traveling tastes. Barribal worked as a
figure and interior painter, as well as a print illustrator
and LNER designer, and was a regularly exhibited artist
between 1919 and 1938. Our other posterist was a
pupil of Fred Taylor and a sailor by training, who was
additionally a brilliantly talented English painter, posterist and decorative artist. Graphically speaking, he is
best known for his work executed for the British railway

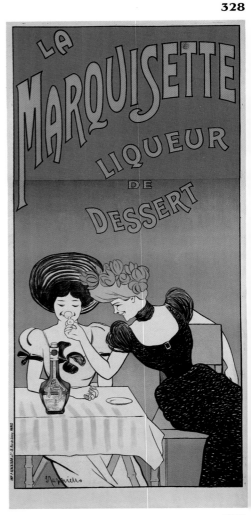

331

and maritime industries. *This is the smaller format of
the Shoesmith design.*
Est: $1,700-$2,000. (2)

LEONETTO CAPPIELLO (1875-1942)
*For another Cappiello poster, see Nos. 50 & 95.
For books of Cappiello's works, see Books & Period-
icals section.*

331. La Marquisette Liqueur. 1901.
38¹/₄ x 81¹/₄ in./97.2 x 206.3 cm
Imp. P. Vercasson, Paris
Cond A.

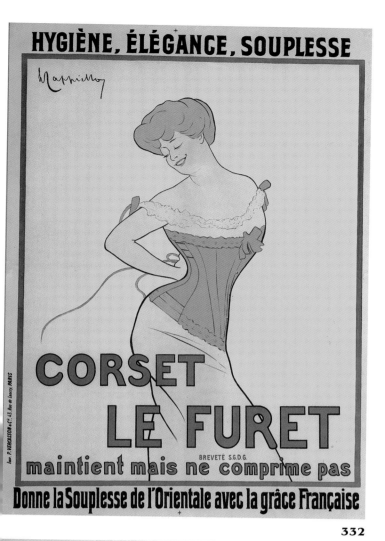

332

333

334

335

333. Champagne de Rochegré. 1902.
$38^3/4$ x $54^1/8$ in./98.3 x 137.5 cm
Imp. P. Vercasson, Paris
Cond B/Slight tears, largely at folds; image and colors
    excellent.
Ref: Cappiello, 247; Menegazzi-I, 433;
    Wine Spectator, 162; PAI-XXIX, 245
"For Champagne de Rochegré, one of the products of
the Chamonard distillery in Epernay, Cappiello has
an elegant woman in a formal black dress taking a
delicate sip as if afraid that too much of the bubbly
might go to her head" (Wine Spectator, 162). One of
Cappiello's most effective and charming designs.
Est: $3,000-$4,000.

334. Pur Champagne/Damery-Epernay. 1902.
$38^1/8$ x 54 in./97 x 137 cm
Imp. Vercasson, Paris
Cond A. Framed.
Ref: Cappiello, 246; Wine Spectator, 160;
    PAI-XXIX, 246
In a letter which Vercasson used in a promotion for his
artist, the director of the champagne association indicates that this poster is "perfect" in that it "clearly conveys the joyful spirit" of someone drinking champagne
from the Champenois region. With the question of
whether or not this is poster perfection out of the way,
the only issue which remains unanswered is what's
more effervescent—the bubbly or the happy redhead
serving it with gusto.
Est: $2,500-$3,000.

335. Grand Kermesse de Charité. 1903.
$38^3/8$ x $53^7/8$ in./97.5 x 137 cm
Imp. Vercasson, Paris
Cond B+/Slight tears at folds. Framed.
Ref: DFP-II, 119; PAI-XIX, 245
This golden lass, daintily carrying a hanging wicker
basket of freshly cut flowers, whisks her way to a
charity event in the Bois de Boulogne. And thanks to
Cappiello's effervescent mastery, we're all but power-
less to follow her in.
Est: $2,000-$2,500.

ef: Schindler, 147; Wine Spectator, 176;
    PAI-XXVIII, 178
n innocent little vignette, a mere trifle—two laughing
adies at a table, sniffing a flower—and Cappiello has
ent the product, an after-dinner liqueur, a sense of
ure untrammeled pleasure. A delightful scene played
ut on a 2-sheet format.
st: $3,000-$4,000.

32. **Corset Le Furet.** 1901.
$9^1/8$ x $54^3/8$ in./99.3 x 138 cm
mp. Vercasson, Paris

Cond B/Slight tears at folds; image and colors
    excellent. Framed.
Ref: Cappiello, 238; Cappiello/St. Vincent, 4.8;
    Wine Spectator, 210; Menegazzi-I, 465;
    PAI-XXVI, 197
A somewhat daring design by 1901 standards. This
corset, which "stays firm but doesn't restrain,"
promises to give its wearer "the suppleness of the
Orient with the charm of France." One of Cappiello's
earliest and most appealing images.
Est: $3,000-$4,000.

CAPPIELLO (continued)

336. Suc du Velay. 1902.
38³/₄ x 53¹/₂ in./98.4 x 135.8 cm
Imp. P. Vercasson, Paris
Cond B/Restored tears at folds.
Ref: Timeless Images, 101; Wine Spectator, 164; Gold, 49; PAI-XXI, 83
"Has a little snifter of Suc de Velay put this woman in a radiant mood or is it that the spirit is the choice of those with a zest for life? Either way, the poster is appealing. And if the figure seems relatively tame compared to Cappiello's usual women, it's because the company wanted to present a dignified upper-class image appropriate for the premium-priced product being marketed to the gourmet trade" (Gold, p. 36).
Est: $2,500-$3,000.

337. Tog Quinquina. 1905.
39 x 54¹/₄ in./99 x 137.8 cm
Imp. Vercasson, Paris
Cond A–/Slight stains at paper edges.
Ref: Wine Spectator, 177
"If a young lady on a horse could sell chocolate (*see* PAI-XXX, 24), why couldn't another one sell an aperitif? Here, the motif is Spanish—the girl's dress, the festive harness on the horse—because Perpignan, where the tonic was made, is close to the Spanish border on the Mediterranean side of the Pyrenees. What she and her horse have to do with Tog Quinquina is not clear—but it is also quite immaterial. We're already captivated" (Wine Spectator).
Est: $2,500-$3,000.

338. Cognac Pellisson. 1907.
45³/₄ x 62¹/₄ in./116 x 158 cm
Imp. Vercasson, Paris
Cond A.
Ref: Karcher, 112; PAI-XXVII, 310
Cappiello in his element, shocking and surprising us with some incongruity—here, a carrot-topped imp car-

rying a monstrous barrel against a stark black background. *This is the larger format.*
Est: $1,500-$1,800.

339. Cinzano. ca. 1910.
50⁵/₈ x 78⁵/₈ in./128.6 x 199.7 cm
Lit del Cinzano, Torino
Cond B/Restored tears at folds; image and colors excellent.
Ref: Wine Spectator, 178; Cappiello/St. Vincent, 33; Cappiello, 281; Menagazzi-I, 419; PAI-XXVII, 312 (var)

Cappiello expresses his technique in a nutshell, allowing the red-and-orange striped zebra to say it all in his design for Cinzano Vermouth. "The Cinzanos have been prominent burghers of Turin since at least the 16th century; however, what really put them on the map was the license to make brandy, obtained in 1757 by brothers Carlo, Stephano and Giovanni Cinzano. Their first concoction, considered the prototype of vermouth, was distilled from raisins, cinnamon, clove mugwart and dittany. Over the next century, the product was developed gradually, becoming a standard

340

341

342

343

344

Ref (Both Var): Célébrities, 63; PAI-X, 129
Since the brewery dates itself to the year 1544, the mincing figure in blue and gold represents Francis I, a popular king whose reign (1515-1547) was marked by an unprecedented flowering of the arts and a buildup of the royal resort of Fontainebleau. And the ornately rendered frame only reinforces the frothy indulgence of the image. The "En Vente Ici" text at bottom indicates that this was a window or in-store display advertisement.
Est: $1,500-$1,800.

343. Bière Schmetz. 1921.
13³/₄ x 17³/₄ in./35 x 45 cm
Vercasson, Paris
Cond B−/Slight tears and stains, largely at paper edges.
Ref: Cappiello, checklist
With a facial flush that nearly bests his scarlet doublet, one suspects that this grinning gourmand may have drained the empty keg lying behind him like another dead soldier in a chugging skirmish without any assistance whatsoever. Not sated however, he plops himself atop another barrel of Schmetz, apparently ready to plunge himself back into the friendly fray. Now that's dedication! The bottom text of this design indicates that it was intended to be an in-store display. *Rare!*
Est: $1,200-$1,500.

344. Cachou Lajaunie. 1920.
38 x 57¹/₄ in./96.5 x 145.4 cm
Imp. Devambez, Paris
Cond A. Framed.
Ref: Cappiello, 291; Marques, p. 43;
   Health Posters, 222; PAI-XXIX, 258
The smoker has just taken a Lajaunie breath freshener to counteract the effects of her cigarette, but it's her dress—with its large sequins in shades reminiscent of autumn leaves—that catches our eye. The product takes its name from the color of its tin—"jaune" is French for yellow—as well as the name of its inventor. "The pharmacist, Léon Lajaunie, set up his pharmacy in Toulouse. After developing several invigorating elixirs, he turned to cachou, as an aromatic for perfuming the breath whose strong flavor covered smoker's breath" (Health Posters, p. 169).
Est: $2,000-$2,500.

345. L'Exhausteur Alimente/Le Nivex Jauge. 1920.
52⁵/₈ x 84³/₈ in./133.6 x 214.2 cm
Imp. Devambez, Paris
Cond B−/Restored tears and stains, largely at folds and
   top text area.
Ref: PAI-VII, 73
The product is a simple pressure cooker gauge—but of course Cappiello finds a way to animate the mundane, incorporating the gauge with a happy human host to cybernetic ends.
Est: $1,700-$2,000

drink of Europe; later, other liquors were added to the line. Cinzano remains a major Italian enterprise whose products are sold in every corner of the world" (Wine Spectator). *An extremely rare, 1st edition version of the image, printed in Italy.*
Est: $8,000-$10,000.

340. Longines. ca. 1911.
45⁷/₈ x 62³/₄ in./116.5 x 159.4 cm
Imp. Vercasson, Paris
Cond B−/Restored tears at folds; image and colors
   excellent.
One is never left with a shortage of verbiage to describe Cappiello's particular genius in any of his varied designs. But in this case, it may be wiser to defer to the observations of a contemporary—art critic, F. Boutet de Monvel, who encapsulated his views for the readers of *Le Monde Illustré* in their December 13, 1913, edition: "Enthroned on clouds like those blissful saints in church windows who are as majestic as God, here's Father Time, as powerfully built as an athlete, contemptuous and blasé in the face of the world's old age. At his feet, the homely hourglass that kept time for our ancestors is casually tossed in a golden ray of sunlight. Farewell, old relic! . . . You're obsolete and Father Time no longer has any use for you. Just like everyone else, he uses a watch. But his can't be like everyone else's. It's a 'Longines' that he has chosen. In a triumphant gesture, as if he's relieved

of a great sadness, he raises it above his head. His watch shows ten-thirty—and you better set yours." *This is the smaller format; there also exists a larger 3-sheet version.*
Est: $2,000-$2,500.

341. Vittel. 1912.
29³/₈ x 41 in./74.7 x 104 cm
Imp. Vercasson, Paris.
Cond A−/Slight tears in borders.
Ref: PAI-IX, 41 (var)
Cappiello puts a face to one of the most flourishing spas of France's eastern Vosges region, personifying the source and setting it into a blue grotto in the mountainside. Exploited commercially since 1845, this textual variant touting the Eastern Railways makes it clear that they provide rapid transport to the mineral springs from both Paris and, grace of connecting service, London.
Est: $1,700-$2,000.

342. Bière du Fort-Carré. 1912.
21³/₄ x 27³/₈ in./55.2 x 69.4 cm
Imp. P. Vercasson, Paris
Cond B/A few restored tears.

351

346

345

347

348

CAPPIELLO (continued)

346. Champagne Vicomte de Castellane. 1922.
$47^{1}/_{8}$ x $62^{3}/_{8}$ in./119.7 x 158.5 cm
Devambez, Paris
Cond B/Slight tears at folds; slightly light stained.
Ref: PAI-XXVIII, 182
Florent de Castellane, a genuine viscount, founded the champagne company bearing his name in 1895; the business, now owned by the Laurent-Perrier group, survives to this day. Other than making wine, the viscount had another passion—collecting Cappiello posters. They have been retained by his estate and are occasionally shown to the public in traveling exhibitions. This pumpkin-pantalooned courtier, wearing the champagne's label as a breastplate, is a charming nod to the origin of the effervescent intoxicant.
Est: $3,000-$4,000.

347. Ecrasez la Tuberculose. ca. 1922.
$19^{1}/_{8}$ x $30^{1}/_{8}$ in./48.5 x 76.5 cm
Imp. Devambez, Paris

Cond B–/Slight tears and stains in bottom area.
Ref: Karcher, 472; PAI-XXI, 94
An institutional effort far from Cappiello's usual joyousness, but no less memorable. Holding an infant aloft, the spirit of France stamps out the menace of tuberculosis. Her white robes cinched with a giant red and blue bow, she resembles a triumphant patriotic angel in stark contrast to the ugly serpentine shape of the disease. *Rare! This is the smaller format.*
Est: $1,700-$2,000.

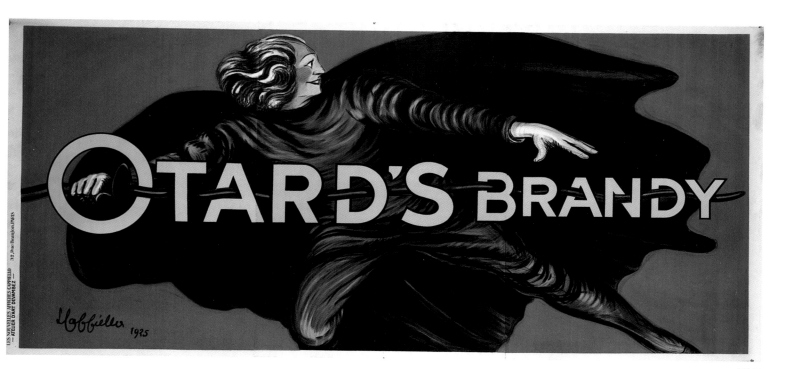

349

350

352

353

348. Exposition Coloniale/Marseille. 1922.
29³/₈ x 46³/₈ in./74.6 x 117.8 cm
Devambez, Paris
Cond B/Restored tears, largely at folds.
Ref: PAI-XXVIII, 184
After 1920, Cappiello's posters shift from Vercasson to Devambez. Here, Cappiello shows us France's benevolent and protective attitude towards its colonies. Inspiring and patriotic, yet surprisingly restrained and literal in comparison to his other works.
Est: $1,200-$1,500.

349. Otard's Brandy. 1925.
135 x 62¹/₈ in./343 x 158 cm
Devambez, Paris
Cond B+/Slight tears and stains at seams and edges.
Ref: Cappiello, 315; Karcher, 113; Boissons, 107;
PAI-XXV, 224
The poster appeared in at least three sizes and two languages, this being the largest, 3-sheet version. While its success is not in dispute, there is a bit of a puzzle as to why a brandy is represented by a mysterious figure cloaked in purple, carrying a long twisted stick. But, since it obviously worked, we won't quibble.
Est: $3,000-$4,000.

350. "SFER.-20" Radiola. 1925.
23⁵/₈ x 31³/₈ in./60 x 79.7 cm

Imp. Devambez, Paris
Cond A–/Slight stains.
Ref: PAI-XV, 169
The young lady is enthralled with the distant reception her new Radiola receiver affords her. What a marvelous collector's item that console would be today! Note how Cappiello takes the radio "waves" literally, giving them not only reality, but also the full prismatic treatment as well.
Est: $3,000-$4,000.

351. Cognac Monnet. 1927.
50⁵/₈ x 78³/₄ in./128.5 x 200 cm
Imp. Devambez, Paris
Cond A.
Ref: PAI-XXVIII, 187
"Sunshine in a glass" is the company's slogan, and Cappiello, with a charming literal-mindedness, depicts exactly that—and, of course, the pure black background makes it stand out prominently. The cognac firm was founded in 1905 by Jean Gabriel Monnet, and is today part of the Hennessy Corporation.
Est: $4,000-$5,000.

352. Nitrolian. 1929.
46⁵/₈ x 62¹/₂ in./118.5 x 158.7 cm
Imp. Devambez, Paris
Cond A.

Ref: PAI-XXVIII, 180
"Watching paint dry" may epitomize unbearable boredom; but with his image of crimson paint being applied a mere step ahead of advancing feet, Cappiello makes it clear that Nitrolian paint is dry in a flash and ready for business.
Est: $2,000-$2,500.

353. La Thermogène.
31 x 46¹/₂ in./78.7 x 118 cm
Dehon, Valenciennes-Paris
Cond A. Framed.
Ref (All Var): Cappiello, 278; Cappiello/St. Vincent, 4.30;
Weill, 210; PAI-IX, 45
A later reprint in a smaller format of the popular 1909 design—completely outside the auspices of the original Vercasson firm in fact—that has become firmly and indelibly associated with this product. It's just the kind of bold overstatement that Cappiello believed would most effectively deliver the message, even with regard to so humble a product as a heating pad.
Est: $1,000-$1,200.

354

355

CAPPIELLO (continued)

354. La Menthe-Pastille. 1929.
45⁵/₈ x 62¹/₂ in./116 x 158.6 cm
Devambez, Paris
Cond B+/Slight tears at folds.
Ref: PAI-XXII, 242
In contrast to the deeply-colored, almost mystical
image Cappiello created for this brand in 1906 (*see*
PAI-IX, 47), the artist gives us this light-hearted social
scene 23 years later. Deep into their refreshing drinks
of green and white mint liqueurs, the two independent
young women don't even notice their waiter eyeing
them suspiciously.
Est: $4,000-$5,000.

355. Docteur Rasurel/Sous Vêtements.
46 x 61⁵/₈ in./116.8 x 156.5 cm
Devambez, Paris
Cond B/Slight tears at folds; image and colors
excellent. Framed.
Cappiello executed several designs for Doctor Rasurel
undergarments, but this conceivably could be an
introductory advertisement. There is a certain dubious
quality to the supposed medical professional standing
behind the mannequin torso in order to best display
his namesake thermal undershirt, something of a char-
latan's smirk gracing his face that confesses to the
fact that he may not be a real doctor—which, in fact,
was true, as the name derived from a clever marketing
scheme rather than an accredited professional. *Rare!*
Est: $3,000-$4,000.

356. L'Oie d'Or.
63 x 47¹/₂ in./160 x 120.7 cm
Devambez, Paris
Cond A.
Ref: PAI-IX, 77
Goose liver pâté gets the royal treatment: the golden
goose wears a crown, and so does the open tin of the
product, and the background is pure imperial scarlet.
But, after all is said and done, what other design
choice could be deemed appropriate for a brand that
claims to be "The Queen of Foie Gras"?
Est: $3,000-$4,000.

356

357. Paris 1937.
31 x 46¹/₂ in./78.8 x 118 cm
Edimo, Paris
Cond A–/Unobtrusive tears.
Ref: Cappiello, 343; PAI-XVII, 160 (var)
For an exhibition of Art and Technology at the 1937
Paris World's Fair, "Two goddesses in blueprint blue
transmit the sacred flame: they stand out against
multi- colored oriflammes (banners, streamers) . . . A
bold conception . . . by a master artist who doesn't
fear audacity" (Vendre, 1937, p. 312). *This is the
smaller format.*
Est: $1,500-$1,800.

358. Le Fusil Darne. 1948.
28⁷/₈ x 38 in./73.3 x 96.5 cm
Imp. Devambez, Paris
Cond B–/Restored tears at folds and edges.
Ref: PAI-XXV, 220 (var)
Earth tones give an autumnal feeling to this poster
advertising a hunting rifle. Designed by Cappiello
before World War II, it was not printed by Devambez
until 1948, six years after the artist's death. *This is
the larger format.*
Est: $1,500-$1,800.

360

361

357

358

359

ERBERTO CARBONI (1899-1984)

359. Boschi Luigi. 1926.
9 x 13¹/₈ in./22.8 x 33.8 cm
Zanlari, Parma
Cond A. Framed.
Sprouting forth from a cental Boschi Luigi canister arrangement that closely resembles an Olympic podium, this ultra-vine of succulent fruit serves as an iconographic reminder of the freshness and big tomato taste of the canned product from whence it sprung. Literal in concept, yet piquantly abstract in design. Carboni had a reputation both as a fine commercial designer and an architect. In addition to Luigi, he worked for many other prominent firms, including Bertolli, Barilla, Olivetti, Campari and Strega.
Est: $1,200-$1,500.

EMIL CARDINAUX (1877-1936)

360. Palace Hotel/St. Moritz. 1920.
35¹/₂ x 50¹/₈ in./90 x 127.2 cm
Wolfsberg, Zurich
Cond A. Framed.
Ref: Cardinaux, 68; Schweizer Hotel, 57; Wobmann, 43; Margadant, 250; Plakat Schweiz, p.34; Timeless Images, 149; Voyage, p. 58; PAI-XXX, 441
A native of Bern, Cardinaux went to Munich at the age of 21 to study law, but the bohemian atmosphere of the town got to him and he turned to art instead. He came under the influence of Franz van Stuck and Ferdinand Hodler, important symbolist painters, and started painting mountain landscapes in their style. But back in Bern, from about 1905 on, he turned to applied graphics as a means of livelihood and eventually became one of Switzerland's most honored posterists. And this poster is one of his classics: The sunlit scene of skaters relaxing at ringside evokes the nostalgia of a cherished holiday snapshot.
Est: $4,000-$5,000

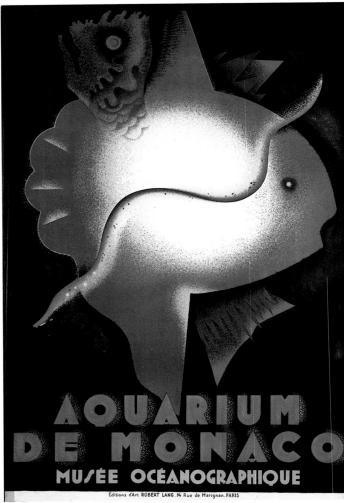

362

364

CARDINAUX (continued)

361. Palace Hotel/St. Moritz. 1922.
36$^1/_8$ x 50$^3/_8$ in./91.7 128 cm
Wolfsberg, Zurich
Cond A.
Ref: Cardinaux, 74; PAI-XVIII,100
Cardinaux had a special talent for landscapes that could easily pass for fine paintings; he never lost the painterly touch in all his graphic work. This is clearly shown in this resort poster: a great impressionistic scene of a golfing party against the impressive alpine panorama.
Est: $3,500-$4,000.

362. Jungfrau-Bahn. 1911.
35$^3/_4$ x 48$^1/_8$ in./90.8 x 122.2 cm
J.E. Wolfensberger, Zürich
Cond A.
Ref: Cardinaux, 22; Alpes, 76; PAI-XXV, 227
The railroad that runs to the Jungfraujoch, a pass near the Jungfrau peak at the height of 11,400 feet, features the highest train ride in Europe, and as a major tourist attraction it advertised often, using a number of the great Swiss posterists. Here, in one of his most stunning designs, Cardinaux shows a climbing party in the high pass beneath the summit.
Est: $3,000-$4,000.

363. Rhätische Bahn/Silsersee. 1916.
35$^1/_2$ x 50$^1/_4$ in./90 x 127.6 cm
J. E. Wolfensberger, Zürich
Cond A.
Ref: Cardinaux, 47; Wobmann, 42; PAI-XXIX, 265
One of Cardinaux's best travel posters, promoting the Rhatisch Railroad in the canton of Graubünden in southeast Switzerland: a landscape with a tranquil lake (Silser) and majestic mountains bathed in the purple hues of a late afternoon sun.
Est: $1,400-$1,700.

363

JEAN CARLU (1900-1997)

For another Carlu poster, see No. 165.

364. Aquarium de Monaco. 1926.
27$^1/_4$ x 40$^1/_4$ in. 69.2 x 112.3 cm
Editions d'Art Robert Lang, Paris
Cond A–/Slight creases at paper edges. Framed.
Ref: Carlu, 12; Timeless Images, 108; Weill, 353; PAI-VIII, 294
This poster for the Aquarium of Monaco is Carlu's finest work: he offers us an aquatic collage, with styl-

365

ized fish and eel silhouettes spotlighted against a stark black background, which works much better by suggesting the underwater mood rather than attempting to depict any particular species. In an interview in 1927, Carlu himself states that he sought to simplify and to impress; if, in the process he abandons scientific accuracy ("Qu'importe l'absence de riguer scientifique?"), he does so to achieve optimum visual effect.
Est: $6,000-$8,000.

366

367

368

365. Pépa Bonafé. 1928.
14³/₄ x 22⁵/₈ in./37.3 x 57.5 cm
Imp. Marcel Picard, Paris
Cond B/Slight tears at folds.
Ref: Carlu, 14 (var); Art Deco, p. 61 (var);
     PAI-XXVIII, 193

Combining curves with straight lines, Carlu creates a stylized, yet recognizable profile of actress Pépa Bonafé. He puts behind her the masks of both comedy and tragedy to show that the source of humor is always close to sorrow. *This is the smaller format.*
Est: $2,000-$2,500.

A. M. CASSANDRE
(Adolphe Mouron, 1901-1968)
For other works of Cassandre, see Nos. 132 & 166.

366. Pivolo Aperitif. 1924.
10¹/₄ x 14¹/₈ in./26 x 36 cm
Hachard & Cie., Paris
Cond A–/Slight staining near edges. Framed.
Ref (All Var except last): Mouron, 2;
     Brown-Reinhold, 3, p. 30; Weill, 338;
     Cassandre/Suntory, 2; PAI-XXIX, 275
Cassandre gave a fine explanation of this design,: "In my work, it is the text, the letter, that sets the process of mental creation into motion and sparks the association of ideas which generates plastic forms. Take *Pivolo*, for example, my favorite poster with *L'Intransigeant*, because they were both spontaneously accepted by my clients in the spirit in which I had conceived and and executed them—accepted without discussion or hesitation. The famous aviation instructor's rule *Et puis vole haut* (keep your altitude), deformed and popularized as *Pivolo* in all aviation schools, suggested to me the pun *Pie vole haut* (magpie, fly high) and led to the stylized black-and-white bird I used to symbolize the new aperitif. A series of verbal connections led me to this formula, which was both aesthetically pleasing and effective publicity, for the public immediately responded to it with a very positive feeling of sympathy" (Mouron, p. 20). The typeface here is Cassandre's as well—the first he ever designed. It showed up in

several of his posters, and in 1929, it was cast at the type foundry of Deberny & Peignot where it was given the name "Bifur." *This is the smaller format.*
Est: $5,000-$6,000.

367. Le Nouvelliste. 1924.
45³/₄ x 62 in./116 x 157.5 cm
Hachard, Paris
Cond B/Slight tears at folds.
Ref: Mouron, ill. 5; Cassandre/Tokyo, 4; PAI-V, 132
One of Cassandre's earliest works for a Lyonaise political daily. The stylized geometric design functions almost like an Art Deco Rorschach test, the combination of the archfully descending bird, beak-delivering the paper from on high, and the tricolored nationalistic sky transmits more than a few abstract notions. But one thing is perfectly clear: *Le Nouvelliste* is precisely the order for keeping up with the events of the day. *Rare!*
Est: $7,000-$9,000.

368. L'Oiseau Bleu. 1929.
24¹/₄ x 39¹/₂ in./61.5 x 100.4 cm
Imp. L. Danel, Lille
Cond A–/Very slight tears at upper right corner.
Ref: Mouron, 18; Brown & Reinhold, 46, Pl. 10; Cassandre/Suntory, 56; Train à l'Affiche, 263; Affiche Réclame, 81; PAI-XXVIII, 202
"Speed is the theme (of this poster) with its cloud of smoke swirling around the checkered red-and-white signal—the only fixed point in the image—standing out against a background of converging telegraph wires. In a highly effective metaphor for speed, a purple martin (*oiseau bleu*) is substituted for the express train hurtling past at full steam" (Mouron, p. 64).
Est: $6,000-$7,000.

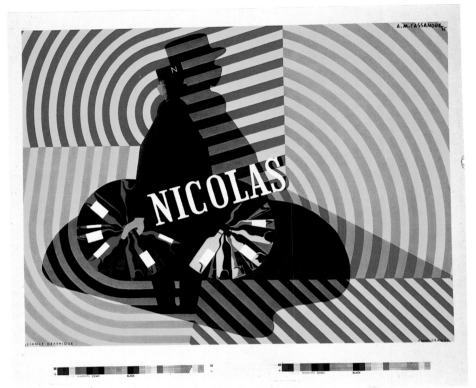

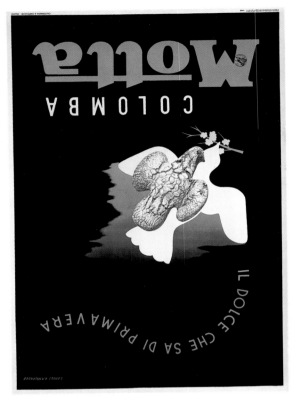

369

370

372

CASSANDRE (continued)

369. Nicolas. 1935.
14⁵/₈ x 13 in./37 x 33 cm
Alliance Graphique
Cond A. Framed.
Ref (All Var): Mouron, 55; Nectar/Nicolas, 41; Weill, 346
Nicolas was—and is—one of the major wine dealers/ distributors in France, and in 1922, the head of the family firm, Etienne Nicolas, asked Dransy—who is given "d'Apres Dransy" credit in the lower right of this piece—to design a poster to show that the company delivers directly to your home. The delivery man, given the name Nectar, became one of the most popular, instantly recognizable images on the walls of France, and was used in dozens of variations. The image was the inspiration for later posters by Iribe, Loupot and Cassandre, among others. And here we see one such inspiration: a hypnotic swirl of sunburst colors inexplicably shading the delivery man while simultaneously casting his violet shadow. Truly spectacular. *Rare printer's proof with color keys at bottom.*
Est: $2,500-$3,000.

370. Colomba Motta. 1936.
27¹/₂ x 39¹/₂ in./70 x 100.4 cm
Calcografia & Cartevalori, Milano
Cond A.
Ref: Mouron, ill. 243 & p. 111;
     Cassandre/Tokyo, 85 (var); PAI-XVIII, 222 (var)
A rare Italian poster, in which Cassandre ingeniously juxtaposes the cookie and its namesake, the dove (*colomba*). *This is the larger format.*
Est: $4,000-$5,000.

371. Italia. 1936.
24¹/₄ x 39¹/₂ in./61.6 x 100.4 cm
Coen, Milano
Cond B/Slight tears at folds and edges.
Ref: Mouron, 192; Brown & Reinhold, 58; Alpes, Pl. 10;
     Cassandre/Suntory, 63A; Cassandre/Tokyo, 83;
     PAI-XIV, 181
Cassandre designed this and two other Italian tourism posters during a working summer holiday on the shore of Lake Maggiore in northern Italy. The Mussolini regime had passed a law banning Italian companies from commissioning French artists; to get around it, Cassandre's future publisher in Italy, Augusto Coen, invited him to work in Italy. Savignac, then Cassandre's assistant, loyally accompanied him and collaborated on the three posters. Though the style was a dead giveaway, Cassandre had to play along with the cha-

371

rade and use the monogram "A.M.C." to conceal his French name. This particular creation centers on a montage of sports and recreational objects against a panorama of Italian topography. From the cobalt-blue Adriatic to the azure of the sky over the Alps, the entire scene is expressed with extreme graphic economy.
Est: $3,000-$4,000.

372. Mentor. 1949.
24⁵/₈ x 33³/₄ in./62.5 x 85.7 cm
Andreasen & Lachmann, København
Cond A–/Unobtrusive tears at left edge.
Ref: Cassandre/Tokyo, 88; Cassandre/Suntory, p. 182;
     PAI-XXX, 455
This rare Cassandre image—one of his last—was done for a Danish encyclopedia. *This is the larger format.*
Est: $3,500-$4,000.

373. Dubonnet. ca. 1956.
47¹/₂ x 66¹/₈ in./120.6 x 168 cm
Axel Andreason & Sonnel, København
Cond A. Framed.
Ref (All Var): Mouron, Cover & 37; Cassandre/Suntory, 31
Cassandre's most famous poster was in fact three posters, a marvelous, witty triptych. His son explains their enduring popularity: "(It) is without question AMC's most popular poster. Three factors can be invoked to explain the popularity of the seated figure: (a) the synthetic simplicity of the design . . . ; (b)the eloquently expressed gesture. . . ; (c) the fact that the theme is treated as an animated sequence in the manner of a comic strip" (Mouron, pp. 157-158). So popular in fact that this version was executed twenty-three years after the design first appeared on the walls of Paris, commissioned by the aperitif company's Danish distributor. The 2-sheet version of the third sheet in the triptych was the only one of the three images to be printed. However, it was never actually posted as it was too large to fit into the designated posting areas.
Est: $2,000-$2,500.

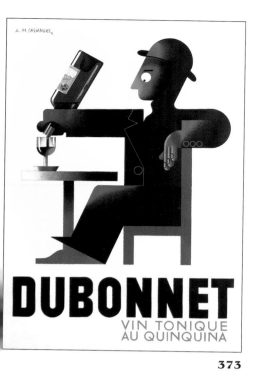

373

374

375

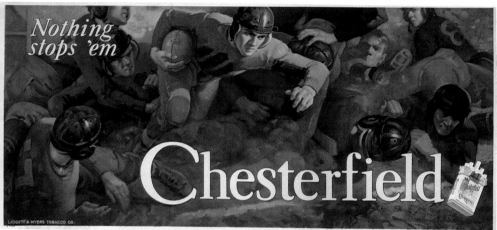

376

377

HENRI CASSIERS (1858-1944)

For other works by Cassier, see Nos. 133-136.

374. Exposition Universelle/Bruxelles. 1910.
34³/₄ x 49³/₈ in./88.3 x 125.3 cm
Imp. J.E. Goossens, Bruxelles, Paris, Lille
Cond A–/Unobtrusive folds.
Ref(All Var): Cassiers, 88; DFP-II, 1004;
  Belle Epoque 1970, 13; Looping the Loop, 35;
  PAI-XIV, 192
A fine bird's eye view of Brussels' Grand Place, with color provided by flags flowing from the balloon above it as well as the flowers below. There are at least three known versions of the poster: one promoting travel by the Belgian State Railways (*see* PAI-III, 61), one advocating the travel benefits of the French Northern rail system (*see* PAI-XIV, 192) and this one, whose belief in the exposition—and the vertiginous artwork—was so strong that it took the stance of, "If you promote it, they will come."
Est: $2,000-$2,500.

MARC CHAGALL (1887-1985)

375. Nice/Soleil, Fleurs. 1962.
23⁵/₈ x 38¹/₂ in./60 x 98 cm
Imp. Mourlot, Paris
Cond A.
Ref: Ref: Sorlier, p. 38; PAI-XXVIII, 220 (var)
A mermaid with a bouquet characterizes the two aspects of Nice of interest to the ministry of tourism which commissioned the poster—the seaside and its exotic flora. A native of Vitebsk, Russia, Chagall arrived in Paris in 1910 and soon made a name for

himself in art circles with his somewhat surreal, poetic vision which seamed best suited for illustrating dreams. Almost all his posters are taken from paintings and prints (the print in this case was titled "The Bay of Angels") which were not originally created as posters, but many of them, because of their bold images and bright colors, turn out to make fine posters nonetheless. *Hand-signed by the artist.*
Est: $2,000-$2,500.

CHARLES E. CHAMBERS (1883-1941)

376. Chesterfield/Nothing stops 'em.
21 x 10¹/₈ in./53 x 25.6 cm
Cond B/Slight tears at folds and edges; image and colors excellent. Framed.
Ref: Poster Design, p. 97
Chambers hammers home the point that when it comes to the narcotic pleasures of Chesterfield cigarettes, "Nothing stops 'em," much like the performance of an all-star fullback. And who better to hawk smokes than professional (or college) athletes. Charles Edward Chambers was born in Iowa and studied at the Art Institute of Chicago and the Art Students League in New York. He was a prolific illustrator (*Harper's, Cosmopolitan, Women's Home Companion, Ladies' Home Journal, McCall's*), and a specialist in oil paintings used as a basis for advertising. Thus, he did a series of musicians' portraits for Steinway which ran for nine years, and the series for Chesterfield which lasted five years.
Est: $1,500-$1,800.

377. Grow White Corn.
21 x 32 in./53.3 x 81.2 cm
Sponsor: American Corn Millers' Federation, Chicago
Cond A–/Unobtrusive folds. Framed.
Relatively speaking, white corn has always been a minor player in the larger corn picture, with white food corn coming in at about one percent of total corn production. There is, however, a good market for the grain, which is used for food products such as tortillas, taco shells, grits and hominy. And the American Corn Millers' Federation wants to spread that message to farmers as a way to increase their profits with the addition of this accessible cash crop. Beyond the obvious color contrast between cob and carrier, Chambers' best design choice was to utilize a baby to make the notion of large white corn returns appear even larger.
Est: $1,500-$1,800.

378

379

380

381

382

383

L. CHARBONNIER

378. Journal de Vichy.
29³/₄ x 46 in./75.7 x 117 cm
Imp. Wallon Frères, Vichy
Cond B/Slight tears and stains at folds.
Artistic Nouveau license is used to spectacular effect by Charbonnier in this advertisement for Vichy's daily newspaper, a publication intended to promote the diversionary offerings of the spa on sale by special vendors within the resort's park. The swirling curlicue wisps of the portal to the conjured casino flow directly into the rocking chair of the clingily clad news buff.
Est: $1,400-$1,700.

G. C. CHAVANNE

379. Cannes Film Festival. 1949.
25 x 38³/₄ in./63.7 x 98.6 cm
Imp. Darboy-Paris
Cond A–/Restored slight loss upper left corner.
A female colossus, dressed in the remnant flags of the global community, towers above the Mediterranean movie Mecca as she holds an unfurling celluloid strip to the sun for her own frame by frame viewing of the film in hand. An excellent design for the second convening of the festival, the first of the post-World War II era.
Est: $1,500-$2,000.

JULES CHÉRET (1836-1932)
For other works of Chéret, see Nos. 54-59.

380. Hippodrome/La Défense du Drapeau. ca. 1876.
16¹/₂ x 22³/₄ in./42 x 57.7 cm
Imp. J. Chéret, Paris
Cond A–/Slight staining in margins.
Ref: Broido, 377 & Pl. 22; Maindron, 299
Patriotic colonialism summed up in three neat colors, the three tones of the French flag reflected in the legionnaire's uniform and fallen steed. Apparently an episodic theatrical experience serialized at the Hippodrome, this installment of "Defending the Flag" focuses on the savagery of Bedouin attacks and the brave Gallic souls set in place to squelch the uprising. How rare is this early Chéret? So rare that even in 1891, Sagot indicated that it was "très rare" and charged one of the highest prices for any of this artist's works: 10 francs (#547).
Est: $1,000-$1,200.

381. A Voltaire. 1881.
16³/₄ x 23¹/₄ in./42.5 x 59.1 cm
Imp. Chaix, Paris
Cond B/Folds show.

Ref: Broido, 763; Maindron, 641
Between 1875 and 1881, Chéret did ten posters for this store promoting everything from children's gifts to apparel for every sex and age. And as the store is named after one of the greatest opponents to intolerance in modern history, their philosophy of affordable fashion equality is put on display in the form of this gent in twill overcoat.
Est: $1,000-$1,200.

382. Aux Buttes Chaumont. 1887.
48¹/₄ x 68³/₈ in./122.5 x 173.7 cm
Imp. Chaix, Paris
Cond B+/Slight tears and stains, largely at folds.
A previously undocumented 2-sheet Chéret promoting a women's and girls' coat sale. Appearing in none of the major Chéret reference materials (Broido, Maindron, the 1891 Sagot catalogue or the 1896 Reims exhibition catalogue), the design features three composed sepia visions of feminine decorum, placidly satisfied with their fashionable choices. *Rare!*
Est: $1,500-$1,800.

383. Une Jeune Marquise. 1889.
33¹/₄ x 47¹/₄ in./84.5 x 120 cm
Imp. Chaix, Paris
Cond B–/Restored tears at folds and edges.
Ref: Broido, 631; Maindron, 518; PAI-XXX, 191

385

386

384

387

385. Cosmydor Savon. 1891.
23^1/$_8$ x 32^3/$_8$ in./58.8 x 82.2 cm
Imp. Chaix, Paris
Cond B+/Slight tears, largely at paper edges.
Ref: Broido, 938; Maindron, 778; DFP-II, 220 (var);
    PAI-XX, 194
A lovely poster for Cosmydor soap, featuring a model
resplendent with exquisite, rich color. The flowers
adorning her dress and hair underline the fresh beauty
that the soap ostensibly brings to her skin. *This is the
smaller format.*
Est: $2,500-$3,000.

386. Palais de Glace. 1893.
32^7/$_8$ x 47^1/$_2$ in./83.5 x 120.6 cm
Cond B+/Slight tears at stains. Framed.
Ref (All Var but Broido): Broido, 362; Maindron, 292;
    DFP-II, 240; Gold, 130; PAI-XXX, 157
"Chéret executed several posters for this popular
establishment, always with a delightful young woman
in the spotlight, accompanied by a shadowy figure of a
gentleman in the background. What we learn from all
the designs is that women were able to enjoy indoor
skating in full street clothes, including elaborate hats,
coats and capes" (Gold, p. 90). In one of the more
complex images of the artist's series for this rink,
Chéret echoes the rhythmic lines of the skater's boa
and coat in the shadowed figures behind her. *This is a
black artist's proof, with several whited corrections.*
Est: $3,000-$4,000.

387. Le Rapide. 1892.
34^3/$_4$ x 49^1/$_2$ in./88 x 126 cm
Imp. Chaix, Paris
Cond B/Slight tears at folds.
Ref: Broido, 568; Maindron, 462; PAI-VIII, 4
A train, a telegraph pole and a soaring vision in red
personifying the newspaper convey the sense that this
publication gets its readership every last journalistic
detail as quickly as humanly possible.
Est: $1,700-$2,000.

The text of this poster advertises "A Young Marquise"
as a novel exploring the life of a neurotic woman.
Indeed, the lass in the foreground does seem rather
distraught, apparently in a quandary about the gentleman taking his leave of her. But other than this visual
clue, we are sadly left without any further information
regarding the literary madness of the heroine of this
tome by Théodore-Cahu.
Est: $1,400-$1,700.

384. Paris Courses. 1890.
33^1/$_2$ x 48^1/$_4$ in./85 x 122.6 cm
Imp. Chaix, Paris
Cond B–/Stains at edges; rounded corners in frame.
Ref: Broido, 520; Maindron, 421; DFP-II, 191;
    Maitres, 61; PAI-XXVII, 344
A young woman in a frilly pink dress rides sidesaddle
on a brown horse in this poster for a racing event at
the Hippodrome. An interesting side note to this is
Sagot's remark that this poster was never placed on
the hoardings as these particular races were canceled.
This is the larger format.
Est: $2,000-$2,500.

JULES CHÉRET (continued)

388. Vin Mariani/Popular French Tonic Wine. 1894.
$33^1/_2$ x $47^3/_4$ in./85.3 x 121.3 cm
Imp. Chaix, Paris
Cond B/Slight tears and stains at folds; iamge and
    colors excellent. Framed.
Ref: Broido, 865; Maindron, 731; DFP-II, 248;
    Maitres, 77; Reims, 540; Wine Spectator, 3;
    Health Posters, 111; Gold, 42; PAI-XXVIII, 254
A "Chéret classic, glowing with irrepressible zest, the
perfect image for a product which earned much of its
renown by clever promotion . . . The founder of the
enterprise was Angelo Mariani (who) came up with the
idea of combining the medicinal properties of coca
leaves with his favorite Bordeaux, thus coming up with
a medicine that didn't taste like one . . . In time (it)
gained an edge on (competitors) partly because of the
intoxicating dash of cocaine in it, but mostly because
of Mariani's unexpected talent as a publicist. Long
before it became a general practice, he shrewdly
recognized the value of celebrity endorsements, and
had doctors, musicians, comedians, respected public
figures and even some minor royalty praising his tonic
in ads and posters" (Wine Spectator). Chéret, besides
designing this lively image, also provided one of the
testimonials.
Est: $4,000-$5,000.

389. Le Punch Grassot. 1895.
$34^3/_4$ x 49 in./88.2 x 124.5 cm
Imp. Chaix, Paris
Cond B+/Unobtrusive tears and stains at folds and
    edges.
Ref: Broido, 876; Maindron, 427; DFP-II, 218;
    Reims, 406; PAI-XXVII, 346
In this masterpiece of three-color printing, Chéret sub-
ordinates the details of draftsmanship to the overall
sweep of the scene. The design itself is rarely seen,
with one of the artist's delightful women airily carrying
a tray of Grassot's best.
Est: $3,000-$3,500.

390. Saxoléine. 1895.
$34^3/_4$ x $49^1/_4$ in./88.2 x 125 cm
Imp. Chaix, Paris
Cond A–/Slight tears and creases at paper edges.
Ref: Broido, 953; Maitres, 13; DFP-II, 261; Reims, 511;
    Gold, 26; PAI-XXVIII, 244
A happy home-maker is so pleased with her choice of
illuminating oil that she fairly waltzes away with her
lamp in this captivating design.
Est: $2,500-$3,000.

391. Saxoléine. 1896.
$34^5/_8$ x $49^1/_8$ in./88 x 125 cm
Imp. Chaix, Paris
Cond A–/Unobtrusive slight tears ot paper edges.
Ref (All Var but PAI): Broido, 941; Maindron, 780;
    DFP-II, 222; PAI-XXII, 294
Originally created in 1891, this is one of the first of
"Chéret's decade-long campaign for Saxoléine lamp
oil . . . Each of the ten successive annual images
contains a woman and a lamp; the only thing that
changes is their mutual position . . . and of course,

PAPIER A CIGARETTES

JOB

Hors Concours

PARIS 1889

Théâtre de l'Opéra

CARNAVAL 1896
Samedi 11 Janvier
1er. Gd. BAL·MASQUÉ

392

393

Taverne Olympia

Restaurant
OUVERT TOUTE LA NUIT

ORCHESTRE
DE DAMES

MONTAGNES RUSSES

28, Bould des Capucines & 6, Rue Caumartin

394

Saxoléine

PÉTROLE DE   SÛRETÉ

EXTRA·BLANC · DÉODORISÉ · ININFLAMMABLE
en Bidons Plombés de 5 litres

395

he color of the dresses and lamp shades also vary.
till, it takes talent to be able to make ten images
ook distinct from each other and make them interest-
g enough so that some people actually looked for-
ard to see what next year's Saxoléine poster would
ook like" (Gold, p. 19). As always, warm tones persist,
ith the golden dress and crimson lampshade fairly
ursting off the midnight blue background.
st: **$2,500-$3,000.**

392. Job/Papier à Cigarettes. 1895.
32⅞ x 46⅜ in./ 83.5 x 117.8 cm
Imp. Chaix, Paris
Cond A. Framed.
Ref: Broido, 1028; Maindron, 850; Maitres, 1;
  DFP-II, 255; Reims, 465; Wine Spectator, 6;
  PAI-XXIX, 290
The defiant gesture of an emancipated woman daring
to flout conventional manners is caught with perfec-

tion; the fact that it happened over a century ago
adds to its piquancy. One of Chéret's best and most
famous designs.
Est: **$5,000-$6,000.**

393. Théâtre de l'Opéra/Carnaval 1896/11 Janvier.
  1895.
34⅝ x 49 in/88 x 124.4 cm
Imp. Chaix, Paris
Cond B+/Slight tears at folds and edges;¾ inch loss,
  lower right corner; colors exceedingly fresh.
Ref: Broido, 293; Maitres, 9 (var); DFP-II, 251 (var);
  Reims, 528; PAI-XXIV, 235 (var)
Like virtually all of the posters Chéret did for the
dances at this theater between 1892 and 1897, the
design features a profiled woman in a billowing dress
looking out over her shoulder as a shadowy male figure and other revelers dance around her. Chéret
would do a single design each winter and it would be
repeated with varying text throughout the season. For
1896, the charmer's dress is striped in two shades of
green and she gestures to her escort with a fan. It is
interesting to see how Chéret, reworking the same
visual ingredients, always keeps us interested.
Est: **$5,000-$6,000.**

394. Taverne Olympia. 1899.
35½ x 47⅝ in./85 x 120.2 cm
Imp. Chaix, Paris
Cond B−/Restored tears at folds and edges. Framed
Ref: Broido 848; Maitres, 217; DFP-II, 226; PAI-VIII, 105
Two couples proffer a hearty toast while a respectful
waiter hovers nearby, prepared to satisfy their every
dining and drinking desire—a vivacious scene to
advertise an all-night restaurant.
Est: **$1,700-$2,000.**

398

399

JULES CHÉRET (continued)

395. Saxoléine. 1900.
$33^3/4$ x $48^1/2$ in./85.7 x 123.2 cm
Imp. Chaix, Paris
Cond B/Slight creasing near edges; unobtrusive tears
along folds. Framed.
Ref: Broido, 958; DFP-II, 208; Gold, 28; PAI-XXIX, 302
"Long before advertising science began to talk of
product recognition, Chéret was creating it with his
Saxoléine posters. He started out by creating a homey
atmosphere with warm friendly colors around the lamp:
he then placed an attractive homemaker in close
relation to the lamp and let her show her pleasure at
having such a bright light to illuminate the room. The
product itself . . . is not shown. But Chéret knew that
women would aspire to the beauty and high spirits of
his model" (Gold, p.20).
Est: $2,500-$3,000

EMILE CLOUET

396. Pneumatique G & J/L'Acatène Métropole.
$36^5/8$ x $49^1/2$ in./93 x 125.6 cm.
Imp. Kossuth, Paris
Cond B+/Slight tears and stains at paper edges.
In all previously seen posters for the Acatène Métropole bicycle, there has always been clear mention
made that their product was outfitted with G & J tires.
This, however, marks the first time that the treaded
pneumatics have headlined their own poster— a poster-
within-a-poster, as a matter of fact—and one which
boasts their enduring superiority in the current world
record of covering an impressive 563 miles
plus in a twenty-four hour period. Clouet's approach
is somewhat reminiscent of Pal's wall and women
approach to promote Whitworth cycles (see PAI-XXV,
446), but goes even further by not including a representation of the tire anywhere in his design.
Est: $1,200-$1,500.

396

JEAN COCTEAU (1889-1963)

397. Ballets Russes de Diaghilew. 1939.
$32^1/2$ x 60 in./82.5 x 152.5 cm
Cond A–/Unobtrusive tears at left margin.
Ref: PAI-XXX, 477
Poet, novelist and historian, Cocteau was also closely
affiliated with the world of dance and theater, as writer,
painter and decorator. In 1911, Cocteau created a
beautiful pair of large posters for the Ballet Russe, in
one depicting Najinsky in a pose from *Le Spectre de
la Rose* (see PAI-XXIX, 315) and in the other, Tamara
Karasavina (*see* PAI-XI, 179), his partner in both the
aforementioned Fokine ballet and the poster set. It is

39

that drawing of Karsavina that is reproduced here for
1939 exhibition of the Ballet Russes in Paris.
Est: $2,000-$2,500.

400

401

402

PAUL COLIN (1892-1986)
For another work of Colin, see No. 61.

398. Signoret.
46¹/₈ x 62 in./117.2 x 157.5 cm
Imp. H. Chachoin, Paris
Cond B–/Restored tears and losses at folds and margins.
Colin adapted his Art Deco bent over the years into his own unique style, evolving as he embraced symbolism and abstraction. He was a master of depicting movement in deceptively simple ways, frequently calling upon multiple exposure to reveal various facets of personality or a variety of experiences. He designed dozens of posters for performers in all media, reflecting the history of Paris show business and public life during his lifetime perhaps better than any of his contemporaries. In this poster for an appearance of Marius Signoret (1872-1937), Colin utilizes a charcoal-sketched chorus of self-realized character creations to flesh out the talents of the central-portraited performer. Signoret was a stage actor of great repute whose talents were recognized by the film industry, embracing him as a master of creating gritty secondary characters.
Est: $3,000-$4,000.

399. Damia. 1930.
15¹/₂ x 23¹/₄ in./39.3 x 59 cm
Imp. H. Chachoin, Paris
Cond B/Slight tears and creases, largely at edges.
Ref: Colin, 55; Colin Affichiste, 88; PAI-XV, 235
"Maryse Damien—Damia—was born, like Colin, in 1892. She is frequently called 'the grande dame' of French song. She developed her precise and self-assured movements as a member of Loïe Fuller's group; later she appeared in revues at the Folies-Bergère, acted in theater, and starred in films . . . 'She was quite a singer,' Colin tells us. 'Her outfit consisted of a black dress. That's all. The dress had a plunging neckline and her arms were bare. I said to myself, 'For her, I'm going to install a black velvet curtain.' Well, a black curtain had never been seen in theater before. The producer was opposed, but I won out. And in the end it was very successful and she sang like this on stage all her life. The audience would see her arms, the neck and her face. The projector was on her and the white skin stood out against the black backdrop. The effect was very good. It was a new idea then, but it is being done all the time now" (Colin, p. 9).
Est: $2,700-$3,000.

400. Week End Cigarettes. 1933.
15⁵/₈ x 23¹/₂ in./40 x 59.6 cm
Signed gouache and ink maquette.
Few alterations were made on the journey of this gouache and ink maquette on its journey to poster-hood (*see* PAI-XXVIII, 268). In fact, the rougher textures of the original artwork bring a certain roguish charm to the trio of *soigné* smokers, blissfully indulging themselves with a sunny nicotine break from the comfort of their respective reclining canvas deck chairs, having chosen Week End cigarettes, the brand in the snazzy hinged dual-compartment pack, as their preferred puff. Colin Art Deco chic at its finest.
Est: $3,000-$4,000.

401. Grand Guignol/Le Main de Singe. 1930.
44 x 59¹/₄ in./111.7 x 150.4 cm
Imp. H. Chachoin (not shown)
Cond B/Trimmed to image; slight tears at folds.
Ref: Colin, 60
"Horror reigned at the Grand Guignol and people flocked in, not knowing or caring much about the plot of the play they were about to see, but taking comfort in the certainty that they were going to be frightened out of their seats" (Colin, p. 10). In this case, the frightfest in question was one of the all-time horror classics, "The Monkey's Paw," a tale that all but created the phrase, "Be careful what you wish for." "Asked about his unusual, almost photographic, treatment in this poster, Colin says: 'You can interpret Mistinguett or plays and actors in various ways, but for a drama whose sole purpose is to frighten, the poster itself must become terrifying and gruesome and this does require a realistic treatment'" (Colin, p. 10). Thus, he adds a rotary printing press to the arsenal of horror weapons.
Est: $5,000-$6,000.

402. La Granero. 1935.
46⁵/₈ x 62¹/₂ in./118.5 x 157.5 cm
Joseph-Charles, Paris
Cond B/Unobtrusive creasing and tears.
Ref: Colin Affichiste, 90; PAI-XV, 227
The dancer Granero assumes the classic Spanish stance; her white dress, the red flowers in her hair and buff accents stand out in sharp contrast to the black background.
Est: $1,700-$2,000.

403

405

406

PAUL COLIN (continued)

403. La Liberation. 1944.
46⁷/₈ x 63¹/₂ in./119 x 161.2 cm
Cond B/Slight tears at folds; offsetting of ink in
    background.
Ref: Colin, 70; Colin Affichiste, 163; PAI-XIII, 181
The most emotional and perhaps the best remembered of all Colin's posters, this image of the Marianne,
her hands still pierced with the stigmata of German
barbarism, yet already looking forward to a better
future, was prepared and printed in secret several
days before the victorious Allied troops actually
marched into Paris. As a result, it was already being
posted all over the jubilant city as the last of the occupying Nazis scurried ignominiously in retreat.
Est: $2,500-$3,000.

404. Afrique Occidentale Française. ca. 1948.
20¹/₂ x 39¹/₄ in/61.5 x 99.7 cm
Editions Diloutremer, Paris
Cond A–/Unobtrusive horizontal fold. Framed.
Ref: PAI-XXIV, 253
A startling, imaginative design promoting travel to
what was then called French West Africa and is now,
among other countries, Benin. The outline of a giraffe
is filled with silhouettes that simultaneously evoke
local sights and suggest the animal's distinctive
splotches. The background has all the hues of sunset
from the last orange glow at top to blue-green shadows at bottom. The image was also used with different
text to promote visits to the region's wildlife parks.
Est: $1,500-$1,800.

405. Vichy/Demandez Votre Quart. 1948.
46 x 62⁷/₈ in./117 x 159.5 cm
Imp. Bedos, Paris
Cond A.
Ref: Colin, 106; PAI-XXVI, 270
A bottle of Vichy mineral water at every occasion is
clearly the message. The green bottles are the only
element rendered realistically here; everything else is
stylized in form and color.
Est: $1,700-$2,000.

PLINIO COLOMBI (1873—1951)

406. Bremgarten-Dietikon-Bahn. 1912.
39⁵/₈ X 28³/₈ in./100.6 X 72 cm
Kümmerly & Frey Bern.
Cond A.
Ref: Margadant, 244; PAI-XXV, 281
The composition has all the feeling of a painting—
note, for example, the meticulous attention paid to
the shimmering reflections in the water—and yet it
makes a most effective promotion for the railroad by
instilling a need to enjoy picturesque vistas like those
available at the Reuss River bridge firsthand.
Est: $1,200-$1,500.

A. COMETTI

407. Nougat Croc. 1924.
45¹/₄ x 60⁵/₈ in./114.7 x 154 cm
Affiches Camis, Paris
Cond B/Slight tears and stains at fold and edges.
Ref: PAI-XX, 224
If, as the poster says, "you can find this candy anywhere," we wonder why Mr. Fox doesn't leave Little
Red Riding-Kerchief alone and go buy his own. But as
foxes don't have pockets, it may be a question of
change rather than bad manners. Cometti left behind
a large and worthy body of work for Paris advertisers

404

407

408

409

410

411

of the 1920s and 1930s (the Bibliothèque Nationale has 265 posters by him), yet nothing is known about the artist himself.
Est: $1,200-$1,500.

L. CONCHON

408. Liqueur Ste. Barbe.
46³/₄ x 62³/₄ in./119 x 159.3 cm
Affiches Louis Galice, Paris
Cond A.
One hears about any number of liqueurs originating in the monasteries of the world, but it's not that often—if at all up to this point—that one comes across one whipped up in a *convent*. But that's exactly the case here, with an aperitif so devilishly good that Satan himself needs to theatrically sneak in under the cover of darkness in order to procure a few bottles of the

stuff for those interminable nights in the depths of hell, leaving behind a no-doubt dubious contract as he steps out into the night.
Est: $1,700-$2,000.

EDOUARD COURCHINOUX (1891-1968)

409. Le Touquet Paris-Plage. 1925.
24¹/₄ x 39¹/₈ in./61.5 x 99.4 cm
Imp. Lucien Serre, Paris
Cond A.
Ref: Sport à l'Affiche, 212 (var); Train à l'Affiche, 213; PAI-XVIII, 102 (var)
A rather visible little caddy flags a golfer up-course at Le Touquet, on the Chanel coast below Boulogne. "If the Northern Railroad takes you to Le Touquet-Paris-Plage and its golf, the red caddy caught from behind by Courchinoux has become a veritable institution: feet planted solidly, flag in left hand, bag crammed with the necessary woods and irons, he doesn't lack for customers" (Sport à l'Affiche, p. 166). And this version of the poster spells out enough of the featured amenities in order to tip the scales for any of those still on the fence: 45 holes of golf, 30 tennis courts, racetrack, sable beach and the most beautiful pool in Europe, filled with heated sea water. I'm sold.
Est: $1,700-$2,000.

410. El Menzah. 1929.
31¹/₂ x 47 in./80 x 119.5 cm
Imp. Grav. Nergi & Cie, Lille
Cond B+/Restored tears in margins.
Courchinoux's design for El Menzah superior red wine is right on the mark, its google-eyed chef—who we suspect may have already been dipping into the El Menzah well already—proclaiming the wine "Excellent!" as he heads in for more. Courchinoux, a graphic artist with at least one-hundred posters to his credit, was the founder of the Académie de l'Affiche, the first institution in Paris devoted purely to poster art.
Est: $1,000-$1,200.

411. Biere de Marle. 1933.
30¹/₂ x 46 in./77.5 x 117 cm
Affiches Courchinoux/L. Grau, Lille
Cond A-/Unobtrusive folds.
Long live the Queen! A precious design that places Marle beer at the top of the pilsner pecking order, cloaking the tumbler with ermine without the distraction of any greater head than the foamy one already present.
Est: $800-$1,000.

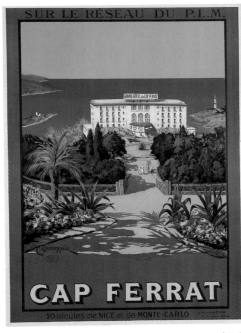

412

413

414

417

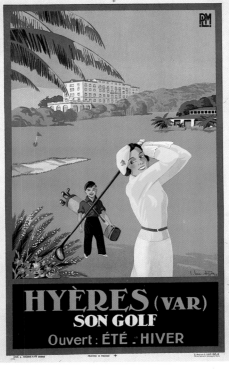

418

419

C. COURONNEAU

412. Cap Ferrat. 1922.
29¹/₂ x 41¹/₄ in./75 x 104.7 cm
Affiches Edia, Paris
Cond A.
Ref: PAI-XXIX, 325
Still thriving today, the Grand Hotel du Cap-Ferrat is located on the French Riviera between Nice and Monaco in a fourteen acre private park of perfumed pines at the very tip of the Cap-Ferrat peninsula facing the Mediterranean. Though unquestionable beautiful, our very own Terry Shargel reports back that the rooms in the resort are a bit on the small side. Which only goes to show that even on the Côte d'Azur, sometimes you can't have everything. However, Couronneau would have you know that the best way to arrive at this singular refuge for all seasons is via the rail network of his employers, the P.L.M.
Est: $1,500-$1,800.

CYRK

413. Polish Circus: 5 Posters. 1963-1969.
Each approx.: 26¹/₂ x 38¹/₄ in./67.2 x 97 cm
Cond A,
Ref: PAI-XV, 471 (var)
Perhaps no other country has had such a concentration of poster talent in the post-World War II period as

Poland—and in circus posters, these artists have had a particularly good opportunity to freely indulge their talents. This group of posters prove it to anyone's satisfaction: "They are filled with exuberance, humor, joy, spontaneity, freedom, whimsy. They want to shock and mock, as well as entertain and please" (*Circus Posters*, p. 15). The five artists represented here are: Tadeusz Jodlowski, Jan Mlodozeniec, Anna Kozniewaska, Waldemar Swierzy and Liliana Baczewski, all of whom indulge their Big Top fantasies from lions to performing poodles and everything in between.
Est: $1,400-$1,700. (5)

414. 100th Anniversary of Polish Circus 1883-1983: 5 Posters. 1983.
Each approx: 26¹/₂ x 37 in./67.3 x 94 cm
Cond A.
During the golden era of the Polish School of Posters, the most recognized subject and most highly acclaimed posters were Cyrk posters, which, during their approximate quarter-century of design supremacy, achieved a remarkable artistic quality as well as an unmatched

degree of popularity. These five posters—created by Marek Freudenreich, Maciej Urbaniec, Tomasz Szulecki, Waldemar Swierzy and Witold Janowski—commemorate the centennial celebration of the Polish entertainment institution with designs ranging from the traditional to the cartoonish to the Cubist, with Urbaniec's reversible happy/sad clown face being perhaps the most ingenious of them all.
Est: $1,200-$1,500. (5)

VERNEY L. DANVERS

415. Sunny Worthing. 1947.
25¹/₈ x 40¹/₄ in./64 x 102.3 cm
McCorquodale, London
Cond B/Slight tears at folds and edges.
"Sophisticated Worthing" might be a better catch phrase for this Danvers' design for the Southern Railways service to the coastal hamlet, once a small coastal fishing village that became the largest town in West Sussex. The posterist takes a turn for the cultural in this design that shows off the Municipal Orchestra and concert hall to prove the point that Worthing is a year-round getaway destination—not just when it's

415

416

420

unny. Danvers ran a commercial art school and was
ommissioned by several fashion and interior design
ouses in addition to his work for the LNER, SR and
ondon Transport.
Est: **$1,700-$2,000.**

.16. Folkestone. 1934.
5³/8 x 40¹/2 in./64.5 x 103 cm
IcCorquodale, London

Cond B+/Slight tears at folds.
Danvers chic hits pay dirt once again in this tiered
masterpiece for the Southern Railways destination
Folkestone, located eight miles west of its one-time
ferry port rival Dover. Our vertiginous perch gives us a
great view of The Leas, the clifftop grassy promenade
laid out in the mid-19th century at the height of the
resort's heydey, and the seaward panorama which on
clear days extends all the way to France.
Est: **$2,500-$3,000.**

ANDRE DAUDE (1897-1979)

417. Pianos Daudé. 1926.
46³/4 x 62¹/8 in./118.8 x 157.8 cm
Publicité PAG, Paris
Cond A–/Unobtrusive tears at paper edges.
Ref: Art Deco, p. 94; PAI-XXX, 486
The creator of this stunning poster for the piano store
on Avenue Wagram in Paris (still there today) is none
other than the former president of the company. It is
an inspired design: The diagonal placement of the
piano instantly animates the entire scene, and the
overhead view of the baldheaded pianist adds just
the right note of humor.
Est: **$2,500-$3,000.**

L. LUC-DÈJE

418. Hyères. 1933.
24³/8 x 39 in./62 x 99 cm
Imp. L. Serre, Paris
Cond A.
Ref: PAI-XVII, 354
Acres of fresh green—helped by a sunshine sweater,
blue sky and red tile roofe—evoke perfect days of fair
weather golf, "summer (and) winter" in the resort town
of Hyères on the Côte d'Azur. Hyères still boasts the
18-hole course of de Valcros. Luc-Dèje was a children's
book illustrator as well as a posterist. He published

much of his own work, either under his real name,
Lucien Dejoie, or that of his Paris firm, Les Creations
L. Luc-Dèje.
Est:**$1,400-$1,700.**

EDGAR DEROUET (1910-1999)

419. Loterie Nationale/Joyeux Gagnants. 1937.
31¹/8 x 46³/4 in./79 x 118.7 cm
Imp. Lafayette, Paris
Cond A–/Unobtrusive tears at paper edges.
Ref: Derouet, 15; PAI-XXIX, 331a (var)
His ingenuous, nearly cartoon-like style brought him
recognition, and he produced a great many posters for
films, products and events; but perhaps none of his
work had more popular appeal than his series for the
Lottery in the 1930s. Regardless of persona and pursuit (there were more than 25 in the series), the jolly
winning characters were always shown the same way:
with their legs akimbo and their arms raised in tri-
umph. *This is the larger format.*
Est: **$1,000-$1,200.**

ALEX W. DIGGELMANN (1902-1987)

420. PKZ/Burger-Kehl & Co. A.G. 1935.
35¹/2 x 50³/8 in./90 x 127.8 cm
Wolfsberg, Zürich
Cond A–/Slight creases at edges.
Ref: Margadant, 333; Plakat Schweitz, p. 137;
    PAI-XVI, 217
The usual PKZ understatement—we know the quality's
in the box from the Swiss clothier's reputation, as well
as from the dignity of the design. Diggelmann started
out as an elementary school teacher, then studied art
in Leipzig and Paris. He established himself in Zurich
as a posterist specializing in travel and sports, and
won awards for poster designs for the 1936 Berlin and
1948 London Olympics.
Est: **$2,500-$3,000.**

421

422

423

JEAN-GABRIEL DOMERGUE (1889-1962)

421. Monte-Carlo.
24³/₄ x 38¹/₂ in./62.9 x 97.8 cm
Imp. Nationale, Monaco
Cond A.
Ref: PAI-V, 161a
Very little information is given and very little is needed with such a comely invitation perched atop a diving board to lure anyone with an appreciation for the female form to Monte Carlo. Domergue's posters are populated with beautiful women in glowing colors, portrayed with chivalrous flattery at their seductive best by someone to whom beauty was an inexhaustible well of inspiration. Domergue lived a life nearly predisposed to that kind of attitude: his home was Monte Carlo and the Cote d'Azur where Europe's most glamorous women were frequently seen, with Domergue himself a member of the smart set he so often portrayed.
Est: $800-$1,000.

MSTILAV DOBUZHINSKY (1875-1957)

422. Kaunas/Lithuania.
23³/₄ x 38³/₄ in./60.2 x 98.3 cm
"Spindulio" Ofsetas, Kaunas
Cond B+/Slight tears at edges.
Kaunas is the second largest city in Lithuania, second only to the capital, Vilnius. Founded in the 12th century and owing its existence to its favorable geographic location at the confluence of the Nemunas and Neris rivers, the city has become a major center of the country's spiritual resistance and struggle for national identity. For twenty years, between 1920 and 1940,
it served as the provisional capital of Lithuania while the nation remained under Polish rule. An old world charm pervades this Dobuzhinsky design which extends its invitation to the English-speaking world with architectural serenity, featuring the early Gothic Vytautas Church, late Gothic Perkanus House and the St. Trinity churches. A painter who specialized in book illustration, watercolors and engraving, Dobuzhinsky ultimately gave himself over to stage design, notably for Diaghilev and the Ballets Russes. His paintings hang in many Russian museums, but in 1920, he left his native country and never returned. He spent the rest of his life working in England, France, Belgium and the U.S.
Est: $1,000-$1,200.

JEAN DROIT (1884-1961)

423. Touring Club de Belgique. ca. 1911.
15⁵/₈ x 24⁵/₈ in./39.7 x 62.5 cm
J. Goffin Fils, Bruxelles

Cond A–/Unobtrusive slight tears and stains at edges.
Ref: PAI-XXV, 294
Although snuggled closely with her escort, the young lady is giving us a most encouraging smile, as if suggesting there's always hope for us if we play our cards right. With such prospects, who wouldn't join the Belgian Touring Club? Droit was a French illustrator and caricaturist; he contributed copiously to various magazines, drew cartoons for *Le Rire,* illustrated a number of books and did some posters for the performing arts. In 1911, he made a trip to Belgium where he produced a few posters.
Est: $1,200-$1,500.

DUBOUT & PAGNOL

ALBERT DUBOUT (1905-1976)

424. Marius. 1950.
23¹/₂ x 37⁵/₈ in./59.8 x 80.4 cm
Imp. Monégasque, Monte-Carlo
Cond B/Slight tears and stains at folds.
Ref: Dubout, p. 15
The film trilogy—*Marius* (1931), *Fanny* (1932) and *César* (1936)—has been re-released at least five times, and the following nine posters come to us from the 1950 reissue of the films. An ardent populist, Pagnol lovingly depicted the lives of colorful characters of the Marseilles waterfront. The whole saga is filled with warmth, humor and compassion, plus a true insight into the motivations behind the concept of honor among ordinary citizens. Hollywood attempted to condense the trilogy into a single film in 1938, titled "Port of the Seven Seas" as a Wallace Berry vehicle, but the director, James Whale, didn't have the acute powers of observation to make the protagonists really come alive the way Pagnol and his excellent cast did in the original. Dubot's famous humorous caricatures are perfectly suited to Pagnol's style; he created posters for the original releases of all three parts, as well as for the 1950 reissue. The film tells the story of Marius, the son of a Marseilles tavern owner who longs for the sea, but is reluctant to leave his childhood sweetheart, Fanny, the waterfront fishmonger. As Fanny is also being wooed by a wealthy widower, she feigns indifference for Marius, knowing that his heart is set on the sea and doesnt wish for him to have any qualms about leaving. As the sea is the thing, Dubout sagely provides us with the single sail and riggings of the ships that sing out their siren song to Marius.
Est: $1,200-$1,500.

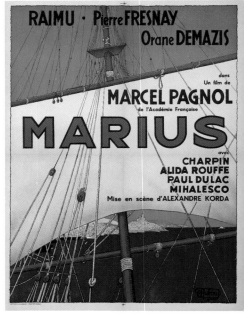

424

425. Marius. 1950.
47¹/₂ x 62⁵/₈ in./120 x 159 cm
Imp. Monégasque, Monte-Carlo
Cond B+/Slight stains at folds.
Ref: Dubout, p. 13
That Honoré Panisse was Marius' rival for the affections of Fanny in this first installment has already been covered. However, the true genius of Pagnol shines through in the real-life wrinkle he tosses into the mix: Not merely a patron of César's Bar de la Mer, Honoré is a widowed sail maker who is one of César's three friends who play cards with him interminably, the other two being Felix, a local ferry captain, and Brun, a customs inspector. A perfect complication to add genuine everyday appeal to the film's premise, and an ideal, 2-sheet foursome for Dubout to exploit, cartoonishly exposing the alcoholic indulgence and comfy corruption with which such gatherings play themselves out. At this bottom of this poster, there appears the following line of text: "Les chefs d'oeuvre n'ont pas d'age" (Masterpieces never age.") As much as this message was intended for Pagnol's trilogy, it refers just as equally to Dubout's masterful designs used to promote it.
Est: $1,700-$2,000.

425

426

428

427

426. Marius.
Artist: **H. Cerruti**
91¹/₄ x 62¹/₂ in./231.7 x 158.7 cm
Imp. de la Cinematographie Française, Paris
Cond B/Slight stains at folds,
Another interpretation of the film series' ongoing boys' night out, this time by illustrator Cerruti. By lessening the playful exaggeration of Dubout's creations, the designer arrives at a somewhat homier destination, giving into a nostalgic bonhomie that facily brings the warm camaraderie of the game to the fore without striking a single false note. The card game itself becomes something of a running joke in the trilogy, showing up again in *César*, supposedly twenty years later, with a hastily recruited substitute filling in for the deceased Panisse.
Est: $3,000-$4,000.

427. Fanny. 1950.
47 x 62¹/₂ in./119.5 x 158.7 cm
Imp. Monégasque, Monte-Carlo
Cond B+/Slight stains at folds.
Ref: Dubout, p. 17
Discovering that his son left Fanny pregnant, César comforts the heartbroken girl and urges her to marry his good friend Panisse, who is both smitten with her and able to give the child a normal home. The same advice is given to her with a tad more shrillness by her mother—one of the funniest figures in the movie, a critically acclaimed hilarious performance by Alida Rouffé—aided by a neighbor woman—which Dubout recreates in this 2-sheet design with characteristic overblown aplomb.
Est: $1,700-$2,000.

428. Fanny. 1950.
23¹/₂ x 31³/₄ in./60 x 80.6 cm
Imp. Monégasque, Monte-Carlo
Cond B+/Slight tears and stains at folds.
Ref: Dubout, p. 23
Such humanity pervades Dubout's cartoon creations that it's hard to imagine any other artist better suited to create promotional material for the films of Pagnol. Here, César and Fanny ponder the contents of a letter no doubt sent by the seafaring Marius. The pair strikes the perfect balance of poignancy and caricature while avoiding cloying sentimentality. In desperation, Fanny decides to accept the courtship of the widower, Panisse, and marries him, bringing up the child as if it were their own son.
Est: $1,500-$1,800.

429

432

430

431

433

DUBOUT/PAGNOL (continued)

429. César. 1950.
$47^{1}/_{4}$ x $31^{3}/_{4}$ in./119.8 x 80.5 cm
Imp. Monégasque, Monte-Carlo
Cond B/Slight tears and stains at folds; image and
colors excellent.
Ref: Dubout, pp. 60 & 61; Cinema Français, p. 65;
PAI-XXVII, 393
This dockside funeral procession may seem a bit irrev-
erent; however, it is in fact the initiating event which
brings the Marseilles saga to a happy conclusion.
César takes place twenty years after the events of the
previous two films. The processional is, in fact, for
Panisse, and Fanny's son, who has learned the truth
about his heritage, manages to reunite his biological
parents—with a bit of help from grandfather César—
for a satisfying and happy ending.
Est: $1,500-$1,800.

430. César. 1950.
47 x $62^{1}/_{4}$ in./119 x 158.1 cm
Imp. Monégasque, Monte-Carlo
Cond B+/Slight stains at folds.
Ref: Dubout, p. 25; Musée d'Affiches, 100;
Memoire du Cinema, p. 64; Phillips I, 206
The element that truly elevates Dubout's designs,
separating them from mere saccharine caricature and
turning them into actual character studies, is their
ability to unflinchingly capture the complete personality of the characters portrayed. Nowhere is this
more abundantly clear than in his design for the trilogy
ending *César*, and its warts-and-all portrait of Raimu as
César. The character, as portrayed by the distinguished
actor, is, in turn, wise, consoling, a bit of a homey
philosopher, but also capable of fits of temper and
given to discourses about people's character and
behavior. Dubout's haughty take on the character is
nothing short of spectacular.
Est: $1,700-$2,000.

431. César. 1950.
$23^{1}/_{2}$ x $31^{1}/_{2}$ in./59.7 x 80 cm
Imp. Monégasque, Monte-Carlo
Cond B/Slight tears and stains at folds.
Ref: Dubout, p. 27
Raimu, in all his larger-than-life glory, is the focus in
this design for the movie that bears his character's
name. None too pretty, but immediately accessible,
we get an effortless sense of the nature of the character from Dubout's caricature—regardless of whether or
not one has seen the film itself. The design generates
a tangible interest, drawing the viewer in with a desire
to further explore the nature of what makes this particular individual tick. A superb example that shows
that the everyday need not be lifeless and dismissible.
Est: $1,400-$1,700.

432. César Vu Par Dubout. 1950.
$31^{1}/_{2}$ x $22^{3}/_{4}$ in./80 x 57.7 cm
Imp. Monegasque, Monte-Carlo
Cond A–/Slight tears and stains at folds.

MARCEL PAGNOL

Though not precisely a household name in the
United States, Marcel Pagnol (1895-1974) was a
playwright and filmmaker whose essential folksy
world view made him in many ways the French
Frank Capra. Born in Aubergne near Marseilles—
his father a school principal with gently humanistic,
anticlerical views—young Pagnol at first followed in
his father's footsteps, becoming a teaching assistant by the age of 19. At first plying his educational
trade in the Marseilles area, he would transfer to
Paris in 1922. There, he gravitated to the theater

and cleverly used his academic background to write
"Topaze," a play revolving around a teacher who
reinvents himself as a smooth operator. It became
a huge success and enabled Pagnol to devote
himself full-time to a career in writing. The warm
humanism he inherited from his father colors a
majority of his projects, most especially his next
play, "Marius," an affectionate portrait of the people
in Southern France that he knew in his youth, populated with Marseilles actors, most notably Raimu,
a big bear of a man who became Pagnol's close

collaborator. The play ran for a year and made the
writer a wealthy man in his mid-30s. At this point he
turned his attention to the movies which had just
added sound. Turning "Marius" into a film—with the
stage cast and script virtually intact—led to worldwide success and spawning two sequels. Most of
the technical crew and many of the actors who
made the original installment in the trilogy were
retained by Pagnol in gratitude and remained with
him for the life of his producing company.

435

436

434

Ref: Dubout, p. 68

A series of ten black-and-white Dubout interpretive sketches are paneled to promote the César re-release of 1950. The storyboard recreations are actually extracted panels from an illustrative publication executed by Dubout of the trilogy—essentially an expertly crafted comic book version of the films—published by "Les Editions du Livre" firm of Monte-Carlo. And, in essence, ten delightful posters merged into one.
Est: $1,000-$1,200.

433. Le Schpountz/Fernandel. 1952.
471/2 x 63 in./120.6 x 160 cm
Imp. Monégasque, Monte-Carlo
Cond B+/Slight loss at top paper edge; slight stains at folds.
Ref: Dubout, p. 43; Phillips IV, 236
This toothsome rube loaded down with what would appear to be an estate's worth of accouterments expertly sums up with graphic shorthand the story line of *Le Schpountz*, Pagnol's comic tale starring Fernandel as a humble grocery clerk who envisions himself as the perfect actor to portray great tragic heroes on film. However, when he finally tries to break into the industry, his bumbling efforts at acting make him instead an instant success as a knockabout comedian. Fernandel was one of the Pagnol's favorite character actors.
Est: $1,500-$1,800.

434. Fernandel/"Topaze". 1950.
47 1/2 x 63 in./120.7 x 160 cm
Imp. Monégasque, Monte-Carlo
Cond B+/Slight tears and losses at paper edges.
Ref: Dubout, p. 41 (var)
Metaphorically, this image of Fernandel as a somewhat distracted teacher unaware of the system breaking down at his feet, encapsulates the measured chaos of the Pagnol film, *Topaze*. The story of a timid, naively honest schoolteacher flattered into accepting a position as the head of a crooked enterprise who in time turns the tables on the corrupt—going so far as to steal the chief villain's girlfriend—was an audience favorite since Pagnol first presented it as a play some twenty-three years earlier. But by 1951, this was the third French film version, with an additional two Broadway versions and two American filmings under its belt. Talk about a crowd pleaser.
Est: $1,500-$1,800.

MARCELLO DUDOVICH (1878-1962)

435. Grado. ca. 1933.
24 1/4 x 39 1/2 in./61.5 x 100.3 cm
Studio Editoriale Turistico, Milano
Cond B/Restored margins.
Ref: Dudovich, 280 (listing)
Wrapped up in a moment of ecstasy, this stunning bather prepares to take the plunge in this Dudovich promotion for the Northern Italian port city of Grado. Keeping things to a graphic minimum, the artist hits the highlights of the seaside resort with a growing reputation—nothing but fields of the deepest blue and the reverse silhouette of the Old Quarter; in other words, the surrounding waters of the lagoon, that give the town a certain grandeur, and the Cathedral of Santa Eufemia, that steeps the berg in tradition. At the age of 19, Dudovich arrived in Italy from his native Trieste. After an initial stint at Ricordi, he was hired at Chappuis in Bologna. He stayed in their employ until 1905, at which point he rejoined Ricordi, where he established himself as Italy's premier posterist, largely as a result of his refined, yet lively, posters for the Mele department store.
Est: $2,000-$2,500.

JEAN DUPAS (1882-1964)

436. Bordeaux. 1937.
24 1/8 x 39 1/4 in./61.3 x 99.6 cm
Imp. Rousseau Frères, Bordeaux
Cond A.
Ref: Weill, 317; Affiche Réclame, 98; PAI-XXI, 165
In all of his posters, Dupas presented highly stylized, very fashionable people in idealized and extravagant settings. In this poster created for the 1937 World's Fair, he gives us an allegorical composition in which the nude representing the city samples of its best achievements: fine architecture, shipping and, of course, the famous Bordeaux wine.
Est: $3,000-$4,000.

EGGLESTON

437. Pennsylvania Railroad/Washington.
24⁷/₈ x 39³/₄ in./ 63.2 x 101 cm
Cond A.

The stacked perspective may not be geographically
accurate, what with every monument and important
landmark in the District of Columbia being visible
from a single vantage point. But, it does, however,
make for a compelling and persuasive poster for the
Pennsylvania Railroad's service to the Nation's Capital.
It also was something of a motif when it came to the
railroad's advertising scheme for "The City Beautiful"
(see PAI-XXVIII, 561). Eggleston doesn't include a locomotive in his design—that might have got in the way of
the exquisitely struck balance between elegance and
monumental style. So why not let a leggy passenger
provide all the railway information necessary with the
mere act of deboarding. An exquisite memento of a
more gracious era.
Est: $4,000-$5,000.

LUDWIG L. EHRENBERGER

438. Bonbonnerie. ca. 1910.
35³/₄ x 49³/₄ in./90.7 x 126.4 cm
J. G. Velisch, München
Cond A.
Ref: DFP-III, 716

Ehrenberger's dates are not known, but he was very
active in the Munich graphic arts scene between 1905
and 1939, working for the magazine *Jugend* and other
publications, including the Berlin-based *Elegante
Welt*. And the elegant world is precisely where he
takes us in this poster for the Bonbonnière, advertised, in fact, as "Germany's Most Elegant Cabaret."
And the opulent decadence on display is perfectly
suited to the milieu, a dismissive submergence into

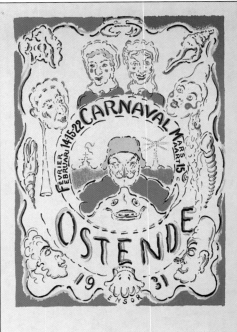

an availability of pleasures so intense as to leave the
chilly revelers in a joyous state of ennui. All for our
voyeuristic pleasure, since after all, life is a cabaret.
Est: $5,500-$6,500.

JULIUS USSY ENGELHARD (1883-1964)

439. Boccaccio. 1920.
35³/₄ x 47³/₈ in./90.8 x 120.3 cm
Oscar Consee, München
Cond A.

A moody hysteria pervades this design, helped in no
small part by the swirling mauve shadow cast by a

439   440

443

pair of high-spirited dancers, reveling with disciplined abandon in order to promote a revival of an operetta loosely based on the life of Italian Humanist prose and poetry writer Giovanni Boccaccio (1313-1375). Penned by "Franz von Suppé (1819-1895) . . . (who) was in many ways the father of Viennese operetta . . . *Boccaccio* . . . (was) one of those happy ones set in Italy, allowing for all sorts of native dances. . . . The role of Boccaccio was taken by Antonie Link (women would traditionally play the part until the 1920s) and

Rosa Streitman was his beloved Fiametta in a clever libretto which placed the actual poet Boccaccio in his own Florence . . . Boccaccio's name alone must have intrigued a good many theatergoers to visit the many theaters all over the world in which Suppé's *Meisterwerk* played" (*Operettas: A Theatrical History*, by Richard Traubner, pp. 104-109).
Est: $3,500-$4,000.

440. Fries, München. 1922.
34⁷/₈ x 49¹/₈ in./88.7 x 124.8 cm
Kunst im Druck, München
Cond B+/Slight tears at folds and edges; image and
       colors excellent.
Ref: PAI-XXIV, 271
Born in Sumatra, Engelhard returned to his parents' native Germany where he studied in Munich with Franz von Stuck. Settling there and becoming a busy posterist and illustrator, he contributed to *Simplicissimus* and all the leading fashion magazines of this period. We can see here why he was such a favorite of these publications: The handsome profiles, assured postures and generally elegant air of this male trio wordlessly reinforce the claim that Fries is *the* men's tailor in Munich.
Est: $2,000-$2,500.

441. Deutschland. ca. 1928.
24⁷/₈ x 39¹/₄ in./63.2 x 99.6 cm
Reichsbahnzentrale für den Deutschen Reiseverkehr, Berlin
Cond B+/Slight tears at folds and edges; image and
       colors excellent.
Ref: Sachs, 111; Voyage, p. 57; Phillips I, 216
Contrasted nicely off the gunmetal beast of iron rail transport, this Art Deco beauty couldn't seem more simultaneously alien and at home in her surroundings. The combination of towering power and fashionable lilt make for an ideal fit in this tourism poster for the German cause, that clues us in with no uncertain terms that Germany is the perfect travel destination.
Est: $1,700-$2,000.

JAMES ENSOR (1860—1949)

442. Carnaval/Ostende. 1931.
12 x 16¹/₂ in./30.5 x x41.9 cm
Cond A. Framed.
Ref: PAI-XXV, 299
With a border made up of eccentric faces, sea creatures and shells, Ensor indulges his predilection for the slightly offbeat drawings that look like they were somewhat hastily sketched, yet show a great ingenuity and inventiveness. At other times, this unpredictable Belgian designer could easily change his mood to impressionism, dreamy lyricism, realism or biting satire, yet always remain an original. *Rare!*
Est: $1,200-$1,500.

HANS RUDI ERDT (1883-1918)

443. Lloyd George. 1908.
37 x 55¹/₂ in./94 x 141 cm
Hollerbaum & Schmidt, Berlin
Cond A/Slightly mismatched sheets.
A rather distinguished looking 2-sheet bit of promotion for "Lloyd George in Berlin" that undoubtedly plays upon the more salacious aspects of the British politician's lifestyle rather than the rather dry historical visit George made to Berlin in 1908 to discuss a national health insurance proposal being considered by the Kaiser. This very rare and virtually forgotten short film regarding the British political maverick in his salad days starred German silent film character actor Albert Paulig, running probably no longer than two reels, while poking fun at the impeccably English attired international playboy. Though Mr. George (1863-1945) acquired a reputation for cutting a wide swath among susceptible ladies—both at home and, especially, abroad—it's key to remember that the Welsh firebrand was thoroughly despised in Germany, as he served as British Prime Minister during WW I, and was largely credited for bringing about the defeat of Germany by persuading the United States to enter the War. Hence, the unflattering celluloid tomfoolery presented in flattering Erdt fashion.
Est: $2,500-$3,000.

445

446

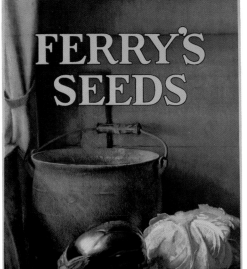

447

448

450

HANS FABIGAN (1901-1975)

444. Rainerdiele.
33 x 46³/₄ in./84 x 119 cm
Piller Druck, Wien
Cond A–/Slight tears and stains at paper edges.
A few scattered blossoms, twin snifters and a classic Baby Grand, all laid down with Art Deco simplicity by Fabigan. The implied romance and tony attitude is all the evidence necessary to convince the passerby that it's always summer in the Rainerdiele, a Viennese piano bar. Educated at the Graphic Study and Research Institute in Vienna, Fabigan would move to Berlin in 1927, becoming active in fashion design, cartoon illustrations and poster work. During the early '30s, he would move back to his native Vienna, continuing to work with great success and became a member of the Vienna Secession in 1951.
Est: $1,000-$1,200.

L. LUCIEN FAURE (1892-?)

445. Claudine. 1901.
39⁷/₈ x 54⁷/₈ in./101.2 x 139.5 cm
Imp. Charles Verneau, Paris
Cond A.
Ref (Both Var): Gold, 83; PAI-XXX, 194
In the full text version of this poster, "Two books about Claudine, a popular schoolgirl literary heroine

around the turn of the century, are offered for three-and-a-half francs each. (Their authorship here is attributed to the newspaperman and playwright Willy, who, in fact, stole the credit from his wife, Colette). Faure chose to advertise them by depicting the dynamic and controversial Polaire, who played the role on stage. Endowed with a generous bosom, the actress defied convention from the start of career . . . by refusing to confine her figure in the corsets prescribed by fashion dictates . . . predictably pushing her career ever higher" (Gold, p. 60). *This is the before-letters version.*
Est: $1,000-$1,200.

G. FAVRE

446. Peugeot.
31³/₈ x 47¹/₈ in./79.6 x 119.7 cm
Affiches Gaillard, Paris
Cond A.
Peugeot's trademark was the lion—note the gender distinction. So it's interesting that it's a lioness seen here, padding her way across the grid-marked globe with a Peugeot bicycle grasped as tenderly in the fangs of her powerful jaw as if it were a newborn cub. A wonderful conjunction of might and finesse. An imaginatively stylized design from an artist who produced a large body of posters, but neglected to leave any biographical information. The Bibliothèque Nationale has

44 Favre posters in its collection; this image is not among them.
Est: $1,200-$1,500.

FERRY'S SEEDS

447. Ferry's Seeds. 1923.
Artist: **Anonymous**
20¹/₂ x 27³/₄ in./52 x 70.5 cm
Cond B+/Slight tears at folds.
Dexter Mason Ferry of New York State grew up in the early-19th century, accumulating a great deal of agricultural knowledge, as was fairly common for men of the period. When he was nearly twenty, he went off to seek his fame and fortune in Detroit, which at that point was a center of horticultural interest. In 1856, Mr. Ferry, along with Milo T. Gardner and Eber F. Church founded the seed firm of Gardner, Ferry & Church. Their first price list preceded the United States Department of Agriculture by almost thirty years. Eventually evolving into the D. M. Ferry & Co., the name Ferry Seeds became synonymous with gardening quality. This rustically composed offset-printed design—copyrit by the company in 1923—conveys an ideal, no-frills comestibility that the company wished to associate with their vegetative line.
Est: $1,000-$1,200.

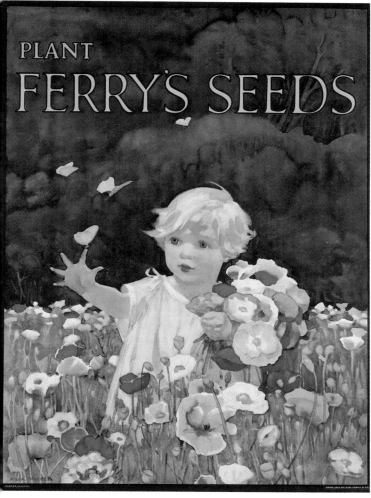

449

452

451

48. **Ferry's Seeds.** 1925.
rtist: **Anonymous**
0³/₈ x 27³/₄ in./51.7 x 70.5 cm
ond A–/Unobtrusive slight tears.
Reputation is a growing thing, and our reputation has
een growing since 1856." This quote from the 1953
erry-Morse catalogue points up the firm grasp the
ompany held in their sowing niche, and the poster
om some thirty years earlier prettily reinforces that
ie seed concern had occupied that place for some

time, able to promote themselves with the simple
beauty of flourishing hollyhocks and the unaffected
charm of their tender. Until Mr. Ferry began packaging
garden seeds in small envelopes, there had been no
such business on the market. He began offering
assortments of packets for store owners which were
tailored to the growing conditions in each shop's vicinity and frequently relying on florid posters to plant the
seed of commerce in the minds of the consumer.
Est: $1,200-$1,500.

449. Ferry's Seeds. 1925.
Artist: **Milda Belemer**
20¹/₂ x 27³/₄ in./52 x 70.6 cm
Cond A–/Slight tears at edges.
This Ferry seeds design from a previously unseen artist
overflows with a whimsical tenderness that could only
have come from a female hand, delicate and sure, at
once maternal and nostalgic. The unjaded simplicity
of the pitch—the sunny young girl, fascinated by her
bucolic surroundings and absorbed with her butterfly
encounter—opiates the viewer as they join in on this
romp through a field of posies. Simply lovely.
Est: $2,000-$2,500.

GEORGES DE FEURE (1868—1943)

450. Paris-Almanach. 1894.
23³/₄ x 31¹/₄ in./60.5 x 79.5 cm
Imp. Bourgerie, Paris
Cond A.
Ref: DFP-II, 342; Maindron, p. 64; Abdy, p. 155;
      Timeless Images, 40; Defeure, p. 72; Gold, 79;
      PAI-XXX, 195
"The advertised booklet was a guide to Paris attractions
published by Ed. Sagot, which de Feure shows in the
hand of a woman traveling alone and wishing to sample
the pulse of the city. As always, the artist manages to
suggest hidden depths. Although looking at the merry
throng, the figure remains a bit apart, oddly aloof, and
slightly mysterious" (Gold, p. 58). DeFeure, the con-
summate designer, created not only this poster, but
the fashionable garb on the arresting viewer.
Est: $2,500-$3,000.

H. J. FLEMMING

451. Hermanwile Clothes.
24 x 36³/₄ in./61 x 92.7 cm
Hayes Litho. Buffalo, N. Y.
Cond C+/Tears and stains, largely at edges. Framed.
Ah youth. That sweet, fleeting time when a spiffy set
of new clothes and a passing smile from a pretty gal as
she drove by was enough to put the spring back into
the old step. And though we get a peak at the Hermanwile women's clothes, it's the hand-tailored men's
"Freshman Clothes" that take center stage in this
Flemming design. And if the clothiers at Hermanwile
could make peg-legged suits perfectly suited to these
two storkish fellas, then just think what they could sew
for the normally proportioned male.
Est: $1,500-$1,800.

FOÄCHE

452. La Garonne. 1898.
20 x 27 in./51 x 68.7 cm
Imp. Cassan Fils, Toulouse
Cond A.
Ref: DFP-II, 359 (var); Abdy, p. 148; PAI-XXX, 500
In this rare, before letters version, it was a limited-
edition print offered by Cassan Fils printers to its
valued clients; in another edition, it was a full-fledged
poster for the printer, with his name in large type at
the bottom of the design. "Foäche was an artist from
the south of France, who worked in Toulouse. His
poster for 'La Garonne' has close affinities with Mucha's
second 'Salon des Cent' poster, yet it has independent
merit. As befits the portrayal of a water goddess, the
coloring is aqueous, pale blue, and pale green. The
sky in the background is streaked with gold. On the
panel on the right he combines two favorite symbols
by gently transforming a star into a narcissus" (Abdy,
p. 149). *The best specimen of this image that we
have ever seen!*
Est: $2,500-$3,000.

453

454

455

456

458

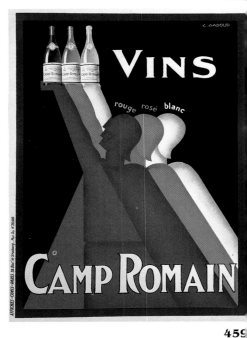

459

HENRY CLAUDIUS FORESTIER (1875-1922)

453. Societé Suisse de Publitité. 1896.
29³/₄ x 47¹/₄ in./75.7 x 120 cm
Societé Suisse d'Affiches Artistiques, Genève
Cond B+/Slight tears at folds.
Ref: Genève, 11
Shouting himself into distortion, this crier hits the cobblestones, noisemaker in hand, to spread the word about the Swiss Society of Artistic Posters, a fraternity founded in order to promote the Genovese printing firm of the same name. Primarily known for his wood-cut illustrations, Forestier also produced illustrations for various publications. Later in his career, he turned to still life, landscapes and figure studies.
Est: $1,200-$1,500.

GUSTAVE (1849-1923) & GEO. FRAIPONT

454. Paris à Bruxelles.
29¹/₄ x 42¹/₈ in./74.3 x 107 cm
Affiches Artistiques, Paris
Cond B+/Slght tears and stains near edges.
Though the Northern Railway is promoting their under-four hour Paris to Brussels daily express service, there is a relaxed, homey feel to the design not usual for something promoting express transport. The French sophistication/Belgian rusticity angle—Brussels is a major European center of commerce, correct?—is a particularly interesting one coming from Brussels-born artist Gustave Fraipoint—working here in conjunction with his brother George—who was a painter and illustrator in Paris, where he collaborated on *Le Courrier Français* and other publications. He also created numerous posters, largely for the French rail, most of them between 1891 and 1896. He was named a Knight of the Legion of Honor in 1892. Unfortunately, no such biographical depth could be discovered for his brother.
Est: $1,200-$1,500.

GEO FRANÇOIS

455. Evian les Bains. 1929.
25 x 39⁷/₈ in./63.5 x 101.3 cm
Lucien Serre, Paris
Cond A.
Ref: PAI-XVIII, 104
The view of the course at the famous spa resort of Evian is lined up like a good golf stroke in order to show to best advantage the superb site overlooking the town and Lac Leman (also known as Lake Geneva), with Switzerland on the far shore. The designer's rich color scheme of greens, golds and turquoise virtually causes it to pulsate with an inner glow. Both in coloring and composition, François recalls the far better known Broders.
Est: $1,500-$1,800.

DOUDOW FRAPOTAT

456. Gourdant. 1933.
31 x 46¹/₈ in./78.8 x 117.2 cm
Imp. Reunies, Lyon
Cond A-/Slight tears in top corners.

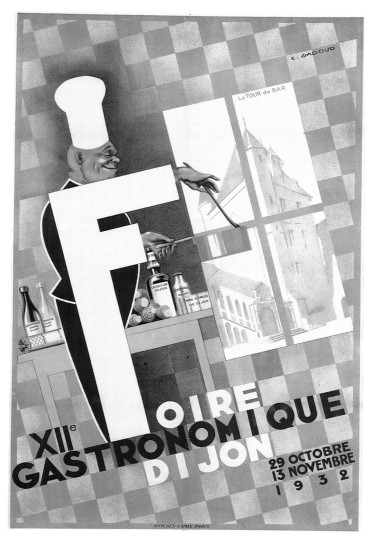

457

460

461

tion, hinting at everything, but in truth revealing nothing. And in case there is any confusion as to the location of the store, it's situated not in Vienna, but rather in Vienne, France, a sunny spot on the east side of the Rhône, overlooking the bend in the river as it makes its way through the crystalline rocks marking the last outposts of the Massif Central.
Est: $1,000-$1,200.

M. FRESSINET

457. Great Skating Rink.
$31^5/8$ x $47^3/4$ in./80.3 x 121.7 cm
Imp. Moullot, Marseille
Cond B/Unobtrusive tears at folds and edges.
Ref: PAI-XXV, 313
The skating rink advertises its services in St. Etienne, in the Rhône Valley, in English, possibly hoping it may enhance its appeal to the sophisticates. There is a Cappiello-like feeling about the design: first of all, the use of plain black as the backdrop, secondly the the-atrical-caricature faces of the skaters, and finally a certain flamboyance of the postures. Despite the designer's obvious competence, we have been unable to obtain any information about him.
Est: $1,700-$2,000.

GABY

458. La Presse.
$30^1/2$ x 46 in./77.4 x 117 cm
Lemercier, Paris
Cond B–/Restored tears at folds and edges.
A very straightforward advertisement for subscriptions to *The Presse*, a Paris daily enjoying its fifty-ninth year of publication. Not only are the savings significant for both local and out-of-town delivery, but two editions of

the paper will economically arrive on your doorstep daily. One interesting design feature: notice how the avian adornment of the woman's hat is subtly echoed in the bird-in-flight presentation of the gazette, imply-ing both speedy delivery and vaunted journalistic goals.
Est: $1,200-$1,500.

C. GADOUD

459. Vins Camp Romain.
$46^1/2$ x $62^1/2$ in./118 x 158.7 cm
Affiches Camis, Paris
Cond A. Framed.
Ref: PAI-X, 236
Stylish Art Deco image of three centurions raising three bottles of the product—red, rosé and white. With the trademark "Roman Field," the reference is obvious.
Est: $2,000-$2,500.

460. XIIe Foire Gastronomique/Dijon. 1932.
$30^3/8$ x $46^3/8$ in./ 77.2 x 117.8 cm
Affiches Camis, Paris
Cond B+/Slight tears and creases at folds and edges.
Framed.
Ref: Karcher, 504
Three years after Beauville sentenced a chicken to an untimely demise for our gustatory pleasure (*see* No. 307), Gadoud plots out a more refined repast in this spit and polish kitchen cast against a blue-toned gridwork in the name of the Twelfth Dijon Gastronomic Fair, whose window of tourism opens onto the heaven-bound glory of the Bar Tower. And as Gadoud has incorporated the capital consonant of the event with the satisfied cook, I think a fair question to ask is whether the chef makes the fair or if the fair makes the chef? Either way, it's the attendee who wins.
Est: $1,700-$2,000.

smart pair of Art Deco apparitions appear to be get-ting ready to paint the town rosé. And who better than couple of spirits to advertise the wares available at he Gourdant haberdashers, for only such sleek silho-ettes could fashion such a stylishly abstract promo-

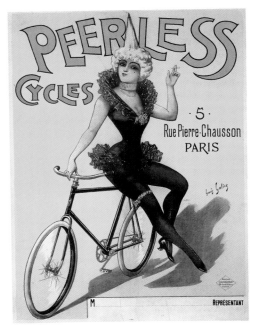

462

463

464

H. GALDIKAS

461. Lithuanie.
24¹/₂ x 39 in./62 x 99.2 cm
"Spindulio" Ofsetas, Kaunas
Cond A–/Slight tears at edges.
A postimpressionistic quietude breezes through this design with whisper-soft promises of unharried leisure awaiting in the popular Lithuanian summer resort town of Palanga on the shore of the Baltic Sea. From our perch atop Birutes Kalnas, Galdikas' sun-shaded vista soothes the mind and unburdens the soul. This hill, incidentally, is named after a prominent pair from Lithuanian mythology. According to legend, there was a pagan shrine at the foot of the hill during the 14th century. That shrine was where a beautiful priestess named Birute used to light ceremonial fires. Having heard about Birute, Kestutis, the Grand Duke of Lithuania, rode over on his horse to take her for his wife. However, Birute wanted no part of his plan and answered that she had promised the gods to guard her virginity as long as she lived. Undeterred, Kestutis took her by force back to his capital of Trakai, where he married her. Some historians allege that after Kestutis' tragic death, Birute returned to Palanga and served the Gods until she died. She is supposedly buried in the hill which is now named in her honor.
Est: $1,000-$1,200.

LOUIS GALICE

462. Peerless Cycles.
38⁷/₈ x 53⁵/₈ in./98.7 x 136.2 cm
Affiches Louis Gallice, Paris
Cond B–/Restored tears at folds.
The disarming coiffure of this smoking stunner hawking the Peerless bicycle reminded us of a curvaceous horseback rider that Pal used to promote the Cirque Molier (see PAI-XXX, 147). You be the judge, but the association is an intriguing one. Though the identity of this stunning equestrian is not known to the contemporary eye, it's very possible that she made quite a splash in the turn-of-the-century collective consciousness. And as she was known for her riding skills in one arena, wouldn't she then be an excellent spokesperson for the pedal-powered mount? Recognized as one of the graphic chroniclers of the Montmartre scene, Galice was also a prolific illustrator and successful printer.
Est: $1,400-$1,700.

ANDRE GIROUX (1895-1965)

463. Auvergne. 1938.
24³/₈ x 39¹/₈ in./62 x 99.3 cm
Editions Paul Matial, Paris
Cond A.
Giroux takes to the skies in order to promote travel to the Auvergne region, an area which forms the core of France's Massif Central. An ironic choice as the graphic enticement for the National French Railway Society

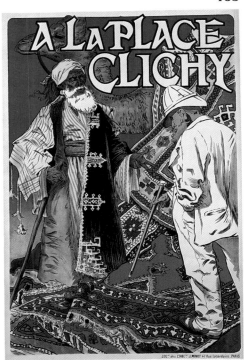

465

and its well-grounded service to the volcanic locale, but an inspired one at that. From this aerial view, the designer focuses our attention on the rugged dormant domes heaving skyward and their cratered lakes, providing a mere glimpse of the vicinity's Romanesque architecture and dropping only the subtlest possible hint of the actual rail service with a far-off trestle.
Est: $1,000-$1,200.

A. GODEFROY (1854-?)

464. Yacht Club de France.
22⁷/₈ x 31 in./58 x 78.7 cm
Imp. Gaston Lefèvre, Havre
Cond A–/Unobtrusive tears at folds.
Godefroy provides the viewer with a porthole view into the physically rigorous, yet aesthetically captivating world of competitive yachting in this promotion for the week long French Yacht Club's Grand Prix International Regatta being held in Deauville. Atypically for advertising material with a global slant, no national flags are

466

flown or hoopla generated for the host country—the man versus nature physics of the event rebuffing all patriotism. Godefroy was the pseudonym of either one of two artists: M. Vallet or Auguste Viollier, between whose identity the historians are evenly divided. This design poses something of a deviation for an illustrator best remembered for his childlike imagery and humorous contributions to *Rires et Grimaces*, *La Galerie Comique*, *le Bon Vivant*, *La Caricature*, *Le Chat Noir*, *Cocorico* and *Le Rire*.
Est: $1,500-$1,800.

EUGENE GRASSET (1841-1917)

465. A la Place Clichy. 1891.
30¹/₂ x 46¹/₄ in./77.5 x 117.4 cm
J. Minot, Paris
Cond A.
Ref (All Var): DFP-II, 401; Reims, 683;
  Berthon & Grasset, p. 37; Maîtres, 18; PAI-XXX, 511
Grasset did much to introduce the concept and practice of Art Nouveau in France. In fact, Grasset "brought Art Nouveau to the aid of the poster: it was to become a worldwide vehicle of the art of advertising. In France, Grasset was the pioneer of an attempt, like that of William Morris in England, to reconcile art and indus-

467

469

468

H. GRAY (Henri Boulanger, 1858-1924)
For other Gray posters, see Nos. 63 & 101.

466. Georges Richard/Automobiles & Cycles.
46³/₄ x 71¹/₂ in./118.7 x 181.5 cm
Courmont Frères, Paris
Cond A–/Unobtrusive folds.
Tally ho! The practicality of trading your steed in on a bicycle for a fox hunt doesn't seem to make a whole lot of horse sense. However, sense sometimes has very little to do with advertising and the image of this tri-corned huntress preparing to leap over the rail between her and her prey is a stunning conceit. Not to mention that the audacity of the idea has the spaniel closest to her rolling about the fields in what looks to be a fit of laughter. At the very least, this new mount has elimi-nated the annoyance of riding sidesaddle. Gray exe-cuted at least one other poster for the automobile and bicycle manufacturer (*see* PAI-XXII, 21), that time focus-ing totally on the company's shamrock trademark.
Est: $1,700-$2,000.

467. Le Tréport. ca. 1897.
28⁷/₈ x 41¹/₂ in./ 73.3 x 105.5 cm
Imp. E. Bougard, Paris
Cond B/Slight tears and stains at folds and paper edges.
Ref (All Var): Train à l'Affiche, 32; Sport à l'Affiche, 161;
    Tourism/Suntory, 72; Affiches Publicitaires, 63;
    PAI-XXVI, 312
A buxom bathing beauty in a frilly thigh-length suit lures us to the seaside resort only "3 hours from Paris" on behalf of the Northern Railroad. Tréport is on the English Channel, 171 km. northwest of Paris between Dieppe and Abbeville. This is a third version of this image that we have come across: this "naughty" one with extensive departure information, another "wanton" one where she is being admired from afar by two favorably impressed dandies (*see* PAI-XXVI, 312) and a censored version which has a sheer little skirt cover-ing the woman's bare thighs (*see* PAI-XXIII, 277).
Est: $2,000-$2,500.

P. F. GRIGNON

468. Pianos A. Bord/Blondel.
18¹/₈ x 25¹/₈ in./46.2 x 63.8 cm
Imp. P. M., Paris
Cond B/Slight stains near edges.
The elements are few, but they add up to the only required components to create an evening concerto of musical distinction—an A. Bord Grand, an untamable-haired maestro and an exquisite composition, here labeled "Melisande," no doubt a movement from Debussy's operatic masterwork, "Melisande and Pelleas." The text medallion at left informs us that the piano makers have produced 132,000 of their opulent stringed instruments as of the time of this poster's production and that serious inquiries as to how to obtain them may be directed towards one Mr. Blondel, their regional sales agent.
Est: $1,200-$1,500.

JULES-ALEXANDRE GRÜN (1868-1938)
For other Grün posters, see Nos. 64 & 65.

469. Chimay-Villegiature. 1900.
33¹/₄ x 49¹/₈ in./84.3 x 125 cm
Imp. Chaix, Paris
Cond A–/Unobtrusive folds.
Ref: PAI-IX, 303
The three visitors to Chimay take advantage of the free skeet shooting instructions, one of the attractions offered by this Belgian resort in the Ardennes hills. You've got to admire the pluck of the Annie Oakley in red, drawing a bead on her clay pigeon and ready to mix it up. Her striped-togged friend on the other hand looks more like a viewer than a shooter, dressed for-mally and taking in the action from the spectator side of her lorgnette.
Est: $2,000-$2,500.

try . . . Interested as he was in all the applied arts, he came naturally to the poster" (Weill, p. 32). This detailed slice of exotica clearly illustrates the fact that the Place Clichy department store was the premiere importer of oriental merchandise, with this unsigned version of Grasset's exquisite creation covering that notion without the extraneous clutter of sales copy. The oft used design went through several printings and editions, beginning in 1891. *This is the smaller format.*
Est: $1,200-$1,500.

470

472

473

471

GURTLER

470. Zebraline.
44^1/$_2$ x 60^1/$_2$ in./113 x 153.7 cm
S.M.I., Paris
Cond B+/Slight tears at folds.
Precisely why this product takes its name from the fleet striped equine is left to conjecture as Zebraline no longer graces the market. Perhaps the cleaning polish for frying pans and ranges was so labeled because it contained a blended mixture of some sort of abrasive material swirled together with a bleaching agent. Whatever the meaning behind the moniker, this high-hoofing zebra with the punky bristle brush mane looks game for any scrubbing challenge that comes his way.
Est: $1,200-$1,500.

L. GUY

471. Bal des Etudiants. 1901
33^5/$_8$ x 97^7/$_8$ in./85.4 x 248.6 cm
Imp. G. Gounouilhou, Bordeaux
Cond A.
Ref: PAI-XXVII, 425
This 2-sheet poster is a mind-blowing tribute to what a Bacchanalia the Students' Ball of February 2, 1901, must have been. As an extravagantly attired female reveler positions herself beneath an ornate archway—

unaware that the Devil is lurking beneath her skirt or that one of his impish legion is carefully unlacing her outfit—a tag-team of rogues does their best to ply her with bubbly, one of them distracting her, while the other keeps her glass constantly filled to the rim. A magnificent nod to unbridled merriment, open to any number of lascivious interpretations.
Est: $2,500-$3,000.

SIKKER HANSEN (1897-1955)

472. Davre-Gryn. 1945.
24^1/$_4$ x 33^1/$_4$ in./61.8 x 84.3 cm
Permild & Rosengreen, Køpenhagen
Cond A/P.
There's nothing in this design to give the viewer the slightest hint as to the product being advertised. It is, however, quaintly beautiful, its sun-dappled impressionism and broadly sketched pastoral scene striking a most appealing chord. Who would guess, unless you speak Danish of course, that it's for a brand of grits? The only connection being that something this natural would naturally be an excellent source of healthful nutrition for your children. Hansen was a painter and book illustrator whose work was greatly influenced by folk art. He made many drawings for the Danish jour-

nal *Politiken* from 1932 on. This poster, as well as the following, comes from his most active poster producing period of the 1940s and '50s.
Est: $1,000-$1,200.

473. Cirkel Kaffe. 1955.
33^3/$_8$ x 24^1/$_8$ in./84.8 x 61.4 cm
Permild & Rosengreen, Copenhagen
Cond A/P.
Ref: PAI-XXVI, 318
The exotic image of a beautiful, unapologetically ethnic, long-necked Black woman, accented solely with the flat white of her dress straps, hair bands and jewelry make for an arresting and unforgettable image to promote Cirkel coffee. The identical image was also utilized by the beverage firm in a vertical format.
Est: $1,200-$1,500.

HAUSLER

474. Franck Cichorie.
36^1/$_8$ x 49^1/$_4$ in./91.7 x 125 cm
Atelier Häusler, Bern
Cond A–/Unobtrusive folds.
Calling upon the coffee manufacturer's trademark burnt umber and navy color scheme, Hausler snags

ED. SAGOT

ESTAMPES & AFFICHES ILLUSTRÉES
39 bis Rue de Chateaudun, Paris

476

474

475

477

the viewers' attention with an unassuming ease while quietly informing us that Franck has been catering to the caffeinated needs of the beverage consuming public for a full century. In addition to their iconographic coffee grinder, the artist sets to paper an unexpectedly coquettish spokesmodel—a sly allusion to the chicory concern's century of service—utterly enveloped in layered antiquity, yet openly flirtatious and invitational in an overtly contemporary manner. All told, a perfectly suited image to the piquant coffee additive, so popular that at times, it even served as a coffee substitute. **Est: $1,500-$1,800.**

FRANK HAZENPLUG (1873-?)

475. The Chap-Book. 1896.
14 x 20¹/₈ in./35.6 x 53.8 cm
Cond B+/Slight tears at folds and paper edges.
Ref: Lauder, 100; Margolin, p. 100; Keay, p. 28; Reims, 1234; PAI-XIV, 283
Active mostly as an illustrator for the Chicago publisher Stone & Kimball, Hazenplug produced three posters for the *Chap-Book*, plus a few others. He liked flat expanses of color without much reliance on drawn lines. Here, we have a blissful reader whose satisfaction comes either from the wine she's consumed or the *Chap-Book* she leans against her goblet. **Est: $1,000-$1,200.**

PAUL C. HELLEU (1859-1927)

476. Ed. Sagot: 3 Versions. 1900.
Each Approx: 29 x 41 in./73.7 x 104.2 cm
Imp. Chaix, Paris
Cond A.
Ref: DFP-II, 466; Affichomanie, 3; Takashimaya, 25; Gold, 34; PAI-II, 173; PAI-XXX, 80
"The customer of Sagot's, one of the principal print and poster dealers in Paris, considers several pieces of artwork. Even though we see only her back, we can tell from the way she leans forward how intensely she's concentrating. Sagot was an early convert to the lure of posters and contributed substantially to the emergence of posters as collectible art in the 1890s" (Gold, p. 23). All three known versions of this design together in one convenient lot: the before letters version, the complete text version and a third version with olive tones injected into the normal sepia design. The reason for this has never been uncovered; however, it may have been a trial print, produced, but never widely distributed. **Est: $1,700-$2,000.** (3)

ARMAND HENRION (1875-?)

477.Grandes Régates Internationales. 1900.
26³/₄ x 35¹/₄ in./68 x 89.5 cm
Gordinne, Liège
Cond B/Restored tears at folds.
Ref: Belgique Sportives, 59
"The artificial lake in Warfuuz (Belgium) was created during the reign of Léopold II, when it was determined that it was necessary to construct a dam at Wayai. . . . Spa remained, above all, a vacation spot, and Henrion's poster, far from insisting on depicting the highly competitive character of the oar, radiates to the contrary a pleasant side: an amiable playful flirtation during one sun-kissed day between a young athlete and a charming damsel" (Belgiques Sportives, p. 62). Henrion was a Belgian still-life and landscape painter who eventually moved to France and became naturalized there; his posters are few and rare. He had a long standing relationship with the Liège printing house, Charles Gordinne and Son. **Est: $1,400-$1,700**

478

479

ADOLFO HOHENSTEIN (1854-1928)

478. Monaco/Exposition de Canots Automobiles.
1900.
33 x 47³/₈ in./84 x 120.2 cm
G. Ricordi, Milano
Cond B+/Unobtrusive slight tears at folds.
Ref: Ricordi, 168; Menegazzi-I, 124;
   Manifesti Italiani, p. 67; Timeless Images;
   Gold, 135; PAI-XXX, 234
Hohenstein's design for a motorboat exhibition and race is simple but spectacular: from aboard a boat, looking across the bows of a smart helmswoman, we see the waters off Monaco teeming with craft and sparkling in the sun. The artist returns to his trademark method for balancing the visual interest of a distant background versus a large format figure: he allots most of the color to the former, and renders the latter in a few sparse lines and the brown of the paper.
Est: $7,000-$9,000.

479. Monte Carlo/Tir aux Pigeons. 1900.
34¹/₄ x 49⁵/₈ in./87.2 x 126 cm
G. Ricordi, Milan
Cond A–/Unobtrusive folds.
Ref: Menegazzi-I, 304; Affiches Azur, 306; Ricordi, 167;
   Riccione, 2; PAI-XXIV, 323
Monte Carlo never permitted gambling to be an advertised drawing card, and, in fact, the city offered all sorts of sporting and social events to the well-heeled winter traveler seeking diversion in a Mediterranean climate. Here, in the rosy glow of sunset, Hohenstein's shotgun-toting gentleman makes a strong appeal on behalf of the pleasures of pigeon shooting. Hohenstein divides the design in half diagonally with an extravagant Art-Nouveau swirl of flat color that also serves as background for the text.
Est: $2,500-$3,000.

LUDWIG HOHLWEIN (1874-1949)

For another Hohlwein poster, see No. 179.
For a book on Hohlwein, see Books and Periodicals.

481

**480. Münchener Künstlerfarben-fabrik Dr. Karl
   Fiedler.** 1907.
16¹/₄ x 32³/₄ in./41.2 x 83.2 cm
Vereingte Druckerein & Kunstanstalten, München
Cond B+/Slight creasing and tears, largely near edges;
   image and colors excellent.
Ref: DFP-III, 316; Wember, 407; Hohlwein/Stuttgart, 4;
   PAI-I, 127

480

482

483

484

Weill comments that "Beginning with his first efforts, Hohlwein found his style with disconcerting facility; it would vary little for the next forty years. The drawing was perfect from the start: . . . nothing seemed alien to him, and in any case, nothing posed a problem for him. . . . His figures are full of touches of color and a play of light and shade that brings them out of their background and gives them substance" (pp. 107-110). Here, he takes a rather literal tack for Dr. Karl Feidler's Munich Artist Color Works, his palette backed by a fiddler of such stern institutional stolidity that the concept turns amusingly on itself.
Est: $3,000-$3,500.

481. Monopol La Falce.
$11^1/_2$ x $17^1/_2$ in./29.2 x 44.5 cm
Vereinigte Kunstanstalten A.G.: Kaufbeuren (Bavaria)
Cond A–/Slight stains near edges.
Ref: Hohlwein/Frenzel
As this Italian-language sales pitch for Monopol scythes already proclaims the sickle to be the preferred brand of farmers, we can only assume that Hohlwein's poster is intended to bring weekend gardeners and recreational tillers into the fold. And he does a magnificent job, breathing intense vitality into his earthy ambassador and filling the entire design with a giddiness with which most gardening implements never come in contact. *Rare!*
Est: $1,200-$1,500.

482. Zoologischer Garten München. 1912.
12 x $16^3/_8$ in./30.5 x 41.5 cm
Vereinigte Druckereien, München
Cond B/Slight tears and stains at edges. Framed.
Ref (All Var): DFP-III, 1408; Hohlwein, 123; Hohlwein/Stuttgart, 68;
   PAI-XXI, 231
During the most productive period of Hohlwein's career—his years in Munich—he made posters for many city institutions, including several for the zoo. This broadly-blocked image of a leopard and a panther shows the artist's powers of abstraction and reaffirms his celebrity as an animal painter. *This is the rare smaller format of this famous image.*
Est: $3,000-$4,000.

485

486

487

488

489

LUDWIG HOHLWEIN (continued)

483. Zoologischer Garten München. 1912.
36¹/₄ x 49¹/₄in./92 x 125 cm
Vereinigte Druckerein & Kunstanstalten, München
Cond B/Slight tears at folds.
Ref: DFP-III, 1407; Hohlwein/Stuttgart, 67; Hohlwein, 180; Wember, 420; PAI-XXVII, 456
Although Hohlwein's specialty was to portray the upper crust of German society in his early posters, he was a sportsman who enjoyed being with and portraying animals; it can be said that he was as much at home depicting the flora and fauna of the wilds as that of the metropolitan boulevards. For the Munich Zoo he produced five posters; this version, graced with the stately bearing of two eagles, is one of the best of the series.
Est: $3,000-$4,000.

484. Burger-Kehl & Co./PKZ. 1911.
37¹/₂ x 50³/₄ in./ 95.3 x 129 cm
Gebr. Fretz, Zurich
Cond B+/Horizontal folds. Framed.
Ref: Hohlwein/Stuttgart, 53; PAI-VI, 299
The light tan suit goes perfectly with the celadon green of the topcoat, tie and hat, as well as the purple of the gloves. Perhaps to emphasize the point about color coordination, Hohlwein goes to the extreme of having the man's face match the gloves! Only the fox terrier escapes the coordination movement, sticking to his own russet patches. This is the last of three posters that Hohlwein executed for PKZ.
Est: $4,000-$5,000.

485. Hauser's Hotel. ca. 1921.
34¹/₄ x 47 in./87 x 119.3 cm
Kunst in Druck G. M. B. H., München
Cond A-/Unobtrusive slight stains at pape edges.
Ref: Hohlwein Posters, Cover & p. 8;
    Hohlwein/Stuttgart, 192; PAI-VII, 182
Hohlwein's more than one thousand posters made German *Gebrauchsgraphik* (commercial art) a leading force of poster design in the 1920s and 1930s. "His special way of applying colors, letting them dry at different times, and printing one on top of the other, producing modulations of shading, has often been copied, but never equaled. He belonged to no school or group, his art and personality are an unprecedented phenomenon in the history of German poster art" (Rademacher, p. 22). His full command is evidenced in this elegant couple enjoying a cocktail in the bar of the prestigious Reichsadler Hotel, one of Munich's finest. In this rare Hohlwein, the woman's flaming coif provides the ideal contrast for her evening's escort, a shadowy gentleman suffused in purple intrigue.
Est: $2,500-$3,000.

486. Kaloderma. ca. 1925.
35⁵/₈ x 48⁷/₈ in./85.3 x 121.6 cm
Herm. Sonntag, München
Cond B/Reatored tears & stains, largely at edges.
Ref: Hohlwein/Stuttgart, 230
The sophistication level of this Kaloderma shaving soap and cream promotion is truly unfathomable. Not to gush like someone who has never seen a well-conceived poster before, but the refined level that Hohlwein achieves on a consistent basis in the name of crass commercialism is nothing short of mind-boggling. And he gives the viewer just enough information to actively draw them in, to make them, as it were, more than just consumers in the purchasing equation. He creates a graphic invitation, filled with unspoken potential, allowing the mere spectator to become a part of his lithographic dance. Brilliant.
Est: $2,000-$2,500.

SUZANNE HULOT

487. Sables d'Or les Pins.
24³/₄ x 39¹/₄ in./63 x 99.6 cm
Imp. Gaillic-Monrocq, Paris

Cond B+/Slight tears at folds and edges.
Ref: PAI-XVI, 297
For a resort on the north shore of Brittany, boasting a magnificent beach and other attractions, Hulot shows a genial midseason scene with horseback riders, golfers, fisherman and sunbathers, together with a few sailboats lazily floating about in the background.
Est: $1,200-$1,500.

HUNTER

488. New Hampshire.
21¹/₄ x 34 in./54 x 86.3 cm
Cond B+/Slight tears at folds.
As understandable as a street sign containing a white capital "H" against a field of blue, this iconographic equation asks the viewer what happens when you add a skier to an oversized snowflake to the state of New Hampshire. The obvious answer: winter fun in the Granite State.
Est: $1,000-$1,200.

JACK

489. Astailor. ca. 1925.
46⁵/₈ x 62¹/₄ in./118.5 x 158.2 cm
Imp. Kossuth, Paris

490

491

492

493

494

Cond A.
A posterist simply remembered as Jack in all likelihood produced this poster for the Astailor line of men's and boys' clothing during his (or her) mid-1920s period when the artist was employed by Paris' Kossuth printing firm. The spiffy creation doesn't shy away from a certain amount of fashionable conceit, allowing for the fact that Astailor clothes are the perfect choice for either youthful swagger or adult sophistication. Jack would continue to be active well into the 1950s, but no other specifics have been left for us to retrieve.
Est: $1,400-$1,700.

LUCIEN-HECTOR JONAS (1880-?)

490. Aix-Les-Bains. 1933.
24 1/2 x 38 5/8 in./62.2 x 98 cm
Imp. H. Chachoin, Paris
Cond B/Slight tears at folds.
Ref: Le Tennis; Montagne, p. 238; PAI-XXIX, 424
Jonas, a painter known for his historical subjects and genre scenes, is called into service by the PLM railway Bains. Caesar himself oversees the opening of newest

for its southeastern French resort destination of Aix-les- thermal establishment through the sepia mists of time as the blue-and-white smart set head for the beach. As the town's alum and sulfur springs have been used since Roman times in the treatment of respiratory ailments and rheumatism, the poster provides a stunning marriage of artist to subject matter, which clearly demonstrates that everything classically old is new again.
Est: $1,500-$1,800.

ADOLFO DE KAROLIS (1874-1928)

491. Turin/April-November 1911.
18 7/8 x 26 7/8 in./48 x 68.4 cm
Lith. Chappuis, Bologne
Cond B+/Slight creases.
Ref: Bolaffi, p. 73; PAI-XXVI, 339
This poster for the 1911 International Exhibition of Industry and Trade, held in Turin to honor the 50th anniversary of the Unified Kingdom of Italy, was printed in several languages; this is the German version. Bronzed figures on a hill overlooking Turin hold symbols of various trades and the Italian flag. Like his fellow members of the Italian artists' group "In Arte Libertas," Karolis was strongly influenced by the principles of the English Pre-Raphaelite Brotherhood.
Est: $1,500-$1,800.

MCKIBBEN

492. Ulster.
25 1/4 x 37 7/8 in./64.2 x 96.2 cm
S. C. Allen & Company, Belfast & London
Cond B+/Unobtrusive tears at top edge near "T" and in lower left corner.
Though no specific town or village is singled out for vacation relaxation, this McKibben design rolls out the green pastoral carpet for Northern Ireland's Ulster county. None of the area's cities (Belfast, Newry or Banbridge to name a few) are transferred to paper; however, the various outdoor recreations afforded the wandering soul pepper the landscape. But it is the scenery that takes priority, the profound beauty of the Irish countryside that is the focal point for potential tourists. And with a shrug, the bluffside walker makes it clear that she can't understand why it took her and her Airedale so long to make this traveling discovery.
Est: $2,500-$3,000.

J. A. KRAL

493. Mistrovství Sveta/Praha. 1933.
24 3/8 x 36 3/8 in./61.9 x 92.5 cm
Cond A.
With a chilling Aryan stoicism perfectly suited to the sport in which he excels, this gloved ice Templar gives a face to the 1933 World Ice Hockey Championship (*Canadian* hockey in the Czech text) being held in Prague, the silhouette of the host city cast against the azure sky like an architectural mountainscape.
Est: $800-$1,000.

TOMISLAV KRIZMAN

494. Guber-forrás.
36 3/4 x 49 1/8 in./93.4 x 124.7 cm
Cond B+/Unobtrusive tears, largely near paper edges.
A poignant, and rather peculiar, image for a product called arsenic water bottled from the Guber hot springs of Srebenica. The woman in the foreground, the very picture of health in her traditional Bosnian peasant dress, is obviously the end product of a healthy lifestyle, whose regime no doubt includes Guber arsenic water, the antidote for weak nerves, insomnia and anemia. In truth, the water was the Bosnian equivalent of snake oil, a stinky little potion that didn't do much of anything for the consumer. An interesting feature of the poster is the small tringular-roofed structure standing to the right of the first house on the left. Although no hoopla surrounds it, that's a grave marker, a not so subtle indication of where one will be headed sooner rather than later without the benefits of the Guber elixir.
Est: $1,500-$1,800.

495

496

497

498

500

CHARLES KUHN (1903-?)

495. Chocmel/Kohler. 1930.
35³/₄ x 50¹/₄ in./90.8 x 127.6 cm
Wolfsberg, Zurich
Cond B/Restored tears at folds.
A design as tempting as the chocolate treat it calls our attention to. The oversized honey almond bar is rendered with near-photographic perfection, and the color scheme is fabulous. By keeping the female chocoholic to a mere shadow, anyone can place themselves into the silhouette and the spray of blossoms gives just the right touch of romantic sophistication. Kuhn went to work for Wolfensberger in Zurich in 1922 and remained for 23 years. He opened his own atelier in 1945, and made something of a specialty of designing wine labels.
Est: $1,200-$1,500.

EDGAR KÜNG (1926-)

496. Ruder Weltmeisterschaft. 1962.
35³/₄ x 50¹/₈ in./91 x 127.3 cm
Keller, Luzern
Cond A.
Ref: Olympics, p. 170; Swiss Posters, p. 156;
PAI-XXIII, 316a

If the Bauhaus were alive today, this is what its work would look like: geometric images and crisp typography, stressing clarity and simplicity. The poster, created by the prize-winning graphic and advertising designer Edgar Küng, announces the first World Rowing Championship. The event was held in Lucerne on the city's famous Rotseecourse with 389 oarsmen in 102 shells competing.
Est: $1,200-$1,500.

JULIEN LACAZE (1886-1971)

497. Vallée d'Ossau.
29¹/₈ x 42¹/₂ in./74 x 108 cm
Affiches Courbet, Paris
Cond A.
Although no rail line is mentioned by name, this is unquestionably a great example of the many fine travel posters that Lacaze produced for the French Railways from 1910 to 1930. Though the Ossau Valley is the sole geographical mention given in this partial text version of the poster, the village being admired across the chasm by the lone hiker could be any of the six villages nestled within the hollows of the Barétous Valley, all of which benefit from the serene undulation of the Pyrénées piedmont whose gentle landscape contrasts with the austere and lunar beauty

of the high chalky massifs. Although the Barétous Valley, both a plane and mountain, neighbors the Pays Basque and Spain, it remains firmly attached to its Béarn origins through its culture and history.
Est: $1,000-$1,200.

PIERRE LAGARRIGUE

498. Souscrivez/Bons d'Armement. ca. 1939.
31⁵/₈ x 46⁷/₈ in./80.3 x 119 cm
Imp. Schuster, Paris
Cond B/Slight stains at folds.
A rare photomontage appeal to the French citizenry to hold up their end of the effort and subscribe to war bonds, in the process greasing the wheels of freedom while keeping the armaments of liberation rolling on or flying high. A rather patriotic petition, focusing on the tidier glories of war rather than its grizzlier aspects, which, though more accurate as to the nature of conflagration, may have lacked the widespread appeal the subscription board was after. In addition to the credit he receives for creating the cut-and-paste design, Lagarrigue is also given photo credit, along with another shutterbug named Parnotte.
Est: $1,000-$1,200.

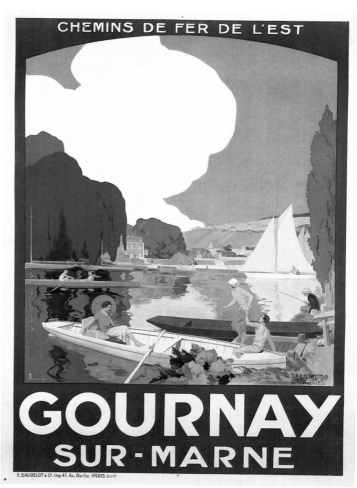

499

502

501

BERNARD LANCY (1892-1964)

499. La Grande Illusion. 1937.
$23^5/8$ x $31^1/2$ in./60.1 x 80 cm
Delattre, Paris
Cond A–/Slight tears at folds.
Ref: Cinéma Franççais, p. 9; Capitaine, 139;
   Belles Affiche, p. 93; PAI-XIII, 281
This is the smaller format of one of the most profound posters created for a film. Few films have conveyed such a powerful antiwar sentiment as Jean Renoir's "La Grande Illusion," and none have surpassed it for a compassionate insight into human nature in crisis. Underscoring its strong condemnation of the inhuman-

ity of war, the film was banned in Germany and Italy, which were at the time being whipped into a frenzy by their fascist governments. Lancy gives us one of the most moving—and today one of the rarest—film posters ever created. In a radical departure from standard film promotional rules, Lancy portrays neither the actors nor the action, but presents, instead, an allegorical antiwar composition.
Est: $2,500-$3,000.

ANTON LAVINSKY (1893-1968)

500. Gekelberi Finn (The Adventures of Huckleberry Finn). ca. 1920.
$36^7/8$ x $28^1/4$ in./93.6 x 72 cm
Goskino, Moscow
Cond B+/Restored tears, largely in borders.
The predecessor of Paramount Studios, Famous Players-Lasky Corp., created a hybrid of the Huck Finn classic that combined elements of Mark Twain's "The Adventures of Tom Sawyer" and "The Adventures of Huckleberry Finn" for this 1920 release. In this version, Huck's ne'er-do-well father kidnaps him in the hopes of extorting money from the Widow Douglas, spiriting away on a raft. He escapes and is joined by a Jim, a runaway slave, who is later seized by two vagrants and sold to a plantation owner named Phelps. Enter Tom Sawyer, who is related to the Phelpses, who joins Huck in an attempt to free Jim. During the botched rescue, Tom is shot in the leg. When the Phelps family learn what has happened, they take care of Tom, release Jim and return Huck to the widow Douglas. The rescue attempt made for a thrilling climax and the artist rightfully chose this as the key element of his design. Lavinsky was head of the sculpture department at the Higher Arts Studio in Moscow. He went on to create the political Rosta posters, working closely with Mayakovsky. In 1928, Lavinsky collaborated with El Lissitzky in designing exhibition interiors of the Soviet pavilion at the Cologne International Press exhibition.
Est: $4,000-$5,000.

LUCIEN LEFEVRE (ca. 1850-?)

501. Cacao Lacté. 1893.
$34^5/8$ x $48^7/8$ in./88 x 124 cm
Imp. Chaix, Paris
Cond B/Slight tears and stains at folds and edges.
Ref: Maindron, p. 83; Reims, 797
Obviously the concept of sharing hasn't made its way into this hot chocolate loving lad's lexicon as of yet. But can you really blame him. We're not talking about any old cocoa here. That's a bowl of Cacao Lacté he's keeping from the begging pup at tongue's length, "the most superior of all known chocolates and cocoas," no doubt made that way from the kiss of milk hinted at in the beverage's name. While only producing posters posters since 1893, Maindron wrote in his 1896 book that Lefèvre, who received his training from Chéret, was mapping out an active career in which he was showing not only much promise, but an individual style whose work to date (including this image) could only be judged as "outstanding" (pp. 82-83).
Est: $1,400-$1,700.

RENÉ LELONG (1860-?)

502. Gournay-Sur-Marne.
$29^3/4$ x $41^3/8$ in./75.5 x 105.2 cm
Imp. E. Baudelot, Paris
Cond A–/Slight tears at paper edges.
Ref: PAI-XXIX, 443
Let's say that the hustle and bustle of Paris has gotten to you and you need to get away. But not too far away. Maybe just an afternoon's sojourn to restore your sanity in a wide open space. Maybe do a little boating or some fishing. Well my friend, the Eastern Railways has the perfect suggestion: Gournay-Sur-Marne, a quaint village just thirteen kilometers from Paris, situated on a wide bend of the river and ideal for soothing a city-addled psyche. An eye-pleasing poster from the designer best known for adapting the iconic English "Kodak girl" for the European market.
Est: $1,500-$1,800.

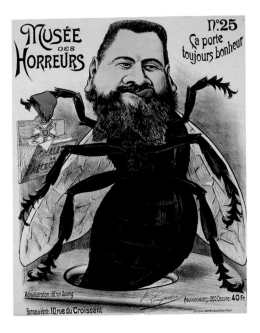

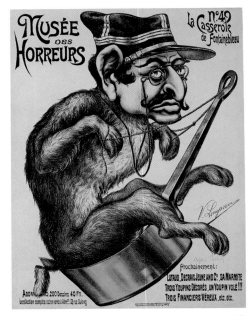

504

LEM

503. Palais du Costume. 1899.
28⁷/₈ x 41 in./73.3 x 104.2 cm
Imp. Chaix, Paris
Cond B/Slight tears and stains at folds and edges.
Situated at the foot of the Eiffel Tower—a fact mentioned but not recreated for this design—the Costume Palace of the 1900 Paris World's Fair was a fashion feast for the couture inclined, showcasing to the collective populations the supremacy of French clothing since the time fashion first became in vogue. Though it's unclear what the exact station of the Empire trio observing the throngs file into the exhibition may be—models in waiting, chic time travelers or spectacularly rendered window dressing—their retro chic is unsurpassed.
Est: $1,700-$2,000.

V. LENEPVEU

504. Musée des Horreurs: The Complete series of 51 Posters. 1899-1900.
Each approx.: 19³/₄ x 25¹/₂ in./50.2 x 64.9 cm
Imp. Lenepveu, Paris
Cond B+/Restored tears and in some cases, slight
    paper loss, largely at edges.
Ref: Dreyfus, Pl. 169-177; DFP-II, 518-551;
    La Propagande, p. 59
An officer of Jewish descent in the French artillery,

503

505

Captain Alfred Dreyfus (1859-1939), was accused and convicted of betraying military secrets to the Germans. The treasonous act earned him a lifetime prison sentence to Devil's Island in 1894. There was just one problem with the open-and-shut case—Dreyfus was an innocent man, framed by the real traitor, Major Esterhazy. And though evidence was uncovered attesting to Dreyfus' innocence, it was suppressed by the military, leading to the most divisive, anti-Semitic occurrences in French history. Finally pardoned in 1906 by the *Cour de Cassation*, he became a symbol of injustice for liberal intellectuals who vigorously opposed the right-wing reactionary forces of the military and the church—most particularly Emile Zola, whose infamous "J'Accuse!" treatise, though potentially libelous, focused national and global attention to the disturbing case. "V. Lenepveu's *Musée des Horreurs*, a series of fifty-one political posters defaming prominent statesmen, journalists, Dreyfusards, and Jews, appeared weekly in Paris, starting in the fall of 1899, after the retrial at Rennes. The series was stopped by an order of the Ministry of the Interior about one year later (Dreyfus, p. 244). All fifty-one of the graphic attacks—printed by the artist himself, no less!—are offered here. The denigrating bestial menagerie naturally include vile caricatures of Dreyfus and Zola, but also target such prominent figures as lawyer Fernand Labori, journalist Caroline Rémy Guebhard (who wrote under the pseudonym Séverine), socialist leader Jean Jaurés, Grand Rabbi Zadoc Kahn, *Le Siècle* publisher Yves

506

Guyot, Joseph Reinoch, banker Nathan Rothschild, as well as many others who bore the brunt of the artist's misplaced ire. An astounding testimonial to the naked power of art—regardless of the lunacy of the creator's convictions.
Est: $8,000-$10,000. (51)

GEORGES LEPAPE (1887-1971)

505. Parfum Rosine/Mam'zelle Victoire. 1918.
14⁷/₈ x 19³/₄ in./37.7 x 50.3 cm
Cond B+/Slight staining in margins.
There's absolutely nothing pretty about war. But once the shooting stops, sister, it's time to dust yourself off and get back in the swing of things. And you get the feeling that's precisely what this oversized Gallic rooster and sprightly Marianne are crowing about in Lepape's hand-colored design for Paul Poiret's post-war

507

508

509

510

from the French lever ("to rise," as in sunrise, meaning the East) is comprised of the countries along the eastern Mediterranean shores. A common use of the terminology sprung from the Venetian and other trade routes that established commerce with cities such as Tyre and Sidon as a result of the Crusades. The far reaching appellation is steeped in a tradition of commercial compromise, a meeting place for greater economic goals for which divergent cultures would set aside their differences in the name of active trade. These two posters for Tel Aviv's 1936 Levant Fair celebrate this tradition with bold iconography, united by both sense of purpose and the fair's emblematic Pegasus, soaring over the event with graceful austerity.
Est: $2,000-$2,500. (2)

ANDRE LHOTE (1885-1962)

509. Ausstellung Französischer Kunst. 1931.
35³/₄ x 50 in./91 x 127 cm
Wolfsberg, Zurich
Cond B/Slight tears at paper edges.
Ref: PAI-XXIII, 338
A masterful design for an exhibition of French art at the gallery owned by Zurich lithographer Wolfsberg (where fine exhibitions are held to this day). The elements here are very simple—a French tricolor, a French sailor and his girl—but they are superbly composed and rendered. Lhote was a well-known and prolific cubist painter who was also an enormously influential theorist, critic and teacher; he founded his own school in Paris in 1918. It is likely that Wolfsberg went all the way to Paris to choose Lhote because some of his own work was included in the exhibition.
Est: $2,000-$2,500.

ROY LICHTENSTEIN (1923-1997)

510. Lincoln Center/4th New York Film Festival.
1966.
29¹/₈ x 44³/₄ in./74 x 111 cm
Cond A. Framed.
Ref: Lincoln Center, 22; Modern American Poster, 170;
PAI-XXX, 548
This is one of the best of the New York Lincoln Center posters produced under the sponsorship of the List Art Poster program established by Albert and Vera List in 1963 to commission posters for important cultural institutions by major artists. Normally, that would mean little, since many of these posters are irrelevant embarrassments. But this is one of the exceptions that proves the rule and is, in fact, one of the best posters produced by this popular artist—a bright Pop-Art image that evokes the glamour of the old Art-Deco movie palaces. Approximately 500 copies were printed, and it is quite scarce today. Roy Lichtenstein studied at the Art Students League in New York and received degrees in Fine Arts from Ohio State; he taught art at SUNY Oswego and at Rutgers University. His paintings are part of the permanent collections of the Whitney, the Guggenheim and MOMA. As one of the foremost graphic designers of the 60s, he helped to define the emerging pop art with its whole array of visual effects.
Est: $3,000-$4,000.

perfume celebration, Mam'zelle Victory. The French couturier (1879-1944) was the first fashion designer to market his own perfumes in the 1910's, named after one of his daughters, Parfums de Rosine. Poiret was the most fashionable dress designer of pre-World War I Paris, whose most lasting contribution to the world of fashion was his introduction of the hobble skirt—a vertical, tight-bottomed style that confined women to mincing steps. Before striking out on his own, the designer, who became friends with both Bakst and Diaghilev, had the opportunity to create costumes for the leading actresses of the time, Sarah Bernhardt and Réjane, while in the employ of Jacques Doucet.
Est: $1,500-$1,800.

506. Bal de la Couture Parisienne. 1925.
16 x 31¹/₄ in./40.7 x 79.5 cm
Edia, Paris
Cond B+/Unobtrusive tears near paper edges.
Ref: Art Deco. p. 62; Timeless Images, 127;
PAI-XXV, 380 (var)
Cool colors and a hot design: the combination makes for Lepape's finest poster and one of the most spectacular ones by any artist of this period. "Created . . . for the famous fashion ball at the Théâtre des Champs-Elysées, (this poster) sums up much of the French high style. It was produced in 1925, the year of the Paris exposition. In it, the couple's elegance, aloofness and pride at being among the fashionable set are beautifully rendered" (Art Deco, p. 620). *This is the smaller format.*
Est: $2,500-$3,000.

HERBERT LEUPIN (1916-1999)

507. Two Knie Circus Posters. 1956 & 1957.
Each: 35¹/₄ x 50³/₈ in./89.5 x 128 cm
Hug & Söhne, Zürich
Cond A–/Unobtrusive folds.
Ref: Leupin, pp. 154 & 156; Circus Posters, 77;
PAI-XXV, 383
Leupin was simply the most prolific, influential and award-winning of the postwar Swiss graphic designers. A combination of all that is best in his French colleagues Savignac and Villemot, he created long-running campaigns for his county's favorite products—textbook classics filled with endless variety and delightful humor. And these two posters show the Swiss master at his creative height, with both clown and seal playfully balancing their employer's name, hinting at the fun to be found at the Swiss national circus.
Est: $1,000-$1,200. (2)

LEVANT FAIR

508. Two Posters. 1936.
Artist: **Lachs**
a: 26¹/₂ x 38¹/₄ in./67.5 x 97.2 cm
Monsan, Jerusalem
Cond B/Unobtrusive tears at folds.
b: 18¹/₂ x 26⁷/₈ in./47 x 68.3 cm
Cond: A–/Pinholes at corners; unobtrusive tears at folds.
Biblically speaking, the Levant is the area of land extending from Egypt to Mesopotamia. Historically and economically speaking, the region that takes its name

512

516

AAGE LIPPERT

511. København Zoo/Okapi.
24⁵/₈ x 34¹/₈ in./62.5 x 87.5 cm
Møller & Landschultz, Copenhagen
Cond A.
There's no more surefire way of attracting paying customers to a zoo—or anywhere for that matter—than by giving the public something that they've never seen. Preferably something a little odd to boot. And the Copenhagen Zoo has made a superb choice with their okapi exhibit. Though it looks the world to be a close kin of the mule or zebra as it placidly stands in its pseudo-natural environment, the African mammal is actually a short-necked relative of the giraffe, and one that definitely makes al long-standing impression with its peculiar physical make-up and serene dignity.
Est: $800-$1,000.

PRIVAT LIVEMONT (1861-1936)

512. Cercle Artistique de Schaerbeek. 1897.
31¹/₄ x 41⁵/₈ in./79.4 x 105.7 cm
Cond A–/Unobtrusive tears, largely at edges.
Ref: Belle Epoque 1970, 81; Maitres, 212 (var);
    PAI-VIII, 417 (var)
One of Livemont's idealized beauties appears to be holding a statuette of a young goddess much like herself. The poster was created to advertise the fifth annual exhibition of the Art Circle of Schaerbeek, the small Belgian town where the artist was born and died; in fact, one of his first known posters was for the 1890 exhibition and he would design a total of four promotions for the town's Cercle Artistique. *Rare proof before the addition of letters.*
Est: $3,000-$3,500.

513. Rajah. 1899.
16¹/₂ x 29⁷/₈ in./42 x 75.7 cm
Van Leer, Amsterdam
Cond A.
Ref: Belle Epoque 1970, 87; DFP-II, 1071;
    Wine Spectator, 82; Muller-Brockmann, 31;
    Hillier, 175; PAI-XXIX, 456
"Rajah has the essential Art Nouveau woman, dressed

511

513

in bejeweled opulence, holding a cup of tea whose steam rises to spell out the product's name. The hair is long again, but fairly tame. The Rajah brand name was used for both coffee and tea" (Wine Spectator, 82). Livemont started out as an interior designer in his home town of Schaerbeek, Belgium. He came to poster art after entering a poster contest on a whim and winning it. By 1898, *The Poster* magazine was calling him "the uncontested master of Belgian posterists." Though one of several posterists often assumed to be disciples of Mucha, Livemont's version of Art Nouveau was in fact well-developed before Mucha burst onto the scene in the 1890s.
Est: $5,000-$6,000.

VINCENT LORANT-HEILBRONN (1874-?)

514. L'Hiver à Pau. ca. 1900.
30³/₄ x 46⁵/₈ in./78 x 118.4 cm
Lithographie Nouvelle, Asnières
Cond B/Slight tears and stains at folds and edges.
Ref: PAI-XXII, 390

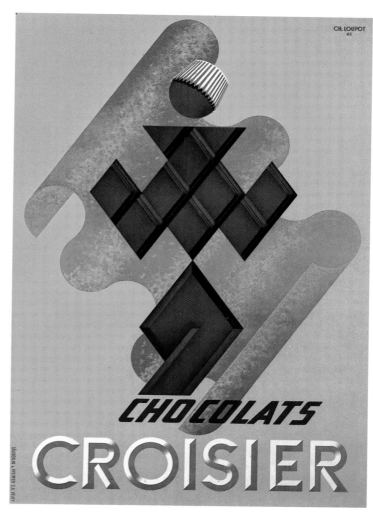

517

518

514

515

The ancient Romans settled at Pau in the Pyrénées-Atlantiques because of its strategic location on top of a mountain ridge. It took the discovery of the town's mild winter climate at the beginning of the 19th century to turn it into a tourist destination. A large English colony developed, and by mid-century, Liszt was giving concerts, fox hunts were regular affairs and a golf course was laid out, older than almost any outside of Scotland. And as if the parasol twirler weren't enticement enough, the Winter Palace is set to open, set against an astonishing chartreuse sky. Lorant-Heilbronn began his career as a posterist for various Paris theaters and music halls. When films came along, he added duties as set designer and assistant director to his graphic responsibilities.
Est: $1,200-$1,500.

515. Orezza.
43³/₈ x 61⁵/₈ in./110 x 156.4 cm
La Lithographie Nouvelle, Asnières
Cond B/Restored tears, largely at folds and edges.
A spectacularly odd design for Orezza digestive liqueur, one with enough Art Nouveau filigrees to keep the purist content, while loading it with a hallucinogenic

portent to please those looking for more than just another pretty lady. Certainly, Lorant-Heilbronn pays respectful lip service to the curative powers of the beverage—the usual run of counter-anemic, pro-kidney claims—but what really catches the eye here is the unusual seduction taking place at the bar. Precisely what "Orezza gives one a "free hand" over isn't thoroughly addressed, and not to change the subject, but what are the exact genders of the patrons of this greenly-lit establishment? A wonderful peek into a decidedly off-kilter universe.
Est: $1,700-$2,000.

CHARLES LOUPOT (1892—1962)

516. Mirus/Poêle a Bois. 1928.
46⁷/₈ x 62⁷/₈ in./119.2 x 159.8 cm
Imp. Chaix, Paris
Cond B/Slight tears at folds.
Ref: Loupot/Zagrodzki, 78A; Loupot, 34; PAI-XXV, 392
Loupot designed two posters in the same period for this stove-making foundry. Both feature symmetry, utmost graphic economy, and a colorful, flower-like flame — "the definitive evocation of a gas or wood burning stove" (Loupot intro). This is the original version; a later one, in smaller format with added text at top, was labeled "d'après Loupot" ("from a design by Loupot;" see PAI-XVIII, 349).
Est: $3,000-$4,000.

517. Cointreau. 1930.
47 x 63 in./119.5 x 160 cm
Les Belles Affiches, Paris
Cond A–/Unobtrusive tears and stains at edges.
Ref: Affiche Réclame, 19; PAI-XXIII, 344
This is the female half of a pair of matching posters designed by Loupot for Cointreau in 1930. The male counterpart is reproduced in the Loupot exhibition catalogue (no. 53) as well as in *Arts et Métiers Graphiques* (1930, No. 20, p. 108). Loupot gives the legendary Cointreau clown his own inimitable twist and colors the whole in shades of the sour orange whose peel flavors this curaçao liqueur.
Est: $5,000-$6,000.

CHARLES LOUPOT (continued)

518. Chocolats Croisier. 1947.
$35^1/2$ x $50^3/8$ in./90 x 128 cm
Sauberlin & Pfeiffer, Vevey
Cond A/P.
Ref: Loupot/Zagrodzki, 110
"The first postwar poster published by Loupot reveals his geometric preoccupation directly linked to his quest for the St. Raphaël mark. One may measure the marked difference in the fashion with which he addresses the difficult subject by comparing it with his image for *Dauphinet* in 1926 (*see* PAI-XXI, 281). It's also another return to his past, as it strikes up an association with one of his printers from the Swiss period" (Loupot/Zagrodzki, p. 94). *Rare!*
Est: $10,000-$12,000.

519. Fêtes de Paris. 1935.
$24^1/2$ x $39^3/8$ in./62.2 x 100 cm
Cond A.
Ref: Loupot/Zagrodzki, 93; Loupot, 54 (var); PAI-XXVII, 482
An old caravel symbolizing trade, along with castle walls which represent old Paris while at the same time form the shape of a crown, are the elements of this design for a Paris trade fair. A cast of thousands and lots of gold ink complete the pageantry. *This is the rare smaller format.*
Est: $1,700-$2,000.

520. La Biere/La Plus Economique. 1927.
$23^1/4$ x $31^1/2$ in./38.9 x 80 cm
Les Belles Affiches, Paris
Cond A.
Ref: Loupot/Zagrodzki, 67; PAI-XV, 362
Loupot studied art at Lyon, but produced his first posters in Switzerland where he stayed for seven years, between 1916 and 1923. He then returned to Paris at the invitation of the printer Devambez, and became one of the top designers of his time. Between 1925 and 1930, most of his work was executed for the agency Les Belles Affiches, founded by two broth-

ers named Damour. He was also Cassandre's partner in the Alliance Graphique. This rarely-seen specimen is an institutional ad for the beer industry, providing sound advice—through straightforward graphic shorthand—about the economic and health benefits of the delectable amber liquid.
Est: $2,500-$3,000.

LUPUS (Hans Wolff, 1892-?)

521. Rikola Bücher. 1924.
$23^3/8$ x $18^3/8$ in./59.4 x 46.7 cm
Cond A-/Unobtrusive tears at top edge. Framed.

Ref: Barnicoat, 93
It's no secret that reading a book has long been promoted as a deterrent to the dumbing down of TV, but it's refreshing to see that the notion was already being advanced in the pre-electronic age. Rikola Books, through the Cubist abstractions of Lupus, encourage the viewer to enter the "fairyland of literature" through the pages of their output, a concept that one of their own tomes has taken to heart, as it sprouts wings in

SAMEDI 13, LUNDI 15, MARDI 16 OCTOBRE.

TOILETTES D'HIVER

IMP MAURICE DUPUY et Cᵉ PARIS.

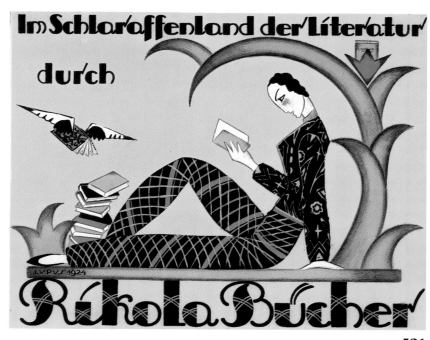

Im Schlaraffenland der Literatur durch

Rikola Bücher

521

525

526

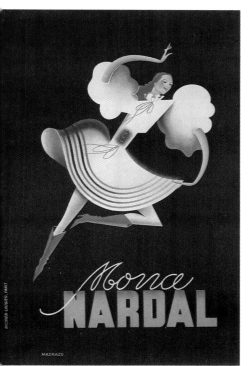

Mona NARDAL

MADRAZO

523

...rder to soar through the golden skies of self-pro-
pelled imagination.
Est: $1,700-$2,000.

TITO LIVIO DE MADRAZO (1899—1979)

522. Esmeralda.
30³/₄ x 45⁷/₈ in./78 x 116.6 cm
Cond B+/Sight tears at folds.
Ref: PAI-XXVIII, 394
...f Madrazo's color choice is any indication, Esmerelda
...as a red-hot dancer. Some of the most beautiful the-
...atrical and dance posters of the 1930s were executed

by the Spanish painter Madrazo, who arrived in Paris
in 1923. He takes all the graphic liberties necessary to
achieve motion with a singular clarity. There are about
a dozen posters for various performers which Madrazo
created, each sharing the same flair—terse, eloquent
caricatures that capture the essence of the personality
in sparse, fluid lines and shapes. Now very sought and
very rare, these works mark a glorious end to the Art
Deco style.
Est: $1,700-$2,000.

523. Mona Nardal.
29⁵/₈ x 45¹/₂ in./75.3 x 115.6 cm
Richier-Laugier, Paris
Cond B+/Slight tears at folds.
Ref: PAI-XXVII, 492
Against an indigo backdrop, Madrazo launches dancer
Nardal skyward, freeing her from gravity's shackles
and, in the process, turns her flouncing sleeves into
soft billowing clouds, with her skirt transformed into a
ringed parachute for delaying her return to the con-
fines of the earth.
Est: $1,500-$1,800.

BURKHARD MANGOLD (1873-1950)

524. Schutzenhaus Bale/Restaurant. 1917.
27³/₄ x 39¹/₄ in./70.5 x 99.6 cm
W. Wassermann, Basel
Cond A.
Ref: Mangold, cat. #85; Schweizer Hotel, 62; PAI-XX, 311
A master of many styles, Mangold chose a soft, almost
smudged technique to render this romantic restaurant
located in an historic Basel guardhouse. A twosome
sharing drinks on the terrace under the flowering trees
frame a vignette of French doors opening onto the
interior where sconces shed a flattering light, beautifully dressed men and women dine on elegant cuisine
and strains of violin music fill the rarefied air. Born in
Basel, Mangold got a thorough grounding in the pre-
vailing Jugendstil while studying in Munich from 1894
to 1900. After his return to Switzerland, he produced
easel paintings, glass paintings, illustrations, wood-
cuts, lithographs—and some 150 posters. Margadant
calls these "delicately perceived, humane, sometimes

witty but then almost lyrical again but always pro-
foundly painterly," and Mangold himself, "the most
highly individual poster pioneer of Switzerland."
Est: $1,700-$2,000.

GUSTAVE MARIE

525. La Lithographie.
33³/₄ x 11³/₄ in./85.7 x 29.7 cm
Cond B+/Slight tears at folds and edges.
A beautiful, if not somewhat incomprehensible, allegorical nod to the potency of Art Nouveau lithography.
Not that it isn't clever, what with its variations on a
floral theme echoing throughout and the abrupt
appearance of a steering wheel in place of one of
the spiked bottom border motif half-wheels. But the
question remains: has this lava-tressed stunner been
enthroned at the lithographic helm or is she merely
guarding it? And is she gazing at a poster of herself or
a like-minded decorative sister? Marie was best known
for his magazine illustrations and as an editor for the
short-lived magazine, *L'Art et la Scène.*
Est: $1,200-$1,500.

ANDRE E. MARTY (1882-1974)

526. Toilettes d'Hiver. 1923.
30¹/₈ x 46⁷/₈ in./76.5 x 119 cm
Imp. Maurice Dupuy, Paris
Cond A–/Slight tears at edges.
Ref: Affiche Réclame, 40 (var); PAI-XIX, 414
A terrific poster for a three-day winter clothing sale at
Paris' Au Louvre department store (in another version,
the store's name appears instead of the sale dates).
"This poster displays a most original layout. The two
figures have been pushed to the left; the little girl's
hoop leads the eye toward the tiny bird, which almost
takes the starring role. Marty arranges the characters
in order of descending size, which lends the composition great strength, and keeps the mother's height
from overshadowing the little bird" (Affiche Réclame.
p. 69). Marty was a very popular illustrator whose work
appeared in all the leading fashion magazines in the
1920s. In the early '30s he produced some memorable posters for the London Transport.
Est: $2,000-$2,500.

527

531

528

529

530

532

533

SASCHA MAURER (1897-1961)

527. The New Haven Railroad/Greater Power.
27³/₄ x 41¹/₂ in./70.6 x 105.5 cm
Latham Litho, Long Island City, N.Y.
Cond B+/Slight tears at edges.
In its heyday, the New York, New Haven & Hartford Railroad's main line sizzled with famous trains shuttling tycoons and business leaders between Boston's South Station and New York City's Grand Central Terminal. The line's extra-fare flagship train, *The Yankee Clipper*, served afternoon tea to Boston Brahmins as it raced along the curving Shore Line route. In the 1930's, the New Haven ordered a fleet of steam locomotives of the Hudson type (four lead wheels, six drivers, and four trailing wheels). These massive engines took advantage of the latest in steam technology, providing increased tractive effort and horsepower for more rapid acceleration and faster speed. To further help matters, The New Haven joined a trend in the industry and specified a streamlined shroud of sheet metal over the locomotives to reduce wind resistance. Note the smooth contours over the pilot ("cow catcher") and down the sides of the boiler. Streamlining would soon lead to lighter, smooth-sided passenger cars, along with modern diesel locomotives, and the iron horse would be led out to pasture. The artist, Maurer, specialized in sleek, railway graphics during the 1930s. *Rare!*
Est: $2,000-$2,500.

LUCIANO ACHILLE MAUZAN (1883-1952)

528. Bertozzi. 1930.
39¹/₄ x 55¹/₈ in./99.7 x 140.2 cm
Mauzan Morzenti, Milano
Cond A.
Ref: Mauzan/Treviso, p. 76; Mauzan, p. 99;
PAI-XXIX, 499
Mauzan goes for a touch of the grotesque in publicizing Bertozzi cheese, but does it with such chutzpah that the overall effect is pleasing. And with three judges putting their olfactory reputations on the line, it can be safely assumed that although justice may be blind, it is quite keen in the other senses. Mauzan produced well over 2,000 posters during the course of his long, prodigious career. Born in France, Mauzan would begin his life as an illustrator in Italy in 1909, working for Ricordi and other topnotch printing firms. He remained there until 1927, when he and his wife were invited to Buenos Aires. There he continued a frantic pace of poster production until 1933, when the Mauzans returned to France, where he would continue his work for the rest of his days. His boundless imagination is a

landscape of ingenious concepts and incongruous associations working in harmony. He lays on color freely, but what marks his designs as unique is his sense of humor, by turns witty, grotesque, mad, pungent, charming and openly affectionate.
Est: $4,000-$5,000.

529. Prestito della Liberazione. 1917.
39³/₈ x 56¹/₂ in./100 x 143.5 cm
G. Ricordi, Milano
Cond B/Restored tears at folds and edges.
Ref: Menegazzi-I, 57; Menegazzi-II, 18;
    Mauzan/Pinerolo, p. 11; Mauzan/Treviso, p. 19;
    Mauzan/Paris, p. 37; Bocca, p. 97; PAI-XVIII, 359
During World War I, in which Italy was on the Allied side, Mauzan designed a number of posters for Italian war bonds. In this one, for what best can be translated as Liberty bonds, a solemn-faced allegorical figure of Italy, winged and laurel-wreathed, extends a sword to which arms reach in the ancient Roman oath-swearing gesture. On a banner, a quote from Italy's wartime leader Orsini obliquely refers to "the return of what was ours"—conquered Italian territory, and, perhaps, Italian pride.
Est: $2,000-$2,500.

A. MELLIÉS

530. Les Femmes Jockey.
19¹/₂ x 56 in./49.6 x 142.4 cm
Gouache-and ink hand-signed maquette.
Proclaiming the newest profession open to the female population—that of jockey—might have been something of a smidgen of wishful thinking as the competitive horse racing world, as least from a rider's standpoint, has always been something of a Little Man's Club. It's a bit difficult to assess whether or not this was intended to be a rather good-natured gibe or not—and the chortling jackass looking up at her in amused disbelief doesn't help matters much. Regardless of the reason for this artistic output, the unapologetically feminine rider looks as confident as can be atop her mount, totally in command and a picture of equestrian beauty in her peach silks.
Est: $1,700-$2,000.

LUCIEN METIVET (1863—1932)

531. Martigny. 1909.
29 x 41¹/₂ in./73.5 x 105.3 cm
Imp. Minot, Paris
Cond A–/Slight tears and stains at paper edges.
Ref: Chemins de Fer, 48 (var); PAI-XXVIII, 409

One of Metivet's finest and rarest, this charming railway poster advertises the resort of Martigny, in the Voges mountains of northwest France. Executed in sun-dappled impressionistic colors and brushstrokes, we see a pair of fashionably dressed women by the river bank with a watchful caddy standing by, while the bottom text area clearly spells out extensive ticketing information. This prolific magazine and book illustrator did few posters; most notably, one for Eugénie Buffet (*see PAI-XXX*, 138) and the winning entry in Century's Napoleon poster contest (*see PAI-XXII*, 411). *This is the smaller, one-sheet format.*
Est: $3,500-$4,000.

LEOPOLDO METLICOVITZ (1868-1944)

532. Fleurs de Mousse. 1899.
31¹/₈ x 43 in./79 x 109 cm
Moullot, Marseilles-Paris
Cond B/Slight tears at fold and edges; image and
    colors excellent.
Ref: Ricordi, 154 (var); Gold, 8; PAI-XXX, 83
In one of the finest works by the prolific Metlicovitz, a French perfume is advertised with a nude sylph in a reverent pose, enraptured with the fragrance from a small vial which "is so potent that the artist imagines it attracts even butterflies. How could a woman resist such an appealing message?" (Gold, p. 7). This is a subsequent edition of the image, printed by the Moullot firm of Marseilles. Metlicovitz was born in the Adriatic port city of Trieste, and appears to have become a painter and portraitist without any formal training. In 1891, he showed up in Milan at Ricordi's print shop as a lithography trainee, proving to be such a quick study he was promoted to technical director within a year.
Est: $3,500-$4,000.

CHARLES METZGER

533. Strandbad Lindau.
42 x 31¹/₂ in./106.8 x 80 cm
Druck de Dr. Karl Höhn, Lindau
Cond A.
Ref: PAI-VI, 173
The warm sand, inviting water and a relaxing bather in an emerald one-piece beckon us to sample the attractions of Lindau at Lake Bodensee, which just happens to be, loosely translated, "The Most Beautiful Spot to Sun On the Bodensee"—as if there ever were any doubts! The golden buff tone of the beach, sky and skin dominates the design, easily conveying the soothing sensation of sunshine.
Est: $3,000-$4,000.

534

535

537

536

538

GEORGES MEUNIER (1869-1942)

534. A la Place Clichy/Étrennes. ca. 1896.
33⁷/₈ x 48¹/₂ in./86 x 123.4 cm
Imp. Chaix, Paris
Cond A–/Slight tears at edges.
Ref: PAI-XXII, 414
Meunier, a Beaux Arts-trained painter and decorative artist, also designed 56 known posters that are executed much in the manner of Chéret—not surprisingly, since he worked at the master's printing plant, starting in 1894. Meunier executed several designs for Christmas sales at the Place Clichy department store, all featuring a woman or girl on a rocking horse. This one is perhaps the liveliest and certainly one of the rarest. However, this time it's a rocking *mule* called upon to serve as the stationary steed, with a clown and a lady in red riding through a shopper's fantasy field of gifts represented by Japanese dolls, masks and assorted trinkets.
Est: $2,000-$2,500.

535. Bullier. 1895.
16 x 23⁵/₈ in./40.6 x 60 cm
Imp. Chaix, Paris

Cond A–/Slight stains at paper edges.
Ref: Meunier, 13; DFP-II, 580; Reims, 853; Maitres, 147; Gold, 142; PAI-XXX, 139 (var)
What distinguishes Meunier from his mentor, perhaps, is a particular lightness of spirit, much in evidence in this poster for the Bullier dance hall. He gives us plenty of action with this flirtatious dancer whose cavorting earns her a tip of the hat from an equally torqued male patron. *This is the smaller format.*
Est: $1,200-$1,500.

HENRI MEUNIER (1873-1922)

536. Rajah. 1897.
30³/₄ x 25 in./78 x 63.4 cm
Lith. Gouweloos, Bruxelles
Cond A–/Unobtrusive stain at fold.
Ref: DFP-II, 1082; Maitres, 156; Belle Epoque 1970, 93; Belgique/ Paris, 47; Weill, 95; Wine Spectator, 99; PAI-XXIX, 507 (var)
This design for Rajah coffee is a classic of Belgian Art-Nouveau poster art; it was called Meunier's "best work" and "a masterpiece" by *L'Estampe et L'Affiche*

in 1898 (p. 227). Appropriately, a strong coffee tone dominates the color scheme.
Est: $3,000-$4,000.

L. E. MITCHELL

537. New Zealand.
24⁵/₈ x 39³/₈ in./62.4 x 100 cm
Cond A.
So convinced is New Zealand's Tourist Department of the untouched splendor of their Marlborough Sounds that all they ask of designer Mitchell is to show the rest of the world precisely what they're missing. And he does so with quiet splendor, laying Queen Charlotte Sound out from an isolated arboreal vantage point. With its fascinating maze of bays and inlets, its sheltered inlets and excellent fishing, the Sound is the boater's paradise of New Zealand. And set as we are in the lush coastal forest with bluffs rising golden about us, the peace and unspoiled beauty of the region translates

539

540

542

541

beautifully to the page and more than compensates for unpictured amenities doubtlessly soon forgotten.
Est: $1,000-$1,200.

THEODORUS MOLKENBOER (1871-1920)

538. St. Franciscus. 1917.
29¹/₂ x 43¹/₄ in./75 x 109.8 cm
Lith. Lankhout, Den Haag
Cond A.
Ref: Dutch Posters, 147; PAI-XXII, 423
Many of the best Dutch posters being done at this time were for cultural events rather than commercial products. Molkenboer's design for a pantomime at the Hague on the life of St. Francis is gravely elegant—strict in composition, perfect in symmetry and daring in conception. The image alludes to the belief that St. Francis was the first to manifest the stigmata of Christ on his hands and feet. The two figures are combined into a crucified phoenix, promising resurrection as the drops of blood become roses; the roses, in turn, evoke the "little flowers" associated with the saint and also refer back to the branch of thorns at the top. The text indicates that Molkenboer—a painter and graphic artist—was responsible for the scenario, sets and costumes. He was the younger brother of Antoon Molkenboer, a portrait painter and applied artist who created several posters as well.
Est: $2,000-$2,500.

HENRY LE MONNIER (1893-1978)

539. Claverie.
51¹/₄ x 78³/₄ in./129.9 x 200 cm
Affiches Lutetia, Paris
Cond B+/Slight tear at folds.
If one were to look too quickly at the artwork laid down here, one might walk away with a rather grim impression of a somewhat grisly scene of dangling appendages. But if you stop and take a closer look—if you weren't put off by your hasty first impression—then you would see that it was in fact the exact opposite, a vision of great hope to the disabled of the world. For this is an advertisement for Claverie, the premiere source for orthopedic prostheses, corsets and hernia support, known worldwide, yet located in Paris. And Le Monnier's warm face of medical benevolence is on the scene to pass out the necessary supplies to the walking wounded. Le Monnier created a large body of posters for films and commercial products during the period from 1924 to 1954, but little biographical
information on him remains.
Est: $1,200-$1,500.

JOSÉ MORELL (1899-1949)

540. Spanien. 1941.

24³/₄ x 39¹/₂ in./63 x 100.4 cm
Seix y Barral, Madrid
Cond A–/Very slight staining and tears in margins.
Ref: España, 984 (var)
When advertising the given sizzle of Andalusian beaches, it's best to avoid extraneous detail and go with precisely what one will find: unsullied sun-baked stretches of sand, family fun, a sleek set or two of tanned, flawless legs and the colorful swirl of protective parasols pin-wheeling skyward. Although Morell created a great number of travel posters during the 1920s and 30s, these works generally avoid the trap of mere decoration and exhibit the same strong graphic qualities we see here. *This is the German version.*
Est: $1,400-$1,700.

SIR CEDRIC LOCKWOOD MORRIS (1889-?)

541. Summer Shell. 1938.
44³/₄ x 29⁷/₈ in./113.7 x 75.8 cm
Baynard Press, London
Cond A–/Unobtrusive tears at paper edges.
Ref: PAI-XVIII, 30
Gorgeous against a deliberately muted landscape, two butterflies of summer circle a Shell symbol as though deciding whether or not it's a flower. This is one of at least three Shell posters by Morris; it was also reproduced as a postcard. The son of a Baronet, he spent his early years farming in Canada, and after service in World War I, became a noted landscape, still life and nature painter. Like Kauffer and a number of other Shell artists, he was for a time associated with the avant-garde London Group.
Est: $1,700-$2,000.

ALBERT GEORGE MORROW (1863-1927)

542. Illustrated Bits. ca. 1895.
19¹/₄ x 28¹/₂ in./48.8 x 72.3 cm
Cond B/Restored tears at folds and edges.
Ref: Hiatt, p. 271, Reims, 1394;
    Affiches Etrangères, p. 71; PAI-XXIX, 520
A gamboling dancing girl, swept along by a self-induced whirlwind of chiffon bearing the name of the magazine she represents, was, according to *The Poster* of January, 1899, the first work by designer Albert Morrow to call attention to his posters and make the public take notice of his commercial skills. A popular English posterist at the turn-of-the-century, his design for *Illustrated Bits* was described by his contemporaries as having "lots of 'go'" (Rogers, p. 47) and as "a radiant affair" (Hiatt, p. 249). Hiatt even went so far as to say of Morrow that "his works should certainly be collected" (p. 249). We couldn't agree more.
Est: $1,000-$1,200.

544

THESE PEOPLE USE SHELL

BLONDES AND BRUNETTES
YOU CAN BE SURE OF SHELL

C. MOZLEY

543

CHARLES MOZLEY (1915-)

**543. These People Use Shell/Blondes and
      Brunettes.** 1939.
44⁷/₈ x 29³/₄ in./113.8 x 75.5 cm
Cond A–/Slight tears in top text area.
Ref: PAI-XVIII, 31
Mozley contributed several posters to the "These People Use Shell" series, usually featuring broad human
categories rather than particular occupations. This
one, for example, claims the better part of the human
race as Shell users.
Est: $1,700-$2,000.

ALPHONSE MUCHA (1860-1939)
For another Mucha work, see Salon des Cents.

544. The Seasons. 1896.
Each: 21¹/₄ x 35¹/₄ in./54 x 89.5 cm
Cond A–/Unobtrusive stains. Framed.
Ref (All Var but PAI): Rennert/Weill,18; Lendl/Paris, 62;
      Mucha/Art Nouveau, 42-44; PAI-XI, 323
This rare set of the four season panels printed on
linen is identical to their on-paper counterparts. The
cloth surface gives a special depth and softness to the
image. This version was done to create ready-made
screens by printing directly onto the material. "One of
Mucha's most endearing and enduring sets. . . Spring
is a blonde sylph who seems to be fashioning a make-
shift lyre out of a bent green branch and her own hair,

with some birds as interested spectators. Summer, a
brunette, sits dreamily on the bank of a pond, cooling
her feet in the water and resting her head against a
bush. Autumn is an auburn lady, making ready to par-
take of the ripe grape. Winter, her brown hair barely
visible as she huddles in a long green cloak, snuggles
by the snow-covered tree trying to warm a shivering
bird with her breath" (Rennert/Weill, p. 90).
Est: $7,000-$9,000. (4)

545. Lorenzaccio. 1896.
14³/₄ x 39⁵/₈ in./37.5 x 100.7 cm
Imp. F. Champenois, Paris
Cond B+/Unobtrusive tears at folds and edges. Framed.
Ref: Rennert/Weill, 20; Lendl/Paris, 4; DFP-II, 626;
      Maitres, 144; Mucha/Art Nouveau, 7; PAI-XXX, 586
"The character of Lorenzaccio, in the play by Alfred de
Musset, is based on Lorenzo the Magnificent (1449-
1492), the most powerful of the Medicis, who ruled
the city state of Florence. In the play, Lorenzaccio
struggles desperately to save Florence, which had
grown rich during his reign, from the grip of a power-
hungry conqueror. Mucha represents this tyranny by a
dragon menacing the city coat of arms and portrays
Lorenzaccio pondering the course of his action. Sarah
Bernhardt adapted the play, first written in 1863, for
herself, and the new version, for which this poster was
produced, opened December 3, 1896. Never afraid to

545

tackle a male role, Bernhardt made Lorenzaccio into
one of the classic roles of her repertoire" (Lendl/Paris,
p. 18). *This is the smaller format.*
Est: $4,500-$5,000.

546

547

548

546. Biscuits Lefèvre-Utile. 1896.
$17^1/_2$ x $24^1/_2$ in./44.6 x 62.2 cm
Imp. F. Champenois, Paris
Cond A–/Horizontal fold. Framed.
Ref: Rennert/Weill, 22; Lendl/Paris, 17; Weill, p. 42;
    Gold, 59 (var); PAI-XXIX, 529
"One of Mucha's most personable young ladies, her hair cascading irrepressibly in fine style, is offering a dish of wafers in this exquisite design. The calendar for 1897 is imprinted on a semi-circular base. Note the initials LU in that part of the golden ornamental border that protrudes into the picture at right. The design of the girl's dress incorporates sickle and wheat emblems, . . . appropriate to the subject" (Rennert/Weill, p. 113).
Est: $9,000-$11,000.

547. Bières de la Meuse. 1897.
$37^3/_4$ x $57^3/_8$ in./96 x 145.8 cm
Imp. F. Champenois, Paris.
Cond B+/Slight tears and stains at folds and edges.
    Framed.
Ref: Rennert/Weill, 27; Lendl/Paris, 37;
    Timeless Images, 36; Maitres, 182; DFP-II, 633;
    PAI-XXVII, 528
"The jovial beer drinker has her long flowing tresses adorned with some appropriate beer ingredients, including barley stalks and green hops, and field poppy flowers indigenous to northeastern France.

This is another one of Mucha's characteristic designs featuring a beauty, semi-circular motifs, and artfully meandering hair" (Rennert/Weill, p. 126).
Est: $15,000-$18,000.

548. C. S./Y.W.C.A. 1922.
$7^1/_2$ x $11^3/_4$ in./19 x 29.8 cm
V. Neubert a Synové, Smíchov
Cond A. Framed.
Ref: Rennert/Weill 107, Var. 1; Lendl/Paris, 90;
    PAI-XXIV, 450
"This poster was used for fund raising for the Czechoslovak YWCA. . . . The movement came to Czechoslovakia after Alice Masaryk, the daughter of the first Czech president, Thomas Masaryk, became acquainted with its work while she stayed at the YWCA Settlement House in Chicago, where she was attending the University of Chicago during 1918 and 1919 . . . (A) Prague branch of the World YWCA was opened in May 1920 and achieved an enrollment of 500 in its first membership drive. . . . Mucha's poster was a part of the organization's efforts to enroll more members and find the funds to build more homes for girls in the major cities in the country" (Rennert/Weill, p. 356). *This is the smaller format.* Hardly bigger than a standard sheet of writing paper, it was probably meant for use on bulletin boards and other eye-level display, or perhaps as a handbill.
Est: $4,000-$5,000.

ART NOUVEAU: 1890-1914

The excellent exhibition, inaugurated at the Victoria & Albert Museum in London, moves to the National Gallery of Art in Washington, D.C., from October 8, 2000 to January 28, 2001. All the leading posterists of the period are included in this well-rounded show.

ALPHONSE MUCHA (continued)

549. Byzantine Heads. 1897.
Each: 14³/₄ x 21 in./37.5 x 53.5 cm
Imp. F. Champenois, Paris (not shown)
Cond A–/Slight staining on brunette. Framed.

Ref (All Var but First): Rennnert/Weill, 40, var 1.;
    Lendl/Paris, 67; Mucha/Paris, 37-38;
    Mucha/Art Nouveau, 48;PAI-XXX, 595
"The mastery evident in creating two archetypes of the
female form against a decorative background confirms
Mucha's artistic maturity. Both women, portrayed in

profile, have their heads decorated with beautiful
jewelry, the richness and oriental nature of which suggested the name *Byzantine Heads* for the series. The
subtle differences in details between the paintings are
worth noticing. For the first time appears the perfect
form of Mucha's often-used motif, circle framing each

head interrupted by a strand of hair. With this device, it is as if Mucha's unreachable beauties have broken the magic border between themselves and their admirers and suggest the possibility that they might, perhaps, meet." (Mucha/Art Nouveau, p. 192). In this version, Mucha added corners filigreed with curves to the original circular designs in order to create the standard rectangular shape of decorative panels. *This is the rarest of all Têtes Byzantines variants.*
Est: $20,000-$25,000. (2)

550. Ivy: Metal Plate. ca. 1901.
Diameter: 12 in./30.5 cm
Cond A–/Slight scratches. Framed.
Ref (All Var): Rennert/Weill, 76; Lendl/Paris, 75;
        Mucha/Art Nouveau, 53a; PAI-XX, 329
One half of the decorative pair, "Reminiscent in concept to the Byzantine Heads, this is a coupling of two girls' profiles in cameos. Since they both represent leafy garden plants they are framed in pale green . . . rich foliage. The backgrounds behind the girls in their respective cameos feature mosaic patterns. The decorative use of foliage of this sort was characteristic of many of the design which appeared in Mucha's *Documents décoratifs* portfolio . . . The circular part of the design was also imprinted on stamped metal plates" (Rennert/Weill, p. 280). This would be an example of one such plate. "It is possible that Mucha was inspired by the dancer Lygie for the panel *Ivy*. This is indicated in the similarity . . . with the poster, also produced in 1901, advertising her performance in *Tableaux Vivants* (Living Pictures), which was based on the themes of Mucha's decorative works" (Mucha/ Art Nouveau, p. 203).
Est: $3,000-$4,000.

551. Laurel: Etched Glass. ca. 1901.
$10^1/_4$ x $10^1/_4$ in./16 x 16 cm
Framed.
Ref (Both Var): Rennert/Weill, 76; PAI-XXX, 594
The laurel image of the decorative pair—Laurel and

Ivy—has been flip-flopped in this signed, etched glass version of the design. Mucha frequently worked in this medium, whether designing stained-glass windows or fine jewelry.
Est: $4,000-$5,000.

552. The Flowers. 1898.
Each: 17 x 41 in./43.2 x 104.1 cm
Imp. F. Champenois, Paris (not shown)
Cond B+/Very slight tears and stains near edges.
        Framed.
Ref: Rennert/Weill, 49; Lendl/Paris, 69;
        Mucha/Art Nouveau, 50; PAI-XXVIII, 434
"One of the fundamental premises of art nouveau was to look for inspiration in nature, and in 'The Flowers' set Mucha produced one of the best arguments for it. The four ethereal sprites represent (from left to right) the Rose, the Iris, the Carnation, and the Lily, respectively, and it is a clear case of Beauty celebrating beauty in each instance. By using only soft pastels and harmonious composition, Mucha imbued each scene with a sense of tranquility and quiet enjoyment" (Lendl/Paris, pp. 86-87).
Est: $25,000-$30,000. (4)

553. The Flowers/Rose. 1900.
$17^1/_4$ x 41 in./44 x 104 cm
Cond A–/Slight tears at paper edges.
Ref: Rennert/Weill, 49d; Lendl/Paris, 69a;
        Mucha/Art Nouveau, 50b
One flower rises above the rest when the air is filled with romance: the rose. And Mucha's personification of that fleshy blossom stands on its own, "proud and closed in her strictly formal pose" (Mucha/Art Nouveau, p. 196). But lest we judge this constrained beauty too harshly, let's not forget that the rose, of all the avidly sought blooms, is the only one equipped with thorns to protect her from the uninvited. Mucha's alluring, yet restrained vision calls to the fore artistically what is often overlooked in casual observations of nature.
Est: $10,000-$12,000.

ALPHONSE MUCHA (continued)

554. Moët & Chandon/Grand Crémant Impérial.
1899.
9¼ x 24 in./23.5 x 61 cm
Imp. F. Champenois, Paris
Cond A. Framed.
Ref: Rennert/Weill, 65; Lendl/Paris, 32;
Wine Spectator, 68; Mucha/Art Nouveau, 28;
PAI-XXVI, 443
"In their relentless pursuit of excellence, Moët and
Chandon was among the first business concerns to
recognize the genius of Mucha . . . The Imperial came
in three grades, 'Dry', 'Crémant' and 'Grand Crémant,'
and all of them have been advertised by the same
design, with the lettering adjusted as needed. Note
the Byzantine ornamentation and elaborate jewelry
on the dark-haired girl: Mucha was as an imaginative
jewelry designer with highly original ideas" (Wine
Spectator, 68).
Est: $11,000-$13,000.

555. Sea Holly. 1902.
11 x 26½ in./28 x 67.5 cm
Imp. F. Champenois, Paris (not shown)
Cond B+/Slight tears and creases. Framed.
Ref: Rennert/Weill, 80; Lendl/Paris, 77 (var);
PAI-XXX, 590
One half of the Heather and Sea Holly decorative
panel set—reprinted with calendars for various years
as well—that proved to be one of Mucha's most popu-
lar designs. "Both the plants and the costumes worn

by the ladies are representative of two ancient sea-
coast provinces of northwestern France, Brittany and
Normandy. Mucha himself, according to his son Jiri,
always referred to the pictures as 'la Bretonne' and
'la Normande' . . . The thistle depicted here, however,
is a common European plant of the eryngo family
named Sea Holly—the real thistle would be too prickly
for the girl to carry in her hands without discomfort"
(Rennert/Weill, p. 290). *Rare!*
Est: $4,000-$5,000.

556. Flirt. 1899.
10¾ x 24 in./37.4 x 61 cm
Imp. F. Champenois, Paris
Cond A. Framed.
Ref: Rennert/Weill, 72; Lendl/Paris, 18 (var);
L'Art du Biscuit, p. 9; Gold, 63; PAI-XXX, 44
This is the original printing of a point-of-purchase display in 1899; after the 1900 World's Fair in Paris, the
poster was reprinted with an added line of text refer-
ring to a prize won by the product on that occasion.
"To bring home the name of the product, Mucha
created a discreet flirtation which embodies the 19th-
century ideal of a romantic encounter: the girl demure
and coy, the gentleman persuasive, the setting a
fragrant garden. But he didn't forget the sponsor:
The wrought-iron gate carries the name, and the girl's
dress features a print pattern of the letters L-U, a
subtle decorative reminder" (Gold, p. 46).
Est: $6,000-$7,000.

557. Pendant Design.
5¼ x 9¾ in./13.5 x 24.8 cm
Signed ink-on-paper design. Framed.
Mucha's sensitive jewelry designs were seen in his
compositions in the *Documents Décoratifs* book and
their practical applications were evidenced in the

559

560

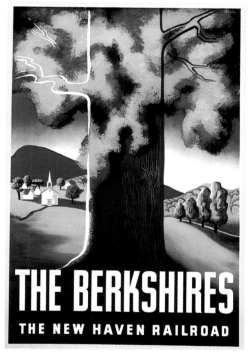

561

562

objects he created for Georges Fouquet's incredible art nouveau boutique in Paris, preserved today in that city's Musée Carnavalet. The Mucha estate stamp appears on the far bottom right of the image.
Est: $4,000-$5,000.

WILLY MUCHA (1905-)

558. Ouistreham Riva Bella. 1934.
24¹/₄ x 39 in./61.6 x 99 cm
Imp. H. Chachoin, Paris
Cond A.
Ref: PAI-XII, 346
No relation to the better known Mucha, Willy was basically a painter who exhibited some of his work at the Salon des Independents. In time, he veered toward Art Deco and abstraction, and this excursion poster is one of his very best designs in that vein, with the primary colors neatly sprucing up the sparse elemental nature of the design.
Est: $1,500-$1,800.

ALFRED MULLER (1869-?)

559. Peacocks.
63¹/₄ x 25¹/₈ in./160.7 x 63.8 cm
Cond A.
Ref: PAI-XXVIII, 442
Born in Livorno in 1869, Italian-native Alfred (or Alfredo) Muller was active as a painter and watercolorist at the turn of the century in both his homeland and France, specializing graphically in the production of decorative panels. These colorful and elegant peacocks, at once both integrated into and decorously separate from their lush surroundings, amply demonstrate Muller's natural flair. Steinlen, in his poster for the magazine "Cocorico" indicated that Muller was one of its contributors, but no work of his appears in any issue.
Est: $1,700-$2,000.

560. Swans.
62¹/₂ x 22 in./158.3 x 55.8 cm
Cond A.
Ref: PAI-XXX, 597
The romance of the only feathered paramours who mate for life is reflected by Müller with Art Nouveau grace amidst the calming quietude of lily pad and rush.
Est: $1,700-$2,000.

BEN NASON

561. New Haven Railroad/The Berkshires.
28 x 41³/₄ in./71 x 106 cm
Cond A-/Slight tears at bottom edge.
Ref: PAI-XV, 412 (var)
Berkshire County, the westernmost county in Massachusetts, is conveniently located within a two-and-one-half hour drive to New York City and Boston. Surrounded by the Berkshire Hills to the east and the Taconic Mountains to the west, the splendid area that also offers numerous lakes, rivers and streams has become a summer and leaf-peeping haven for the affluent and those who merely would like to be perceived in that light. Nason's spectacular—and mildly abstract—vision of verdant simplicity for the New Haven railroad tempts the nearby city dwellers with expansive freshness with room to roam.
Est: $1,200-$1,500.

JACQUES NATHAN-GARAMOND (1910-)

562. Ducretet-Thomson. 1939.
30¹/₄ x 46¹/₂ in./76.8 x 118.2 cm
Printel, Paris
Cond B-/Slight stains in image; restored tears in margin.
Oh, the places you'll go. And thanks to Ducretet-Thomson, you'll go there without ever leaving the confines of your parlor. The Nathan-Garamond design for the short-wave marvel is a rather unique photomontage effort, in that instead of utilizing a photographic image of the product being touted as "The Voice of the World," he instead places a pictured sculpture of a waif putting ear to a seashell at the center of a global compass, in the process creating for the viewer the possibility of becoming the master of their listening universe grace of his employers. Nathan-Garamond was an interior designer and posterist of the Constructivist school and is best known for the many posters he created for L'Habitation, the Paris home show.
Est: $1,000-$1,200.

563

564

566

NEW YORK WORLD'S FAIR—1939.

563. New York World's Fair/John Weidman.
Artist: **Anonymous.**
15 x 20 in./38 x 51 cm
Cond A.
Ref (Both Var): Trylon, p. 19; PAI-XXVIII, 448
During the first part of the 20th century, the Brooklyn Ash Removal Company turned Flushing Meadows into an odoriferous wasteland. Despite this, "plans were announced in 1935 to reclaim the land for a colossal world's fair that would 'demonstrate the wonders of contemporary life now within the reach of the man of the millions as well as the man with the millions.' Such a scheme would have been impossible if not for the Fair's president, Grover Whalen. In a typically grand speech before his fellow boosters, Whalen said: "I remember way back, in studying advertising some years ago, that . . . in Julius Caesar's time they had plumbing. Nobody knew anything about it (then) because there was no means of communicating the fact. . . . It was sixty years ago that we got plumbing in the White House. Why has it advanced to the point it has today? Because of . . . advertising and salesmanship. We have a product to sell . . . the New York World's Fair of 1939. How are we going to sell it? We must go to the country . . . we want every store . . . to put out a World's Fair flag . . . and we'd like all the merchandise to be Fair-inspired—its color scheme and everything else" (Trylon, p. 19). Case in point: this spectacular stock poster, bursting with the marvels of the World's Fair, distributed to Pennsylvanian merchants. Here, the John Weidman dealership advertises its fuel and fertilizer wares while unabashedly hawking the Fair.
Est: $1,000-$1,200.

564. New York World's Fair. 1939.
Artist: **John Atherton (1900-1952)**
20 x 30¹/₂ in./50.9 x 77.5 cm
Grinnell Litho Co., N.Y.C.
Cond A–/Slight crease at lower left corner.
Ref: Trylon, p. 18; American Posters, p. 42; PAI-XXX, 600
The Trylon, Perisphere and Geosphere—otherwise known as Earth—all in the lap of Liberty are the elements of this striking Fair poster. Atherton went on to design some memorable "home front" posters during World War II (see PAI-XXVIII 136). Highly recognized as a magazine and advertising illustrator, he was responsible for many national campaigns including Packard, Lincoln and General Motors cars.
Est: $1,200-$1,500.

565. New York World's Fair/World of Tomorrow. 1939.
Artist: **Joseph Binder (1898-1972)**
20 x 30¹/₄ in./50.8 x 76.9 cm
Grinnell Litho Co., NYC

568

Cond A–/Slight tears at edges.
Ref: Art Deco, p. 113; Weill, 427; PAI-XXX, 601
The Trylon and Perisphere, ubiquitous symbols of the Fair, glow like celestial objects against a night sky. Airplanes, searchlights, skyscrapers and an ocean liner provide other signs of modernity in this design, first-prize winner of the poster contest organized by the Fair's sponsors. Binder was born in Vienna and trained there and in Munich. After a term as professor at the Municipal Institute in Frankfurt, he returned to Vienna to teach at the Academy. On the eve of World War II, he joined the exodus of talented, politically incorrect Germans and Austrians to America where he became a leading designer of posters for the war effort. He also won acclaim for his historical paintings and portraits.
Est: $2,500-$3,000.

566. New York World's Fair 1939.
Artist: **Albert Staehle (1899-1974)**
20 x 30¹/₂ in./50.9 x 77.5 cm
Grinnell Litho. Co., NYC
Cond A.

Ref: Trylon, p. 39; PAI-XXVIII, 453
Fireworks, brilliant lighting and a happy wave from an official hostess greet us at the Fair's opening ceremonies. An image befitting "the grandest illusion of the century" (Trylon, p. 39) that was The World of Tomorrow.
Est: $1,700-$2,000.

HANS NEUMANN (1888-1960)

567. Josephine Baker Revue. 1928.
9³/₈ x 12³/₄ in./23.8 x 32.5 cm
Cond B/Restored tears at edges. Framed.
This in-store placard advertising Josephine Baker's 1928 Vienna appearance sizzles with the thrill of flesh and feathers one has come to inseparably associate with the enigmatic performer, topped off with a smile as unforgettable as the exoticism she embodied. Multiply this erotic zest exponentially with the addition of a chorus line of Josephinettes and you've created the equation for an irresistible promotional lure. Or so it would seem. The actual details of this Austrian engagement are nowhere near as frivolous as the adverting or the show itself. "A petition to ban

'Then I started to dance, the way I always have danced' . . . and every night for a month, the sold-out (Johann Strauss) theater had to turn . . . them away" (Josephine Baker, pp. 155-157).
Est: $1,700-$2,000.

BEN NICHOLSON (1885-1982)

568. These Men Use Shell/Guardsmen. 1938.
$44^{3}/4$ x 30 in./114 x 76.2 cm
L. Weiner, Ltd., London
Cond A–/Slight tears and stains in borders.
Ref: Shell, 77; PAI-XXV, 73
Palace guards use Shell, and they know their duty: Perhaps anyone who doesn't deserves to be thrown into the Tower of London, shown on the right. Nicholson was a widely exhibited painter from about 1920 to 1940. His mother, Mabel Nicholson, was an artist too, as was his father, Sir William Nicholson, who with brother-in-law James Ferrier Pryde comprised the Beggarstaff Brothers.
Est: $1,000-$1,200.

NODING

569. Championnats d'Europe d'Athletisem 1958.
$24^{5}/8$ x $39^{1}/4$ in./62.5 x 99.7 cm
Tornbloms Bengtsons Litogr, Stockholm
Cond A.
Neatly sandwiched between the 1956 and 1960 Olympic competitions, this European athletic championship convening in the Swedish capitol doubtlessly helped to keep the flame of physical competition burning strong on the Continent. The previously unseen designer arrives at an ingenious conclusion when it came to transferring motion and speed to the design: let the background do all the work for you. By unevenly streaking the victoriously-toned backdrop, the implied speed makes it appear as if the racing statuary are the ones surging their way to glory.
Est: $1,000-$1,200.

570

569

Josephine's 'brazen-faced heathen dances' was circulating, and there ensued a debate in Parliament . . . Josephine was supposed to have opened at the Ronacher theater, but the city council said no. . . . Catholic priests were still preaching against her. Ostentatiously she began attending services every day . . .

But the authorities remained unconvinced of her fitness to entertain a population as moral as the Viennese; she still had to appear before a committee that would judge her act. . . . Diaghilev. . . offered Josephine advice: She should audition by dancing on toe. She did, and was granted a work permit. . . . She came on in a long gown, buttoned to the neck, to a 'second of total silence and surprise,' and began to sing a blues song called 'Pretty Little Baby.' The applause that followed was wild; it seemed the theater would crumble.

572

573

NYK

570. Hendaye-Plage. ca. 1900.
28^1/$_8$ x 39^3/$_4$ in./71.5 x 101 cm
Imp. F. Champenois, Paris
Cond B+/Unobtrusive tears, largely at edges and top
    text area.
Ref: Train à l'Affiche, 90
In the extreme southwest of France, Hendaye is the
last French town you'll encounter before crossing the
border into Spain. Confined on the edge of both the
Atlantic Ocean and Pyrenees Mountains, its exceptional beauty is enhanced to an even greater degree by
an immense fine sand beach. Delightful beyond compare, this encounter between the crisp refinement of
Biarritz and the sultry grace of San Sebastian at the
Basque confluence for the Central and Paris/Orleans
rail lines—a meeting that charmingly can be taken as literal or metaphorical—commands attention with such
subtle surety that no textual pitch is even required.
And just in case the subtlety of the rendezvous is lost
on the few pedestrians not susceptible to seduction, a
panoramic map of the area is graciously included at
the poster's bottom.
Est: $1,500-$1,800.

EUGENE OGÉ (1869-1936)

571. La Lanterne. 1902.
54^1/$_4$ x 78 in./137.7 x 198 cm
Affiches E. Bougard, Paris
Cond B+/Slight staining and tears at fold, seam and
    edges.
Ref (All Var but Ogé): Ogé, 235; Musée d'Affiche, 43;
    Dreyfus, 5; Phillips II, 447
An imposing 2-sheet design for the publication that
would become a major Dreyfusard vehicle. "This composition for a Republican magazine, which posts without ambiguity its anticlerical stance, is the only known
creation of Ogé's where he abandons his habitual
good nature. The cleric, transformed into a vampire,
clutches the Sacré-Coeur with powerful talons, spreading his shadow over the town. Further elements,
historic and personal, permit one to decipher this
extremely charged image, which in one fell swoop
stigmatizes the recent and condemnable role of the
church in the Dreyfus Affair (*see* No. 504), the existence of this Montmartre basilica, the expiatory monu-

571

ment thrown disgracefully in the face of the common
people, and the educational responsibility of the
priesthood in the disastrous destiny of their brethren.
This poster is without a doubt the origin of the split
between Ogé and Charles Verneau" (Ogé, p. 219).
This is the larger format.
Est: $1,500-$1,800.

MANUEL ORAZI (1860-1934)

572. Job.
18^3/$_4$ x 24^1/$_8$ in./47.6 x 61.2 cm
Cond A. Framed.
Job, a manufacturer of rolling paper that later ventured
into all-out cigarette production, always turned to the

574

greatest poster artists of the time to promote their
smoldering output—Jane Atché, Bouisset, Cappiello,
Chéret, Meunier and, of course, Mucha. But none of
these premier posterists created a design so rare, so
exquisite, that only one known copy remains in existence—and that version would be on *silk* no less! No,
that distinct honor would fall to Orazi, an accomplished painter, illustrator and designer, for whom
exotic themes were a specialty. And it is indeed nearly
impossible to imagine a cigarette girl more exotic than
the one he presents us with here. Byzantinely arrayed
and cool as an ornate cucumber, this princess puffer
exudes refinement and excess, an inspired combina-

ORSI (1889-1947)

573. Beethoven.
47 x 62³/₄ in./119.3 x 159.3 cm
Imp. H. Chachoin, Paris
Cond B/Slight tears at folds.
Orsi launches the brooding genius of the German composer into the celestial sphere, where his visage is allowed to take its proper place in the cosmos around which the moon and the stars revolve in this promotion for a bio-play of the bombastic visionary playing at Théâtre de la Porte St. Martin. The posterist known only as Orsi produced hundreds of posters, many of them for the theater, and all with strong, eye-catching designs. "In the history of this art, his name must occupy an important place because of the innovative character of his esthetic . . . and the importance of his work" (Benezit).
Est: $2,000-$2,500.

PAL (Jean de Paléologue, 1860-1942)

574. Bouffes-Parisiens/Mam'zelle Carabin. 1894.
24¹/₄ x 37 in./61.5 x 94 cm
Imp. Paul Dupont, Paris
Cond B–/Restored tears at folds.
Ref: Spectacle, 120a
Alas. No one seems to have found it consequential enough to record the melodramatic goings-on during the run of "Mam'zelle Carabin" at the Bouffes-Parisiens. It would appear to have been an operettic evening, filled with teary-eyed reconciliation, dastardly deeds and a high-spirited international costume fête whose title translates, somewhat surprisingly given the poster vignettes, as "Miss Medic." This is actually one of two posters Pal created for the theatricality that were assuredly just what the doctor ordered. *Rare!*
Est: $1,200-$1,500.

575. Dufayel/Administrations. 1894.
38¹/₂ x 55 in./98 x 139.8 cm
Imp. H. Laas, Paris
Cond B+/Slight tears at folds and edges.
Ref (Both Var): DFP-II, 705; PAI-XXVIII, 472
A poster for the Grand Magasins Dufayel—an early

Parisian version of a shopping mall containing over 400 stores and an early movie house—is being papered about Paris by a fetching poster hanger, who also happens to be pulling double-duty as a distributor of the venue's sales catalogue. The only problem is that she would seem to be ill-garbed for such a sticky situation in her revealing summer dress. Not that we're complaining, mind you.
Est: $2,000-$2,500.

576. Fernand Clément & Cie. 1895.
41³/₈ x 58¹/₄ in./105 x 148 cm
Imp. Paul Dupont, Paris
Cond B/Restored tears, largely at folds.
Ref: DFP-II, 685; Petite Reine, 49; Reims, 941;
   Gold, 68; PAI-XXX, 14
"The voluptuous beauty in ecstasy expresses the feeling of unrestrained freedom which the bicycle could bring into a 19th-century woman's life. Now able to cover distances under their own power, women felt there was a whole new frontier opening to them, as indeed there was. Pal gives the euphoria palpable substance" (Gold, p. 48).
Est: $7,000-$9,000.

577. Rayon d'Or. ca. 1895.
31³/₄ x 47³/₄ in./80.6 x 121.2 cm
Imp. Paul Dupont, Paris
Cond A.
Ref: DFP-II, 688; Reims, 951; Timeless Images, 22;
   Weill, 71; Femme s'Affiche, 154;
   Wine Spectator, 129; Gold, 21; PAI-XXIX, 566
"Rarely has a product so humdrum as a kerosene lamp been promoted with such uninhibited zest—but then Pal, given free rein to his imagination, could be relied to come up with something featuring one of his incomparably alluring nymphs every time. The secret of his success is the fact that even though he makes it clear in some way—such as the gossamer wings here —that these are purely imaginary spirits, the loving care with which he draws every curve and flesh tone gives them a sensuality much too solid for make believe" (Gold, p. 17).
Est: $2,500-$3,000.

ion for addictive advertising. The
rt Nouveau background—an element that frequently
ivals the primary focus—against which she indulges
erself can't even compare with the ensemble which
Orazi has chosen for her—a jewel-encrusted shift that
nay as well be armor for all its baubles, the earrings
hat defy accessorized plausibility and the peacock
hapeau, an item to which words should not be
pplied. Unbelievable! *Extremely rare!*
st: $12,000-$15,000.

578

579

580

581

PAL (continued)

578. Patin-Bicyclette/Richard-Choubersky. ca. 1899.
36^1/$_8$ x 50^1/$_2$ in./91.7 x 128.4 cm
Imp. Paul Dupont, Paris
Cond B+/Slight tears at folds.
Ref: Gold, 124; PAI-XXX, 172
Obviously, this precursor to roller blades made a big enough impression on the conventionally skating gent to have him wind up on his keister. It would take, however, over eighty years before the mainstream fitness-conscious public caught up with this prescient idea. The exercise angle matters very little to Pal—the product was merely an excuse to create another graphic vixen, which he does here with sophisticated understatement.
Est: $2,500-$3,000.

579. Liberator Cycles & Automobiles. ca. 1899.
42^7/$_8$ x 57^1/$_2$ in./109 x 146 cm
Cond A–/Slight loss lower left corner.
Ref (All Var): DFP-II, 696; Bicycle Posters, 48;
    Petite Reine, 33; PAI-XXVII, 21
Faced with the concept of "Liberator," other designers might have thought of a male figure (as, in fact, can be seen on the firm's logo), but Pal finds a way to inveigle one of his curvaceous beauties into the scene. A most definitive sign of the popularity of this design is the fact that abundant reprintings were executed by several different firms utilizing the talents of various other posterists to do nothing but *redraw* Pal's original artwork, such as the Charles Tichon variant (*see* PAI-XXVII, 21) with thistles in the lower right, Émile Clouet's version (*see* next lot) or this version executed by an unidentified designer who merely juggled the bottom text. What remains identical in every version is the resolute "Don't mess with me, Mister!" look of the sturdy "Soldat Gaulois," standing guard with her awesome armory of sword, shield, Liberator helmet, and, of course, Liberator bicycle. Rarely has the saying "If it ain't broke, don't fix it" been applied with such resolute beauty.
Est: $1,700-$2,000.

PAL & EMILE CLOUET

580. Liberator Cycles & Motocycles.
51 x 79^1/$_4$ in./129.5 x 201.4 cm
Imp. J. Simon Weisshoff, Paris
Cond A–/Unobtrusive folds.
Ref: DFP-II, 696 (var); Bicycle Posters, 48 (var);
    Petite Reine, 33 (var); PAI-XXIX, 77
It's a bit curious as to why Liberator bicycles would hire the services of a capable designer to create a poster for their product and then have him simply redraw an image from a successful earlier campaign. But that would definitely be the case with this Clouet

work for the company, which leaves the central image virtually untouched—hence the "d'après Pal" credit—while removing all of the background. *This is the larger format of the previous image.*
Est: $2,000-$2,500.

581. Loterie. 1900.
31^1/$_4$ x 46^1/$_2$ in./79.4 x 118 cm
Imp. Chardin, Paris
Cond B/Slight tears at left.
Ref (Both Var): DFP-II, 697; PAI-XXVII, 548
Where else but in France would the public be encouraged to take chances on a lottery for the benefit of dramatic artists? Holding the wheel of progress in one hand, the maiden representing dramatic arts stands girded with the masks of comedy and tragedy and not much else. Note how Pal arranges the lighting to show the lady's charms to the very best advantage. *This is the medium format.*
Est: $1,500-$1,800.

M. PALLANDRE

582. Thermes de Cauterets. 1898.
39^3/$_4$ x 50^3/$_4$ in./98.5 x 128.7 cm
Affiches Camis, Paris
Cond B/Slight stains in lower right corner; unobtrusive folds.
Ref: Chemins de Fer, 36; Train à l'Affiche, 82;
    Tourism/Suntory, 84; PAI-XXIX, 574 (var)
A beauteous hiker takes a moment's repose from her jaunt in order to mull over life's little foibles amidst the natural rapture of the Jeret Valley, located in Cauterets, the French sulfur springs resort on the Spanish border. The combined rail systems of France don't hedge their bets one iota, having obviously instructed Pallandre to shoehorn every possible attraction the spa has to offer into his design. And he does a splendid job of it, fanning out the features from the Espagne Bridge to its various thermal stations, while dropping in various locales in cameo, amazingly executing this crammed directive without creating a hint of claustrophobia. *This is the larger format.*
Est: $1,400-$1,700.

583

585

584

sufficiency. In 1858, with a religious revival sweeping the Northeast, this group of college-educated, Protestant women of varying denominations concerning themselves with this humanist commitment named their group the Young Women's Christian Organization. Working together toward their unified goals of improving the quality of female life, they became the first women's organization in the United States. The goal of this early group sought a common vision: peace, justice, freedom and dignity for all people. In 1907, the National Board of the Y.W.C.A. was incorporated in New York. Their goals were lofty, but the sense of sisterhood that they strove for never excluded the pleasures of camaraderie, a spirit reflected admirably in this Parkhurst poster, showing two such young female travelers fashionably setting off down the friendly road to success. It's interesting to note that approximately the same time of the production of this design, the first women's pension fund in the U.S., the Y.W.C.A. Retirement Fund, was initiated. Chicago born Parkhurst was a member of the Artists' Guild and the Society of Illustrators. She is perhaps best remembered for her work featured on the covers of *The Saturday Evening Post* and *Colliers*.
Est: $2,000-$2,500.

RENÉ PÉAN (1875-1940)

584. Tout le Monde à Paris. 1898.
$23^3/_4$ x $32^1/_4$ in./60.3 x 82 cm
Imp. Chaix, Paris
Cond B+/Slight tears and stains at folds and edges.
Thanks to the technomagic of cable and satellite television, you can practically bring the entire world into your living room. But once upon a time—and not that long ago in a cosmic sense—people had to actually *travel* to see the larger picture the globe could afford. So imagine the opportunity to see all the world in one

city. Sound impossible? Not if you knew about the 1900 Paris World's Fair it wasn't. This poster for the French Fair Society doesn't really make much ado over that city-swelling factoid, taking the more understated approach of allegorical curvaceousness sweeping her laurels in a welcoming gesture. What is impressive is the week-long Parisian stays they're offering, including lodging, round-trip rail tickets for this package ranging from 1.25 to 3.60 francs, depending on the class of service and place of departure. But note the small print: That's the weekly charge over a seventeen-week period, so the range is 21.25 to 61.20 francs—still a great deal!
Est: $1,000-$1,200.

585. Paris-Valence. 1905.
$42^1/_2$ x $62^3/_8$ in./108 x 158.4 cm
Imp. Chaix, Paris
Cond B+/Slight stains at paper edges.
Valence's remarkable geographical location makes it an ideal stopping place along the Rhône Valley and a hub of life and exchanges with the Alps and Massif Central regions. With a rich cultural tradition, this beautiful canalled city, peppered with parks and spectacular architecture, makes for an ideal winter vacation destination, one from which the urbane Parisian could either make winter sport excursions, or simply wallow in peaceful sophistication. So, with little more than the lilt of her head, this fox-stolled socialite turns us in the right direction for wintering in Valence. Péan was a pupil of Chéret, working under him at the Chaix printing firm and this piece definitely reflects the master's influence. He specialized in theater and cabaret posters from around 1890 to 1905. After being among the first to produce posters for the fledgling movie industry, he faded into obscurity.
Est: $2,500-$3,000.

ANITA PARKHURST (1892-?)

583. Y.W.C.A./The Friendly Road. ca. 1924.
$19^5/_8$ x $26^1/_2$ in./49.7 x 67.2 cm
Rode & Brand, N. Y.
Cond A.
In the late-1850s, a small, concerned group of perceptive women began to sense the anxiety of the young women relocating to the larger cities across the country from rural areas in search of work and self-

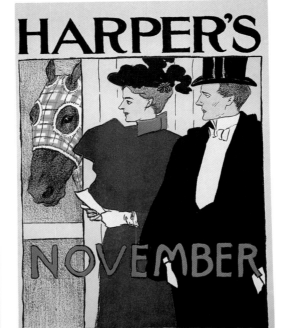

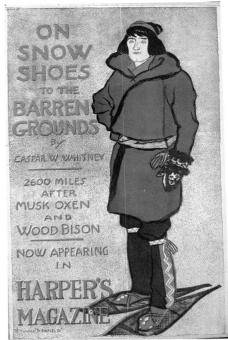

586

587

588

Country Carts Series No.1 Copyright 1900 by Edward Penfield   EXERCISING CART   Published by R.H.Russell   New York

589

Country Carts Series No.1 Copyright 1900 by Edward Penfield   HACKNEY CART   Published by R.H.Russell   New York

590

Country Carts Series No.1 Copyright 1900 by Edward Penfield   A KENTUCKY BREAKING CART   Published by R.H.Russell   New York

591

Country Carts Series No.1 Copyright 1900 by Edward Penfield   MEADOW BROOK CART   Published by R.H.Russell   New York

592

M. PELTIER

586. Imprimerie A. Barbière. 1900.
$14^1/_2$ x $20^1/_2$ in./36.7 x 52 cm
Imp. A. Barbière, Toulouse
Cond B+/Slight tears and stains at edges.
There's something utterly pleasant about this promotion for the Barbière printing firm of Toulouse. Complete with a 1901 calendar, there's an ease present that doesn't necessarily accompany Art Nouveau creations, from the modest foliage and wild flower bou-

quet to the simple line and cut of our calendar cutie's outfit. In every aspect, it's Mucha redux, with one major exception—the hair, which is swept away in an untamable decorative incongruity not in line with a single other element of the design. As the company's *spécialité du maison* is promotional fans, they include five of the calendar month panels on the advertising waver for good measure.
Est: $1,200-$1,500.

EDWARD PENFIELD (1866—1925)

587. Harper's/November. 1895.
$11^3/_4$ x $16^1/_4$ in./30 x 41 cm
Cond A.
Ref: DFP-I, 350; Lauder, 171; Reims, 1267; PAI-XXVI, 493
One of the best of our native talents, Penfield is well-known for the decade 1891-1901, during which he was the art director of *Harper's*. For five of these ten years, he produced posters for each month's issue of the then-popular magazine. His drawings are deceptively

593

594

595

simple, with flat colors and clear lines, but they always manage to convey class and refinement. Penfield's posters are models of effective composition and economy of expression. Here, an elegant couple appraises a thoroughbred—as always a subtle suggestion that people of breeding read the magazine.
Est: $1,200-$1,500.

588. Harper's/On Snow Shoes. 1896.
11³/₈ x 18¹/₈ in./29 x 46 cm
Cond A–/Slight tears at edges.
Ref: DFP-I, 366; Reims, 1278; Lauder, 189
A droll Penfield take for Harper's. Removed from his customary urbane milieu and thrust into the frigid savagery of the frozen tundra, all in the name of a feature entitled "On Snow Shows to the Barren Ground," running in that month's issue of the magazine, it looks as if Penfield took one of his collegiate dandies and dressed him up in freshly store-bought cold-weather hunting gear.
Est: $700-$900.

589. Exercising Cart. 1900.
22¹/₈ x 15¹/₂ in./56.2 x 39.5 cm
Published by R. H. Russell, New York
Cond A.

Throughout his illustrative life, Penfield "incorporated coaches in some of his *Harpers*' posters, as well as in the work for other clients. Studying coach design and history was a favorite hobby, and he later became a collector of these vehicles, and wrote about them for *Outing*. The unfinished manuscript of a book on coaches survives among his family papers" (Penfield, p. 13). This attraction to early vehicular transport wends its way across the next four decorative panels, titled "Country Carts Series #1," no doubt part of a larger portfolio devoted to horse drawn conveyance. Here we are given your basic exercising cart, nothing fancy just high-wheeled dependability for traveling over frequently muddy roadways. Though Penfield renders horse and driver with masterful surety, it's his attention to detail that makes him a superior chronicler of his time, such as the boater clasp attached to the driver's hat to prevent blow away damage.
Est: $1,000-$1,200.

590. Hackney Cart. 1900.
22¹/₂ x 15¹/₂ in./56.2 x 39.5 cm
Cond A–/Slight tears and stains at edges.
By definition, a cart is a two-wheeled vehicle drawn by a draft animal for the transportation of freight, agricultural produce, refuse, and people. The hackney cart seen here—drawn by a spectacular chestnut draught horse—elevates the driver further off the road, providing him with an even better view of what lies ahead.
Est: $1,000-$1,200.

591. A Kentucky Breaking Cart. 1900.
22¹/₂ x 15¹/₂ in./56.2 x 39.5 cm
Cond A–/Slight tears and stains at edges.
Carts have been made in several ways, with emphasis usually placed upon simplicity of construction. As far as simplicity goes, not much could top the straightforward construction of this Kentucky Breaking cart, currently braking along the road, affording its chiseled roan a moment's rest. For the first time, Penfield allows his driver to break the "Fourth Wall" of the poster and gaze directly at the viewer.
Est: $1,000-$1,200.

592. Meadow Brook Cart. 1900.
22¹/₂ x 15¹/₂ in./56.2 x 39.5 cm
Cond A.
With some cart models, the shafts were frequently but extensions of the framework of the body, and, depending upon the nature of the load to be hauled, the body itself might simply consist of a sturdy wooden box. A better summation couldn't apply to this Meadow Brook cart, with room for two and maybe a pooch. Interest-

ingly, in this series of four panels, Penfield opted to show the male horsemen in motion, while he kept the female drivers at rest. Though no aspersions are being cast, one can't help but wonder whether his motives were chivalrous or chauvinist.
Est: $1,000-$1,200.

593. Y. W. C. A. ca. 1918.
29⁵/₈ x 24⁵/₈ in./75.2 x 62.5 cm
United States Printing & Lithograph Co., New York
Cond A. Framed.
Ref: American Posters, 63; Theofiles, 211; Phillips I, 487
"The dramatic image Penfield made for the Young Women's Christian Association late in his career exemplifies his use of flattened shapes and bold composition. In contrast with his early work, here he reduces the decorative elements and focuses on the broad planes of color to make silhouettes of the figures carrying a hoe, a rake, and harvested vegetables. Despite their competence with tools and farm animals and their khaki-colored uniforms that evoke thoughts of the boys gone off to war, these 'girls' remain feminine in face and manner" (American Posters, p. 101).
Est: $1,400-$1,700.

PEPSI

594. Grossenbrode Kai-Gedser.
23¹/₂ x 32⁷/₈ in./59.8 x 83.6 cm
Offsetdruckerei Emil Falke
Cond A–/Slight tears near paper edges.
Rending an opening into the flat midnight-blue sky like a portal to another dimension of travel, this bridge linking Germany to Denmark reflects off the glassine waters where a ferry service also bridges the liquid gap betwixt the two nations, leaving a trail of European unification in her wake. A slick, monumental design for the German Railways.
Est: $1,000-$1,200.

PIERRE PERON (1905-1988)

595. 1 Pote/Anis Breton Surfin. 1936.
46¹/₂ x 62¹/₂ in. 118 x 158.6 cm
Imp. Depêche, Brest
Cond A.
Ref: PAI-XXIX, 579
A glass of this potion will clearly bring a glow to your face, clearly expressed here with graphic delight. The simple lines and bold statement remind us somewhat of Paul Colin's approach, but this artist has quite a flair all his own. And as there is a nautical theme in full effect; a deep sea-blue dominates the color scheme.
Est: $1,700-$2,000.

597

601

CELESTINO PIATTI (1922-)

596. Dimitri/Knie. 1973.
35¹/4 x 50 in./89.5 x 127 cm
Reutsch, Trimbach
Cond A–/Unobtrusive slight tears and stains at edges.
Ref: Circus Posters, 80; PAI-XIII, 373
The famous clown Dimitri appears at the Knie Circus in a design which simulates a multicolored crayon drawing. The style comes easy to one of Switzerland's best and most prolific contemporary graphic designers and posterists, Celestino Piatti, who has, among other things, illustrated a number of children's books, some written by his wife, Ursula. It is a style he rarely uses in his posters, which tend to rely on bolder, woodcut-like outlines and broader coverage of color. Of the more than 400 posters produced by him, this is regrettably the only one for the Knie Circus.
Est: $800-$1,000.

ALESSANDRO POMI (1890-?)

597. Cicli Attila.
38¹/4 x 54⁷/8 in./97.2 x 139.4 cm
Sacchetti, Milano
Cond B/Restored tears at folds and paper edges;
      image and colors excellent.
Come and worship at the altar of gear-driven technology to a product forged by man, yet so superior, so infinitely more divinely-constructed than any other pedal-powered vehicle that mighty fleet-footed Apollo himself must supplicate, caduceus and all, at the foot of the anvil, resigned to his newfound secondary status. All hail Attila, a bike above the rest! Consumer idolatry at its most spectacular. Pomi studied at the Venice Academy of Art under Ettore Tito. He went on to produce landscape and portrait paintings as well as frescos and was represented in worldwide exhibitions. In the 1920s he produced posters of great interest and distinction. *Rare!*
Est: $3,500-$4,000.

596

JULES DE PRAETERE (1879-1947)

598. Carlton Restaurant. 1915.
34⁷/8 x 49¹/4 in./88.5 x 125 cm
Gebr. Fretz, Zürich
Cond A–/Unobtrusive stains; horizontal fold.
Ref: Schweitzer Hotel, 41
A sumptuous repast awaits you at Zurich's Carlton

598

Restaurant, and de Praetere knows when to leave chic-enough alone, surrounding his classically overindulgent champagne and lobster feast with a framing bower of stocky vines, sumptuous fruit and pouting blossoms. The upscale eatery, located in the Carlton Hotel, still stands today at Bahnhofstrasse 41.
Est: $1,400-$1,700.

599

600

602

MOST HUMOROUS PAPER. 1D. *Weekly.*

PICK-ME-UP

603

SHOES & SHIPS AND SEALINGWAX

AT DERRY & TOMS KENSINGTON W.8.

604

RENE PREJELAN

599. Ponctua.
46⁷/₈ x 63¹/₄ in./119.2 x 160.7 cm
Publicité Wall, Paris
Cond A.
A Lilliputian Scotswoman turns a Ponctua precision pocket watch into an instrument of percussion with highlandish glee in order to drum up business for the chronometer that's not only the best, but the least expensive. And if she isn't but a wee lass, then that's one huge watch. Préjelan created a handful of posters while writing and illustrating for Parisian satiric magazines around 1910. Little else is known about him—a pity.
Est: $1,400-$1,700.

LESLIE RAGAN (1897-1972)

600. A Century of Service/Norfolk and Western.
1938.
22¹/₄ x 28 in./56.5 x 71 cm
Cond A.
Ref: PAI-XXVI, 503
The past is the present, with the dream of a yet-to-be-realized powerful engine riding like a phantom on the

smoke of the technological marvel of a coal-burning locomotive in a scene from the 1830s, the very first decade of railroading in the United States. Ragan, an Iowa native who studied painting and illustration in Chicago before moving to New York City, spent most of his career creating posters for the Norfolk & Western and the New York Central railroads.
Est: $1,700-$2,000.

601. Union Terminal Cleveland/New York Central.
26³/₄ x 40¹/₈ in./68 x 102 cm
Latham Litho, Long Island City, N.Y.
Cond A-/Slight tears at edges.
Since the late 1800s, railroads had been constructing train stations of monumental proportions, featuring a variety of classical design elements. In the 1920s, it was time for Cleveland, Ohio, to gain such a structure, and for railroad passengers to gain the convenience of a single union station, eliminating the need to transfer across town when changing between trains of different rail lines. In 1925, the firm of Graham, Anderson, Probst and White was engaged to engineer the proposed structure, having completed Chicago's Union Station earlier that year. Their design included an office building that, upon completion in 1930, became the trademark feature of Cleveland's skyline. The

superb passenger trains of the New York Central Lines paused here on their luxury runs connecting New York City and Boston with the Midwest, and the terminal also played host to the fine trains of the Baltimore & Ohio and the Nickel Plate. For many years, Terminal Tower was the tallest building in the city, at 708 feet, and it stands today, attractively illuminated each evening, and still a Cleveland landmark overlooking Lake Erie. This poster is part of a series the artist created for the N.Y. Central celebrating cities that it served.
Est: $2,500-$3,000.

AAGE RASMUSSEN (1913-1975)

602. DSB. 1937.
24¹/₄ x 39¹/₂ in./61.8 x 100 cm
Andreasen & Lachmann, Copenhagen
Cond A-/Slight tears in border.
Ref (All Var): Weill, 469; Danish Posters, p. 228; PAI-XXVIII, 498
Arguably the most stunning Danish poster ever created, this design for the Danish State Railways was printed in several versions, with the name fully spelled out in various languages; this is the rare French-language version. An absolutely unforgettable image. Rasmussen, one of Denmark's finest posterists, was as greatly involved with the Danish state railway as Cassandre was with the French.
Est: $1,700-$2,000.

LEONHARD RAVENHILL (1867-1942)

603. Pick-Me-Up. 1894.
19³/₈ x 29⁵/₈ in./49.2 x 75.4 cm
Cond B/Slight tears at folds.
Ref: DFP-I, 107; Schindler, 63
"Leonhard Ravenhill must be regarded as a successor to Dudley Hardy, perhaps with a degree more elegance and virtuosity. The superior draftsman captured the characteristic female type of the turn of the century in all media, youthfully pert, playful or openly coquettish. His posters are magnificently conceived. The color pattern and the functional typography result in the exciting effect that the poster client is looking for. The lady in the orange coat on the boulevard bench perfectly embodies the title of the weekly she is promoting, *Pick-me-up*" (Schindler, p. 78). Illustrator, etcher and posterist Ravenhill studied in Paris and was greatly influenced by English caricaturist, Charles H. Keene. He became one of the most important contributors to *Punch* and *Pick-me-up*, for which he designed numerous posters.
Est: $1,000-$1,200.

606

610

607

PREBBLE RAYNER (1886-?)

604. Derry & Toms/Shoes & Ships. ca. 1918.
38³/₈ x 59¹/₄ in./97.4 x 150.5 cm
Cond B−/Restored tears and losses at folds and edges.
Ref: PAI-XXIV, 485

For the first three-quarters of this century, Derry & Toms was one of the great department stores on Kensington High Street in London. It was certainly the one with the oldest history: Various members of both the Derry and Toms families had small shops on the street as early as 1828, and in the 1850s the two clans merged by marriage. Rapid expansion followed and by 1900 Derry & Toms was a full-fledged department store with 200 *live-in* staff. Growth continued until the World War I slump. By 1916 the store was struggling—surely one of the reasons, along with the growth of the Underground as an advertising medium—that the store turned to poster advertising. From 1917 until the firm was taken over in 1920, the store commissioned 20 or so artists and graphic designers to create what turned out to be an enormously successful poster campaign. Whether Derry & Toms sold ships, or for that matter, sealing wax, is questionable; shoes, certainly. Here, based on "The time has come, the walrus said" ditty in *Alice in Wonderland*, ships and shoes float in a sealing-wax sea, with the wax sticks recalling a tangle of masts and rigging. Rayner was a widely exhibited painter of less fanciful landscapes.
Est: $1,200-$1,500.

JOSEP RENAU-MONTORO (1907-1982)

605. Las Arenas. ca. 1932.
27¹/₈ x 39¹/₄ in./68.8 x 99.6 cm
Graficas Valencia, Sevilla
Cond A.
Ref: Weill, 490; Purvis, p. 62; Voyage, p. 66; Publicidad, 1317 & Cover Vol. 2; PAI-XXIX, 466

A most striking design for an illuminated swimming pool in Art Deco style, with fine geometric patterns and indirect lighting that give prominence to the swimmer. The colors are almost fluorescent. Renau was born in Valencia and did much of his best work there during the early 1930s. Many of his posters were for political causes; he fought against Franco (*see* PAI-XXIII, 487), and when the dictator came to power, he left Spain to settle in Germany. Becoming a follower of Dadaist John Heartfield, he added the techniques of collage and photomontage to his designs. When Franco died, Renau returned to Valencia and remained there until his own death in 1982.
Est: $2,000-$2,500.

RENWICK

606. College Years: 2 Posters. 1910.
Each: 13³/₄ x 21¹/₄ in./35 x 55.5 cm
C. G. & S. Inc., Litho, N. Y.
Cond B+/Unobtrusive tears near edges.

It's abundantly clear that both the artist, Renwick, and the firm of Close, Graham & Scully that published the "College Years" poster series, held a rather dim view of the American university institution. Or at the very least, the young "gentlemen" who walked those hallowed halls of higher learning. First we are given the "Soph," a pouty man/child unable to set down the toys of his youth while casting a predatory scorpion's shadow that betrays his inner corruption. Two years later, he has become the "Senior," a disrespectful, arrogant lout who scoffs at his education to such a degree that his sheepskin serves better as a cigar lighter than a proud documentation. One can only imagine what barbs were illustratively cast at the freshman and junior classes.
Est: $1,200-$1,500. (2)

608

609

611

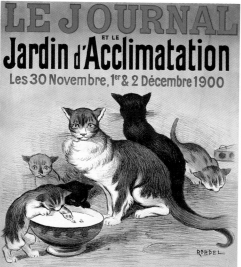

612

VIRGILIO RETROSI (1892-1975)

607. Cesenatico. 1932.
27¹/₄ x 39 in./69.2 x 99 cm
Arti Grafiche, Roma
Cond A–/Slight tears at paper edges.
Though separated by the balmy waters of the Mediterranean, Retrosi found inspiration in the colorful beach umbrellas that pop up like hot house flowers along the shore much in the same manner as his Spanish counterpart, José Morell (see No. 540). The Italian posterist ups the ante, however, by adding in the expansive, gently undulating water and multicolored sails of the skiffs that help to create the "seaside enchantment" of Cesenatico, one of the most prominent towns of the Romagna Riviera, whose canal port was designed by Leonardo da Vinci and is home to not one, but three soft sand beaches: Valverde, Villamarina and Zadina Pineta. Retrosi was a painter, ceramicist and book and periodical illustrator active largely in the 1930s.
Est: $2,500-$3,000.

LOUIS J. RHEAD (1858-1926)

608. The Century Magazine/For June. 1896.
10³/₄ x 21 in./27.3 x 53.3 cm
Cond A–/Slight tears at paper edges.
Ref: DFP-I, 461; Margolin, p. 49; Lauder, 265;
    Keay, p. 98; PAI-XXVI, 515
Rhead places one of his preferred redheads amongst bright yellow roses, giving the impression that she may be serving as a trellis for them as they wrap themselves around her and even adorn her hair. The peaceful pastoral settings of his designs make it perfectly clear that *The Century* is appropriate reading material in every surrounding. Rhead was one of the first poster artists to gain an international reputation. Born in England, he was quite active in London, New York and Paris with equal success; his exhibition of posters in New York in 1895 was America's first, and was well received.
Est: $1,700-$2,000.

C. RICART & R. ABELLA

609. Copa Davis. 1972.
19³/₄ x 27³/₄ in./50.2 x 70.3 cm
Tobella
Cond A–/Unobtrusive tears at paper edges.
Once more, when it comes to the lithographic promotion of tennis, we see that less is definitely more. This Spanish twosome keeps the clutter to a minimum, equitably setting down the nationalistic racquets of the United States and Spain and the net which divides them. No ball is provided, but if you need that much information, perhaps the Davis Cup isn't the sporting event for you. Though the poster announces semifinals competition between the two countries, it was the United States that bested their Spanish rivals in the 1972 *finals*. But just to show that everything that goes around comes around, the Spanish Davis Cup team eliminated our volleyers in the semifinals earlier this year.
Est: $1,000-$1,200.

ALICK P. F. RITCHIE (1869-?)

610. My Girl.
40 x 28³/₄ in./101.7 x 73 cm
David Allen, London
Cond B/Restored tears at folds.
A lacy parasol wouldn't be my first choice of weaponry to fend off a charging Zulu warrior. But then again I'm neither as stern as the seated matron or involved with the theatrical hi-jinks of the Gaiety's production of "My Girl," a play for which no summary has been handed down, but one that most assuredly couldn't have been the inspiration for the 1991 Macaulay Culkin/Anna Chlumsky vehicle of the same name. Regardless of finer plot points, Ritchie's choice of allowing the scene to play itself out in front of a solid orange background makes for a standout, eye-popping experience.
Est: $1,200-$1,500.

ROB

611. Salon de Photo. 1949.
39 x 59 in./99.2 x 150 cm
Imp. Delattre, Paris
Cond B+/Unobtrusive tears at folds.
Beauty is in the eye of the beholder. Or more appropriately when considering the Rob poster for Paris' 20th Photographic and Amateur Cinema Salon, beauty comes from the eye of the beholder. A startling concept for the exhibition, and one that by planting a camera lens as the ocular center of a Grecian statue's vision, combines the contemporary and the classic in a perpetual universal search for harmonious line and form.
Est: $1,500-$1,800.

ROEDEL (1859-1900)

612. Le Journal/Jardin d'Acclimatation. 1900.
29 x 33⁷/₈ in./73.8 x 86 cm
Cond B+/Slight tears at folds an edges.
Ref: DFP-II, 762 (var)
Roedel was a caricaturist, illustrator, watercolorist and lithographer; he aligned himself in Paris with a group of artists of Montmartre such as Willette, Léandre and Caran d'Ache, supplied drawings for *Le Courrier français* and produced posters, mostly for the local cabarets and theaters. The poster seen here is something of a riddle at first; we're given the central image that states that a newspaper and the zoo are partners in an event without stating what the event is. Granted, with the image of these kittens gathered about a bowl of milk, one can surmise that it has something to do with cats. But one should never assume that advertising is a open-faced enterprise. This time, however, the image doesn't lie and was, in fact, used to publicize a cat show, with Roedel's felines taking a lithographic curtain call, as the image had been used two years prior for another kitty fest, thus explaining the lack of text in an already familiar image on the streets of Paris.
Est: $1,700-$2,000.

613

NORMAN ROCKWELL (1894-1978)

613. Four Freedoms. 1943.
Each: 40^1/$_4$ x 56 in./102.2 x 142.2 cm
U.S. Governement Printing Office
Cond A-/Slight tears at folds.
Ref: Rockwell's America, pp. 204-207;
    Rockwell Illustrator, pp. 143-149;
    American Posters, p. 24; PAI-XXVIII, 503 (var)
The Four Freedoms is probably the most ambitious
and serious work by the most famous American illustrator of the 20th century. New York-born and trained,
Rockwell became the artist of small-town America,
best known for the 322 covers he painted for the
Saturday Evening Post between 1916 and 1963. A
supreme draftsman, he had a unique ability to give
visual expression to the American Dream—a talent
that was also employed in major advertising campaigns
including that of the U. S. government for support of
the Second World War effort. It was FDR who had
distilled the cause for which we were fighting into
Four Freedoms. Only Rockwell could have represented
such big ideas in his homey, folksy way without over-
sentimentalizing or trivializing them. He undertook the
paintings on his own initiative; it was only after he had
failed to interest the Office of War Information in them
and they had been published in the Post that the government saw their potential and used them in poster
campaigns for both the general war effort and War
Bonds. The Treasury Department also took the origi-
nals on tour; seen by 1.2 million people, they helped
sell $132 million in bonds. The original paintings form
the centerpiece of the Rockwell Museum in Stock-
bridge, Massachusetts, as well as that of the smash-
ingly successful tour of this artist's work. *This is the
larger format of the series.*
Est: $2,500-$3,000. (4)

NORMAN ROCKWELL EXHIBITION:
Oct. 28–Dec. 31, 2000: San Diego Museum of Art
Jan. 27–May 6, 2001: Phoenix Art Museum
June 9–Oct. 8, 2001: Stockbridge
Nov. 16, 2001–March 3, 2002: Guggenheim Museum, New York City

ARN. V. ROESFEL

614. Reclamebureau Julius Dickhout. 1915.
43^1/$_2$ x 61^7/$_8$ in./110.5 x 157 cm
Druikkerij Kotting, Amsterdam
Cond B/Restored tears at folds.
A bizarre 2-sheet piece of advertising cloaked in a
shroud of normalcy. Not to take anything away from
Roesfel, who does a superior job of laying on sharp
planes of color and utilizing a series of discreetly
placed archways to create perspective to promote the
Dickhout advertising agency, a firm that specialized in
circulars. Not that there's anything strange about
handbills, or at first look, the street scene where
they're being doled out. However, could someone
explain precisely why the Dickhout representative in
the process of offering one of his circulars to the
viewer is equipped with the ears of an elf?
Est: $2,500-$3,000.

615

W. S. ROGERS

615. The London Letter. 1899.
20 x 30^1/$_4$ in./51 x 76.8 cm
Eyre & Spottiswoode, London
Cond B/Slight tears and stains at edges and bottom
    text area.
Ref: The Poster, November, 1899, p. 98 (var)
When commenting on his career as a lithographer,
Rogers, a man of few words, made the following statement: "During my experience as a designer of posters,
I have to complain—like many other brothers of the
brush—of the capricious treatment received from
some of my clients, who would rather I made a hack-
neyed design, than produce an original notion of my
own. Advertisers are generally supposed to know what
they require when they commission an artist to design
a poster, yet I have invariably found it to be quite the
opposite. After one has lighted on a brilliant idea for a
design, it is irritating to have it compulsorily marred by
an alteration to suit the advertiser's idea of effect,
which is of so incongruous a nature as to make the
conception absurd" (*The Poster*, November, 1899, pp.
97-8). The heads of the *London Letter* must not have
been one of these tampering clients as they utilized
Rogers' breezy reader enjoying her weekly dose of the
Letter by the Thames as a stock poster, altering nary a
detail save for the necessary textual changes.
Est: $1,200-$1,500.

616

A. ROMÈS

616. Columbia Chainless. 1897.
40^1/$_8$ x 87^3/$_4$ in./102 x 223 cm
J. Ottman Lithographic Co., New York
Cond A-/Slight teas at folds.
Ref: DFP-III, 4399 (var); PAI-XXVIII, 51
Surely one of the most grandiose concepts for advertising a bicycle—the woman glorifying the machine
with a laurel wreath in a formal setting, the whole
scene in an opulent gold frame. Columbia bicycles
sponsored a poster contest in 1896; the winner was
Maxfield Parrish of Philadelphia, second prize went to
O. Rohn of Montclair, N.J. and third prize (for this
image) went to A. Romes of New York City. It was so
popular that it was reprinted in Germany and in France,
and a frequently seen photo of an 1898 Paris street

614

618

617

619

by the artist for the Zurich art and office supplies business, with the other featuring available art supplies (see PAI-XIX, 475).
Est: $2,500-$3,000.

AUGUSTE ROUBILLE (1872-1955)

618. Spratt's Patent Ltd. ca. 1909.
$45^1/2$ x $61^1/2$ in./115.6 x 156 cm
Imp. Lemercier, Paris
Cond B–/Restored tears and losses at folds and edges.
Ref: DFP-II, 765; Livre de l'Affiche, 24; Gold, 20; PAI-XXX, 95
Spratt's was a major British pet food producer with branches in several countries (their U.S. factory was located in Newark, NJ). Here, the French branch advertises with a poster stressing dog food. "Roubille uses a restrained yet warm style to show a happy mistress dispensing Spratt's treats to her clamoring canines" (Gold, p. 14). The designer abandons the broad caricature style for which he is best known to give us a very charming and appealing poster, reminiscent in character of Steinlen's classic Clinique Cheron (see PAI-XXX, 96).
Est: $8,000-$10,000.

J. JACQUES ROUSSEAU

619. Paris à Londres.
$28^1/2$ x 41 in./72.5 x 104 cm
Imp. Cornille & Serre, Paris
Cond B–/Restored tears at edges.
In his blazing white trousers, red-and-black striped jacket and pipe lip-locked firmly in place, this chap is the archetypical British public school upperclassman—and he engages in a typical English pastime: punting a boat up the Thames, all in the name of promoting the British State and Brighton rail lines' connecting service to the Continent, while at the same time subliminally alluding to the brief shipboard portion of the journey.
Est: $1,200-$1,500.

scene shows four copies of this poster on the wall, next to Mucha's Waverly Cycles. Columbia Chainless is a brand name of the Pope Manufacturing Co.
Est: $1,500-$1,800.

ERWIN ROTH (1886-1963)

617. Gebrüder Scholl/Zürich. 1916.
$35^1/2$ x $50^1/2$ in./90 x 128.2 cm
Wolfensberger, Zürich
Cond A–/Slight tears and creases at paper edges/P.
Ref: Margadant, 220; Affiches Suisse, 9; PAI-XIII, 395

A superb example of an object poster, its desktop elements arranged in such a fashion that, were one to remove the name of the Scholl Brothers firm from the design, it could just as easily be titled "Still Life With Office Equipment." Set within the oval frame (a favorite device of other Swiss designers of the day such as Mangold and Baumberger), Roth's deft touch clearly demonstrates that an "object poster" need not be a stark and dull venture, but rather a graphically compelling montage decoratively assembled. This is one of a pair of posters known to have been designed

RUDD

620. Escargots Ménetrel.
46¹/₂ x 62¹/₂ in./118 x 158.6 cm
Affiches Gaillard, Paris
Cond A.
Ref: PAI-XXVIII, 507
A snail wise enough to spell out the name of one of France's premier packagers of escargot with its viscous trail ought to be keen enough to see that he's in imminent danger of being consumed by an ardent slug lover. But perhaps it's wise enough to know that a snail's pace can never outrun a voracious appetite. Though the Ménetrel brand no longer graces the shelves, its name has lived on in recipe form: Snails Menetrel, a preparation flavored with anchovies and *Quatre-epices*, a spice of West Indian origin.
Est: $1,500-$1,800.

ROBERT SALLES (1871-1929)

621. Voyages Animés. ca. 1899.
23¹/₂ x 31¹/₂ in./59.6 x 82 cm
Imp. Bourgerie, Paris
Cond B/Slight tears at folds and edges.
Even though it's somewhat unclear whether this event being held in conjunction with the 1900 Paris World's Fair is a cartoon expedition or merely a sprightly tour of other fair installations, it matters very little. For any time spent with this diaphanous ambassador of the global presentation is definitely time well spent. A lovely, wistful design from Salles, a member of the

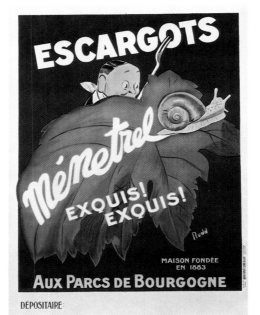

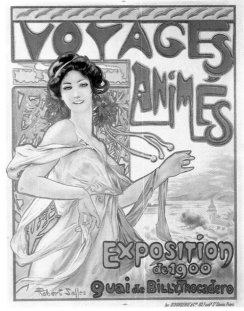

620

621

Société des artistes français, remembered more for his illustration of children's books than for his posters, due exclusively to the lack of quantity.
Est: $1,400-$1,700.

SALON DES CENT POSTERS

The "Salon des Cent" ("Salon of the 100") was the exhibition hall and marketing outlet of the artistic and literary magazine *La Plume*, opened in February, 1894, on its own premises at Rue Bonaparte. The editor, Léon Deschamps, was one of the first art connoisseurs to take posters seriously: he often reproduced them in the magazine, organized special exhibitions of them, and made them available to the public by reprinting them, with or without the advertising text, in various editions.

Artists whose works were on sale at the Salon were, of course, frequently written up in the magazine, and nearly all of them were asked, at one time or another, to design a poster for one of the Salon's exhibitions. In this way, the Salon became the single subject covered by the largest number of individual artists in poster history. There were about 43 exhibits in the brief period of the Salon's existence (1894-1900), with 40 artists creating posters for them. Maindron, writing in 1895, urges his readers to collect "all the charming posters" of the Salon des Cent for "they will make a most valuable collection." He was, as always, quite right.

PIERRE BONNARD (1867-1947)

622. Salon des Cent. 1896.
17³/₄ x 24³/₄ in./45 x 62.9 cm
Imp. Chaix, Paris
Cond A. Framed.
Ref: DFP-II, 79; Salon des Cent, p. 53;
    Salon des Cent/Neumann, p. 35; Marx, 45;
    Bouvet, 39; Word & Image, p. 27; PAI-XXIII, 163
The drawing of a woman admonishing her dog appears only half-finished, with the right side remaining a blank, but all the pertinent elements are there—the fashionable veiled hat, the gesture of the gloved hand and the attentive pose of the pooch. A charming way to invite us to the 23rd show of the members of the Salon des Cent. *Rare!*
Est: $12,000-$15,000.

FERNAND FAU (1858-1917)

623. Salon des 100. 1894.
15³/₄ x 25 in./40 x 63.3 cm
Chamerot et Renouard, Paris
Cond A–/Slight tears and stains in margins.
Ref: DFP-II, 330; Reims, 604; Salon des Cent, p. 34;
    Salon des Cent/Neumann, p. 67; PAI-XXV, 307
The woman in a trailing blue print dress and a white cape is so consumed by the artwork she's been inspecting with her lorgnette that she seems to have unknowingly dropped her exhibition catalogue. Fau was a painter and illustrator of books; he contributed to several journals like *Le Chat Noir* and *Le Rire*, produced only a handful of posters and participated in performances at the "Chat Noir" cabaret.
Est: $1,700-$2,000.

ANDHRÉ DES GACHONS (1871-?)

624. Andhré des Gachons/Salon des Cent. 1895.
15³/₄ x 23¹/₂ in./40 x 59.6 cm
Typ. A. Davy, Paris
Cond A.

623

624

Ref: DFP-II, 378; Reims, 651; Salon des Cent, p. 39;
    Salon des Cent/Neumann, p. 41; PAI-VII, 366
For an exhibition of his own work, Gachons gives us a long-haired woman watering some flowers at a fountain. Gachons was a symbolist painter who took a very personal mystical and religious direction in his work. As with several others in this series, this poster was produced by pochoir (stencil) colors over letter press. Gachons also has the distinction of being the sole artist to benefit from the exposure of two exhibitions of his work at the Salon des Cent.
Est: $1,000-$1,200.

622

626

625

627

ARSENE HERBINIER (1869-?)

625. Salon des Cent. 1898.
15³/₄ x 23⁷/₈ in./39.8 x 60.6 cm
Cond B/Slight tears and stains at edges.
Ref: Salon des Cent, p. 78;
    Salon des Cent/Neumann, p. 42; PAI-XXIX, 399
In this design for the January 1899 exhibition, Herbinier sets down a woman in peril of becoming entwined in the embrace of the flowering vines which

have attracted her fancy. That year's *L'Estampe et l'Affiche* described the poster as follows: "A woman, clad in green, arranges a branch of wild roses, whose coilings pass for a corsage and loose themselves in her hair. Simply executed in flat colors with encircling lines like those of a leaded stained glass window that give added weight to the profile and hands" (Salon des Cent, p. 78).
Est: $1,500-$1,800.

ALPHONSE LEVY (1843-1918)

**626. Exposition d'Oeuvres d'Alphonse Levy/
    Salon des Cent.** 1897.
19³/₈ x 25³/₄ in./49.2 x 65.3 cm
Imp. Chaix, Paris
Cond A–/Slight tears and stains at edges.
Ref: DFP-II, 540; Salon des Cent, p. 59 (var);
    Salon des Cent/Neumann, p. 79 (var); PAI-X, 289
With its full text, the poster informed the public that an exhibition of Levy's work was being held at the Salon de la Plume (better known as the Salon des Cent) from January 25 to February 14, 1897. This pertinent information was added to the portrait of a synagogue worshipper, one of Levy's many illustrations from Jewish life. He faces the Hebrew word "Mizrach," meaning "the place where the sun rises," as traditionally the faithful have faced East, towards Jerusalem, when praying. *This version of the poster is #9 in a limited-edition of 50 hand-signed and numbered posters.*
Est: $3,000-$3,500.

RICHARD RANFT (1862-1931)

627. Salon des Cent/Exposition Richard Ranft.
    1894.
15¹/₂ x 23¹/₄ in./39.4 x 59.1 cm
Cond B+/Slight tears and stains in margins.
Ref: DFP-II, 729; Reims, 976; Salon des Cent, p. 23;
    Salon des Cent/Neumann, p. 32 (var); PAI-XVI, 433
An over-the-bare-shoulder view of a text-only poster-within-a-poster all set against an amusing mice-on-the-run wallpaper serves as Ranft's calling card to the sixth exhibition of the Salon des Cents. Ranft started out as a landscape painter in his native Geneva, but already by the age of 18 he had relocated to Paris where he earned a living as a book and magazine illustrator as well as a posterist. He even penned a novel, "Mademoiselle d'Ochar," which he naturally self-illustrated.
Est: $1,200-$1,500.

628

629

SALON DES CENT (continued)

P. H. LOBEL

628. Salon des Cent. 1897.
15⅝ x 23⅜ in/39.6 x 59.3 cm
Imp. Chaix, Paris
Cond A–/Slight tears and stains at edges.
Ref: DFP-II, 542; Schardt, 982; Wine Spectator, 60 (var);
Salon des Cent, p. 66; Salon des Cent/
Neumann, p. 37; PAI-XXVIII, 384 (var)
Considering the woefully inappropriate billowing dress
she is wearing, this tennis player is making a game try
at returning the ball over the net. Is there something
in this poster that reminds you of Toulouse-Lautrec?
In discussing the master, Weill comments that there
were only three poster artists who might be considered
his disciples: Jacques Villon, Maxime Dethomas and
"Lobel (of whom nothing is known) for the *Salon des
Cent* and *Pierrefort* poster" (p. 35).
Est: $3,000-$3,500.

ALPHONSE MUCHA (1860-1939)

629. Salon des Cent/Juin 1897.
17¾ x 25½ in./45.3 x 64.7 cm
Imp. F. Champenois, Paris
Cond A. Framed.
Ref: Rennert/Weill, 36; Lendl/Paris, 101;
Mucha/Art Nouveau, 25; DFP-II, 638; Maitres, 114;
Salon des Cent, p. 65; Salon des Cent/
Neumann, p. 49; PAI-XXVIII, 429
Mucha, for his own exhibition at the Salon des Cent,
drew a "life-like girl with a twinge of homesickness; it
is a decidedly Slavic face, with a bonnet featuring one
of the embroidered regional patterns that distinguish
the folk costumes in his part of the world, and her hair
is adorned with daisies—symbol of the Moravian fields
where Mucha spent his youth" (Rennert/Weill p. 150).
Est: $8,000-$10,000.

G. BOUTROU

630. Salon des Cent. 1899.
17¾ x 24¼ in./45 x 61.5 cm
Cond A. Framed.
Ref: Salon des Cent, p. 82 (var);
Salon des Cent/Neumann, p. 52; PAI-XI, 130
A very rare poster in the distinguished Salon des Cent
series, and it's quite marvelous: the pink of our
painter's left nipple is ingeniously positioned so as to
make it appear as if it is but another stunning color
on her palette. *This is the version before letters, on
china paper.*
Est: $1,700-$2,000.

LOUIS J. RHEAD (1858-1926)

631. Salon des Cent. 1897.
15¾ x 23⅝ in/40 x 60 cm
Imp. Chaix, Paris
Cond A–/Slight tears at edges.
Ref: DFP-I, 468; Vleeshuis Museum, 54;
Affichomanie, 29; Salon des Cent, p. 61;
Salon des Cent/Neumann, p. 53; Gold, 198;
PAI-XXIV, 488
This is Rhead's announcement for his Paris exhibition
which preceded Mucha's at the famed showplace. It
consisted of 60 maquettes, all of which are listed in
the April 15, 1897 issue of "La Plume." The design is
one of Rhead's best, showing the artistic muse in contemporary dress with a triumphant wreath of laurel in
her hair. The handsome scheme of three colors is
carried out in the daubs on her palette. A critic writing
in the issue of "La Plume" a month later, had high
praise for Rhead's restrained color play: "Nothing is
more powerful in achieving a variety of effect than
limitation of means. See how often this economy and
methodic restraint create, as a result, the development

630

of nuances. Rhead has banished half-tones, and by
juxtaposing a blue with other colors, he has created a
whole chromatic range. In the panel, for example, you
seem to see greens, blues and violets; you notice their
freshness and . . . you're continually astonished to dis-
cover that there is one and only one color!" (Salon des
Cents, p. 61).
Est: $1,500-$1,800.

631

632

633

634

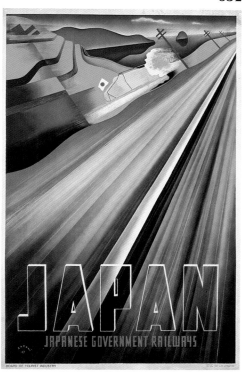

635

ANDREW K. WOMRATH (1869-?)

634. Salon des Cent. 1896.
15³/₄ x 21¹/₂ in./40.2 x 54.5 cm
Cond B+/Unobtrusive folds.
Ref: DFP-II, 895 (var); Salon des Cent, p. 58;
    Salon des Cent/Neumann, p. 68; Gold, 196;
    PAI-XXX, 251
"Andrew Kay Womrath was an American artist who
studied in New York, London and Paris. This is his only
known poster, showing a woman leafing through some
prints while a man admires a vase. She is dressed
conventionally enough, while the man, judging by his
Van Dyke and floppy cravat, is either an artist or would
be bohemian" (Gold, p. 134). The broad appeal of the
artwork on display hinted at would seem to be rein-
forced by the February/March tip-on included on this
version of the poster: Originally slated to run only for
the month of January, the popularity of the event
demanded a two-month extension.
Est: $800-$1,000.

EDMOND A. ROCHER (1873-?)

632. Salon des Cent. 1895.
16⁵/₈ x 23¹/₂ in./42.2 x 59.7 cm
Imp. Bougerie, Paris
Cond A.
Ref: DFP-II, 756; Reims, 995; Salon des Cent, p. 26;
    Salon des Cent/Neumann, p. 44; Gold, 194;
    PAI-XXX, 245
"The woman is examining the print with intensely
critical concentration—she might be an art student or
even a painter herself" (Gold, p. 132). This was the
only poster by Rocher in the historic 1896 Reims
exhibition. The brown-on-beige gives the piece a duo-
tone effect that is achieved by printing pochoir over
letterpress. In addition to his work as an illustrator,
lithographer and engraver, Rocher also indulged his
muse by way of poetry.
Est: $1,200-$1,500.

GASTON ROULLET (1847-1925)

633. Salon des Cents. 1895.
15³/₄ x 23⁵/₈ in./40 x 60 cm
Cond A.
Ref: DFP-II, 766; Reims, 1000; Salon des Cent, p. 27;
    Salon des Cent/Neumann, p. 71
Primarily a painter of maritime scenes, Roullet turns
out a realistic—in feel if not in photographic execution
—man-versus-nature portrait that smacks of an intimate
knowledge of the subject matter to promote an exhibition of his works at the Salon. Deeply impressed by
his exhibit, art critic Léon Maillard expressed his feel-
ings in *La Plume* of February, 1895: "His studies . . .
aren't futile and transient expressions, they are living
affirmations of light. They are an homage to a pene-
trating artist returning to the unseizable sea, always
finding nuances of color more alive and more profound" (Salon des Cent, p. 27).
Est: $1,200-$1,500.

MUNETSUGU SATOMI (1900—1995)

635. Japan. 1937.
25 x 39¹/₄ in./63.5 x 99.7 cm
Process Seihan Printing Co., Osaka
Cond B/Slight tears and stains, largely in borders;
    image and colors excellent.
Ref: Art Deco, p. 56; Livre d'Affiche, 149; PAI-XXVII, 581
Satomi could be called—quite unpatronizingly, indeed
in high praise—the Japanese Cassandre; both excelled
in distilling a subject down to its essence, blending its
pictorial representation and the lettering into near-
pure graphic design. Here, the Japanese countryside,
seen from the car of a streaking Japanese Government
Railways' train gives us a colorful, albeit blurred,
image of the lush landscape and terraced hills in this
promotion published by the Board of Tourist Industry.
Est: $2,000-$2,500.

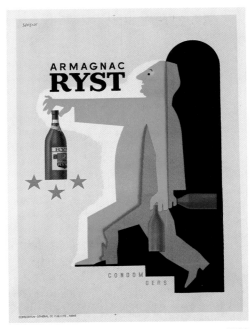

636

637

638

RAYMOND SAVIGNAC (1907-)

636. Armagnac Ryst.
$46^1/_2$ x $63^3/_8$ in./118 x 161 cm
Consortium Général de Publicité, Paris
Cond A–/Slight stains.
Savignac is the enfant terrible of French poster art,
who, along with the late Bernard Villemot, has had
more impact on that country's graphics of the past 40
years than any other artist. As for his style, there are
no displays of technical virtuosity that might compete
with the wit—only disarmingly simple, almost childish
brushwork, basic colors and uncluttered design. Take
his design for Ryst armagnac, for example. Emerging
from the depths of his private stock into the light of
tasteful consumption, this bon vivant has obviously
fallen under the sway of the superior cordial. A hyp-
notically good design that leaves little doubt that Ryst
is an alcoholic step up.
Est: $1,200-$1,500.

637. Paris. 1951.
$24^1/_4$ x $39^1/_4$ in./61.7 x 99.5 cm
Imp. S. A. Courbet, Paris
Cond A–/Slight crease at top edge.
Ref: Savignac/Paris, 9; Savignac/Japan, 4
The former pupil of Cassandre explained his method
this way: "If I express myself with gags, whims and
pirouettes, if my posters are graphic clowning, it's first
of all because the public is so bored in its daily rou-
tine that I think advertising should amuse them"
(Weill, p. 303). To that end, he provides us with two
immense Parisians scaling the monumental French
calling card to the world, enamored with their city, and
surrounded by enough blanched open air to create the
appropriately nationalistic color scheme in this open
invitation to celebrate the French capital's 2,000th
anniversary. The lighthearted proposition was also
printed with English text.
Est: $1,200-$1,500.

638. Ducotone. 1960.
27 x $39^1/_2$ in./68.5 x 99.8 cm
Cond B/Unobtrusive tears and stains, largely at fold
and edges; image and colors excellent.
Ref (Both Var): Savignac A-Z, p. 89; Savignac/Key, 25
An architectural construct in the name of Ducotone
paint executed with such simplicity that it nearly glosses
over the inspirational genius required to take such a
basic idea and colorfully translate it to the advertising
medium. Composed of little more than flat planes of
vibrant color and overlapping L-shaped wedges, Savignac creates perfect perspective as his painter obliterates the darkness, giving a sense of the infinite to a
finite universe. *This is the smaller format.*
Est: $1,000-$1,200.

641

EGON SCHIELE (1890-1918)

639. Secession/49. Kunstausstellung. 1918.
$20^7/_8$ x 27 in./53 x 68.5 cm
Albert Berger, Wien
Cond B/Slightly light-stained; unobtrusive slight tears
and stains at paper edges/P. Framed.
Ref: Modern Poster, p. 75; Weill, p. 118;
Denscher, p. 56; PAI-XXVIII, 524
Along with Klimt, Schiele was a stellar figure in Viennese art at the turn of the century. But unlike his older
friend, whose often-erotic figures were swathed in fabulous textiles and rendered in a highly decorative
manner, Schiele created images of the human body
that reflected his own tortured, tubercular state.
Naked, feverish and curled up in private hells, they
were found brilliant, but scandalous. The Secession
dedicated an entire room to his work, but only a few
months before his premature death during an

642

influenza epidemic. He must have been touched by
the honor: This scene showing the fellowship of like
minds is uncharacteristically serene.
Est: $12,000-$15,000.

ALEXANDER SCHINDLER (1870-?)

640. Kunstlerische Arbeiten für die Mitglieder.
1901.
33 x $23^1/_2$ in./83.8 x 59.7 cm
Cond B/Unobtrusive folds; slight-offsetting in
background.
Ref: DFP-III, 2907; Plakate München, 80
A powerful Schindler design for a society of turn-of-
the-20th-century contemporary and illustrative Munich
artists which combines the fluid lines and elegant
grace of Art Nouveau with the uncluttered formalism
and sparse ornamentation of Art Deco. The hybrid
membership announcement solicits submissions with
the assistance of the unflinching gaze of a shadowy
beauty who, in concert with the more decorative
elements of the design, creates an abstraction of
disarming impact. *Rare!*
Est: $2,000-$2,500.

639

643

640

V. SCHUSTER

642. Pyrol.
45³/₄ x 62¹/₄ in./116.2 x 158.2 cm
Publicité Wall, Paris
Cond B+/Slight tears and stains at edges.
Die, bugs, die! This call to insect irradiation by Pyrol insect powder declares that it strikes down any creepy-crawly creature it comes in contact with. The choice of exterminator in the poster is an interesting one—some form of reptilian monstrosity that looks as if it stands a pretty good chance of becoming as much of a nuisance as the skittering pests it's just eliminated. We know nothing about the artist—in fact, we're not even sure whether his first initial is "V" or "N"—but we do know that the only two other posters of his that we've seen were done in an equally amusing style.
Est: $1,400-$1,700.

PIERRE SEGOGNE (?-1958)

643. Paquita Sol.
30¹/₄ x 46¹/₂ in./77 x 118 cm
Publicité Stella, Paris
Cond B/Restored tears at folds and edges.
Segogne, an artist whose typical output strictly adheres to a geometric Cubist sensibility, assembles a facial mask for Spanish entertainer Paquita out of subdued shadings and geometric opposition, creating a visage that is at once world-weary and openly naive. He softens the rougher edges with flips of hair and melancholy eyes and transforms her into a performance beacon that radiates with the Art Deco intensity of the star with which she shares a name.
Est: $2,000-$3,000.

ERNST EMIL SCHLATTER (1883-1954)

641. Rhätische Bahn. 1911.
28¹/₈ x 41¹/₄ in./71.5 x 104.8 cm
J. E. Wolfensberger, Zürich
Cond A–/Unobtrusive tears at folds and edges
Ref: Wobmann, 61; Margadant, 243; PAI-XX, 421
Using a painterly style, Schlatter produced some of the best Swiss landscapes in all posterdom—many for the national railway. In this picturesque scene, a graceful railroad viaduct of the Rätische Bahn and its rustic cousin, a covered wooden bridge, leap a chasm and rushing stream in Graubünden, Switzerland. After Schlatter studied lithography in Zurich and then Stuttgart, he returned to his native city around 1910 to work for Wolfensberger where he introduced several important innovations in the application of color lithography to poster art. From 1917 to 1920, he taught lithography and landscape painting at Zurich's Kunstgewerbeschule. In 1920, he moved to Uttwill to devote himself to freelance art.
Est: $1,500-$1,800.

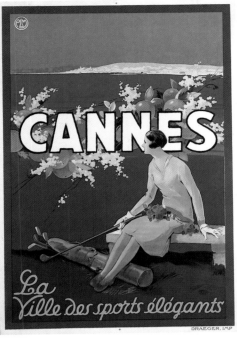

645

646

644

647

648

Marseilles in 1898 did he venture to Paris where he charmed the city folk with his talent.
Est: $1,700-$2,000.

G. SEIGNAC

644. Emprunt National. 1920.
29³/₄ x 46 in./75.5 x 116.9 cm
Imp. Joseph-Charles, Paris
Cond A–/Slight tears at edges.
The bountiful harvest of peace is reaped—in more ways than one—in this image for what was to be the last national French bond drive of the post-World War I era. Though it's possible to interpret the work in two ways—a return of dividends or an entrusting of one's financial future—the feeling of prosperity flowing off the Seignac design comes much more from the rosy-cheeked embodiments of France and the United States than it does from the overflowing coffer. The unsullied *paysanne* was Seignac's allegorical contribution to the national drive, utilizing her services several times, always with her apron overflowing with the abundant harvest, her hair interwoven with poppies and wheat and her nationalist color scheme seemingly more a necessity than an overt act of patriotism.
Est: $1,000-$1,200.

SEM (Georges Goursat, 1863-1934)

For other works by Sem, see Nos. 43-45.

645. Cannes. 1930.
28 x 40 in./71 x 101.6 cm
Imp. Draeger, Paris
Cond A. Framed.
Ref: Affiches Azur, 118; Mer s'Affiche, p. 113; Karcher, 452; PAI-XVIII, 113
As noted in *Affiches d'Azur* (p. 93), the three chief themes in posters for Cannes were elegance, sports and flowers. This poster has all three: orange blossoms, a golfer, and the slogan "The City of Elegant Sports." Elegant, too are the colors—serene deep blues, rose, orange. The orange branch and the unusual placement of the title across the middle recur in a companion poster by Sem of the same year (subtitled "The City of Flowers and Elegant Sports"). The career of caricaturist Sem started modestly enough in his home town of Perigueux where he published his first collection of local celebrities' portraits in 1895. Only after doing the same for Bordeaux in 1897 and

F. SERRACCHIANI

646. Cinquantenaire du Carnival. 1928.
30⁷/₈ x 47 in./78.5 x 119.3 cm
Imp. Moullot, Marseille
Cond B+/Slight tears at folds.
Ref: Affiches d'Azur, 88
Commonly described as "the chief pleasure city of the Riviera," the popular, if expensive Côte d'Azur resort announces its 1928 Spring Carnival with a shimmering kaleidoscope of unbridled revelry. The carnival promotion for the 50th celebration of this famous pre-Lent fête is brought to graphic life by Serracciani who calls forth the three elements most closely associated with the city: the aching-blue sky of a balmy climate, the fleshy decadence of lush flora and the salacious portent of anonymous hedonism. All told, three ideal reasons to leave behind a life of normalcy and plunge headlong into the debauchery.
Est: $1,500-$1,800.

649

651

650

KENNETH DENTON SHOESMITH (1890-1939)

647. Lowestoft.
49¹/₄ x 39⁵/₈ in./125.2 x 100.6 cm
Jarrold and Sons, Norwich and London
Cond B/Slight stains in bottom text, slight tears at folds.
Ref: PAI-VII, 447
The bright green sea and the cinnamon sails give a festive appearance to this nautical scene observed by

holiday visitors to the North Sea boating and beach resort. Shoesmith was a brilliantly talented English painter, posterist and decorative artist. Graphically speaking, he is best known for his work executed for the British railway and maritime industries.
Est: $2,500-$3,000.

ROGER SOUBIE (1898-1984)

648. Vichy. 1928.
30¹/₄ x 42 in./ 77 x 107 cm
Lucien Serre, Paris
Cond A.
Ref: Sportissimo, p. 68; Train à l'Affiche, 214 (var); PAI-XXVI, 538
In this first edition poster, while the slogan touts Vichy as the famous thermal spa, Soubie chooses to glorify the golf. And a glorious course it is, overlooking the Allier, the town of Cusset and the hills of the Massif Central beyond. Soubie is best known for movie posters, but he produced some lovely travel posters as well. Particularly admirable here is the foliage: lush but shot through with autumn colors, which are echoed in the outfits of the foreground golfers.
Est: $1,700-$2,000.

SPANISH FESTIVALS

649. Sevilla.
Artist: **Juan Balcera**
42 x 63³/₄ in./106.7 x 162 cm
Imp. y Lit. Ortega, Valencia
Cond A–/Slight tears at folds.
Ref: España, 42; PAI-XXVII, 265
Nowhere does the word "fiesta" apply as completely as it does to Seville's spring festival. As the center of Andalusia, Seville of all Spanish cities retains most of the charm of old Spain. Every year during the third week of April, the city justifies its reputation with a

grand fiesta which lasts six days and has been celebrated since 1847. In the big park, Prado de San Sebastian, a whole city of small huts (*casetas*) pops up, nonstop dancing and revelry and the drinking of *manzanilla* which gleams like the gold of the setting sun. At night the stalls are all lit up, sparkling like jewels among the palms and the rhododendron bushes. This rich pageant of Seville's splendor is sumptuously captured by Balcera, his golden goddess blessing the festival while luring us into her sensual embrace.
Est: $1,700-$2,000.

650. Sevilla. 1932.
Artist: **Juan Balcera**
27¹/₄ x 39 in./69.3 x 99 cm
Imp. Ortega, Valencia
Cond A–/Slight unobtrusive tears.
Ref: España, 43; PAI-XXIX, 635 (var)
Seville's spring festival is once again opulently promoted by Balcera, who creates a rich tableau of luminous color and hypnotic patterns, flattening the perspective to such an extent that the raven-haired señorita observing the goings-on becomes one with the seductive carnival tapestry. *This is the smaller format.*
Est: $1,200-$1,500.

651. Sevilla/Fiestas de Primavera. 1932.
Artist: **Enrique Estela-Anton**
42³/₄ x 61³/₄ in./108.5 x 156.8 cm
Imp. Lit. Ortega, Valencia
Cond B+/Slight tears and stains at folds.
Ref: España, 44; PAI-XXV, 305
A wonderfully eye-catching poster—exploiting the contrast between the brightly illuminated dancer and the tender shadows of a starlit night in the city—invites us to take part in the spring fiesta in Seville. An expertly composed, flawlessly executed piece of work.
Est: $1,700-$2,000.

652

653

655

656

657

SPANISH FESTIVALS (continued)

652. Seville 1929-30.
Artist: **Gustavo Bacarisas**
24³/₄ x 39¹/₄ in./63 x 101 cm
Lits. Dura, Valencia
Cond A–/Slight tears and stains in margins only.
Ref: España, 730 (var)
Though the style of this Bacarisas design is decidedly Spanish in nature, an overriding sense of global sensibility fills the design for Seville's Hispano-Americain Exposition, due in large part to the presence of a United Nations' worth of flags flying high above the Barrio de Santa Cruz—central of which is Old Glory—and the overwhelming sense of welcome. This version of the design informs the English speaking invitees that their best way to the fair is by Wagons Lits and Cooks; presumably, other language versions exist offering similar advice in a variety of tongues.
Est: $1,400-$1,700.

653. Valencia/Festes de les Falles. 1932.
Artist: **A. Vercher**
45³/₄ x 64¹/₄ in./116 x 163.2 cm
Imp. y Lit. Ortega, Valencia
Cond B/Many vertical tears at top edge; slight creasing and tears in bottom text area.
Ref: España, 383; PAI-VII, 345 (var)
Valencia, Spain's third largest city, holds a week-long carnival every year during the week preceding March 19th. The tradition of the festival originates in the Middle Ages, when on the Feast of St. Joseph, the carpenters of Valencia burned their accumulated wood shavings in bonfires known as *fallas*, a word which finds its origins in the Latin *fax*, or "torch." The word became synonymous with the festival for which, in time, objects were made solely for burning—particularly effigies of the less popular members of the community. The effigies in time were replaced with floats produced by the different quarters of the town. Prizes are awarded every year for these creations and the general festivities include fireworks, bullfights and processions before everything goes up in flames on the evening of the 19th. Vercher appropriately shows a pair of dummies hanging about in a silly fashion as they await their date with the flames. A most original and amusing approach. *This is the Castilian version.*
Est: $1,500-$1,800.

654. Festividad de las Fallas/Valencia. 1936.
Artist: **Marco Vincente Ballester**
45³/₈ x 64 in./115.2 x 162.5 cm
Imp. y Lit. Ortega, Valencia
Cond B+/Slight tears at folds.
Ref: España, 390
It's rather fitting that this puffing puppet enjoys his last smoke as he is lowered into the bonfire's inferno of Valencia's festival of flames. Resigned to his fate, the pleasantly nightmarish vision of simultaneous destruction and redemption suits the celebration's atmosphere to a tee.
Est: $1,700-$2,000.

655. Cáceres/Concurso de Ganadas. 1935.
Artist: **Burgos Capdevielle**
27⁷/₈ x 40¹/₈ in./70.7 x 102 cm
Imp. Lit. Ortega, Valencia
Cond A–/Slight tears at fold.
Ref: España, 159
It comes as no surprise that the walled city of Cáceres would play host to an agricultural exposition, featuring livestock judging and an exhibition of rural products,

seeing as the lively town in the Spanish southwest is the capital of an agricultural province known for its stock rearing and cereal grain production. And Capdevielle's colorful feeding time design capably captures both the spirit and patience of a country community. And though all the elements make perfect sense, one has to wonder exactly what farming yarns were featured in the fair's literary competition, prominently featured as one of event's major attractions.
Est: $1,500-$1,800.

656. Exposicion General Epañola. 1929.
Artist: **Rafael de Penagos Zalabardo (1889-1954)**
26 x 39 in./66 x 99 cm
Lit. Mateu, Madrid
Cond A–/Slight tears and stains in borders.
Ref: España, 744 (var)
As a lifelong resident of Madrid, Penagos was the ideal choice to create the publicity for this countrywide celebration of all things Spanish, anchored by Barcelona in the east and Seville on the western front, with the designer firmly situated as an artistic fulcrum in the central capital. And what a creation it is. Rooted solidly to the unseen earth like a pagan high priestess of culture, the entire design practically dripping with rich tones of gold and crimson, it is immediately evident

654

658

659

that resistance is futile—one must surrender to the magnificence. The powerful image encompasses every aspect of national pride one could wish for—from the athletic to the scholarly to the purely beautiful—and obviously proved to be an effective marketing tool as the crowned enchantress was employed on several occasions, indicated by the artist's mark that designates the design's premiere appearance to 1926.
Est: $800-$1,000.

J. STALL

657. Mirus.
46³/₄ x 62⁵/₈ in./118.7 x 159 cm
Imp. Joseph-Charles, Paris
Cond B-/Restored tears and losses at folds; image and colors excellent.
Sure. It's easy to thumb your nose at Old Man Winter when you've got a Mirus wood-burning stove at your disposal to heat your hearth and home. Still, you'd think that this bubbly lass with the Princess Leia hairdo might be a bit more gracious knowing that she's got such an unfair advantage over all things frigid. But, I guess when it comes right down to it, all's fair in love and warmth. *For Loupot's approach to this subject, see No. 516.*
Est: $1,700-$2,000.

THEOPHILE-ALEXANDRE STEINLEN (1859-1923)

658. Lait pur Stérilisé. 1894.
38¹/₄ x 54 in./97.2 x 137 cm
Imp. Charles Verneau, Paris
Cond B+/Slight tears and stains at folds.
Ref: Bargiel et Zagrodzki, 16. A1; Crauzat, 491;
  Wine Spectator, 112; Maitres, 95; DFP-II, 783;
  Abdy, p. 97; Weill, 63; Gold, 56; PAI-XXX, 50
"Nowhere does Steinlen's humanity shine with a greater glow than in 'Lait pur Sterilisé,' a poster for a milk distributor. His daughter Colette is . . . the subject . . . she carefully tastes the milk she's giving the family cats to make sure it isn't too hot for them." (Wine

Spectator, 112). The humble dairy of Quillot Brothers in the village of Montigny sur Vingeanne could not have had the slightest notion that, to advertise their sterilized milk, they caused Steinlen to produce one of the all-time most endearing poster images ever created.
Est: $10,000-$12,000.

659. Le Journal/Les Mystères de la Tour Pointue.
  1899.
22⁷/₈ x 31 in./58 x 78.5 cm
Imp. Charle Verneau, Paris
Cond A-/Slight tears at folds.
Ref: Bargiel & Zagrodzki, 38B; Crauzat, 506;
  PAI-XV, 502
This charming little scene of a Parisian lowlife doing away with the sugar daddy of a woman of questionable repute—with her full consent, of course—was apparently based on a true story taken from the memoires of Marie-François Gordon. The biographical installment series—this particular chapter, "The Mysteries of the Pointed Tower" sounding like the inspiration for a "Hardy Boys" adventure—ran in the pages of *Le Journal*. "After being a traveler and explorer throughout South America, (Gordon) became police commissioner, and afterwards chief of security for all of Paris. Before he turned fifty, he retired in 1894, turning command over to Armand Cochefort . . . (He) then became a journalist and novelist, serializing his memoires . . . before publishing them in four volumes . . . in 1897 with a preface by Émile Gautier" (Collectionneur, p. 149).
Est: $2,000-$2,500.

STEINLEN (continued)

660. A la Bodinière/Exposition T. A. Steinlen. 1894.
31 x 23⁵/₈ in./79 x 60 cm
Imp. Charles Verneau, Paris
Cond B/Restored tears at folds and edges; slight
    staining at edges.
Ref: Bargiel & Zagrodzki, 14; Crauzat, 492; DFP-II, 782;
    PAI-XXVIII, 550
To advertise his important first exhibition of paintings,
drawings and posters at the Bodinière gallery, Steinlen
returns to a favorite subject: his cats. The simple but
masterful sketch justly remains one of the great posterist's most famous and beloved images.
Est: $7,000-$9,000.

661. Le Journal/Paris/Emile Zola. 1898.
77⁵/₈ x 54¹/₈ in./.197 x 137.5 cm
Imp. Charles Verneau, Paris
Cnd B/Restored tears at folds and edges.
Ref: Bargiel & Zagrodzki, 29; Crauzat, 501; Steinlen, 95;
    DFP-II, 791; Dreyfus, p. 119; PAI-XXVII, 590
Olive green tones dominate this large, two-sheet
poster announcing the serialization of Zola's novel
Paris in the daily *Le Journal*. It "depicted such aspects
of Parisian life as the political machinations of those
in power and the squalor of the poor . . . (Steinlen)
created a powerful political image with a mythic view
of the capital, seething with corruption, violence and
lust . . . Below the somber cityscape speckled with
golden rays of light, a mass of naked bodies were
locked in struggle. Their fierce arms and fists, ready to
strike, rose up from the crowd. On the left, a large figure carried a jug over his head from which coins fell,
as eager hands grabbed wildly for them. In the right
foreground a savage-looking man grinned at the young
girl he was embracing. Truth rose above the heap of
humanity in the form of a female nude with flowing
hair" (Steinlen, pp. 125-126).
Est: $2,000-$2,500.

STENBERG BROTHERS (Vladimir, 1899-1982; Georgi, 1900-1933)

662. Tainstvennaya Gatcienda (Secret Hacienda).
    1927.
27¹/₂ x 39⁷/₈ in./70 x 101.2 cm
Sovkino, Moscow
Cond B/Slight tears at folds and edges.
Ref: Russian Films, p. 52
The Stenberg Brothers were Russian designers and
poster artists who embraced Constructivism and became major figures in the avant-garde of Soviet art
during the turbulent revolutionary era after 1917.
"Under Soviet auspices the film industry was encouraged as a leading communications medium . . . The
head of poster production, an artist named Yakov Ruk-
levsky, recruited a brilliant group of avant-garde Constructivist designers. Of these, the most prolific and
talented were the brothers, Vladimir and Georgi Stenberg . . . . While techniques of film and photomontage
were the point of departure for their posters, the . . .
brothers, masters of color and lithographic process,
preferred to draw their images. The facilities available
for printing photographic images simply did not give
them the sharpness and color they desired. However,
the photographic quality of their renderings was
achieved with a primitive method of projecting film
and photographic images to the desired size and then
drawing over them" (Modern Poster, pp. 29-30). In their
poster for the 1925 Soviet release of an American film
originally titled "The Fighting Demon," for its 1925 release, the Stenbergs geometrical frame Richard Tal-
madge in the role of "John Drake, a college athlete who
has been promised a job in South America. On the ship,
he meets and falls for the banker's daughter Dolores
(Lorraine Eason). In South America, he discovers he
has been hired by a criminal gang to help them rob
her father's bank. Drake fights off the criminals, locks
them in the vault and wins the heroine's love. The
poster depicts Drake leaping from the bank vault in
his best 'fighting demon' form" (Russian Posters, p. 52).
Est: $6,000-$7,000.

663. The General. 1929.
28¹/₈ x 42¹/₂ in./71.2 x 108 cm
Sovkino, Moscow
Cond B+/Unobtrusive slight tears and stains. Framed.

660

661

Ref (All Var): Revolutionary Russia, p. 67;
    Russian Films, p. 100; Stenberg/Moma, p. 91;
    PAI-XI, 399 (var)
"This comedy masterpiece was about a railroad engineer during the Civil War who is rejected from serving
in the Confederate army because he is more valuable
as an engineer than as a soldier. Unaware of the cir-
cumstances, his fiancée and family think him a cow-
ard. When his train,'The General,' is stolen by Union
agents with his fiancée aboard, Keaton saves them
both and defeats the Union troops in the process. He
is rewarded with an officer's commission in the Confederate Army and the renewed love of his fiancée"
(Russian Films, p. 100). An off-the-charts Stenberg
Brothers' classic, calling upon a repeated locomotive
motif to evoke the inevitable comedic crash course of
the protagonist's subtextual life, and a poster more
than equal to the task of promoting what is arguably
one of the greatest comedies ever made: "Another
favorite device for the sense of conveying a moving
picture was the use of repetition, frequently an important design element, as in the case of of the locomotives in the Stenberg's poster for the Buster Keaton
film *The General*" (Avant Garde, p. 76). Also note that
the top border contains a handwritten notation that
announces that the movie will be shown on the 18th
at 4:30 PM at an unnamed venue. *Rare!*
Est: $20,000-$25,000.

FRANCISCO TAMAGNO (1851-?)

664. Extrait de Viande Liebig.
38 x 54¹/₄ in./96.6 x 137.6 cm
Affiches Camis, Paris
Cond B–/Restored tears at folds.
Ref: PAI-XXVI, 544
When inventor Justus Liebig introduced this beef ex-
tract in 1852, it bore the claim "between 30 and 50
kilograms of beef chunks go into every kilogram of
Liebig." Relieved of the time consuming task of making
their own *glace de viande*, essential for enriching sauces
and stews, grateful French cooks snapped the stuff up
and continue to do so today. In Tamagno's steamy
kitchen scene, a boyish chef finds the product "indis-
pensable." Liebig must have found the poster indispens-
able, too: an earlier version of the image exists—same
design with a much brawnier chef (*see* PAI-XXIII, 495).
Est: $1,700-$2,000.

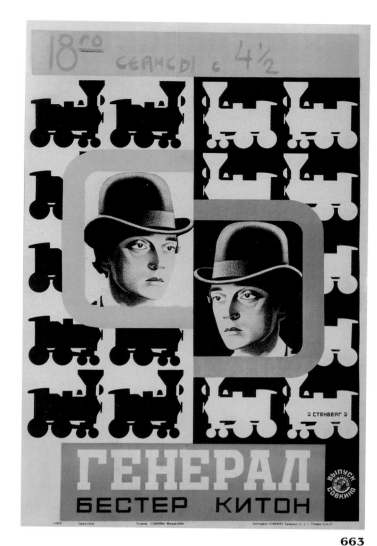

662

663

664

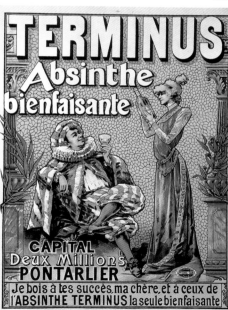

665

666

665. L'Absinthe Cusenier Oxygénée. 1896.
36⁷/₈ x 51 in./93.6 x 129.4 cm
Affiches Camis, Paris
Cond A–/Unobtrusive folds.
Ref: DFP-II, 807; Reims, 1042; Absinthe, p. 107; Boissons, 285; PAI-VIII, 322
A young woman peering into a cafe window gets an invitation from the actor Albert Brasseur (1862-1932) who is going through the ritual of preparing his absinthe potion. Warm indoor tones are used to

offset the pale drink to which our attention is drawn. *This is the larger format.*
Est: $2,000-$2,500.

666. Terminus Absinthe. ca. 1905.
38³/₈ x 51 in./97.5 x 129.6 cm
Imp. Affiches-Camis, Paris
Cond B/Slight tears at folds and paper edges.
Ref: Absinthe, p. 46; PAI-X, 408
Tamagno used the likenesses of two famous stage personalities to move "beneficial" Terminus Absinthe

off the shelves: Constant Coquelin and Sarah Bernhardt, apparently enjoying a post-performance toast. According to Barnaby Conrad III, author of "Absinthe: History in a Bottle," the actors were not asked to give permission for the commercial use of their images and Ms. Bernhardt, incensed went to court; as a result, the posters had to be removed from the walls of Paris. Though unsigned, the distinctive style of the design has led to its general Tamagno attribution. *This is the larger format.*
Est: $1,200-$1,500.

667

669

FRED TAYLOR (1875-1963)

667. Scarborough.
49⁵/₈ x 39¹/₂ in./126 x 100.4 cm
Chorley & Pickersgill, Leeds
Cond B/Tears at folds and edges.
While much of Europe's railroad advertising focused on the glamour or modernity of the ride itself, the British rail always emphasized the destination. Here, in its favored horizontal format (so conducive to landscapes), the LNER invites travelers to experience one of the very best places in Britain in which to savor the atmosphere of the Victorian seaside. Taylor's expansively tiered panorama gives every attraction its due: promenades, pavilions, cafes, chalets, pretty little shelters, the elegant bulk of the Spa, the ruins of the 12th-century castle built around a Roman signal station and the luxurious pool, situated smack-dab in the middle of the popular sandy beaches of the South Bay, a stone's throw from the North Sea. Taylor was one of the principal, and finest, designers for the London Underground, creating 60 posters between 1908 and 1960. He also produced prolific work for rail and shipping clients.
Est: $2,500-$3,000.

TEJADA

668. Espagne.
26⁷/₈ x 39¹/₄ in./68.4 x 99.6 cm
Graficas Reunidas, Madrid
Cond B+/Tears and stains, largely at folds.
Ref: España, 900 (var); PAI-VII, 324
The town square is a stylized sunny plaza lined with orange and palm trees, but framing it in the graceful arch of a colonnade is an inspired device to localize it in Spain. The light warm shades also help, as does the adobe beige of the structure. A tourist poster par excellence from an otherwise little known artist.
Est: $1,200-$1,500.

PAUL TELEMANN

669. Die Moderne Eva. ca. 1911.
37 x 27¹/₂ in./94 x 69.8 cm
Hoflith. Robert Müller, Potsdam
Cond B+/Unobtrusive tears near edges; slight staining in background; colors very fresh.
Ref: DFP-III, 3254
Temptation, thy name is woman. Ever since the day that biblical mythology so neatly planted the image in the collective mind of the Western world that Eve gave in to serpentine seduction, women have borne the brunt, deserved or not, as the purveyors of instigation. And seeing as the flames are fanned ever higher by the merest mention of women's liberation, it comes as no surprise that popular entertainments spring up to feast on such an exploitable topic. Thus, we are left with the charming bite of "The Modern Eve," an Art Nouveau tapestry used to promote the operetta penned by Georg

668

671

Okonkowsky and Schönfeld with music by popular Viennese composer Jean Gilbert. The tuneful theatricality explored the comic possibilities of the suffrage movement of the early-20th century and the spectacular poster gives us the three classic elements that inevitably lead to an expulsion from The Garden: a conniving femme-fatale, a groveling simperer and a gargantuan snake of liberated thought. A superlative work by commercial artist Telemann, a craftsman best known for his book jacket designs and theatrical posters.
Est: $1,700-$2,000.

ALEARDO TERZI (1870—1943)

670. Rom-1911/Internationale Ausstellung.
15⁵/₈ x 23 in./39.8 x 58.6 cm
E. Chappuis, Bologna
Cond A.
Ref (Both Var): Menagazzi-II, 49; PAI-XXVI, 546
Considered one of the masters of early poster design in Italy, Terzi takes a symbolist approach in publicizing an expo in Rome. He was born in Palermo on the island of Sicily, but by 1900 we find him doing draw-

ings for the Rome daily *La Tribuna Illustrata*. From then on, he starts working in posters, first for the printer Instituto d'Arte Graphiche in Bergamo, later for Ricordi in Milano and others. His draftsmanship as well as his feeling for colors are impeccable, his designs always pictorially fascinating. Here he lends his talents to the International Exposition, featuring displays of art, archeology, music, Italian ethnography and sports. It was produced in several languages; here we are presented with the German version. *This is the smaller, in-store display format, used with metal strips top and bottom.*
Est: $1,700-$2,000.

WALTER THOR (1870-1929)

671. Cycles Griffon.
31¹/₂ x 46¹/₄ in./80 x 117.4 cm
Imp. Elleaume, Paris
Cond B-/Restored tears and stains at folds and edges.
Thor designed at least two other posters for Griffon bicycles (*see PAI-XX, 51 & PAI-XXVII, 26*), both of which are charming, but don't even begin to approach the evocative nostalgia of this lakeside encounter. The

670

672

673

namesake mythological winged-lion of the chain-driven transport is nowhere to be found; what is clearly present is a sense of anticipation and camaraderie in a tale primarily told in earth tones. Thor's composition s nothing short of brilliant, creating a splendid visual ension smattered with enough details so as to allow he viewer the opportunity to create a narrative of heir own for the imminent meeting.
Est: $1,200-$1,500.

HENRI DE TOULOUSE-LAUTREC (1864-1901)

672. Divan Japonais. 1893.
24 x 31³/₈ in./61 x 79.7 cm
Imp. Edw. Ancourt, Paris
Cond B/Restored tears at folds and edges. Framed.
Ref: Wittrock, P11; Delteil, 341; Adriani, 8; DFP-II, 824;
    Maîtres, 2; Wagner, 3; Modern Poster, 5;
    Wine Spectator, 41; PAI-XXIX, 657
"Of all the female entertainers Lautrec celebrated in his posters, Jane Avril and Yvette Guilbert were the two with whom he maintained the longest friendships. He portrayed them both together in one of his most brilliant posters, *Divan Japonais* . . . Although Guilbert was the performer at this rather shabby cabaret when it opened in the spring of (1893), Lautrec made the half-Italian Avril the focal figure in his composition. Under a shock of red-orange hair topped with a pagoda-shaped hat and towering plume, her black, silhouetted figure dominates the frontal plane as she assumes a regal pose and an attitude of hauteur. Neither she nor her companion, Edouard Dujardin, the distinguished founder of the Symbolist *Revue Wagnerienne,* deign to look at Guilbert on stage, whom Lautrec has portrayed as acephalous, probably as a witty response to her complaint that he caricatured her and made her ugly" (Wagner, p. 21). This image show's Lautrec's mastery of bold design and simplification of line and color. To appreciate the revolutionary aspect of this design, one need only compare it to other Divan Japonais posters of the period, such as those of Maurice Millière (*see* Nos. 67 & 68). One of the methods which accomplished this stark contrast was Lautrec's "good use of spatter, a technique which adds another dimension to poster art: here, for example, it effectively separates the solid black of Jane's dress from the less important dark mass of the bar and the orchestra. Spatter can also add depth and three-dimensionality, and Toulouse-Lautrec was to use it in much of his lithographic work; yet, surprisingly enough, it is rarely if ever employed by other posterists, perhaps because

of the sheer technical difficulty of it. But he, having acquired the skills of a lithographer, could work right alongside the printing plant employees and achieve whatever effect he desired" (Wine Spectator, 42).
Est: $25,000-$30,000.

673. Le Matin/ Au Pied de l'Echafaud. 1893.
23³/₄ x 32³/₈ in./60.4 x 82.2 cm
Imp. Chaix, Paris
Cond B+/Slight tears at folds.
Ref: Wittrock, P8; Delteil, 347; Adriani, 14;
    DFP-II, 830; PAI-XXVIII, 571
This design advertises the serialization in the newspaper *Le Matin* of an 1891 book, "At the Foot of the Scaffold," written by a former prison chaplain. The grim-visaged prisoner being led to the guillotine strikes the keynote, with the dark silhouette of the detachment of the witnessing soldiers, the somber priest and the executioner adding dramatic overtones. All known copies of this image are trimmed at the bottom.
Est: $5,000-$6,000.

674. Aristide Bruant Dans Son Cabaret. 1893.
39¹/₂ x 54¹/₂ in./100.4 x 138.3 cm
Imp. Charles Verneau, Paris
Cond B/Restored paper losses at edges; slight tears at
    folds. Framed.
Ref: Wittrock, P9A; Delteil, 348; Adriani, 12-I;
    Wagner, 10; DFP-II, 827 (var); PAI-XXIX, 656
Bruant was a strong, forceful, and in many ways vulgar entertainer of intimate cabarets—the kind of places where fashionable society went "slumming" for their thrills. Toulouse-Lautrec catches this brutal quality of the performer and the disdain with which he treated his audiences by having him show us the broad of his back. The red scarf forms an exclamation point, punctuating the black expanse, and the pose itself makes a complete, self-contained statement. Toulouse-Lautrec at his graphic best. *Rare proof before the addition of letters.*
Est: $50,000-$60,000.

TOULOUSE-LAUTREC (continued)

675. Jane Avril. 1893.
35^1/$_4$ x 49^1/$_4$ in./89.5 x 125 cm
Imp. Chaix, Paris
Cond A–/Unobtrusive tears and stains at extreme edges. Framed.
Ref (All Var): Wittrock, P6B; Delteil, 345-I; Adriani, 11-I; Wagner, 7; DFP-II, 828; Maitres, Pl. 110; Wine Spectator, 41; PAI-XXVII, 602

Ebria Feinblatt indicates, with good reason, that this "is universally considered his most brilliant and successful design" (Wagner, p. 22). Toulouse-Lautrec shows "Jane Avril on stage doing her specialty, which, according to contemporaries, was essentially a cancan that she made exotic by making a pretense of prudery—the 'depraved virgin' image aimed at arousing the prurience in the predominantly male audience. The sexual innuendo was captured by the artist by contrasting the dancer's slender legs with the robust, phallic neck of the bass viol in the foreground—a masterly stroke that not only heightens our perception but also creates an unusual perspective: we see the performer as an orchestra member would, and this allows Toulouse-Lautrec to show, as if inadvertently, how tired and somewhat downcast she looks close-up, not at all in keeping with the gaiety of the dance that is perceived by the audience. It is clear, as Maindron has pointed out, that she is dancing entirely for the viewer's pleasure, not hers, which makes it a highly poignant image. Seemingly without trying, Toulouse-Lautrec not only creates a great poster but makes a personal statement: Only a person who really cares about his subject as a human being would portray her with such startling candor" (Wine Spectator, 41). *This is one of only two known existing copies with the key stone printed in olive-green. Wittrock refers to this trial proof as an "incomplete drawing on wove paper." Extremely rare!*
Est: $50,000-$60,000.

676. Troupe de Mlle Eglantine. 1896.
31^1/$_8$ x 24 in./79 x 61 cm
Cond A. Framed.
Ref: Wittrock, P21C; Delteil, 361; Adriani, 162-III; Wine Spectator, 43; DFP-II, 850; Wagner, 23; PAI-XXIX, 658

"At the height of the cancan's popularity, dancers formed groups which offered their services as a unit; whether the troupe of Mlle Eglantine was the best of them we don't know, but it is certainly the only one publicized by the best. Toulouse-Lautrec did it at the request of his friend, Jane Avril. From left to right, we see Jane Avril, Cléopatra, Eglantine and Gazelle. As with his Moulin Rouge poster, he lets the white of the petticoats, punctuated by stockinged legs, do most of the talking, but he also offhandedly gives each girl a

677

678

679

"In the poster Belfort is framed by long black curls under an enormous cap, her hands hiding most of a yellow-eyed kitten. Lautrec presents her on a diagonal plane, her brilliant orange-red dress slanting to the left, her shoulder brought forward in the picture plane to place her in a frontal position. The flat sweep of her gown bellow the frilled, green-splattered sleeves is, taken by itself, merely a red sail or banner" (Wagner, p. 27). Julia Frey's excellent biography gives some interesting background to this: " May Belfort, whom Henry represented in at least ten works, had gained a reputation for corrupt innocence by appearing onstage dressed as a baby holding a black kitten in her arms, and 'miaowing or bleating' her popular song, 'Daddy Wouldn't Buy Me a Bow-Wow,' whose lines had a dou- ble meaning which was not lost in the French-speaking audience: 'I've got a pussycat, I'm very fond of that.' Henry, enthusiastic, later wrote letters to friends trying to find a mate for the cat, and even got a cat himself" (Frey, p. 382).
Est: $25,000-$30,000.

678. May Milton. 1895.
23³/₄ x 30¹/₂ in./60.3 x 77.5 cm
Cond A–/slight tears at edges. Framed.
Ref: Wittrock, P17B, Delteil, 336; Adriani, 134-II;
    DFP-II, 836; Timeless Images, 55; Wagner, 18;
    Wine Spectator, 45; PAI-XXVII, 606
According to Adriani, "May Milton was an English dancer with a pale, serious face and strong chin who appeared at the Moulin Rouge." Toulouse-Lautrec is almost brutally frank in depicting her face, neither pretty nor youthful, and pointing out the inappropriate- ness of the white debutante's dress with puffed sleeves which she wore on stage. Yet the point is made with such gentle irony that it may have been missed, or ignored, by the performer herself, as she apparently used the poster for personal publicity.
Est: $22,000-$26,000.

distinct character in only a few lines limning their facial expressions" (Wine Spectator, 43). The poster was designed for the group's London appearance at the Palais Theatre; Jane Avril asked her friend Henri at the last minute to leave the name of the venue out of the design, hoping that it would be a success and travel to other theaters as well. Unfortunately, the Troupe was not well received and they went no fur- ther. But the cancan, which was usually performed at the time in a formation of four dancers, as shown here, continues to live in our imagination due to the lively, fresh and original composition of this poster. *This is the finest specimen of this poster ever seen!*
Est: $35,000-$40,000.

677. May Belfort. 1895.
23⁵/₈ x 31 in./60 x 78.8 cm
Kleinman, Paris
Cond B+/Restored tears and losses at edges. Framed.
Ref: Wittrock, P14 (iv); Delteil, 354; Adhemar, 116;
    Adriani, 126-IV; DFP-II, 837; Wagner, 16;
    PAI-XXVIII, 568

680

681

TOULOUSE-LAUTREC (continued)

679. L'Aube. 1896.
31³/₄ x 24³/₈ in./80.6 x 62 cm
Imp. Edw. Ancourt, Paris (not shown)
Cond B+/Slight tears and stains at edges.
Ref: Wittrock, P23; Delteil, 363; Adriani, 184; Wagner, 25; DFP-II, 845;
PAI-XXIV, 540
To advertise a socialist periodical titled *L'Aube* ("The Dawn"), which started
publishing in May of 1896, Toulouse-Lautrec designed a scene in turquoise,
using his spatter technique to suggest the grainy quality of the day's early
light. He conveys the drudgery of these downtrodden souls with poignancy,
creating the sympathetic desire to read about their plight. Ebria Feinblatt
points out that "the robust female pushing the cart illustrates Lautrec's mastery of movement, here almost geometrized in her shape" (Wagner, p. 29).
Est: $10,000-$12,000.

680. La Vache Enragée. 1896.
23 x 32 in./58.4 x 81.2 cm
Imp. Chaix, Paris
Cond B+/Slight tears and stains at top and bottom edges. Framed.
Ref: Wittrock, P27A; Delteil, 364; Adriani, 175; Abdy, p. 85; DFP-II, 844;
Wagner, 26; PAI-VII, 335 (var)
First state, before letters, of the poster advertising Willette's magazine,
La Vache Enragée, which lasted for only a single year. Wittrock, who rates
the rarity of this state as "uncommon," also indicates that "the image in
the poster was drawn by Toulouse-Lautrec in imitation of the style of A.
Willette" (p. 808). This is one of the few Lautrec posters with movement:
the runaway cow is the centerpiece of a remarkable caricature depicting
sheer panic in some, curious complacency in others—an obvious reflection of the world that swirled around the artist.
Est: $25,000-$30,000.

682

683

684

681. La Revue Blanche. 1895.
35¹/₂ x 50¹/₄ in./90.3 x 127.5 cm
Imp. Edw. Ancourt, Paris
Cond A. Framed.
Ref: Wittrock, P16C; Delteil, 355; Adrianni, 130;
    Maitres, 82; DFP-I, 835; Gold, 92; PAI-XXX, 213 (var)
When Toulouse-Lautrec chose to advertise the art and
literary magazine *La Revue Blanche* by using a portrait
of Misia Natanson, wife of coeditor Thadée Natanson,
it was because the brainy, redheaded beauty was the
real mover behind the throne. Her house was the mecca
of the *literati*, and it was she who coaxed some of the
major celebrities of the day—Catulle Mendès, Paul
Valéry, Léon Blum, Octave Mirbeau, Claude Débussy,
André Gide, Colette and Toulouse-Lautrec himself—to
contribute to the publication's success. The original
design for this poster had a small remarque printed at
left which made it clear that Misia was being shown
skating. In her biography of the artist, Frey writes that
"many people feel (this poster) is (Toulouse-Lautrec's)
strongest individual work. . . . The strength of this work
comes in large part from the fact that, as in many of
Henry's posters, the figure is cut off by the lower edge
just below the knees. . . . The entire poster is like a
little joke, as if Henry were amusing himself by proving
that he could show an ice skater without ever showing
her skates" (p. 408).
Est: $30,000-$35,000.

682. Elles. 1896.
18³/₄ x 23¹/₂ in./47.8 x 59.8 cm
Cond A–/Slight tears at edges.
Ref: Wittrock, 155, 3rd state; Delteil, 179;
    Adriani, 177-IV; DFP-II, 842; PAI-XXIX, 659
This image of a woman taking her hair down advertises the portfolio of ten lithographs of Lautrec's
scenes of Paris brothels as well as their exhibition at
the gallery of *La Plume* magazine. The ladies' occupation could not be openly named any more than it
could be depicted. They are simply called "Elles" (Those
Women), and their business is indicated merely by a
gentleman's hat on the bed. Adriani calls Lautrec's
Elles series "one of the high-points of nineteenth-cen-
tury art" (p. 222).
Est: $20,000-$25,000.

683. Napoleon. 1895.
18¹/₈ x 24 in./46.2 x 61 cm
Cond A. Framed.
Ref: Wittrock, 140; Delteil, 358; Adriani, 135;
    DFP-II, 841; Wagner, 20; Abdy, 89
Provenance: Collection of Nelson A. Rockefeller.
"In the summer of 1895 a competition was held by the
art-dealers Boussard, Valadon et Cie. for a poster to
advertise a biography of Napoleon by William Milligan
Sloan, which was to be published in the *Century Magazine* in New York in 1896. No doubt encouraged by
Maurice Joyant, a friend from his youth and director of
Boussod and Valadon, Lautrec entered the competition . . . Although the handling of the motif should
actually have appealed to the specially selected jury—
the successful society painters Detaille, Gérôme and
Vibert, and the Napoleon scholar Frédéric Masson—
the design was not judged worthy of a prize. From the
21 entries, Lucien Métivet, a minor illustrator and former fellow student of Lautrec's in the Atelier Cormon,
won the prize. The rejection of Lautrec's work is all
the more astonishing since Lautrec, no doubt with the
jury in mind, produced a composition in full sympathy
with the elevated traditional image of the great man,
and aimed to give an accurate representation of the
historic facts, even down to the details of the uniforms.
After vain attempts to sell the design elsewhere, the
artist decided to have an edition printed at his own
expense" (Adriani, p. 190). *Of this self-published
edition of 100, this is No. 38, numbered and hand-
signed in black crayon. Exceedingly rare!*
Est: $100,000-$120,000.

TOULOUSE-LAUTREC (continued)

684. L'Estampe Originale. 1893.
28⁵/₈ x 22¹/₄ in./72.7 x 65.5 cm
Imp. Edw. Ancourt, Paris
Cond A. Framed.
Ref: Wittrock, 3; Delteil, 17; Adriani, 9;
    Color Revolution, 32; PAI-XXII, 529
Provenance: The Claude Roger-Marx Collection.
"By 1893 if there were any doubts that there was a
printmaking renaissance and that lithography domi-
nated this general print revival, those doubts were qui-
eted forever by a new publication entitled *L'Estampe
originale* . . . From March 1893 to early 1895, in collaboration with (critic) Roger Marx, (André) Marty published . . . a series of quarterly albums of ten prints
each (except for the last which contained fourteen
prints) in the media of etching, drypoint, mezzotint,
woodcut, wood engraving, gypsography and lithography. In all, the publication encompassed ninety-five
prints by seventy-four artists representing the young
avantgarde such as Lautrec and the Nabis, as well as
their established mentors including Gauguin, Puvis de
Chavannes, Redon, Chéret, Whistler, Bracquemond
and Lepère. *L'Estampe originale* offers a remarkable
cross-section of the most advanced aesthetic attitudes
in *fin de siècle* French art" (Color Revolution, p. 22).
Marty felt that Lautrec "deserved 'a place of honour in
the golden book of the modern print' . . . (and he)
accorded Henri exactly that place, using him as the
artist for the cover of the first issue" (Frey, p. 323).
Lautrec shows us his favorite model, Jane Avril, at his
favorite lithographic workshop, Ancourt, studying a
proof pulled by Père Cotelle, the experienced printer
at the Bisset press behind her. Wittrock knows of only
three proofs "not used as a cover, unfolded, with key
stone printed in olive-green and colour stones in
beige, salmon-red, red, yellow and black"—this is one
of them and it bears the stamp of the Claude Roger-
Marx estate in the lower right.
Est: $40,000-$50,000.

685. The Ault & Wiborg Co. 1896.
12¹/₂ x 15⁷/₈ in./31.7 x 40.3 cm
Courier Lithographic Co., Buffalo (not shown)
Cond A. Framed.
Ref: Wittrock P28B; Delteil, 365; Adriani, 196-II; Wag-
    ner, 27 (var); PAI-VIII, 527 (var)
Lautrec's smallest poster is also the only one executed
by him on zinc plates and the only one printed in the
United States. He sent the plates to the Cincinnati ink
and printing company, Ault and Wiborg, who commis-
sioned it from him. It represents the actress Emilienne

685

686

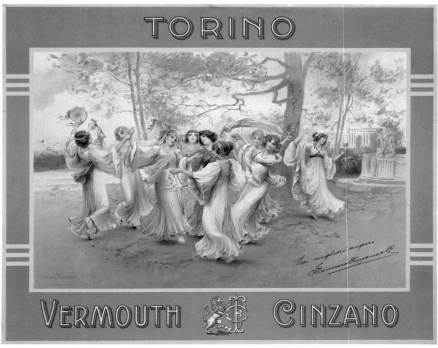

687

688

689

690

d'Alençon and Lautrec's cousin, Dr. Gabriel Tapié de Céleyran in a loge. Lautrec also printed a small edition under the title "Au Concert" in Paris. *This is the extremely rare French version before letters, signed and with the Sagot stamp, executed before the plates were sent off to the Cincinnati printing house. Adriani estimates this edition consisted of approximately 20 copies.*
Est: $60,000-$70,000.

686. The Ault & Wiborg Co. 1946.
13¹/₂ x 15⁵/₈ in./34 x 39.7 cm
Cond A. Framed.
Ref: Wittrock, P28/Note; Adriani, 196/New edition;
    Wagner, 27 (var)
Once Ault & Wiborg printed their Lautrec poster for mass consumption, they donated the original plates to the Art Institute of Chicago. On the occasion of the 50th anniversary of the design's execution "In 1946, the Art Institute of Chicago Print and Drawing Club published for its members an edition of 100 impressions of this poster on china paper, numbered x/100. These images were printed offset and the zinc plates and proofs of this re-edition are in the print room of the Art Institute of Chicago" (Wittrock, p. 810). *This poster represents # 24 of the limited edition run with an attached verso note which attests to the statements made by Wittrock with regard to this edition of the design.*
Est: $7,000-$9,000.

FERNAND TOUSSAINT (1873-1955)

687. Vermouth Cinzano/Torino.
23 x 18⁵/₈ in./58.4 x 47.3 cm
O. de Rycker & Mendel, Bruxelles
Cond B+/Slight creasing and tears in border. Framed.
To the rhythmic rattle of the trusty tambourine, this passel of vestal virgins tastefully whips themselves into a frenzy in the name of Cinzano vermouth. Though they seemingly share a very narrow plot of common ground—ostensibly the gamboling waifs could be Italian and they appear to be prancing about a Romanesque ruin—their tenuous connection hardly matters when the results are as lovely as those seen in this promotional lithograph, complete with the stone-etched well-wishes of Francesco Cinzano himself. Toussaint had a long and productive career in Belgium as a painter, but unfortunately produced few posters.
Est: $2,500-$3,000.

ABEL TRUCHET (1857-1918)

688. Louvre/Jouet/Etrennes. 1910.
47¹/₄ x 63¹/₂ in./120 x 161.2 cm
Eugene Verneau & Henri Chachoin, Paris
Cond B+/Slight tears and stains at folds.
Look! In the sky! It's a bird! It's a plane! Actually, it's a little of each, but it certainly does attract one's attention to the fact that the Louvre department store is having a toy and gift sale. The rearing rolling stallion and his equally wooden handler also add to the unde-

niable fun of the design. "Truchet was primarily a painter, but he also mastered the techniques of illustration, etching, and lithography and produced a few posters of undoubted merit" (Gold, p. 139).
Est: $1,500-$1,800.

FLORIMOND VAN ACKER (1858-1940)

689. Station Balnéaire. 1897.
39 x 27¹/₈ in./99 x 69 cm
Lith. A. Bernard, Liège
Cond B–/Slight tears at folds and edges. Framed.
Ref: Côte Belge, 127
How does one create a winning Art Nouveau design to promote a Belgian seaside resort? Easy. Combine two parts Cassiers inspiration with one part Livemont decorative flair and, Voila! "This poster, the work of Bruges painter and posterist Florimond Van Acker, was affixed to the walls of Liège in July of 1897 and enjoyed a successful life with the 'affichophile' collectors of the era. It was presented at an international poster exposition held in St. Petersburg in December, 1897. Isi Collin, in his article about the life and career of the painter Van Acker, announced precisely that this very beautiful poster was seen everywhere. And English critic W.S. Rogers gave his stamp of approval to the 'sketching Lady' d'Oostduinkerke, 'a very appropriate and well-drawn advertisement" (Côte Belge, p. 179).
Est: $1,500-$1,800.

JEAN-DOMINIQUE VAN CAULAERT (1897-1979)

For other Van Caulaert works, see Nos. 9 & 10.

690. Pot Pourri de Valses 1900. 1934.
30³/₄ x 11⁵/₈ in./78.2 x 29.5 cm
Gouache, pencil and ink maquette. Framed.
Though Van Caulaert's specialty was portraits—barely a luminary of his time escaped his particular brand of immortality—he shows in this maquette that his imagination and skill were as powerful as his ability to capture a personality. The unpublished design for a celebration of turn-of-the-century waltzes inventively utilizes flat-black as a background, an artistic maneuver which allows the gentlemen's tuxedoes to conceal themselves while allowing their faces and partners' wardrobes to soar off the page, thereby creating a spectacular sense of movement and unconcealed enjoyment.
Est: $1,500-$1,800.

691

693

696

N. VAN DEN EEDEN

691. Maison d'Art. 1898.
39³/₄ x 26¹/₂ in./101 x 67.5 cm
Gouweloos, Bruxelles
Cond B+/Slight tears and stains at vertical fold and edges.
When promoting an exhibition of your own works, it's always best to allow one's muse to speak on one's behalf, permitting them to quietly call attention to the event rather than bellowing heavy-handed boasts. Or at least that would seem to be Van Den Eeden's philosophy in this poster announcing a showing of his paintings and sculptures at Brussels' Art House, his watercoloresque inspiration painting the way with focused concentration.
Est: $1,200-$1,500.

W. M. VAN HASSELT

692. Rugby.
45³/₈ x 61¹/₈ in./115.2 x 155.2 cm
Affiches Kossuth, Paris
Cond C+/Restored tears, largely at folds and edges.
The far-more brutal, grueling and regulation infested cousin of American football gets a vigorous going over in this Van Hasselt design that served as a stock poster for whichever rugby match wise enough to allow the design to draw in the masses with its astute combination of athleticism and artistry.
Est: $1,200-$1,500.

THEODORE VAN RYSSELBERGHE (1862-1926)

693. La Libre Esthétique/Arts Graphiques. 1896.
28 x 39 in./71 x 99 cm
Imp. Ve. Monnom, Bruxelles
Cond A–/Unobtrusive folds.
Ref: DFP-II, 1126; Reims, 1502; Belle Epoque, 1970, 132; Weill, 84; PAI-XXVIII, 518
"Van Rysselberghe exerted a positive force for the revitalization of the decorative arts at the turn of the century, but his posters are not numerous; those he created for *La Libre Esthétique* are unquestionably the finest. The elegant feminine figures of his posters, very knowingly placed on the page, seem to be the pretext for Van Rysselberghe to balance large spots of red-orange against their greenish or bluish complementaries. The text is beautifully drawn and gracefully integrated into the design of the posters" (Belle Epoque 1970, p. 86). *Estampe et Affiche* spoke highly of the "impressionist painter (who) painted on an azure background, a charming young lady with red hair, whose languid arms and white neck spring from a large, violet dressing gown" (1898, p. 203). It is an impressively tasteful, delicate design. This is the version before the addition of lettering to the lower right text panel.
Est: $8,000-$10,000.

OTTO VAN TUSSENBROEK (1882-1957)

694. Volksuniversiteits Bibliothek.
17¹/₄ x 24¹/₂ in./43.8 x 62.2 cm
Druk Emrik en Binger, Haarlem
Cond A.
The decorative central shield of this poster for the Haarlem university extension libraries and their affiliation with local booksellers and publishers sets forth the flame of knowledge with a calculated abstraction, surrounding the corralled conflagration of academia with Van Tussenbroek's trademark proliferation of text. The artist was the director of an industrial arts school in Haarlem.
Est: $1,200-$1,500.

ERNST SIGMUND VON SALLWÜRK (1872-1944)

695. Ausstellung Kunstwerken. 1902.
31³/₄ x 50 in./80.6 x 127 cm
C. A. Kaemmerer, Halle
Cond B/Slight tears and stains at seam and folds.
A very expressive poster for an exhibition of the Halleschem family's private art collection—one whose scrutinizing viewer could either be a discerning critic or, quite possibly, the artist himself.
Est: $1,700-$2,000.

692

697

694

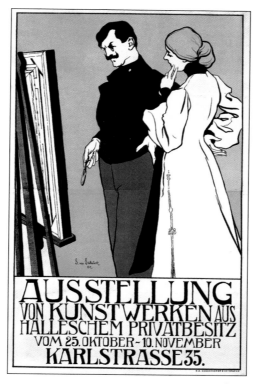

695

698

MARCEL VERTES (1895-1961)

696. Frou Frou. 1922.
62³/₄ x 47 in./159.4 x 119.5 cm
H. Bataille, Paris
Cond A–/Unobtrusive folds.
Ref: PAI-XI, 423
A charming design for a satirical magazine. Every element works—the flirty miss, the ogling oldster, the prototypical battle-ax—even the handle of his umbrella enjoys the view. And the coloring is perfection as well —zesty background, proper seductress-scarlet, envy-green wife. The poster is for the postwar revival of the publication, which enjoyed its original run between 1900 and 1914. Vertès, a highly talented painter and illustrator, was born in Budapest. After an initial stint designing political posters in his home town following World War I, he settled in Paris, chronicling the city life during the Roaring Twenties. Later, he would relocate once more, this time to the United States.
Est: $2,000-$2,500.

VIC

697. Shellubricate.
44³/₄ x 30 in./113.8 x 76.2 cm
Cond A–/Unobtrusive tear in bottom text area.
In order to keep the wheels of progress turning with the proper viscosity, the gears of modernity must be thoroughly greased. And what better product than Shell, the purveyors of petroleum with a long-standing tradition of credibility, both in motorized and poster circles. Vic keeps things to an ideal minimum to advertise the "Modern Oil For Modern Motors," his interlocked gears dipping smoothly into their slickening pool with the subtlest shadings of implied movement. Although he was an active graphic artist from about 1930 to 1960, little is known of Vic save his monosyllabic moniker. *Rare!*
Est: $2,500-$3,000.

RENÉ VINCENT (1879-1936)

698. Underwood.
16³/₄ x 24¹/₈ in./42.5 x 61.3 cm
Cond B+/Slight tears and stains, largely at folds.
Vincent became a posterist for the smart set by virtue of his long connections with fashions, from the *belle epoque* of the turn of the century to the Art Deco styles of the late Twenties. An apostle of elegance, his posters are graced with sleek, stylish women, filled with the exhilarating images of these goddesses elevating their surroundings. He was also quite capable of utilizing this graphic command to transform the most mundane of products into something exceptional with his eye for charm and impeccable skill. Case in point, this wonderful design for Underwood typewriters, a work which encapsulates all the artist's strengths as he renders the durability of the fast, precision office machine with spectacular detail and combines it with the breezy flirtation and fine fashion sense of a frizzy-haired gal from the steno pool.
Est: $1,200-$1,500.

699

700

RENÉ VINCENT (1879-1936)

699. Valentia/La Poule.
19¹/₄ x 17³/₈ in./49.5 x 44.2 cm
Imp. J. Céas & Fils, Valence
Cond A–/Slight stains near edges; mounted on board.
    Framed.
Vincent, an advocate for ultimate elegance and style,
creates a design that manages to make operating
industrial machinery look like a white collar profession.
With his hand on the crank of this pasta-spewing
marvel, capable of churning out the complete line
of Valentia egg noodles in one miraculous process.
We're given an in-store macaroni display that brightly
reminds us that these noodles are as much a joy to
eat as they were to produce. All in all, the perfect
pasta poster!
Est: $1,500-$1,800.

BERNARD VILLEMOT (1911-1989)

700. Negrita. Le Rhum. 1974.
85³/₄ x 56 in./218 x 142 cm
Imp. Bedos, Paris
Cond A.
Ref: Villemot, 253; PAI-XIV, 474
Cassandre had said, "The poster is like a telegrapher:
he does not draft messages, he *dispatches* them"
(Mouron, p. 48). And 20 years later, Villemot came to
the same conclusion: "A good poster must be a
telegram" (Villemot, p. 55). And he practiced it thus:
his designs always create instantaneous impressions
that urge themselves on the spectator. Here is a spectacularly clear example of the way he adhered to his
tenet. This is one of the rarest of all his posters today,
in the larger 2-sheet format. Villemot's death in 1989
left a serious void in the world of French poster art,
unsurpassed as he was at setting just the right mood
with a few simple lines and bold colors.
Est: $1,400-$1,700.

VON AXSTER-HAIDHASS

701. Agfa-Travis. 1931.
46¹/₄ x 66⁷/₈ in./117.6 x 170 cm
Carl Werner, Reichenbach
Cond A–/Slight tears and stains at seam.
An advertisement that could just as easily be a promotion for any of the elegant sirens that graced the
Silver Screen during the era of this poster's production
as it is for the hosiery they may have allowed to grace
their gams. The marvelous detail with which the folds
of this silken gown cascade down the curves of this
2-sheet heartbreaker nearly distracts from the fact that
we're supposed to be paying attention to her Agfa-Travis
stockings, the very finest artificial silk product on the
market. Classic German cheesecake at its leggy best.
Est: $1,700-$2,000.

701

ALBERT WEISGERBER (1878-1915)

702. Der Bunte Vogel. ca. 1913.
20³/₄ x 34³/₈ in./52.2 x 87.4 cm
Vereinigte Kunstanstalten, München
Cond A–/Restored tears in margins.
Ref: Schubert, p. 21
One of the most famous of all German posters was
created in 1911 by Weisgerber for the students' and
artists' Bohemian wine bar, Der Bunte Vogel (The
Colorful Bird). This later printing is drawn slightly
differently—a bit smaller and with the addition of the
establishment's telephone number (see DFP-III, 3376;
Schindler, p. 99). Only Professor Schubert's 1927
exhaustive tome, *Die Deutsche Werbe Graphik* repro-
duces this version. Schindler indicates that that Weisgerber was a "powerful natural painter never short of
ideas (who) left behind only a few posters. As a collaborator on the *Jugend*, he stood out for his color-rich
graphics work based on his eminently painterly concepts. He then went to Paris, where the works of
Cézanne and the Paris school changed his views. He
developed a wholly new sense of colors and the rules
of composition . . . (This poster) betrays a confident
style based on French models" (p. 98).
Est: $5,000-$6,000.

703

D. O. WIDHOPFF (1867-1933)

703. Danseuse Espagnole.
35³/₈ x 51¹/₂ in./90 x 131 cm
Imp. Eugène Mauler, Paris
Cond A.
Ref: DFP-II, 875; PAI-XXVII, 616
Clasping a rose in her teeth, the exotic bearing and
lithesome torque of the Spanish dancer, Pilar Montero,
is beautifully caught in this poster by a Russian-born
painter and caricaturist who became a naturalized
Frenchman. A contemporary and close friend of Mucha,
he studied in Munich and later in Paris before starting
work in 1908 as illustrator for *Le Courrier Français*.
He was born in Odessa, and his real name was Davidov;
the extravagant pseudonym "D. O. Widhopff" is simply
his way of presenting his last name as it might be pronounced by a non-Russian reader. No specimen with
letters exists.
Est: $1,000-$1,200.

WIM

704. Paris-Montpellier. 1906.
43¹/₈ x 63 in./109.5 x 160 cm
Imp. Chaix, Paris
Cond B–/Tears at folds and edges. Framed.
This hobby horse appears just about ready to break
free from the shackles of his twin-rocker oppression
and give his young rider a bucking he won't soon for-

702

704

705

get. What a perfect appeal to the unreigned imaginations of the youthful pests the Paris-Montpellier establishment hopes to unleash on the unsuspecting
parents of the region in order to promote their toy
sale, produced with a minimum of color and a maximum of concentrated imagination.
Est: $2,000-$2,500.

NEWELL CONVERS WYETH (1882-1945)

705. Interwoven Socks for Christmas.
60 x 20¹/₂ in./152.5 x 52 cm
Sweeney Litho. Co., Bellerville, N.J.

Cond A.
When the pilgrims first came to the New Country, they
sought freedom. Freedom from religious persecution,
freedom from oppression and the freedom to begin
the tradition of handing out socks as a Christmas gift.
Of course, there isn't a sock in sight in this beautiful
panoramic view of the Christmas ship arriving in New
Amsterdam harbor—printed on light cloth with four
corner grommets for proper in-store display—but the
suggestion of the Interwoven socks stocking stuffer
leads us to believe there might have been a pair or
two stashed in the bales being unloaded on the docks.

Wyeth, a prolific painter, illustrator, muralist and teacher
who created this design, produced more than 3,000
illustrations for hundreds of articles, numerous posters
and more than 100 books. His best-known book illustrations include *Treasure Island* and *Kidnapped* by
Robert Louis Stevenson, *Deerslayer* and *Last of the
Mohicans* by James Fenimore Cooper, and *Robin Hood*
and *Robinson Crusoe* by Defoe. *Included with this
poster is the original tube in which it was sent to
retailers whose label shows the Interwoven Sock
Company was located in New Brunswick, New Jersey.*
Est: $1,700-$2,000.

BOOKS & PERIODICALS

706

706.L'Estampe Moderne. 1897-1899.
Each: 13 x 16 in./30.7 x 41 cm
All 100 plates; includes tissue overlays with
commentaries. Slight fraying on edges of a few.
Ref: PAI-XXX, 698 (var)
The publication distributed by Imprimerie Champenois,
Paris, contains 24 monthly portfolios plus four bonus
plates with covers by Mucha, with four original litho-
graphs in each. Almost all of these lithographs were
commissioned especially for this series, featuring works
by Mucha (2), Donnay, Evenepoele, Rassenfosse,
Louis Rhead, H. Meunier, Léandre, Lepère, Grasset,
Berchmans, Ibels, DeFeure, Robbe, Helleu, Roedel,
Steinlen, Bouisset, Gottlob, Détouche, Boutet, Bellery-
Desfontaines, Lenoir and Willette.
Est: $14,000-$17,000.

707. Nos Actrices, by Leonetto Cappiello. 1899.
13^1/$_4$ x 17^1/$_4$ in./33.6 x 43.8 cm
Published by Editions de la Revue Blanche, Paris
Cond B+/Staining on cover.
Ref: PAI-XIII, 124
Commissioned in 1898, a few short months after
Cappiello's arrival in Paris in the spring of that year,
this collection of theatrical caricatures attests to the
artist's immediate popularity with the French public.
The book consists of 18 plates featuring 17 noted
actresses (Bernhardt is shown in two poses). Other
featured actresses include Réjane, Jeanne Granier,
Marcelle Lender, Lucie Gerard, Simone Girard and
Mariette Sully. In many ways, this book launched his
career, and the bold outline and flat color backgrounds
in them foretell the early Cappiello poster style.
Est: $2,000-$2,500.

708. 70 Dessins de Cappiello. 1905.
11 x 15 in./28x 38 cm
Published by H. Floury, Paris
Cond B+/Slight staining on cover only.
Ref: PAI-XII, 123
This is a delightful collection of insightful character
studies of prominent people from the world of turn-of-
the-century Paris theater, politics and public life. Without resorting to outright ridicule or mockery, Cappiello
captures with an exquisite sense of irony the facial
features and traits that define personalities—so that
whether or not we recognize the names, we are amused
by the skill of the caricaturist. Some of the portraits
amount to revelations—we can detect a certain pom-
posity in Puccini, for example, and a bit of shrewish-
ness in Sarah Bernhardt. All told, the volume contains
64 pages of caricatures, printed by lithography and
pochoir, published in an edition of 1,520 copies, of
which this is #461.
Est: $1,400-$1,700.

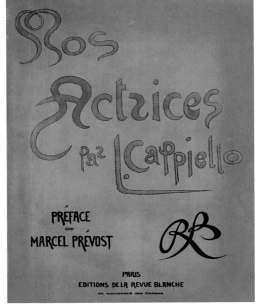

707

708

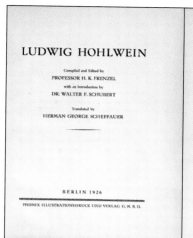

709

710

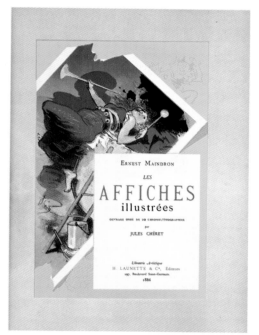

711

712

713

709. Ludwig Hohlwein, by H. K. Frenzel. 1926.
8⁷/₈ x 11³/₄ in./22.5 x 30 in.
Hardcover book published by Phönix Illustrations Druck und Verlag, Berlin. Overall excellent condition, but slight wear on the cover. 298 pages, with 223 of Hohlwein's posters reproduced. Text in both German and English.
Est: $800-$1,000.

710. Les Programmes Illustrés, by Ernest Maindron.
9⁵/₈ x 132¹/₂ in./24.5 x 31.6 cm
Published by the Librairie Nilsson-Per Lamm, Paris

Gold-embossed cover.
"I often ask myself what they, the curious of the year 2000, will think of us, whom we are cut off from by a century of dreadful events; them, knowing that which we don't yet know and that we nearly suspect, what will they say of our old frivolity with all that has passed? Won't they pity us, like we today have pity for the aristocratic society whose ancient prints we refer to with carelessness and levity?" Thus mused Pierre Veber in his prefacing comments for the *Programmes Illustrés*, a hardcover compendium presenting reproductions of some of the most beautiful menus, invitations, busi-

ness cards and announcements of the Belle Epoque. Little could he have known how off the mark his thoughts were, as today we look back at the technical virtuosity these posterists displayed with the limited technology of the time. Along with forty pages of introductory text, the sixty plates—most in color—contained herein include works by the best-known artists of the day, including: Ibels, Misti, Grasset, Rochegrosse, Chéret, Willette, Roubille, De Feure, Toulouse-Lautrec, Casal, Choubrac, Guillaume and Roedel.
Est: $2,500-$3,000.

711. Les Affiches Illustrées, by Ernest Maindron.
1886.
9 x 12³/₄ in./22.9 x 31.8 cm
Published by H. Launette, Paris
Hardcover book in excellent condition.
Ref: PAI-XXX, 696
This first comprehensive history of the poster contains 160 pages and many poster reproductions, including 28 in color (of which 21 are by Chéret). Number 278 of a limited, numbered edition of 525 copies. Maindron's text is erudite and enthusiastic. *A must for the serious collector.*
Est: $2,000-$2,500.

712. Les Affiches Étrangères Illustrées,
by M. Bauwens, T. Hayashi, La Forgue,
Meier-Graefe & J. Pennel. 1897.
8¹/₂ x 12 in./21.5 x 30.2 cm
Published by G. Boudet, Paris
#191 of 1,000 numbered copies on vellum.
This 210-page hardcover classic, complete with 212 reproductions—150 black-and-white and 62 magnificent full-color plates printed by Chaix—acknowledges the global lithographic feats of artists outside the boundries of France, including representative works from Germany, England, Austria, Belgium, the United States and Japan. Accompanying articles by the authors, with text in French and color cover design by Rassenfosse.
Est: $3,000-$4,000.

713. Draeger.
12¹/₄ x 15 in./31 x 38 cm
Overall excellent quality; slight stains at paper edges.
A portfolio of 11 lithographs by Charles Martin (1848-1934) that playfully bestow the printing process of the Draeger firm upon us, with accompanying text by Jean Cocteau. Intended to "glorify the graphic arts industry," the album was naturally printed and published by none other than the Draeger Frères. This particular copy has a dedication to Jacques-Èmile Ruhlman (1879-1933), the famed Parisian cabinetmaker signed by Georges Draeger, one of the three Draeger brothers. Martin was a well-known fashion designer and magazine illustrator for *Gazette du Bon Ton, Femina* and *La Vie Parisienne.*
Est: $2,500-$3,000.

BIBLIOGRAPHY

The following is a list of books used in the preparation of this catalogue. In the interest of brevity, these works have been abbreviated in the Reference ("Ref:") section of the description of each lot. The abbreviations can be found below accompanied by the work's full title, publisher's name, city and date of publication. It should be noted that we have made no reference to the many magazines and annuals which are essential tools in this area, such as *The Poster, Estampe et Affiche, La Plume, Arts et Metiers Graphiques, Vendre, Das Plakat, Gebrauchsgraphik* and *Graphis Posters.*

NOTE: References to prior PAI books are limited to the last auction in which the poster was offered. We refer readers to our book, *Poster Prices V,* which gives the complete record of each poster offered at the first 28 PAI sales.

Abdy
The French Poster, by Jane Abdy. Clarkson N. Potter. New York, 1969.

Absinthe
Absinthe: History in a Bottle, by Barnaby Conrad III. Chronicle Books, San Francisco, 1988.

Adriani
Toulouse-Lautrec: The Complete Graphic Works, by Götz Adriani. The catalogue raisonné, featuring the Gerstenberg collection. Thames & Hudson, London, 1988.

Affiche Réclame
Quand l'Affiche Faisait de la Reclame! Editions de la Réunion des Musées Nationaux, Paris. 1991.

Affiches Azur
Affiches d'Azur—100 Ans d'Affiches de la Côte d'Azur et de Monaco, by Charles Martini de Chateauneuf. Editions Gilletta, Nice, 1992.

Affiches Etrangères
Les Affiches Etrangères Illustrées, by M. Bauwens, T. Hayashi, La Forge, Meier-Graefe & J. Pennel. Boudet, Paris, 1897.

Affiches Publicitaire
Affiches publicitaire: 100 Ans d'Histoire à traverse l'affiche, by Dominique Spiess. Edita, Lausanne, 1987.

Affiches Suisses
Objets-Realisme-Affiches Suisses 1905-1950. Catalogue of the exhibition held at the Bibliothèque Forney, Paris, 1982. Text by Eric Kellenberger.

Affichomanie
L'Affichomanie. Catalogue of the exhibition on the subject of the Postermania of the period 1880-1900 held at the Musée de l'Affiche, Paris, 1980. Text by Alain Weill.

Air France
Air France/Affiches/Posters 1933-1983, by Jérôme Peignot. Fernand Hazan, Paris, 1988.

Airline Artistry
Airline Artistry—Vintage Posters & Publicity, by Don Thomas. Published by the author in Dunedin, Florida, 1992.

Alpes
Les Alpes à l'Affiche, by Yves Ballu. Editions Glenat, Grenoble, 1987.

America for Sale
America for Sale: A Collector's Guide to Antique Advertising, by Douglas Congdon-Martin. Schiffer Publishing Ltd., West Chester, Pennsylvania, 1991.

American Posters
Posters American Style, by Therese Thau Heyman. Harry N. Abrams, New York, 1998.

Art Deco
Art Deco Graphics, by Patricia Frantz Kery. Harry N. Abrams, New York, 1986.

Ateny-Atlanta
Athens-Atlanta: 100 Years of Modern Olympic Games. Catalogue of the exhibition held at the Poster Museum of Wilanów, Poland, under the auspices of the Polish Olympic Committee, 1996.

Avant Garde
The 20th Century Poster—Design of the Avant Garde, by Dawn Ades. The catalogue-book of the exhibition of the Walker Art Center, Minneapolis, 1984. Abbeville Press, New York, 1984.

Auto Show II
2eme Salon de l'Affiche Automobile. Catalogue of the exhibition at the Musée de l'Affiche, Paris, September to October 1979. Edited by Jacques Perier.

Auto Show III
L 'Automobile et la Publicité. Catalogue of the exhibition at the Musée de la Publicité, Paris, 1984.

Bargiel et Zagrodzki
Steinlen-Affichiste. Catalogue Raisonné, by Réjane Bargiel and Christophe Zagrodzki. Editions du Grant-Pont, Lausanne, 1986. (Distributed in the United States by Posters Please, Inc., New York City).

Barnicoat
Posters: A Concise History, by John Barnicoat. Softcover edition reprinted by Thames and Hudson, London, 1985.

Baumberger
Otto Baumberger 1889-1961. Catalogue of the exhibition of Baumberger posters held at the Museum für Gestaltung Zurich, May-July 1988, and subsequently in Basel and Essen.

Belgique/Paris
L'Affiche en Belgique 1880-1980. Catalogue of the exhibition at the Musée de l'Affiche, Paris, 1980. Text by Alain Weill.

Belgique Sportives
Affiches Sportives en Belgique 1890-1940. Catalogue of the exhibition in Brussels, 1981-82.

Belgische Affiche 1900
De Belgische Affiche 1892-1914, by Yolande Oostens-Wittamer. Koninklijke Bibliotheek Albert I, Brussels, 1975.

Belle Epoque 1970
La Belle Epoque—Belgian Posters. The catalogue-book of the touring exhibition of the Wittamer-De Camps collection. Text by Yolande Oostens-Wittamer. Grossman Publishers, New York, 1971.

Belle Epoque 1980
La Belle Epoque. Catalogue of the loan exhibition from the Wittamer-De Camps collection, featuring the works of Combaz, Léo Jo and Livemont. Text by Yolande Oostens-Wittamer. International Exhibitions Foundation, 1980-81.

Belles Affiche
Les Belles Affiche du Cinéma. Atlas, Paris, 1986.

Bernhard
Lucian Bernhard: Plakate, Gebrauchsgrafik, Verpackungsdesign, Buchgestaltung, Schriftentwürfe. Catalogue of the exhibition at the Institut für Auslands-beziehangen, Stuttgart, 1999.

Berthon & Grasset
Berthon & Grasset, by Victor Arwas. Academy Editions, London; Rizzoli, New York, 1978.

Bocca
I Manifesti Italiani: fra belle epoque e fascismo, by Giorgio Bocca. Fratelli Fabri editori, Milano, 1971.

Boissons
Les Boissons/Un Siècle de Réclames, by F. Ghozland. Editions Milan, Toulouse, 1986.

Bolaffi
Catalogo Bolaffi Del Manifesto Italiano—Dizionario Degli Illustratori. Giulio Bolaffi Editore, Torino, 1995.

Bouvet
Bonnard: The Complete Graphic Work, by Francis Bouvet. Rizzoli, New York.

Broders
Voyages: Les Affiches de Roger Broders, by Annie de Montry and Françoise Lepeuve. Syros-Alternatives, Paris, 1991.

Broido
The Posters of Jules Chéret: 46 Full Color Plates and an Illustrated Catalogue Raisonné, 2nd ed., by Lucy Broido. Dover Publications, N.Y., 1992.

Brown & Reinhold
The Poster Art of A. M. Cassandre, by Robert K. Brown and Susan Reinhold. E. P. Dutton, New York, 1979.

Buffalo Bill
100 Posters of Buffalo Bill's Wild West, by Jack Rennert. Darien House, New York, 1976.

Café-Concert
Le Café-Concert 1870-1914. Catalogue of the poster exhibition at the Musée des Arts Décoratifs, Paris, 1977. Text by Alain Weill.

Canadian Pacific
Canadian Pacific Posters 1883-1963, by Marc. H. Choko and David L. Jones.

Capitaine
L'Affiche de Cinéma/Les Plus Belles Stars du Hollywood, by J. L. Capitaine & B. Charton. Frédéric Birr, Paris, 1983.

Cappiello
Cappiello. Catalogue of the exhibition at the Galerie Nationale du Grand Palais, Paris, 1981.

Cappiello/St. Vincent
Leonetto Cappiello—dalla pittura alla grafica. Catalogue of the exhibition in Centro Culturale Saint-Vincent. Text by Raffaele Monti & Elisabeth Matucci. Artificio, Firenze, 1985.

Caradec-Weill
Le café-concert, by François Caradec and Alain Weill. Hachette/Marsin, Paris, 1980.

Cardinaux
Emil Cardinaux (1877-1936). Catalogue of the exhibition at the Museum für Gestaltung Kunstgewerbemuseum, Zurich, August-October, 1985.

Carlu
Jean Carlu. Catalogue of the exhibition of the Posters of Jean Carlu at the Musée de l'Affiche, Paris, 1980.

Cassandre/Tokyo
A. M. Cassandre. Catalogue of the exhibition held at the Tokyo Metropolitan Teien Art Museum, 1991.

Cassandre/Suntory
Cassandre: Every Face of the Great Master, 1901-1968. Catalogue of the exhibition held at the Suntory Museum, Osaka, June-August, 1995.

Cassiers
Henri Cassiers 1858-1944. Catalogue of the 1994 exhibition at the Vleeshuis Museum in Antwerp, Belgium.

Célébrités
Célébrités à l'Affiche, by A.C. Lelieur and R. Bacollet. Edita, Lausanne, 1989.

Chaumont/Exposons
Exposons Affichons: 300 affiches d'expositions. Catalogue for the 5th annual Poster Festival of Chaumont, France. Includes a section on "L'Affiche pour l'affiche" (Posters on Posters) from the Rennert collection. Somogy, Paris, 1994.

Chemins de Fer
100 Ans d'Affiches des Chemins de Fer, by Pierre Belves. Edition NM—La Vie du Rail, Paris, 1980.

Cinéma Français
Affiches du Cinéma Français, by J. M. Borga & B. Martinand. Editions Delville, Paris, 1977.

Circus Posters
100 Years of Circus Posters, by Jack Rennert. Avon Books, New York, 1974.

Colin
100 Posters of Paul Colin, by Jack Rennert. Images Graphiques, New York, 1977.

Colin Affichiste
Paul Colin: Affichiste, by Alain Weill & Jack Rennert. Editions Denoel, Paris, 1989.

Collectionneur
Collectionneur d'Affiches, edited by Laurence Prod'homme. Editions Apogé, Musée de Bretagne, 1996.

Color Revolution
The Color Revolution. Catalogue of the exhibition at Rutgers University Art Gallery, Boston Public Library and Baltimore Museum of Art. Edited by Philip Denis Cate and Sinclair Hamilton Hitchings. 1978.

Côte Belge
Affiches de la Côte Belge 1890-1950, by Marie-Laurence Bernard. The collection of Roland Florizoone. Uitgeverij Marc van de Wiele, Brugge, 1992.

Crauzat
L'Oeuvre Gravé et Lithographié de Steinlen, by E. de Crauzat. Société de Propogation des Livres d'Art, Paris, 1913. Reprinted by Alan Wofsy Fine Arts, San Francisco, 1983.

Crayons
Et aussi des Crayons: Ecriture, Papeterie et Publicité. Edited by Thierry Devynck. Catalogue of the exhibition at the Bibliothèque Forney, 1996. Somogy, Paris, 1996.

Dance Posters
100 Years of Dance Posters, by Walter Terry & Jack Rennert. Avon Books, New York, 1973.

Danish Posters
Den Danske Plakat, by Lars Dybdahl. Borgen, Denmark, 1994.

Deco Affiches
Affiches Art Deco, by Alain Weill. Inter-Livres, Paris, 1990.

Delhaye
Art Deco Posters and Graphics, by Jean Delhaye. Academy Editions, London, 1977.

Delteil
Le Peintre-Graveur Illustré, by Loys Delteil. (Volumes X and XI devoted to Lautrec). Paris, 1920. Reprinted by Collectors Edition Ltd.-Da Capo Press, New York, 1969.

Denscher
Österreichische Plakat Kunt 1898-1938, by Bernhard Denscher. Verlag Brandstätter, Wien, 1992.

Derouet
Derouet & Son Atelier/Affiches et publicités, by Anne-Claude Lelier and Raymond Bacollet. The book of the exhibition held at the Bibliothèque Forney, Paris and published by Agence Culturelle de Paris, 1994.

DFP-I
Das Frühe Plakat in Europa und den USA. Volume I. British and American Posters. Edited by Ruth Malhotra and Christina Thon. Mann Verlag, Berlin, 1973.

DFP-II
Das Frühe Plakat in Europa und den USA. Volume II.French and Belgian Posters. Edited by Ruth Malhotra, Marjan Rinkleff and Bernd Schalicke. Mann Verlag, Berlin, 1977.

DFP-III
Das Frühe Plakat in Europa und den USA. Volume III. German Posters. Edited by Helga Hollman, Ruth Malhotra, Alexander Pilipczuk, Helga Prignitz, Christina Thon. Mann Verlag, Berlin, 1980.

Dreyfus
The Dreyfus Affair: Art, Truth & Justice, edited by Norman L. Kleeblatt. University of California Press, Berkley and Los Angeles, 1987.

Dubout
Affiches Dubout. Editions Michele Trinckvel, Lausanne, 1985.

Dudovich
Marcello Dudovich—Cartellonista 1878-1962, by Roberto Curci. Lint Edizioni, Trieste, 1976.

Dutch Posters
A History of the Dutch Poster 1890-1960, by Dick Dooijes and Pieter Brattinga. Scheltema & Holkema, Amsterdam, 1968.

España
España en 1000 Carteles, by Jordi Carulla and Arnau Carulla. Postermil, Barcelona, 1995.

Fantastic Voyage
Fantastic Voyage: Luxury and Sophistication on the Ocean Liners. Catalogue of the 1996 exhibition at the Suntory Museum, Osaka.

Femme s'Affiche
La Femme s'Affiche. Catalogue of the exhibition of the Kellenberger collection held in Montreux, 1990.

De Feure
Georges De Feure: Maitre du Symbolisme et de l'Art Nouveau, by Ian Millman. ACR Editions, Courbevoie (Paris), 1991.

Fiat
Cinquanta arnni immagini della pui importante industria italiana, by Arbiasino and Gianni Bulgari. Edizioni de Autocritica, Rome, 1984.

Folies-Bergère
100 Years of Posters of the Folies Bergère and Music Halls of Paris, by Alain Weill. Images Graphiques, New York, 1977.

Frey
Toulouse-Lautrec: A Life, by Julia Frey. Viking Penguin, New York, 1994.

Genève
Genève: Encyclopédie de l'Affiche. Selected posters from the collection of Jean-Daniel Clerc, Geneva.

Gold
First Ladies of the Poster: The Gold Collection, by Laura Gold. Posters Please Inc., New York City, 1998.

Golden Age of Travel
The Golden Age of Travel Posters: 1880-1939, by Alexsis Gregory. Cassell, London, 1998.

Health Posters
Posters of Health, by Marine Robert-Sterkendries. Therabel Pharma, Brussels, 1996.

Hiatt
Picture Posters, by Charles Hiatt. George Bell and Sons, London, 1895.

Hillier
Posters, by Bevis Hillier. Weidenfeld and Nicholson, London, 1969; Stein & Day, New York, 1969; Spring Books, The Hamlyn Publishing Group, New York, 1974.

Hohlwein 1874-1949
Ludwig Hohlwein 1874-1949: Kunstgewerbe und Reklamekunst, by Volker Duvigneau and Norbert Gota. Klinkhardt & Bierman, Munich, 1996.

Hohlwein/Frenzel
Ludwig Hohlwein, complied and edited by Professor H. K. Frenzel. Phönix Illustrationsdruck und Verlag, Berlin, 1926.

Hohlwein Posters
Hohlwein Posters in Full Color. Dover Publications, New York, 1976.

Hohlwein/Stuttgart
Ludwig Hohlwein: Plakate der Jahre 1906-1940. Catalogue of the Hohlwein exhibition at the Staatsgalerie Stuttgart in Germany, March-April 1985. Text by Christian Schneegass.

Internationale Plakate
Internationale Plakate 1871-1971. Catalogue of the exhibition at the Haus der Kunst, Munich, 1971. Edited by Dr. Heinz Spielmann.

Italia che Cambia
L'Italia che Cambia: Attraverso i manifesti della raccolta Salce. Edited by Pepa Sparti. Artificio, Firenze, 1989.

Josephine Baker
Josephine Baker: The Hungry Heart, by Jean-Claude Baker and Chris Chase. Random House, New York, 1993.

Kamekura
Exhibition of Works by Yusaku Kamekura. Catalogue of the exhibition held at the Kirin Plaza, Osaka, 1988.

Karcher
Memoire de la Rue—Souvenirs d'un imprimeur et d'un afficheur. Illustrated book of the archives of the Karcher printing firm of Paris with introduction by Alain Weill. WM Editions, Paris, 1986. (Distributed in the U.S.A. by Posters Please, Inc., New York with a translation of text and the addition of an index).

Keay
American Posters of the Turn of the Century, by Carolyn Keay. Academy Editions, London, 1975.

Khachadourian
Motoring: The Golden Years—A Pictorial Anthology—the Khachadourian Gallery. Compiled by Rupert Prior. Morgan Samuel Editions, London, 1991.

Kiffer
Charles Kiffer et le Spectacle. Catalogue of the exhibition at the Centre de l'Affiche, Toulouse, 1900.

Lauder
American Art Posters of the1890s (The Leonard A. Lauder Collection). Catalogue of the exhibition of the Metropolitan Museum of Art, New York, October 1987—January 1988. Text by David W. Kiehl. Harry N. Abrams, New York, 1987.

Lendl/Paris
Alphonse Mucha: La Collection Ivan Lendl. Catalogue of the exhibition at Musée de la Publicité, Paris, 1989. Text by Jack Rennert. Editions Syros/Alternatives, Paris.

Leupin
Herbert Leupin: Plakate, Bilder, Graphiken, by Karl Lüönd and Charles Leupin. Friedrich Reinhardt, Basel, 1995.

Lincoln Center
Lincoln Center Posters, by Vera List and Herbert Kupferberg. Harry N. Abrams, New York, 1980.

Litfass-Bier
Litfass-Bier: Historische Bierplakate-Sammlung Heinrich Becker. Edited by Gerhard Dietrich. Plakat/Konzepte, Hannover, 1998.

Lives of Buffalo Bill
The Lives of Buffalo Bill, by Don Russell. University of Oklahoma Press, Norman, 1960.

Livre de l'Affiche
Le Livre de l'Affiche, by Réjane Bargiel-Harry and Christophe Zagrodzki. A publication of the Musée de la Publicité, Paris. Editions Alternatives, Paris, 1985.

Loie Fuller
Loie Fuller: Magician of Light. Catalogue of the exhibition at the Virginia Museum, Richmond, 1979.

Looping the Loop
Looping the Loop: Posters of Flight, by Henry Serrano Villard and Willis M. Allen, Jr. Kales Press, San Diego, California, 2000.

Loupot
Charles Loupot. Catalogue of the exhibition at the Musée de l'Affiche, Paris.

Loupot/Zagrodzki
Charles Loupot: L'Art de l'Affiche, by Christophe Zagrodzki. Le Cherche-Midi, Paris, 1998. (Exclusive American distributor: Posters Please Inc., N.Y.C.)

Magic Posters
100 Years of Magic Posters, by Charles and Regina Reynolds. Grosset & Dunlap, New York, 1976.

Maindron
Les Affiches Illustrées, 1886-1895, by Ernest Maindron. G. Boudet, Paris, 1896.

Maitres
Les Maitres de l'Affiche 1896-1900, by Roger Marx. Imprimerie Chaix, Paris 1896-1900. Reprinted as *Masters of the Poster l896-1900* by Images Graphiques, New York, 1977, and The Complete "Masters of the Poster," by Dover Publications, New York, 1990.

Mangold
Burkhard Mangold (1873-1950). Catalogue of the exhibition at the Kunstgewerbemuseum, Zurich, 1984.

Manifesti Italiani
Manifesti Italiani: Dall'Art Nouveau al Futurismo 1895-1940, by Giampiero Mughini & Maurizio Scudiero. Posters of the Massimo & Sonia Cirulli Collection. Ricordi, Milano, 1997.

Margadant
Das Schweizer Plakat/The Swiss Poster, 1900-1983, by Bruno Margadant. Birkhaus Verlag, Basel, 1983.

Margolin
American Poster Renaissance, by Victor Margolin. Watson-Guptill Publications, New York, 1975.

Marques
Images de Marques/Marques d'Images: 100 marques du patrimoine français, by Daniel Cauzard, Jean Perret and Yves Ronin. Editions Ramsay, Paris, 1989.

Marx
Bonnard: Lithographie, edited by Claude Roger-Marx. Monte Carlo, 1952.

Mauzan
Mauzan: Affiches/Oeuvres Diverses, by A. Lancellotti. Casa Editrice d'Arte Bestettie Tumminelli, Milan, ca. 1928.

Mauzan/Paris
Achille Mauzan. Catalogue of the exhibition held at the Musée de la Publicité, Paris, 1983.

Mauzan/Pinerolo
Omaggio a Luciano Achille Mauzan: "l'arte del manifesto." Catalogue of the exhibition titled "Omaggio a Luciano Achille Mauzan—l'arte del Manifesto," curated by Mario Marchiando-Pacchiola, and held in Pinerolo in 1984.

Mauzan/Treviso
Manifesti di A. L. Mauzan, by Antonio Mazzaroli. Editrice Canova, Treviso, 1983.

Meisterplakate
Franzosische Meisterplakate un 1900. catalogue of the exhibition of the posters of the Sammlung der Folkwangschule für Gestaltung at the Villa Hugel, Essen, Germany, held November-December, 1968.

Memoire du Cinema
Memoire du Cinema Française, by René Chateau. Les Editions de l'Amateur, France 1991.

Menegazzi-I
Il Manifesto Italiano, by Luigi Menegazzi. Electa Editrice, Milan, ca. 1976.

Menegazzi-II
Il Manifesto Italiano, by Luigi Menegazzi. Arnoldo Mondadori Arte, Milan, 1989 (revised edition).

Mer s'Affiche
La Mer s'Affiche, by Daniel Hillion. Editions Ouest-France, Rennes, 1990.

Meunier
Georges Meunier—affichiste 1869-1942. Catalogue of the exhibition at Bibliothèque Fourney, Paris, 1978.

Modern American Posters
The Modern American Poster, by J. Stewart Johnson. Catalogue of the Japanese exhibition of the posters from the N.Y. Musuem of Modern Art collection, 1983-84. Little Brown, Boston, 1983.

Modern Poster
The Modern Poster, by Stuart Wrede. Catalogue of the exhibition at the Museum of Modern Art, New York, 1988. New York Graphic Society/ Little Brown and Co., Boston, 1988.

Montagne
La Montagne s'Affiche, by Daniel Hillion. Editions Ouest-France, Rennes, 1991.

Mouron
A. M. Cassandre, by Henri Mouron. Rizzoli, New York, 1985.

Mucha/Art Nouveau
Alphonse Mucha: The Spirit of Art Nouveau. Catalogue of the touring exhibition organized by Art Services International, Alexandria, Virginia, 1998. Edited by Victor Arwas, Jana Brabcová-Orliková and Anna Dvorák.

Mucha/Paris
Mucha 1860-1939. Peintures-Illustrations-Affiches-Arts Décoratifs. Catalogue of the exhibition at the Grand Palais, Paris, held February 5 to April 28, 1980. Editions des Musées Nationaux, Paris, 1980.

Müller-Brockmann
History of the Poster, by Josef and Shizuko Müller-Brockmann. ABC Edition, Zurich, 1971 (in German, French and English).

Musée d'Affiche
Musée d'Affiche. Catalogue for the inaugural exhibition titled "Trois Siècles d'Affiches Françaises," Paris, 1978.

Nectar/Nicolas
Nectar comme Nicolas, by Alain Weill. Editions Herscher, Paris, 1986.

Olympics
L'Olympisme par l'Affiche/Olympism through Posters. International Olympic Committee, Lausanne, 1983.

Ogé
Eugène Ogé/Affichiste 1861-1936. Catalogue of the exhibition at the Bibliothèque Fourney, Paris, with text by its director, Anne-Claude Lelieur and Raymond Bachollet. Agence Culturelle de Paris, 1998.

Orientalist
The Orientalist Poster, by Abderrahman Slaoui. Malika Editions, Cassablanca, 1997.

PAI—Books of the auctions organized by Poster Auctions International, Inc.

PAI-I
Premier Posters. Book of the auction held in New York City, March 9, 1985.

PAI-II
Prize Posters. Book of the auction held in Chicago, November 10, 1985.

PAI-III
Poster Impressions. Book of the auction held in New York City, June 1, 1986.

PAI-IV
Prestige Posters. Book of the auction held in New York City, May 3, 1987.

PAI-V
Poster Pizzazz. Book of the auction held in Universal City, California, November 22, 1987.

PAI-VI
Poster Splendor. Book of the auction held in New York City, May 1, 1988.

PAI-VII
Poster Potpourri. Book of the auction held in New York, November 13, 1988.

PAI-VIII
Poster Treasures. Book of the auction held in New York, May 7, 1989.

PAI-IX
Poster Palette. Book of the auction held in New York, November 12, 1989.

PAI-X
Elegant Posters. Book of the auction held in New York, May 20, 1990.

PAI-XI
Poster Passion. Book of the auction held in New York, November 11, 1990.

PAI-XII
Poster Panache. Book of the auction held in New York, May 5, 1991.

PAI XIII
Poster Jubilee. Book of the auction held in New York. November 10, 1991.

PAI-XIV
Poster Extravaganza. Book of the auction held in New York May 3, 1992.

PAI XV
Rarest Posters. Book of the auction held in New York, November 8, 1992.

PAI-XVI
Poster Parade. Book of the auction held in New York, May 2. 1993.

PAI-XVII
Poster Classics. Book of the auction held in New York, November 14, 1993.

PAI-XVIII
Winning Posters. Book of the auction held in New York, May 1, 1994.

PAI-XIX
Prima Posters. Book of the auction held in New York, November 13, 1994.

PAI-XX
Poster Panorama. Book of the auction held in New York, May 7, 1995.

PAI-XXI
Timeless Posters. Book of the auction held in New York, November 12,1995.

PAI-XXII
Positively Posters. Auction held in New York City, May 5, 1996.

PAI-XXIII
Poster Delights. Auction held in New York City, November 10, 1996.

PAI-XXIV
Poster Pleasures. Auction held in New York City, May 4, 1997.

PAI-XXV
Sterling Posters. Auction held in New York City, November 9, 1997.

PAI-XXVI
Postermania. Auction held in New York City, May 3, 1998.

PAI-XXVII
Poster Ecstasy. Auction held in New York City, November 8, 1998.

PAI-XXVIII
Poster Vogue. Auction held in New York City, May 2, 1999.

PAI-XXIX
Posters for the Millennium. Auction held in New York City, November 4, 1999.

PAI-XXX
Poster Allure. Auction held in New York City, May 7, 2000.

Paillard
Affiches 14-18, by Remy Paillard. Privately published by the author. Reims, France, 1986.

Penfield
Designed to Persuade: The Graphic Art of Edward Penfield. Catalogue of the exhibition at The Hudson River Museum, Yonkers, New York, 1984. Text by David Gibson.

Petite Reine
La Petite Reine: Le Vélo en Affiches à la fin du XIXeme. Catalogue exhibition of bicycle posters of the end of the 19th century held at Musée de l'Affiche, Paris, May to September, 1979.

Phillips I
A Century of Posters 1870-1970. The catalogue of the Phillips Auction held November 10, 1979, in New York. Text by Jack Rennert.

Phillips II
Poster Classics. The catalogue of the Phillips Auction held May 10, 1980, in New York. Text by Jack Rennert.

Phillips IV
Poster Pleasures. The catalogue of the Phillips Auction held April 11, 1981, in New York. Text by Jack Rennert.

Phillips VIII
American Circus Posters. Catalogue of the auction held May 6, 1984, in New York City. Text by Jack Rennert.

Plakat Schweiz
Das Plakat in der Schweiz, by Willy Rotzler, Fritz Schärer and Karl Wobmann. Edition Stemmle, Zurich, 1990.

Plakate München
Plakate in München 1840-1940. Catalogue of the exhibition of Munich posters at the Münchner Stadtmuseum, 1975-76.

Plakatkunst
Plakatkunst von Toulouse-Lautrec bis Benetton, by Jürgen Döring. Edition Braus und Museum für Kunst und Gewerbe, Hamburg, 1994.

Plakatkunst 1880-1935
Plakatkunst 1880-1935, by Christiane Friese. Klett-Cota, Stuttgart, 1994.

Poster Design
Poster Design, by J. I. Biegeleisen. Greenberg, New York, 1946.

Propogande/Affiche
La Propogande par l'Affiche, by Laurent Gervereau. Editions Syros-Alternatives, Paris, 1991.

Publicidad
La Publicidad en 2000 Carteles, by Jordi Carulla and Arnau Carulla. Two volumes. Postermil, Barcelona, 1998.

Purvis
Poster Progress. Introduction by Tom Purvis. Edited by F.A. Mercer & W. Gaunt. The Studio, London and New York, ca. 1938.

Rademacher
Masters of German Art, by Hellmut Rademacher. October House, New York, 1966 (Original German edition published in 1965 by Edition Leipzig).

Reims
Exposition d'Affiches Artistiques Françaises et Etrangères. The catalogue of the November 1896 exhibition held in Reims. Reissued in a numbered edition of 1,000 copies by the Musée de l'Affiche in 1980.

Rennert/Weill
Alphonse Mucha: The Complete Posters and Panels, by Jack Rennert and Alain Weill. G. K. Hall, Boston, 1984.

Revolutionary Soviet Film
Revolutionary Soviet Film Posters, by Mildred Constantine and Alan Fern. The John Hopkins University Press, Baltimore, 1974.

Riccione
Capolavoir Italiani nel Manifesto Liberty 1880-1918. Catalogue of the exhibition at the Palazzo el turismo, Riccione, 1988. Text by Jack Rennert.

Richmond
The Technique of the Poster, by Leonard Richmond. Sir Isaac Pitman & Sons, London, 1933.

Ricordi
Grafica Ricordi: Dal Manifesto Storico all produzione d'avanguardia, by Giovanni Sangiorgi, Giorgia Mascherpa and Giulia Veronesi. Ente Premi, Roma, Ricordi, 1967.

Rockwell Illustrator
Norman Rockwell, Illustrator, by Arthur L. Guptill. Watson-Guptill, New York, 1946.

Rockwell's America
Norman Rockwell's America, by Christopher Finch. Readers' Digest/Harry N. Abrams, B.V., The Netherlands, 1976.

Rogers
A Book of the Poster, by W. S. Rogers. Greening & Co., London, 1901.

Russian Films
Film Posters of the Russian Avant-Garde, by Susan Pack. Benedikt Taschen Verlag, Koln, Germany, 1995.

Sachs
Kunst Kommerz Visionen: Deutsche Plakate 1888-1933. Catalogue of the exhibition at the Deutsches Historisches Museum in Berlin, 1992, consisting of the Hans Sachs collection. Edition Braus, Heidelberg, 1992.

Sagot
Catalogue d'Affiches Illustrées, published by Edmond Sagot, Paris, 1891.

Salon des Cent
Le Salon des Cent: 1894-1900. Affiches d'artistes, by Jocelyne Van Deputte. Catalogue of the exhibition held at the Musée Carnavalet, Paris, 1995.

Salon des Cent/Neumann
Les Affiches du Salon des Cent. Catalogue of the exhibition at Fondation Neumann, Gingins, Switzerland, 2000, and Musée des Arts Décoratifs, Bordeaux, 2001.

Savignac A-Z
Savignac de A à Z, by Raymond Savignac, with bibliographical notes by Alain Weill. Editions Hoëbeke, Paris, 1987.

Savignac/Japan
Savignac. Catalogue of the exhibition held at the Seibu Museum, Tokyo, 1989.

Savignac/Key
Savignac/Julian Key. Catalogue of the exhibition held Oct-Nov. 1984 at the Centre d'Art Nicolas de Staël, in Braine-l'Alleud, Belgium.

Savignac/Paris
Savignac au Musée de l Affiche. Catalogue of the exhibition at the Musée de l'Affiche, Paris, 1982.

Schindler
Monografie des Plakats, by Herbert Schindler. Süddeutscher Verlag, Munich, 1972.

Schubert
Die Deutsche werbe-graphik, by Dr. Walter F. Schubert. Verlag Francken & Lang, Berlin, 1927.

Schweizer Hotel
Schweizer Hotelplakate 1875-1982, by Karl Wobmann. Biregg Verlag, Luzern, 1982.

Shell
The Shell Poster Book. Introduction by David Bernstein. Hamish Hamilton, London, 1992.

Sorlier
Chagall's Posters: A Catalogue Raissonné, edited by Charles Sorlier, Crown Publishers, Inc., New York, 1975.

Spectacle
Les Arts du Spectacle en France—Affiches Illlustrées 1850-1950, by Nicole Wild. The catalogue of the Bibliothèque de l'Opera (part of the Bibliothèque Nationale), Paris, 1976.

Sport à l'Affiche
Sport à l'Affche, by Jean Durry. Editions Hoebeke, Paris, 1988.

Sportissimo
Sportissimo: Cent Ans de Grandes et Petites Histoires du Sport, by Françoise and Serge Laget. Editions du Chêne, Paris, 1996.

Steinlen
Théophile-Alexandre Steinlen, by Phillip Dennis Cate and Susan Gill. Gibbs M. Smith, Salt Lake City, Utah, 1982.

Stenberg/MoMA
Stenberg Brothers: Constructing a Revolution in Soviet Design. Catalogue of the exhibition at the Museum of Modern Art, New York, 1997. Edited by Christopher Mount.

Takashimaya
The Poster 1865-1969. Catalogue of the exhibition which opened at the Takashimaya Art Gallery, Nihonbashi, Tokyo, April 18, 1985, and consisted largely of posters from the Deutsches Plakat Museum of Essen, Germany.

Le Tennis
Le Tennis à l'Affiche 1895-1986, by Jean-Pierre Chevallier. Albin Michel, Paris, 1986.

Theaterplakate
Theaterplakate: ein internationaler historischer Überblick, by Hellmut Rademacher. Edition Leipzig, Leipzig, 1990.

Theofiles
American Posters of World War I, by George Theofiles. Dafran House, New York.

Timeless Images
Timeless Images. Catalogue of the touring Exhibition of posters in Japan, 1984-85. Text by Jack Rennert; in English and Japanese. Exclusive American distributor: Posters Please, Inc., New York City.

Tolmer
Tolmer: 60 ans de création graphique dans l'Ile St. Louis. Catalogue of the exhibition at the Bibliotèque Fourney, Paris, 1986.

Tourism/Suntory
Tourism in Posters. Catalogue of the exhibition at the Suntory Museum in Osaka, 1997. Ms. Yukie Takeuchi, curator.

Train à l'Affiche
Le Train à l'Affiche: Les plus belles affches ferroviaires française, by Florence Camard and Christophe Zagrodzki. La Vie du Rail, Paris, 1989.

Trylon
Trylon and Perisphere/The 1939 New York World's Fair, by Barbara Cohen, Steven Heller and Seymour Chwast. Harry N. Abrams, New York, 1989.

Vleeshuis Museum
Affiches Belle Epoque. Catalogue of the exhibition at the Museum Vleeshuis, Antwerp, Belgium, 1979.

Villemot
Les affiches de Villemot, by Jean François Bazin. Denoël, Paris, 1985.

Voyage
L'Invitation au Voyage, by Alain Weill. Somogy, Paris, 1994.

Wagner
Toulouse-Lautrec and His Contemporaries: Posters of the Belle Epoque from the Wagner Collection. Book of the exhibition at the Los Angeles County Museum of Art, 1985.

Wagons-Lits
125 Years International Sleeping Car Company, by Albert Mühl and Jurgen Klein. The history in text and graphics of the Wagons-Lits company, with text in German, French and English. EK-Verlag GmbH, Freidburg, 1998.

Weill
The Poster: A Worldwide Survey and History, by Alain Weill. G.K. Hall, Boston, 1985.

Wember
Die Jugend der Plakate 1887-1917, by Paul Wember. Scherpe Verlag, Krefeld, 1961.

Wine Spectator
Posters of the Belle Epoque: The Wine Spectator Collection, by Jack Rennert. The Wine Spectator Press, New York, 1990.

Wittrock
Toulouse-Lautrec: The Complete Prints, by Wolfgang Wittrock. 2 volumes. Sotheby's, London, 1985.

Wobmann
Touristikplakate der Schweiz (Tourist Posters of Switzerland), by Karl Wobmann, introduction by Willy Rotzler. AT Verlag, Aarau, 1980.

Word & Image
Word & Image. Catalogue of the exhibition at the Museum of Modern Art, New York, edited by Mildred Constantine. Text by Alan M. Fern. New York Graphic Society, Greenwich, Connecticut, 1968.

Where do you find them?

Many of the above cited books and catalogues are available from the
Poster Art Library of Posters Please, Inc.

For a free, fully-illustrated catalogue, please write to
Posters Please, Inc. 601 W. 26th Street, New York, N.Y. 10001
Telephone (212) 787-4000 Fax (212) 604-9175
www.postersplease.com

CONDITIONS OF SALE

The Conditions of Sale in this catalogue, as it may be amended by any posted notice during the sale, constitutes the complete terms and conditions under which the items listed in this catalogue will be offered for sale. Please note that the items will be offered by us as agent for the consignor.

Every potential buyer should read these Conditions of Sale and it will be agreed, acknowledged and understood by such buyer that said buyer has consented to each and every term and condition as set forth herein.

1. Authenticity and Terms of Guarantee.

For a period of five years from the date of this sale, Poster Auctions International, as agent, warrants the authenticity of authorship of all lots contained in this catalogue as described in the text accompanying each lot.

This warranty and guarantee is made only within the five year period and only to the original buyer of record who returns the purchased lot in the same condition as when sold to said buyer; and, it is established beyond doubt that the identification of authorship, as set forth in the description in this catalogue as may have been amended by any posted signs or oral declarations during tire sale, is not correct based on a reasonable reading of the catalogue and the Conditions of Sale herein. Any dispute arising under the terms in this paragraph will be resolved pursuant to final and binding arbitration at the American Arbitration Association.

Upon a finding by an Arbitrator in favor of buyer, the sale will be rescinded and the original purchase price, including the buyers premium, will be refunded. In such case, Poster Auctions International and the purchaser shall be deemed released of any and all claims that each may otherwise have had against the other arising out of the sale of such item.

The benefits of any warranty granted herein are personal to the buyer and are not assignable or transferable to any other person, whether by operation of law or otherwise. Any assignment or transfer of any such warranty shall be void and unenforceable. The purchaser refers only to the original buyer of the lot from Poster Auctions International and not any subsequent owner, assignee, or other person who may have or acquire an interest therein.

It is understood, in the event of disputed authenticity of authorship of any lot results in a rescission of the sale and restitution of the original price and premium paid by such purchaser, stated aforesaid, such restitution is buyer's sole remedy and Poster Auctions International disclaims all liability for any damages. incidental, consequential or otherwise, arising out of or in connection with any sale to the buyer.

Poster Auctions International has provided as much background information for each item listed in this catalogue as possible and has made reasonable efforts to insure the accuracy of the descriptions provided; but Poster Auctions International disclaims any warranty with regard to such descriptions and statements which accompany the listings in this catalogue, including but not limited to, the year of publication, the size, the condition, the printer, the references or any other background information or fact. Accordingly, buyer has due notice that any such information and/or descriptions cannot and will not be considered as material facts to this transaction and will root affect any sales herein.

All items are sold AS IS.

The consignor warrants good title to the buyer. Poster Auctions International and the consignor make no representations or warranty that the buyer acquires any reproduction rights or copyright in items bought at this sale.

Any statements made by Poster Auctions International, whether in this catalogue or by its officers, agents or employees, whether oral or written, are statements of opinion only and not warranties or representations of material facts as to each arid every transaction herein.

2. Auctioneers Discretions.

Poster Auctions International has absolute discretion to divide any lot, to combine any of them, to withdraw any lot, to refuse bids and to regulate the bidding. Poster Auctions International reserves the right to withdraw lots at any time prior to or during the sale. The highest bidder acknowledged by the auctioneer will be the purchaser of the lot. Any advance made on an opening bid may be rejected if the auctioneer deems it inadequate. In the event of any dispute between bidders, or in the event of doubt as to the validity of any bid, the auctioneer shall have the final decision either to determine the successful bidder or to re-offer and re-sell the lot in dispute. If any dispute arises after the sale, the auctioneer's sale record shall be deemed the sole and conclusive evidence as to the purchaser of any lot or item.

3. Transfer of title and property.

Upon the fall of the auctioneer's hammer, title to the offered lot shall pass to the highest bidder, who may be required to sign a confirmation of purchase; and, shall be required to pay the full purchase price. The purchaser shall assume full risk and responsibility for the lot purchased upon the fall of the auctioneer's hammer. Poster Auctions International, at its option, may withhold delivery of the lots until funds represented by check have been collected or the authenticity of bank or cashier checks has been determined. No purchase shall be claimed or removed until the conclusion of the sale. In the event Poster Auctions International shall, for any reason whatsoever, be unable to deliver the lots purchased by the buyer, its liability shall be solely limited to the rescission of the sale and refund of the purchase price end purchaser's premium.

Poster Auctions International disclaims all liability for damages, incidental, consequential or otherwise, arising out of its failure to deliver any lots purchased. Poster Auctions International does not charge extra or sell separately any frame if a poster is so offered; but it is clear that it is the poster and not the frame which is being offered for sale. Poster Auctions International shall not be responsible for any damage to the frame or to any poster within the frame. Generally, framed posters offered for sale were received framed, photographed that way, and Poster Auctions International can make no warranty or representations regarding the condition of the poster in unseen areas of any such frame. All items are sold strictly as is and the purchaser assumes full risk and responsibility for the purchased lot upon the fall of the hammer, as stated aforesaid.

All lots shall be paid for and removed at the purchaser's risk and expense by noon of the second business day following the sale. Lots not so removed will, at the sole option of Poster Auctions International and at purchaser's risk and expense, be stored at Poster Auctions International's office or warehouse or delivered to a licensed warehouse for storage. Purchaser agrees, in either event, to pay all shipping, handling and storage fees incurred. In the case of lots stored at Poster Auctions International's own warehouse, the handling and storage fee will be an amount equal to 2% of the purchase price for each such lot, per month, until removed, with a minimum charge of 5% for any property not removed within thirty days from the date of the sale.

In addition, Poster Auctions International shall impose a late charge, calculated at the rate of 2% of the total purchase price per month, if payment has not been made in accordance with these Conditions of Sale.

Poster Auctions International may, on the day following the sale, remove all unclaimed lots to its offices or warehouse.

Unless purchaser notifies Poster Auctions International to the contrary, purchaser agrees that Poster Auctions International may, at its discretion, use purchaser's name as buyer of the item sold. If the purchaser fails to comply with one or more of these Conditions of Sale, then, in addition to any and all other remedies which it may have at law or in equity, Poster Auctions International may, at its sole option, cancel the sale without notice to the buyer. In such event, Poster Auctions International shall retain as liquidated damages all payments made by the purchaser, or sell the item and/or lots and all other property of the purchaser held by Poster Auctions International, without notice. Such liquidation sale shall be at standard commission rates, without any reserve. The proceeds of such sale or sales shall be applied first to the satisfaction of any damages occasioned by the purchaser's breach, and then to the payment of any other indebtedness owing to Poster Auctions International, including without limitation, commissions, handling charges, the expenses of both sales, reasonable attorneys fees, collection agency fees, and any other costs or expenses incurred thereunder. The purchaser hereby waives all the requirements of notice, advertisement and disposition of proceeds required by law, including those set forth in New York Lien Law, Article 9, Sections 200-204 inclusive, or any successor statue, with respect to any sale pursuant to this section.

4. Buyer's Premium

A premium of 15% will be added to the successful bid price of all items sold by Poster Auctions International. This premium shall be paid by all purchasers, without exception.

5. Order Bids

Poster Auctions International shall make reasonable efforts to execute bids for those not able to attend the auction; and act on the prospective purchaser's behalf to attempt to purchase the item desired at the lowest price possible, up to the limit indicated by purchaser in writing as if the purchaser were in attendance. Poster Auctions International shall not be responsible for any errors or omissions in this matter. Poster Auctions International reserves the right not to bid for any such purchaser if the order is not clear; does not arrive in sufficient time; the credit of the purchaser is not established prior to the sale; or, for any other reason in its sole discretion. An Order Bid Form shall be provided on request.

6. Sales Tax

Unless exempt by law, prior to taking pssession of the lot, the purchaser shall be required to pay the combined New York State and local sales tax, or any applicable compensating tax of another state, on the total purchase price.

7. Packing and shipping

Packing and/or handling of purchased lots by Posters Auctions International is performed solely as a courtesy for the convenience of purchasers. Unless otherwise directed by purchaser, packing and handling shall be undertaken at the sole discretion of Poster Auctions International. Poster Auctions International, at its sole discretion as agent of the purchaser, shall instruct an outside contractor to act on its behalf and arrange for or otherwise transport purchased lots. Charges for packing, handling, insurance and freight are payable by the purchaser. Poster Auctions International shall make reasonable efforts to handle purchases with care, but assumes no responsibility for damage of any kind. Poster Auctions International disclaims all liability for loss, or damages of any kind, arising out of or in connection with the packing, handling or transportation of any lots/items purchased.

8. Reserves.

All lots are subject to a reserve, which is the confidential minimum below which the lot will not be sold. Poster Auctions International may implement the reserve by bidding on behalf of the consignor. The consignor shall not bid on consignor's property.

9. Notices and jurisdiction.

(a)   All communications and notices hereunder shall be in writing and shall be deemed to have been duly given if delivered personally to an officer of PAI or if sent by United States registered mail or certified, postage prepaid, addressed as follows:

From: Poster Auctions International
To: _____(Seller)
         _____
         _____
From: _____(Seller)
To: Poster Auctions International
         601 W. 26th Street
         NewYork, NewYork 10001

or to such other address as either party hereto may have designated to the other by written notice.

(b)   These Conditions of Sale contain the entire understandings between the parties and may not be changed in any way except in writing duly executed by PAI and buyer.

(c)   These Conditions of Sale shall be construed and enforced in accordance with the laws of the State of New York.

(d)   No waiver shalt be deemed to be made by any party hereto of any rights hereunder, unless the same shall be in writing and each waiver, if any, shall be a waiver only with respect to the specific instance involved and shall in no way impair the rights of the waiving party or the obligations of the other party in any other respect at any other time.

(e)   The provisions of these Conditions of Sale shall be binding upon and inure to the benefit of the respective heirs, legatees, personal representatives and successors and assigns of the parties hereto.

(f)   The Conditions of Sale are not assignable by either party without written permission of the other party; any attempt to assign any rights, duties or obligations which arise under these Conditions without such permission will be void.

DESCRIPTION OF THE POSTERS

I. Artist's name.
   Unless otherwise indicated, the artist's name, mark or initials appear on the poster.

2. Year of the Poster.
   The year given is that of the publication of the poster, not necessarily the date of the event publicized or the year that art for it was rendered.

3. Size.
   Size is given in inches first, then centimeters, width preceding height. Size is for entire sheet, not just the image area.

4. Printer.
Unless otherwise indicated, the name of the printer is that which appears on the face of the poster. It should be kept in mind that frequently the establishment credited on the poster is, in fact, an agency, studio or publisher.

5. Condition of the Poster.
   We have attempted a simplified rating of all the posters in this sale. It should be kept in mind that we are dealing in many cases, with 50 to 100-year-old advertising paper. The standards of the print collector cannot be used. Prints were, for the most part, done in small format, on fine paper, and meant to be immediately framed or stored in a print sleeve or cabinet. A poster, for the most part, was printed in a large format, on the cheapest possible paper, and was meant to last about eight weeks on the billboards.
   Most important to the condition of a poster—not eight weeks but often eighty years later—is the image of the poster: is that image (the lines, the colors, the overall design) still clearly expressed? If so, it is a poster worth collecting.
   While details of each poster's condition are given as completely and accurately as possible, blemishes, tears or restorations which do not detract from the basic image and impact should not seriously impair value.
   All posters are lined, whether on linen or japan paper, unless otherwise indicated. But please note that posters received in frames are not inspected out of their frames and therefore no warranty can be made about them.
   All photos are of the actual poster being offered for sale. A close look at the photo and a reading of the text should enable the buyer who cannot personally examine the item to make an intelligent appraisal of it.

   The following ratings have been used:

Cond A   Designates a poster in very fine condition. The colors are fresh; no paper loss. There may be some slight blemish or tear, but this is very marginal and not noticeable. A+ is a flawless example of a poster rarely seen in such fine condition. A– indicates there may be some slight dirt, fold, tear or bubble or other minor restoration, but most unobtrusive.

Cond B   Designates a poster in good condition. There may be some slight paper loss, but not in the image or in any crucial design area. If some restoration, it is not immediately evident. The lines and colors are good, although paper may have yellowed (light-stained). B+ designates a poster in very good condition. B– is one in fairly good condition. The latter determination may be caused by heavier than normal light-staining or one or two noticeable repairs.

Cond C   Designates a poster in fair condition. The light-staining may be more pronounced, restorations, folds or flaking are more readily visible, and possibly some minor paper loss occurs. But the poster is otherwise intact, the image clear, and the colors, though possibly faded, still faithful to the artist's intent.

Cond D   Designates a poster in bad condition. A good part of such poster may be missing, including some crucial image area; colors and lines so marred that a true appreciation of the artist's intent is difficult, if not impossible. There are no D posters in this sale!

The above condition ratings are solely the opinion of Poster Auctions International, and are presented only as an aid to the public. Prospective purchasers are expected to have satisfied themselves as to the condition of the posters. Any discrepancy relating to the condition of a poster shall not be considered grounds for the cancellation of a sale.

Some other notes and designations relating to the condition of a poster:

Framed   Where a poster is framed, this is indicated. In many cases, we have photographed the poster in the frame and the dimensions given are those which are visible within the matting or edges of the frame.

Paper   All posters in this sale are linen- or japan-backed unless the designation "P" appears.

6. Bibliography.
An abbreviation for each reference (Ref) is given and can be found in the complete Bibliography. The reference is almost always to a reproduction of that poster. If a "p." precedes it, it means the reproduction or reference is on that page; if number only, it refers to a poster or plate number. Every effort has been made to refer to books that are authoritative and/or easily accessible.

7. Pre-Sale Estimate
These estimates are guides for prospective bidders and should not be relied upon as representations or predictions of actual selling prices. They are simply our best judgment of the fair market value of that particular poster in that condition on the date it was written.

THE POSTER ENCYCLOPEDIA

MISSING ANY BOOKS?

These hard-cover, auction catalogues form an essential encyclopedia for the poster collector. Each illustrates over 500 posters, with full annotations, bibliography, estimates and prices realized. Price of individual volumes: **$40** each ($45 foreign).

SPECIAL OFFER: All 24 previous catalogues (Auctions I-XXX, excluding out-of-print volumes I, II, III, VI, VII, and XIV) for only **$675** ($725 foreign).

POSTER AUCTIONS INTERNATIONAL, INC.
601 WEST 26TH ST., NEW YORK, N.Y. 10001
TEL (212) 787-4000, FAX (212) 604-9175
www.posterauctions.com　　e-mail: jrennert@angel.net

POSTER POWER
ORDER BID FORM

Please bid on my behalf on the following lots up to the price shown. I understand that all bids are subject to the Conditions of Sale which are printed in the Catalogue.

Poster Auctions International will make every effort to execute bids for those not able to attend and act on the prospective purchaser's behalf to try to purchase the item desired at the lowest price possible up to the limit indicated by purchaser below as if the purchaser were in attendance, but Poster Auctions International cannot be responsible for any errors or omissions in this matter. Poster Auctions International may reserve the right not to bid for any such party if the order is not clear, does not arrive in sufficient time, or the credit of the purchaser is not established, or for any other reason in its sole discretion.

The purchase price will be the total of the final bid and a premium of 15% of the final bid together with any applicable sales tax. Unsuccessful bidders will not be informed but may telephone for sales results.

_____　Date _____
(Signed)

NAME _____

ADDRESS _____

City _____State _____Zip _____

TEL: Home: (　　) _____ Office: (　　) _____ FAX: (　　) _____

BANK: Name _____Telephone (　　)_____

　　　Address _____

　　　Account Number _____Officer _____

REFERENCE _____

Lot #	Artist	Title	BID (excluding premium)
_____	_____	_____	$ _____
_____	_____	_____	$ _____
_____	_____	_____	$ _____
_____	_____	_____	$ _____
_____	_____	_____	$ _____
_____	_____	_____	$ _____
_____	_____	_____	$ _____
_____	_____	_____	$ _____

YES, you CAN
be with us on November 12.

If you cannot attend our New York sale in person, you can nonetheless take advantage of these rare offerings.

BID by MAIL, FAX or PHONE
with confidence.

Simply fill out the form on the reverse side of this page, indicating your maximum bid for each desired lot. It should be in our New York offices no later than Friday, November 10.

You may indicate an "either-or" bid if you want to purchase only a portion of the items on your wish list. You may also indicate a maximum total dollar amount. We execute your bid on your behalf at the lowest price possible.

To bid by telephone, simply fill in the lot numbers and indicate the phone number where we can reach you on Sunday, November 12. When your lot number comes up, we'll call you.

Either way, you bid with confidence: We execute your bid on your behalf at the lowest possible price.

DON'T MISS OUT ON THE POSTER YOU WANT
just because you can't be in New York.

If you need any further information, don't hesitate to call Ms. Terry Shargel—she'll answer all your questions.

We are a bidder-friendly organization!